MOTHERHOOD IN LOCKDOWN

150 MOTHERS ON PREGNANCY, BIRTH & POSTPARTUM IN A PANDEMIC

DAISIE LANE

First published in 2024

Posh Dog Press
www.poshdogpress.com

All rights reserved

© Daisie Lane, 2024
Individual essays © Contributors, 2024

No portion of this book may be reproduced in any form without written permission from the publisher or author.

ISBN 978-1-3999-7935-1

Printed and bound in Great Britain.

For Dad, who instilled my love of books and the written word.
I wish you could have seen this.

And of course, for the Lockdown Mamas -
This one is yours.

CONTENTS

Introduction	9
KATE WATKINSON	18
JESSICA JAIRATH	21
ISABELLA GAMBLE	28
JO CHESTERS	31
ALI BLAND	36
ALLISON ISAAK	38
AMY SLATER-BELL	40
KATE OWEN	41
KAYLEIGH GISSING	44
ANNA CARTER	46
AMY BALDERSTON	54
ASHLEY ROSTRON	59
BETHAN MINTER	61
CARLY ACRES	66
CAROLINE ELLIS	70
CATHERINE GREGORY	74
CLAIRE McNICOL	76
CHLOE BROWN	77
ELEANOR BAGNALL	79
ELIZABETH CLIFF	83
MELISSA HASKINS	84
ELAINE GREGERSEN	86
KATHRYN BRANCH	92
ELENA CHOW	94
GEMMA LEE	98
HANNAH DAVIES	100
ALISHA SAMMS	103
FRANKIE TOWELL	104
HANNAH BURGESS	109
GEMMA HAANK	118
SARAH PICKERING	120
LYNSEY CARROLL	122
MARIA MYERS	124
N. DESAI	127
HANNAH PAGE	129
RACHEL GALLOWAY	132
CHERI ANGHARAD LEWIS	135
CHLOE PRIVETT	137
KERRY LOCKYER	139
KATE BROCK	143

JENNIFER WEBBER	146
JASMINE BUNDOCK	148
LEANNE BOWEN-BRENNAN	150
LAURA GOOCH	152
RACHEL JEAN BIRCH	155
RAJVINDER SHERGILL	157
LAURIE GOLDIE	162
SAMANTHA TAVENDER	164
LEANNE LOWIS	167
LAUREN CLARK	170
SARAH BOYD	174
KATY BENTLEY	178
ESTELLE MOON	180
JO COATES	181
SHELLEY SMITH	183
KIRSTY HEADFORD	185
CAITLIN LANGDON	186
CLAIRE MARTIN-QUIRK	188
CHARLOTTE MORGAN	191
NATALIE COOMBER	193
IONA MAXWELL	197
ELLEN CLAYTON	199
GENEVIEVE BEECH	201
HARRIET CLAY	202
AMANDA ANTHONY	204
CARLY PARTRIDGE TONDEUR	207
NATALIE SHARPE	209
REBECCA JONES	213
JULIA COOPER	215
SARAH HOWARD	219
EMILY LOUISE WALKER-LAKHANI	221
REBECCA DAVENPORT	225
JO MATTHEWS	228
REBECCA BARTLETT	230
DIMPLE MISTRY	235
EMMELINE BAGLEY	237
HAYLEY ANDERSON	239
RACHEL GALE	243
KAYLEIGH STANNARD	245
VICTORIA NICHOLLS	248
REBECCA SAYCE	252
KIMBERLEY CORNWELL	259
TONI GREENWAY	261
HAYLEY CARNE	263

NICOLE FOX	267
CLAIRE UNWIN	270
ALEX RANDLE	273
SARAH PEGRAM	274
RACHAEL FIELD	277
SAMMY KATE MAGGS	279
ALICE ANN TURNER	281
HEATHER CORDINER	284
ANONYMOUS	286
KAYLEIGH	290
LAURA FETTES	292
LAURA MARCIANTE	294
DEANNE LOGAN	296
HELEN McCLEN	299
HANNAH BOYD	300
LAURA YOUNG	304
LIZZIE BRACE	306
RACHEL M	311
LOUISE ACKERMAN-MURPHY	314
NICOLA HAMILTON	316
SARAH STOCKTON	321
CHARLOTTE FOX	323
JANINE RANDALL	326
LAURA WOODLAND	330
ANNA JAMES	335
SARAH LANE	339
VICTORIA GRIFFITHS	343
JESSICA WATSON	348
SAMANTHA	351
SARAH KNAPP	356
CHARLOTTE TOKOLICS	361
HANNAH JG RAMSDALE	367
JULIE COLMAN	371
CLARE LANGER	374
TERRI COLEMAN	378
LARA ALI	381
CHARLOTTE SCANLON	383
KYRIE CLARKE	388
REBECCA FOGARTY	391
VERITY CHANCELLOR	393
EMMA BARRIE	397
SHONA ANDERSON	400
SARAH STOKES	405
MADELEINE ABEL	406

LUCY FAIRBROTHER	411
MAYA LAMPARD	413
KIA BROWN	416
LAURA McALLISTER	418
HANNAH TILLBROOK	420
EMMA MORGAN	425
TORI BEAT	427
SARAH BIRCH	431
ELLIE BRIGHT	434
LUCY HORNE	439
HELEN WHALE	442
REBECCA BRYANT	444
JADE CANNON	450
LUCY WEBB	452
MARTINA BYRNES	456
EMILY HAWKES	458
LEIGH McCOMISH	461
JENNIFER McLAMB	464
HAYLEY ENGLAND	467
KEZIA LOCKHOUSE	470
4AM DOODLES	475
LISA DUBROVINA	476
Acknowledgments	483

INTRODUCTION
By Daisie Lane

By the time I gave birth to my daughter in June 2020, I'd spent so long trying not to die that my mind pretty much checked out. I couldn't blame it. It had been in a constant state of fear for months, trying to keep us both alive, all the more exhausting when the killer you're fighting is invisible.

That's what we were all doing in those days - trying not to die. The country was in a collective survival mode, trying not to catch COVID - the deadly virus that we knew virtually nothing about, except that it was taking thousands of lives every day.

Since March of that year, pregnant women had been referred to as 'clinically vulnerable' and instructed, by our UK government, to stay at home. What followed, were months of uncertainty and hazy guidance, resulting in pregnant women obsessively checking the news and any communications from their local NHS trust. Each trust was able to issue its own policy, underwritten by government advice and guidance. In April, the NHS issued a guide for the temporary reorganisation of maternity care,[1] putting the decision-making responsibility onto local trusts. This led to huge disparities between hospitals and a lack of clarity for expectant parents. The deficit of focus in this area, and the autonomy given to trust administrators, caused inconsistent application of that advice and a vast variation in care. The ambiguity meant those who were supposed to be fountains of knowledge in pregnancy – midwives and obstetricians – struggled to give their patients definitive answers.

BMJ, an online medical journey, published a blog in 2020 titled 'Birth partners are not a luxury,' warning of the lasting negative impact that denying pregnant women access to their support network could have.

> "The early inconsistencies of government and public health policy undermined the confidence of healthcare workers and provided an open platform for conflicting influential opinions. Rather than health services maintaining a holistic approach that balances risks against benefits, paranoia and tunnel vision have flourished in many places. Decisions were taken without due consideration of their wider consequences, leaving person-centred care approaches sidelined. Gaps in knowledge were filled by assumptions. However, what makes us *feel* safe is not always the same as what makes us safer."[2]

I spent almost a week in hospital after the birth of my baby and not one person was allowed to visit. My husband missed the first week of his child's life. Already deeply affected by labouring alone, a traumatic birth and a premature baby, it was the absence of support in these vulnerable key moments that positioned my mental health on a downward trajectory. A recipe for a mental health disaster, I refer to it as now. I spent much of the first few days locked in the hospital toilet, sobbing, until I lost the final shred of inhibition I had left and gave up hiding, returning to my bed to wail behind my blue curtain instead.

Less than a three-hour drive away, staff at 10 Downing Street were gathering for our Prime Minister, Boris Johnson's, birthday, at a time when indoor gatherings were banned.

The following month - July - pubs were permitted to re-open, dubbed 'Freedom Day' by much of the national media, while thousands of women were still screaming, alone, behind blue curtains.

In August, as England was financially incentivised to flock to restaurants with the government's 'eat out to help out' scheme, mothers were still crying, alone, in hospital toilets.

It took six months before NHS England, after significant pressure, published guidance for trusts on how to introduce birth partners and visitors, framework which was vague and continued to put the onus of the decisions very much on the trust. Whilst the infection rates differed from location to location, and therefore some autonomy was understandable, this postcode lottery did little to alleviate women's concerns and bridge the gaps that had begun to appear in maternity care. As hair salons, soft plays and theatres re-opened, many hospitals continued to take the 'worst case' approach, to be on the safer side of what was open to interpretation, and so restrictions on labour and maternity wards remained.

In December, nine months after the announcement of the first lockdown, NHS England issued updated guidance which acknowledged the importance of a birth partner during scans, appointments and birth, encouraging trusts to facilitate this but to make their decisions based on local circumstances. Many women still continued to report visiting restrictions within hospitals.

With midwives being pulled onto COVID wards and the usual supporting structure of visitors eradicated, the needs of patients could not possibly be met due to simple supply and demand. This meant that absolutely everything fell to the mothers, some of whom were recovering from major surgery or had not slept for days. Of course, pain and sleep deprivation may have been typical experiences of many patients across all departments within a hospital, but only within maternity care was that patient solely responsible for a secondary vulnerable human being.

The pandemic also reinforced class inequalities, with those who could afford private scans being able to have their loved ones present, emphasizing the underlying feeling of prioritisation of the economy over health.

The lack of urgency and priority by the government in this area meant that maternity restrictions were some of the harshest and longest-lasting in the UK. Human rights charity Birthrights pushed for more robust guidance ensuring the protection of women, citing "an inconsistent, disproportionate and inhumane response by some NHS Trusts." They argued that any general suspensions on visitors and services within hospitals should not be automatically applied to maternity services, due to the distinct needs of this patient population in comparison.

> "We believe that the restrictions that have been imposed on maternity care, and a failure to communicate them in a timely manner, risk compromising the safety of women and babies and causing serious trauma and psychological damage to pregnant women and their partners."[3]

Alarms were raised, alerting us to a looming maternal mental health crisis, with warnings of the detrimental impact that restrictions could have on mothers, their babies and their families. Yet, despite the continued easing of social measures, we did not see the same consideration for maternity services.

The silence around maternity restrictions made the screaming chants of 10,000 people in a football stadium seem all the louder.

Those in labour were denied their advocate, their distraction and their support, meaning many entered childbirth in a heightened state of anxiety, physiologically detrimental to the process. Over 15,000 pregnant women and mothers were surveyed by the campaign group Pregnant Then Screwed, with an overwhelming 97% of respondents saying lockdown had increased their anxiety around childbirth.[4]

As the messages that mothers mattered less began to penetrate, we started taking matters into our own hands, putting our health and well-being on the line in an attempt to take back some control. In labour, we delayed going into hospital and stayed home for as long as possible, even if it meant dancing with risk, because at least it meant we were not alone and frightened. Because of the 'active labour' rule in place (needing to be 4cm dilated before birth partners were allowed to be present) we asked for more internal examinations - unpleasant, painful and in the most intimate parts of our bodies - our only barometer of how much longer we would have to endure being alone. Elective caesareans increased in popularity to avoid such a rule. In this book, you will read about Rebecca and Victoria, who both reluctantly decided on home births because of the constant unpredictability of whether or not their partners could be present at a hospital. Not only did we decide to completely change the courses of our labours just to decrease the risk of being alone, but even after babies were born, we self-discharged before being medically fit, just to get home to where a shred of support was present.

Sadly, the journey into motherhood, for many, did not turn to rainbows upon getting home. The restrictions and social distancing measures in place meant that respite did not come, and parents missed out on the 'village' that so many talk about as being critical in early motherhood.

The fear I had in pregnancy, of catching COVID and dying, did not disappear when the baby was born. I still had visions of ending up intubated and my husband having to choose whether or not to switch off the life support machine of his newborn's mother. I would look at my baby, so tiny and vulnerable, and almost buckle under the weight of the pressure of keeping her safe from the very air she was breathing. This was not irrational, like the many intrusive thoughts new motherhood can bring. There was a very real chance one of us could become very ill and die and there was very little any of us could do to stop it.

I distinctly remember my anxiety levels skyrocketing at the idea of time passing. Of course, many new mothers feel emotional at the thought of their baby growing, their tiny hands getting bigger… but for me, it was a ticking clock so loud and clear in my mind it kept me awake at night. Tick, tock, when will this end? Tick, tock, when will my parents be able to see my baby? My mind couldn't see the positive of having succeeded in keeping a tiny human alive for another day. Instead, it saw another day where no one had met her. This clouded much of the postpartum period and so I found myself in an endless confusion of wishing the time away and then feeling guilty for doing so.

By the end of 2021, with both the lockdowns and the postpartum fog having lifted, along with the new clarity and hope given to me by in-person support, I began to breathe again. No longer being shown a scatter graph of death on the TV every evening or having to risk-assess every time I left the house, and with COVID becoming less at the forefront of every conversation, it gave me space for processing. It is often only in rest that we can begin the process of healing, and so, after two years of being in survival mode, silenced by fear, I began to reflect on the two years prior.

It wasn't the spiritual awakening that paragraph made it sound like. It was ugly. I felt like I'd been hit by a train. I'd been holding my breath for two years and finally exhaling forced me to my knees. I had a breakdown. My family ushered me to my GP and a prescription was written for anti-depressants.

We'd complied, we'd sacrificed and we'd pushed down our feelings. After all, people were *dying*. And as we held our beautiful, tiny babies we felt we didn't have the right to feel loss or grief or heartbreak.

Except… we *did* have the right.

Suicide is the leading cause of maternal death in the first year postnatally.[5] Protecting and prioritising the mental health of mothers is surely a matter of national importance. By the end of this book, you will see clearly how mothers were failed and what the lasting impact of those failures was. These 150 women are a small window into that trauma. Sadly, there is so much more out there.

In 2022, I set up 'The Lockdown Mama Community' online and the reaction sparked a fire in my belly. It became clear very quickly that there was a huge number of mothers desperate to talk about it. Hundreds contacted me to tell me their stories, their words spilling out hurriedly, palpable relief at the door opening on this subject. Many wanted to thank me for making them feel less alone. They made *me* feel less alone. We were all struggling, broken and not quite the same as we were before.

It became clear a space was needed to talk openly about these experiences, so I contacted Arts Council England for funding support. I proposed a project of community and healing, with the aim of tackling some of the enormous mental health burden left by the pandemic, by encouraging mothers to write about their experiences as a form of therapy. Writing has been proven to have many benefits on mental health and wellbeing, of course, but the most important thing to me was ensuring this demographic of people finally felt *heard*. I wanted to give them the voice that was silenced during the pandemic, and a place to solidify that voice, encapsulated forever in a book.

The funding was granted. That year, I launched Posh Dog Press, an independent publisher dedicated to amplifying the voices of mothers, and pledged that the first book published would be the stories of the lockdown mums. I put out a call for submissions, asking mothers to write their stories about being pregnant, giving birth and experiencing early motherhood in lockdown. There were no rules or style guides, just a 3000-word limit and the prompt that 'your story must show us how your motherhood was impacted by the pandemic.' I hosted workshops on Zoom, where we did writing exercises to get participants comfortable with putting their thoughts onto paper. There were nerves at first, many didn't consider themselves 'writers' and questioned whether they would be good enough for a book. Confidence grew, bolstered by the support within the group. For some, it prompted a newfound love of writing. Some began to share their words online. We cried and laughed together. It was a beautiful thing to see.

By the time submissions closed, I had case study after case study, showing the outcome two or three years on from restricting mothers during their early parenting journeys. I had masses of qualitative information that needed to be put out into the world. The stories were humming with rage and power, the emotions poured from the pages: anger, deep sadness and pain. The writing had been a clear release and for some, made way for healing. Rachael Field writes about this perfectly on page 277.

> "As I let myself go back and relive the experience of pregnancy, birth and postpartum in lockdown, I realised there were things that I hadn't processed or worked through, and some things I was unaware needed to come to the surface. I discovered that I was grieving again, in real time, as I wrote. In writing this, I realise that I never dealt with how lockdown made me feel and the impact it had. Writing this, and grieving all over again, has been the best thing I could have done. If I hadn't, I might never have realised that I was still holding those feelings so deeply."

In this book, you will hear from 150 of those mothers who grew, gave birth to, raised, and in some cases even lost babies, alone. You will read about the extremes they were driven to, from severe depression to suicide attempts, journeying through grief, resentment, injustice, disappointment, loss, fear and rage. Stories move from living rooms to intensive care units, across global virtual support systems, navigating fertility struggles, IVF journeys and relationship breakdowns. We are shown the power and value of human connection and how much it was missed in the most vulnerable moments. Most of all, the unimaginable strength of women shines through.

There's Isabella, who helped to change the restrictions on her local maternity ward to prevent other mothers from going through what she did. Samantha, faced with her husband's cancer diagnosis alongside early motherhood isolation. Rebecca, who, when public transport was rife with COVID, would walk the six-mile round trip every day to deliver breastmilk to her baby in NICU.

Some of the stories will leave you speechless, like Emily, who was left with no choice but to show her vaginal tear stitches to a doctor on a video call, and Rajvinder, who had to pull her baby out of the toilet after being denied her birth partner, and Kate, who learned she had miscarried and had to then deliver the news to her hopeful husband, who had not been allowed to hold her hand.

There are common themes laced throughout each of the stories: dads waiting in car parks, partners who never got to be present for a single appointment, the 'shift' work with babies in NICU where only one parent was allowed to visit, inconsistency of antenatal care, lack of postnatal care including breastfeeding support and the absence of a 'village.'

You will also read about the very real anxieties mothers were experiencing on a daily basis - developing phobias or extreme fears of germs, illness and death, worrying that their child's development would be affected by the lack of outside contact, and experiencing apprehension about having another baby because of how impacted they were by their experience in lockdown. The pandemic caused many new anxieties that are still felt today.

In this book, the words 'anxious' or 'anxiety' appear 141 times.

The words 'fear' or 'scared' appear 247 times.

The words 'alone' or 'lonely' appear 507 times, more than the words 'lockdown' or 'COVID.'

At the end of 2023, deep into the public inquiry examining the UK's response to the COVID-19 pandemic, Helen MacNamara, a senior official at the height of the pandemic, said in her written witness statement it was "clear that the female perspective was being missed in advice and decision making" and "decisions were being taken where the impact on women was either lost or ignored."

We knew it, we felt it... but to hear it from the lips of someone in the inner circle validated our anger.

"There was a disproportionate amount of attention given to more male pursuits in terms of the impact of restrictions and then the lessening of the same (football, hunting, shooting and fishing). There was a lack of guidance for women who might be pregnant or were pregnant... The restrictions around birth and pregnancy care seemed unnecessarily restrictive and were comparatively slow to adapt. I never understood this. Although I appreciated the need to keep hospitals as secure as possible I am sure there would have been kinder ways of managing pregnancy and birth especially given the differential clinical outcomes for women and their babies who become stressed."[6]

To any lockdown mama reading this: We may have been forgotten, but we will never forget. The grief is real. The feelings of loss, even if you didn't lose someone to the disease, are valid, because it's the loss of memories, experiences and precious time. Maternity leave dreams were dashed and it's OK to feel bitter about that. It's OK to feel like you were robbed. It's OK if your friend having a baby in 'normal times' fills you with jealousy. It's OK if you're not 'over it' yet, in a world that feels like it's moved on.

It is my hope that the stories in this book leave you feeling validated, understood, heard and, most importantly, not alone.

As I write this introduction, we have just entered 2024. Many of the women in this book have gone on to have second babies since writing their piece, and now know what it's like to be pregnant in an unrestricted world. Some have gone through various types of mental health support and therapy. Many have received diagnoses of depression, anxiety, obsessive compulsive disorder and post-traumatic stress disorder.

It is important to state that; most people respected and understood the need for restrictions. Should history repeat itself, I would abide by them again, as would many others. But it doesn't mean that everything was done in the right way.

It is essential that we interrogate previous decisions to learn from what happened. We must understand that some things, such as a person's journey to bring a baby into the world, cannot be met with a blanket response. The extremes of existence: the joy of welcoming a life or the heartbreak of saying goodbye to one, should have been prioritised over social pursuits and quick economic gain. We must realise the nuances present within maternity care, to not only consider the immediate risks to physical health, but the long-term ones to mental health. We must never allow bias or sexism to dictate decision making and policy.

We must listen to mothers.

References

[1] NHS. (2020) Specialty guides for patient management during the coronavirus pandemic Clinical guide for the temporary reorganisation of intrapartum maternity care during the coronavirus pandemic. Available at: https://madeinheene.hee.nhs.uk/Portals/0/Clinical%20guide%20for%20the%20temporary%20reorganisation%20of%20intrapartum%20maternity%20care.pdf (Accessed 30th March 2024).

[2] B. Black. J, Laking. J. McKay, G. (2020) Birth partners are not a luxury. Available at: https://blogs.bmj.com/bmj/2020/09/24/birth-partners-are-not-a-luxury/ (Accessed 30th March 2024).

[3] Birthrights. (2020) Human rights implications of changes to maternity services during the Covid-19 pandemic. Available at: https://www.birthrights.org.uk/wp-content/uploads/2020/07/Birthrights-Covid-19-Human-Rights-Committee-Briefing-July-2020.pdf (Accessed 30th March 2024).

[4] Pregnant Then Screwed. (Date unknown) Huge mental health toll that Covid restrictions have had on mothers-to-be is laid bare in a landmark survey. Available at: https://pregnantthenscrewed.com/huge-mental-health-toll-that-covid-restrictions-have-had-on-mothers-to-be-is-laid-bare-in-a-landmark-survey/ (Accessed 30th March 2024).

[5] Tubb, A. (2023) Suicide still a leading cause of maternal death. Available at: https://maternalmentalhealthalliance.org/news/mbrrace-2023-suicide-still-leading-cause-maternal-death/#:~:text=Suicide%20continues%20to%20be%20the,or%20existing%20mental%20health%20condition. (Accessed 30th March 2024).

[6] MacNamara, H. (2023) Witness statement of Helen MacNamara. Available at: https://covid19.public-inquiry.uk/wp-content/uploads/2023/11/03103311/INQ000273841.pdf (Accessed 30th March 2024).

Notes from the author

1. The terms 'women' and 'mothers' have been used throughout this book for convenience. The terms were chosen that best represented the majority of participants in this book who identified as women. We acknowledge that, while the majority of people who get pregnant and give birth are women, not all people who are pregnant and give birth identify as women. If you are reading this book and relate to the stories within - but do not relate to the identities or pronouns used - I want you to know: this is equally for you.
2. All contributors were given the option to include their name or remain anonymous, and to include or exclude a biography.
3. The biographies at the end of each piece were written in March 2023, so the information stated is relevant to that time.

KATE WATKINSON

My daughter was born on 29th March 2020; day six of the first national lockdown. Arriving home that evening with a newborn and her 20-month-old brother, whilst a global pandemic raged and daily headlines screamed 'virus deaths' and 'tougher measures,' was thoroughly daunting. Family and friends were forbidden and midwife visits and breastfeeding clinics were cancelled. Were we supposed to do this on our own now?

At around a week old, our baby developed some unusual health complications. What followed, was the battle to be heard by an NHS in crisis, fear, uncertainty, solo hospital trips, sleep deprivation, postpartum hormones, a bewildered toddler and emotional support via only WhatsApp messages and video calls... It was overwhelming. That first lockdown - my daughter's first months - is a blur, but there are moments that I recall vividly. Snapshots of the stress and sadness, but also the hope and humanity in the midst of what was an intensely surreal and frightening time. I have written about some of them, here.

***

My newborn sleeps on my chest,
peaceful.
The warmth and the weight of her,
delicate breath on my skin and the gentle beating of hearts.
She has silky hair, soft cheeks.

The radio is on and the world might be ending.
Arenas are hospitals now,
makeshift morgues,
medics sweating in hazmat suits.
We Must Stay At Home.
There are dolphins in Venetian canals.

The daily death toll is delivered.
My baby sighs, the sun streams in stripes onto the duvet.

***

My mum leaves a veggie chilli and a box of breast pads in the front garden.
Rings the doorbell, retreats to the gate,
furtive, anxious, is this breaking The Rules?
I listen, exhausted, from the landing.
If I go downstairs I will want her to hold the baby,
hold me.
My toddler will try to run to her.

Everyone will cry.

On my birthday we open the door and wave.
Flowers, strawberries, a Victoria sponge.
The devotion in these doorstep visits.
The desolation.

* * *

I sit on a blue plastic chair,
appear composed.
Day three.
A workman next to me is fixing the automatic doors.
Gloves, toolbox, cup of tea.
I need a cup of tea, with my parents, friends, on the sofa.
Not this stranger in a clinic waiting room.
The injustice feels desperate, piercing,
my heart hammers.

I haven't seen a midwife since my daughter was seven hours old.
This one is stressed and kind and uncomfortable in unfamiliar uniform,
fogged glasses.
I weigh my baby,
grit teeth through a painful latch,
the midwife's hands twitch.
Arms-length abandoned, she rearranges us,
better, a bit.
I say I am okay. We will be okay. It will be okay.

* * *

My husband hides chocolate eggs in our tiny backyard,
finds the eggcups for breakfast.
Our son is thrilled, bemused,
marches soldiers across his plate,
unwraps a mini Lindt bunny, enrapt.
I sob in the shower because we haven't baked an Easter cake together
or cooked a roast dinner
or made cards with yellow finger-painted chicks and cotton wool sheep.
And also because I am scared there is something wrong with my two-week-old baby
and we are in the middle of a pandemic
and all the doors are closed.

* * *

We drive our weeks-old daughter to a London hospital,
deserted motorways, the city eerily silent.
I think someone will stop us, masked, helmeted,
and tell us to turn back.
My husband parks outside,
settles in for an eight-hour wait,
whilst I clutch the car seat and disappear through revolving doors
to take on tests and diagnoses and medication doses
alone.

On the way home I feel invincible
and like if I unclench my jaw I will shatter into pieces.

There is a party at Downing Street that night.

JESSICA JAIRATH

Our eyes meet for the first time, I weep. Overwhelmed.
We hold you, taking in your newborn smell. This moment is shattered, too soon.
Your father is forced out.
The village is absent.

You and I are imprisoned. It is sterile here.
The windows have been locked. Safety feels stifling.
I hear the other babes crying, desperately wanting anyone to hold them.
The village is absent.

My body is broken. I must heal, rest and be whole again.
No one is allowed to join us behind this white curtain. I cannot breathe a sigh of relief.
We must escape. This place has lost its humanity.
The village is absent.

Your cries grow urgent, my voice trembles with fear.
I negotiate the terms for our freedom.
We break out but there is only one place we are allowed to go.
The village is absent.

I had hoped to share the world with you.
I had hoped others would hold you and kiss your sweet cheeks.
We were told freedom could kill us.
The village is absent.

Your guttural screams are too much to bear,
The white coats dismiss me. I'm hysterical, they say.
I am unqualified to perceive your happiness.
The village is absent.

I watch your small chest rise and fall.
The wires flow around your Pyrex bed.
This is not the vindication I wanted for us.
The village is absent.

There are only so many times we can walk this stone path.
Only so many times we can see the same tree.
I wish I could have a semblance of a moment's peace.
The village is absent.

The passage of time no longer feels linear.
The crying. The crying. The crying.
I pour myself a fourth. Alone. They laugh in their groups of six.
The village is absent.

Today, you need me desperately.
I am depleted by the monotony and I want to hide.
I fleetingly wish you were not here.
The village is absent.

It has been 369 days.

Change comes but it is trivial. The damage has been done.
I crumble seeing 10,000 marching to the stadiums. Seeing their laughter on the screens.
I crumble hearing about their parties. Seeing their laughter as their lives seemingly never changed.
I crumble watching them drink in their gardens. Seeing their laughter as we remain caged.
I crumble hearing about their journeys beyond the boundaries. Seeing their laughter as our minds frayed.
I crumble as they hold hands. Seeing their laughter whilst my mother couldn't hold mine.

It has been 477 days. They are opening the world to you, my child.
The pause button turns to play. The village returns, elated.
The village did not see my body change.
The village did not see you as a babe.
The village did not celebrate us or help shoulder the burden.
The village did not help to keep my mind whole.
The village did not hold me as I wept.
The village did not get to know you.
The village is eager to tell me what I am doing wrong.
The village hears my words as I hesitantly relive our time.
The village will never fathom, our experiences seem worlds apart.
The village feels joy so readily and it doesn't understand why I do not.
The village, it seems, has moved on.
My mind remains frozen.
You tumble towards me. The noise feels like chaos to you.
The enormity of the last 477 days crashes into me in waves, I cannot catch my breath.
I needed the world, but you only needed me.
Those lost firsts. Impossible to recreate.
I should look back in fondness, but I grieve instead.

I will never forgive. I will never forget.

When the world was locked down in March 2020, I was 19 weeks pregnant. It felt as though overnight we began living in a dystopian reality. My joy was replaced with crippling anxiety that I would catch a virus which would kill me, or make me lose our miracle baby. I was full of fear that going to buy a bottle of milk was a risk not worth taking.

My partner became relegated to a spectator of my pregnancy. I went to all my prenatal appointments, including the big 20-week scan, alone, while my husband waited at home for hours. He was the last to know that everything was OK.

Our homes became prisons. We were allowed to go outside for one hour of exercise a day. For a pregnant woman, this was torture. Movement was crucial for the relief of pain in my ever-expanding joints. I was questioned several times when I went for a wander around the local park. I was made to feel like a criminal for daring to leave my home. It felt as though my needs were deemed as 'nice to haves.' The world was closing in on me fast and the pregnancy and first-time mum journey I had dreamed of was slipping away.

My mother did not live locally. Under the government legislation, we were not allowed to travel to see each other. My mother never saw her only daughter go through her first pregnancy. My mother never saw her only daughter's belly grow. My mother never saw her daughter give birth. My mother was not allowed to visit her daughter in hospital. My mother never got to hold her daughter's hand to comfort her and guide her through the early weeks of motherhood. My mother never held her grandchild as a baby. My mother was not able to love me or care for me so I could heal and repair. My mother was not able to give her daughter and her grandchild the support needed for us to bond and love each other.

After our son was born, life felt bleak. After two days of labour, my partner was allowed to stay for less than two hours. My son and I were wheeled to the postpartum ward where we stayed there for three days in the middle of a heatwave. Windows were shut and fans were switched off, for fear of spreading the virus. I was on my own in the corner of a ward with cries of other mothers and their babies overwhelming my senses. We were all alone, desperately trying to meet the needs of our children whilst trying to recover physically and mentally. It felt as though no one cared that we may need to go to the toilet or want a minute to eat some food. Without our partners or family there to visit – we had been left. Forgotten.

My first challenge came quickly. My son would not breastfeed easily and my lower back was in excruciating pain. I could not be discharged home until I breastfed successfully. Help was promised but it never came. I couldn't sit, lie or stand without crying from the pain. The baby blues had started and I was going through waves of crying uncontrollably. I thought I was going to go mad with the pain and worrying about the safety of my baby. My son started to go quiet but no one believed me. On the fourth day, I broke down in loud tears and screamed in the middle of the ward for someone to listen. They finally allowed me to sign a self-discharge form so I could go home.

The relief of being reunited with the familiar face of my partner was indescribable. Perversely, I felt safe having finally left the hospital.

Less than 12 hours after being discharged, our five-day-old son was rushed to A&E with severe dehydration. I punished myself for not escaping the hospital sooner.

Any mother will tell you that maternity leave can be isolating and monotonous. It is the ability to leave your home, go for a walk and see others in baby classes or coffee shops that can give you back a shred of sanity. It is having a parent come and stay with you for a few hours, which can give you the strength and ability to recharge. Motherhood is mind, body and life-altering.

From the age of two weeks, until my son was eight months old, he cried and cried and cried. The reality of motherhood felt like a never-ending nightmare. My son was in excruciating pain day in and day out. The hours became unbearable. My only escape was putting him on his mat, putting headphones in my ears and locking myself in the bathroom to cry until no more tears would fall. I desperately needed someone to tell me it was going to be OK. I needed someone to take some of the mental load away, to cook for me or just hold the baby for a little while so I could get some sleep. I had become a walking zombie. My eyes were constantly red and sore from crying. I was one of thousands of mothers who had suddenly been forced to navigate this life-changing ordeal alone.

Doctors had stopped seeing patients face to face. All consultations were done over the phone. For months, I spent hours on the phone feeling like I was fighting the system. I was called hysterical. I was told to "calm down" and that all babies cry and are difficult. My worries were not worthy of attention. I was deemed "over-worried" and "over-cautious."

The daily stand-ups by the government on TV blew my mind. They were full of pomp. They would rattle off all of the economically stimulating packages they were going to provide. People were going to work from home. If they had been laid off work temporarily, they would be provided for. Restaurants and bars were not going to be allowed to go under. The government had decided it was crucial for us all to "eat out to help out." I could not understand it. I would go mad trying to reason why six people were able to go to a pub and have a drink but my son, who was in dire need of help, was left to suffer. How was the need to have a beer more critical? Why was it not deemed crucial to have an infrastructure which supported mothers?

Women have always had to fight to have their medical concerns taken with the same serious consideration as their male counterparts. The pandemic exacerbated this gap in healthcare. I was starting to believe that I wasn't cut out for motherhood and that my son was better off without me. I became a shell of myself. I started to drink and smoke in order to cope. Any hope I had of loving my child had gone. I hated every minute of every hour of every day. I didn't want to wake up in the mornings anymore.

We gave up on our government and the NHS. I looked to find a private consultant for our son and for the pain in my back. We broke the rules and regulations and travelled for over an hour to see this doctor. I do not regret it. I would do it again. I would do anything for my son.

I was vindicated. I found that I had fractured my tailbone through labour which had been the source of my pain for the past six months. My son had severe allergies and structural issues with his digestive tract which could not be cured "with time." Within 4-6 weeks of treatment, my son was a different child. I felt stronger, but more than anything, I felt rage. My natural optimism and ability to see the best in everything had been crushed. It had been replaced by cynicism. I steeled myself. I stopped thinking about how unfair and unbearable life had become. I steadied myself to provide the best for my son, no matter how broken I had become.

Life stayed like this until our son was 10 months old.

In May 2021, the world started to reopen some more. We were allowed to mingle with up to 30 people outdoors and one family indoors but we had to stay local to where we lived. The vaccination programme had only just started in the UK. For our parents, who were deemed vulnerable and lived over two hours away, the change in rules was of no consequence to us. Our lives remained unchanged. All the while, 10,000 spectators were legally allowed to go and watch football in stadiums. I felt unbearable rage at the unjustness of the rules and policies in our country. It had become painfully apparent they were becoming less about contagion and more about monetary value.

Reflecting on the events of March 2020 until July 2021, I have realised our society takes motherhood for granted. It takes the strength of women for granted. Women must keep going, no matter what life throws at them. We have no option to stop and take a moment's breath. We are innately gifted and wired to provide for our children, no matter how much we lose ourselves in the process. We do not think twice about sacrificing ourselves. Society does not seem to think twice about sacrificing us, either.

During the pandemic, mothers were forgotten. We had just brought life into an incredibly uncertain world where the message, "If you leave your home you might die or kill someone else by spreading the virus," was constantly drummed into us. We were expected to raise the future of our society alone. The unjustness of watching the world reopen and much of society get on with their lives as if nothing had happened, or moving on while bragging about the benefits which the pandemic had brought them, such as working from home, enraged me even more. How could they all just move on with so much joy? I was still living the same life as during the lockdowns but now I was having to explain to everyone how and why my experience over the last year had differed so vastly. They simply could not put themselves in my shoes. They could not fathom the enormity of what had happened to me and other first-time mothers.

I know too many women who have been left with lifelong trauma from hospitals. Even now I cannot go onto a ward or go in for treatment without having a panic attack that I will be imprisoned, forgotten and separated from my family.

While the UK government announced lockdowns to prevent a "moral disaster" for the NHS, it felt as though it forgot about the moral disaster unfolding in our care homes, on our maternity wards and in our pre/postpartum care. It felt as though the government viewed the management of the pandemic through the lens of death toll statistics. It failed to recognise that, whilst thousands of us did not lose our lives, we lost our sanity.

To anyone who thinks that motherhood with your first baby can be repeated at any time - I will leave you with this. As a woman, I grew up with a vision of what my life would be like, including starting my own family. Time, thought and planning go into this, for many women. Many of us choose when to start trying for a child, a process which can be exhausting and worrying but equally full of excitement. Choosing to become a mother for the first time is a massive period of adjustment for a woman, both before and after the baby is born. I can confidently say there is nothing else that happens in a woman's life which breaks you so physically and mentally and changes you so extremely, both biologically and emotionally. You break apart and must piece yourself back together into a different and more capable version of yourself. When you fall pregnant you imagine your support network showering you with love, affection and confidence. You need this. It is not just a 'nice to have.' It is necessary so that a mother does not feel alone on this life-changing journey. It sets the tone for the rest of your pregnancy and those first few years of your baby's life, during which you are learning how to navigate new situations. You cannot recreate these moments. No second or third child will bring the same feelings. Of course, they are joyful occasions and those children are equally loved. However – your first baby is the one that changed you forever. Your first baby made you a mother. That can never be recreated. The excitement of seeing your baby doing things for the first time when you have never seen a baby do those things before is indescribable. When you are experiencing this through a lens of isolation and grief, those moments are tainted. You do not get to celebrate your first baby's first birthday ever again. This is one of those things in life where you do not get a re-run. Reflecting on these moments for many women feels like gut-wrenching grief, similar to losing a loved one.

The resentment I feel when I see a first-time mother surrounded by her village, loved and supported, is heartbreaking. The jealousy I feel when I see first-time mothers going to baby classes or going on walks unhindered, watching their babies do something for the first time and then sharing that with their families, is painful. I will never be a first-time mother again and I have learned this through having my second child.

I thought my experience with my second child would heal me from the grief of my experience with my eldest. It did not. If anything, the grief worsened. Society did not treat me as a first-time mother. Society saw my eldest and assumed I did not need to be asked how I was. I was a seasoned professional in their eyes, I had already done this. I was shunned from conversations about what to do if a baby did X, Y and Z. "Oh, you have done this before so you're probably not worried." Yes, I had done this before but I had no one to help or show me what to do. I have so much to learn which I missed the first time around.

I have lost myself over the last few years. I know how to smile but I do not feel the joy it brings. I have been conditioned into surviving and shouldering the burden of motherhood.

Mothers must not become the forgotten victims of the pandemic. We didn't lose our lives but many of us lost our sanity. This must never be allowed to happen again. Society must be more vigilant.

Jessica Jairath, 31, is originally from Manchester and is a proud Northerner. She lives with her husband in the Midlands with their two sons whilst working as a Procurement Manager, Group Leader for Endometriosis UK (in Leamington Spa) and Business Coach for Mothers. She also runs her own business, 'The Mum Club Leamington Spa,' which curates events to bring mothers together to help create a community during a vulnerable time in their lives. Having experienced life as a "lockdown mother" this a real passion project. When she isn't running around, you will find her admiring pictures of her children, completely forgetting the hours it took to get them to sleep that night. @themumclubleamingtonspa and @jessica.jairath

ISABELLA GAMBLE

4.5 Miles

"*What do you need to start to heal from this?*" my mother asked me, gently.

It had been five months since my youngest son, Charlie, was born in September 2021, when my local maternity hospital was restricting partner visits to the postnatal ward to one hour a day. This rule was still in place.

My symptoms included:

1. **Flashbacks** to seeing Charlie so new into the world, red-faced and crying in a clinical-looking, clear, plastic hospital crib next to me. It was only a few hours since he'd been pulled from the warmth of my womb. I still couldn't move my lower body following C-section surgery. The midwives told me to press my bell if I wanted to lift Charlie out of the crib and not to try moving and picking him up myself, but when I pressed my buzzer, nobody came.

   As I watched him cry, the instinct of every single cell in my body wanted to hold my precious baby in my arms. Another mother on the ward asked if she could help. She came over and lifted Charlie out and onto my chest for me - a kindness I wish I could somehow repay, but I was too dazed from the anaesthetic to even remember her name.

   When the midwife came ten minutes later, she apologised for not coming sooner - the pandemic had caused low staffing levels.

   I didn't put baby Charlie back in his cot for 24 hours until I was confident that I had built up the strength to lift him in and out myself. I had not slept for over 40 hours.

   I searched on Google Maps the distance between me and home, where my husband and three-year-old son were. 4.5 miles. I looked at the roads between us, mapped the journey, imagined a length of string travelling the paths to connect us and tried to focus on how home wasn't as far away as it felt.

2. I was carrying a deep **anxiety** since the moment I looked down at my hospital sheets soaking in blood as I experienced what I thought was a haemorrhage. I watched the deep red stain on the sheet growing every second.

I had a serious haemorrhage following the birth of my eldest son two years prior, and all I remember was watching my newborn baby in my husband's arms, and feeling content knowing that whatever was happening to my body, he was safe with his dad.

This time it was just Charlie and me in the hospital bay. I thought I was going to die. Charlie would be alone. My exhausted and scared mind was picturing him as a teenager carrying the burden that he was the only one by his mother's side when she died. My baby, alone in the world, nobody there with him who knew his name. Why couldn't my husband have been there to hold Charlie? To get help? Why was he 4.5 miles away?

I pressed the bell but didn't know if anyone was coming or how long it would take. Luckily this time it was only a few minutes until a nurse came. The bleeding was coming from my fresh C-section incision wound. She applied padding and pressure but my distress didn't subside when the bleeding did.

3. I had only spent one night away from my three-year-old prior to Charlie's birth. He's a sensitive child and I'm his safe place. After returning home I would find myself clinging to him and **crying often**. I tried to gently and carefully explain to him that I didn't abandon him, I was at the hospital 4.5 miles down the road. I couldn't leave and he wasn't allowed to come and see his mum or cuddle his new brother for four days and I missed him so, so much. I had imagined the smell of his hair every time I closed my eyes.

4. My chest would tighten and I'd feel **breathless** at the thought of spending time on my own with Charlie, even now we'd been home for months. I had physically recovered but I'd worry that I'd not be able to take proper care of him and would feel **overwhelmed** by his very normal and healthy baby needs. Whilst we were at the hospital Charlie had become dehydrated and was put on a formula top-up feeding plan. I'd felt responsible for not being able to cope well in those first few days and for not breastfeeding him enough.

Post-Traumatic Stress Disorder (PTSD) was Doctor Google's diagnosis for me.

What about the people making the 'rules' that were in place on 13th September 2021, the night Charlie was born? **Did they have PTSD? Were they haunted by the human consequences of their decisions? Did they, in their comfy beds, wake in the middle of the night and look down at their sheets to check they weren't blood-stained?**

I thought about my mother's question - *what did I need to heal from this?*

I'd been frozen in a moment in time, part of me was stuck in that hospital bed 4.5 miles away, trapped in a moment of fight or flight, but too weak to do either. But I wasn't so weak anymore.

I started doing some research. I found organisations such as Birthrights, But Not Maternity and Pregnant Then Screwed who were challenging COVID-related maternity restrictions. It was almost six months since Charlie was born and my local maternity hospital was one of only three in the country still limiting visiting to one hour a day.

My other job, when I'm not changing nappies, providing endless snacks or making up stories about dragons, is in communications and public relations. Because of this, I'm a confident writer and comfortable speaking to journalists. My husband and I wrote to the CEO of the hospital and our local MP. I found a copy of the letter Birthrights had sent to the hospital trust challenging their decision to still enforce such a cruel policy. I sent the letter to the local press along with some words about my experience. The reporter called me back to chat more about the impact of the restrictions. She was awaiting a response from the hospital before she published her article.

A few days later she called me again to tell me her story had changed. She wanted my reaction to the news that:

"They are lifting all maternity visiting restrictions at the local hospital."

It was no miracle, it was an incredibly overdue decision to change something that should have never been in place, but I was overwhelmed with relief that families would no longer have to endure an experience like mine.

That evening, as it began to get dark, the time when my anxiety normally peaked, my thoughts travelled the 4.5 miles down the road back to the maternity hospital, as they so often had over the last six months. To the fourth bay in the third room on the postnatal ward. But that night, instead of seeing another lonely mother there craving rest and recovery, silently screaming out for her village, I could see somebody with her, somebody who loves her, standing at the foot of that bed, gently rocking and hushing her baby.

I still had work to do, but it was over, and that meant I could finally start healing.

Isabella (Issy) Gamble, 30, lives by the sea in Bournemouth with her husband, Karl, and their two sons, four-year-old Arthur and two-year-old Charlie. She has a degree in Fashion Journalism and works in communications and public relations. In her spare time, she pursues interests including women's history, herbalism and magic. Issy loves beachcombing along the Dorset coast and adventuring in the woodlands of the New Forest with her family.
@isabellajaneee

JO CHESTERS

The day he died was not the hardest day.
It was simply the day the stakes got raised.

2020 – Beginning

Two weeks into lockdown. Seven months pregnant. A two-year-old at home. My 43-year-old brother-in-law dies. He had been on a ventilator battling COVID for the past week. No company. No visitors. No contact. I hear the news and instantly collapse to the floor. At the same time, my two-year-old runs in to tell us there's a helicopter in the sky. From that moment on, the fear is more rational, more intense, just *more*.

People often share their sympathy that it "must be hard to go through it alone." But I *want* fewer people and less contact. I resent extra growth scans. They seem an unnecessary risk. I do not want my husband putting himself at risk too, by coming to appointments. Everything is about minimising risk and giving us time. The world needs time to learn and understand what we are fighting, time to build treatments and maybe even, if we are lucky, vaccines.

I cannot rest. It feels inevitable one of us will get it. What if we do? I don't want to pass it on. I don't want anyone else getting sick. My husband is just like his brother. If he gets it, he surely will die, too. I can't have that happen. I cannot let that happen. I cannot raise two children alone. I don't want to raise two children alone. I must not let that happen.

At 37 weeks the baby is breech. I am asked if I want to book in for a C-section or come back for another scan in a week. I am so relieved. I book the section. I am fully prepared to give birth alone if I have to. After all, who could look after our two-year-old, safely, while I am in hospital? Now I have a day that I can plan for. We plan to break the rules. A friend comes to the house to watch our two-year-old for the day. I am deeply uncomfortable that my husband is coming to the hospital with me, but pleased he will be there. He is kicked out the moment I can stand. The ward is quiet and lonely. I like it. My perfect new baby sleeps soundly in the hospital crib and I'm able to video call the grandparents. They were meant to be here for this, not 200 miles away. Thank goodness for technology.

We have to complete some tests to be able to go home. The doctor keeps a safe distance and gets me to handle the baby so he doesn't have to. I do as much as I can, but my baby is not co-operating. We'll have to come back for a hip scan in a few weeks. More contact to dread. I want to go home. I want to get back to my safe space.

We sit at home with a calendar and look at appointment dates. When will there be two weeks without any contact with anyone, to be able to isolate, and then safely have visitors? We plan it out. If nothing goes wrong, my parents can visit in four weeks. They start planning their five-hour drive. Where will they stop? Where will they wee? 'She-wees' are discussed. En-route layby knowledge is shared. They arrive dehydrated, tired and hairier than I remember.

Travel restrictions mean the baby will be 13 months old before meeting the other grandparents. There will be no tiny baby cuddles for them.

By the time others can hold her she's scared of everyone and screams until she's handed back. What have we done to her? How did we let this happen? We should have done more. I should have done more. I should have taken her out. I should have put aside my fears and given her more experiences. But... It wasn't safe.

Restrictions ease a little. We're allowed to meet with friends in the park but I'm too scared. I make my apologies and they go without me. I beat myself up. I try to be rational but I know my husband will die and I cannot let that happen. How would I ever cope? How would I explain to his family that it took another of theirs and it was all my fault? I cannot afford to slip up. I have to keep us safe.

So, we play, at home. It's nice. We video call family. We stay home. Even when we no longer have to, we still do. We take regular walks around the park. We know every inch of that park. It's so beautiful in Autumn with the red leaves and the waterfalls. We're lucky to have it so close by.

As the days shorten, not sharing the load is beginning to drain me. The longer this goes on, the harder it gets. Simple things like having a friend round for a chat and letting the kids play, Mum popping up on the train to stay for a few days, taking the kids to shopping centres, soft play, museums, the zoo... I miss these things more than I thought I would. I wish I could do these things. But I can't. Even when we can, I can't. It's still not safe. Not for me. Not for us.

My husband works from home throughout. He has the freedom to shower, go to the toilet and have a break whenever he wants, under the guise of work. I can hear the shower and his movements upstairs. I resent his freedom. There's no escape from it. At 4:30 pm every day I am watching the clock. Every second past that time I get more frustrated. Where is he? I need him. He's supposed to be done. He should be here to help me now. Why haven't I eaten today? When can I go to the toilet?

I potty train our son. My daughter rolls and tries to crawl. It is the run-up to Christmas. I am so empty that I start to experience periods of derealisation. I clock out, mentally. We make plans to isolate for several weeks so we can share Christmas with my parents. We make plans for the journey with a baby and a newly toilet-trained pre-schooler. The day before leaving, Boris announces Christmas is cancelled. The latest reshuffle of the rules means we can form a 'bubble.' My father describes this as "a loophole in the guidance." We try to persuade him it is OK. We've been careful. We've isolated. We're safe. But he's not happy. He doesn't like how it might look to the neighbours. I give him an earful and then several more. I cry. A lot. I am clutching. I need this Christmas trip, if only to see some different walls. I fight, argue and cry. I throw a few things at a few walls. No one seems to understand how much I NEED this escape. How much I'm sinking under the weight of not being able to share the load and the weight of responsibility to keep my unit safe. It's been so long. We sleep on it. The next day, the loophole is deemed acceptable to everyone. We can make the trip.

The journey is hard. She doesn't like being in the car, she's not used to it. She wants to wriggle. She throws up several times. We stop at some services but we can't go in. We bounce, we cuddle, we feed, we bounce again, we change the nappy on the car seat, we eat the pre-prepared snacks, we leave. At the end of the journey, we're greeted by happy grandparents. Everyone is cautious about cuddles at first but a toddler and a baby soon take over and everything feels weirdly normal.

Normal? I'm not sure I know what normal means anymore.

Everything is meticulously planned. Every meal, every trimming, every day. It all must be included in the shopping delivery. No one can visit a shop. It's not safe.

The time with family is precious, but it's also hard. I know I'm lucky. I should be grateful we can do this. But still, it's hard. I don't handle it well. This has all been too much for too long and I'm ready to break. Christmas isn't the smooth, happy day it should be. I get frustrated. Eventually, I snap. I'm not proud. I've hurt my hand. I feel awful. I am so drained.

2021 - Broken

January brings a fresh start and a new lockdown. I find this comforting. Everyone is back in the same boat. I'm not the outlier or the weirdo. My guilt of not doing things eases for a while. Relatives get their first dose of the vaccine. Things feel more positive for the first time in nearly a year. But this lockdown has come too late. People weren't behaving like us before Christmas. People are dying again. The news is grim. I'm furious at the people for not taking it seriously. I'm furious at the government for not doing more or acting sooner. I'm furious at the world for bringing this on us. I'm broken, angry and extraordinarily sad. Just very, very sad.

The days are really long and really dark. Everyone is weary. This new lockdown isn't as sunny as the first one. No one knows how long it will last. The vaccine roll-out is chugging along and I can see that flicker of a light at the end of a distant tunnel. Better times are coming, aren't they?

But it drags. On. And on. And on.

I am at peak parenting fatigue. I try to find some relief. A coping mechanism. I'm gifted 30 minutes each day, a lunch break, to shut myself away and not be Mummy. My working husband will use his lunch break to take over childcare duties for a bit. I wonder if he's doing too much, then I remember the freedoms he gets. Most days I just sit in a quiet room and do absolutely nothing.

When minute 29 ticks by, the anxiety builds. I go back to my parenting duties. We build another train track. We make new playdough. We paint. We play. We dance. We sing. We watch TV. We can't go out. We have no visitors. It's just us. In our space. The weather is shit. We rarely leave the house, even to the garden, which is now a muddy quagmire.

This period (January – April 2021) is a grey cloud of fog in my mind. It all blurs into one horrible mess. Dark, rainy days of arguments, nappies, feeds, train tracks. I cannot think of a single moment of real happiness. I'm sure there were some, maybe even plenty, but I don't remember them. They weren't the headline stories of the time.

In mid-March, my husband receives his first dose. It's like a weight is lifted. I get mine a few weeks later and literally skip home. I can't tell if I'm more relieved at being vaccinated or that I got to be out of the house alone for a full hour.

I start to consider things we can do, safely. I'm still uneasy about being around people. I try to adjust my mindset. I need to start believing that if we get it, he won't die. He'll be OK now. But this is hard. I'm still scared. I've been away from everyone for so long. My son is back at preschool. They've noticed he backs away from other children when playing outside. We've done this to him. We've taught him this behaviour. I feel awful. I wonder if he'll ever be OK.

The preschool hours allow for some baby time. They're brief, but they're precious. They remind me of what I lost and missed out on. All the things I thought I'd get and didn't. Those early days are gone now and there is no getting them back. She's not a baby any more. She's crawling, eating solid foods and babbling. Her birthday is approaching and she's never been in a shop or eaten out before.

Time crawls by and I'm due back at work soon. I'm still not fully vaccinated. I don't feel ready. I don't think she's ready for nursery. I'm not ready for nursery. I don't like the risks it involves. I look into our options. Maybe I should just quit my job. But we can't afford that. I apply for some extra weeks of unpaid leave. I do the calculations; we can make it work, if we're careful. I vow to make use of the time, to try and get out and have some experiences before the time is gone. I also manage to arrange two full days that I can have just for myself.

We rent a caravan for a weekend and take the kids to the beach. It's perfect. We take them out to eat in a casual restaurant. Being inside with other people makes me uneasy. I leave as soon as I can. I worry about the exposure we've had. Was it safe? How clean was that cutlery? Did that waitress get too close? Were those kids at that other table coughing?

Day 1 to myself - I cycle a favourite trail. Being outside and alone is amazing therapy. Day 2 - I drive myself to the beach. The time in the car is wonderful. I can listen to whatever I want. I don't have to keep checking over my shoulder for children being sick. It's windy and pouring with rain. I'm getting sandblasted as I walk. I'm enjoying every second. Even when I get stuck in the mud and start to panic, I'm still smiling. The whole experience is cleansing for the brain. Just being able to switch off. I start to realise: I'm ready.

2022 – Reflection & Recovery.

Returning to work is a new challenge. Being forced into indoor office space with new people means a loss of control over my risks. Not knowing who to trust or how worried to be. I discover work means I get time to think for myself, about something other than parenting. My supportive manager helps with arranging a CO_2 monitor for the room. I can sit next to an open window. Sorry, colleagues, but we'll be keeping this open all winter. It makes me feel safer. With time to think, I recognise I've never actually dealt with any of it. Not really.

People around me are having babies. They're able to pass them around. They meet family and then share photos. I find myself uncontrollably crying every time I'm confronted with one of these images. I'm not resentful. I'm happy for these new babies and their families. But I'm so sad that mine missed out, that they didn't get to hold my tiny baby or form a close bond early on. Stories of friends' antenatal appointments trigger memories of my own experiences. I remember how scared I was, sitting alone in that waiting room. I didn't want to be there. I didn't want anyone coming near me. The memory of this makes me sob. My reaction is so intense that it surprises me.

Through it all, I'm still grieving. The loss of my brother-in-law. The uncle that my children will never know. We show them photos and talk about him. Each Christmas I remember his last visit. December 2019. He bounced my then two-year-old, Jacob, on his knee and said, "next year, I'll take you to panto."

I'm also grieving something else, less specific: the experiences. The walks, the cafes, the friends, the visitors, the excursions, the baby swimming. All the things we couldn't do. I grieve the loss of these things.

I visit a friend and her newborn. I walk around the house carrying the tiny baby. I cry as I carry. This is what no one else got to do with mine. I explain this, through tears, to my friend, explaining my grief, and as I bounce the tiny baby in my arms I realise it's getting easier. I've reached a point of acceptance. I can accept what happened. It may still make me sad sometimes. Some very random things will trigger a memory or a response that catches me off guard. The latest triggers have brought me full circle. My baby daughter, Riley, now two years old, is getting to do things my eldest didn't get to do when he was that age! But I'm OK. We're OK. We're going to be OK.

Jo Chesters lives with her husband and two children in Derbyshire. She enjoys countryside walks with the family, and hilltop sunrises.

ALI BLAND

In the words of the great Charles Dickens, "It was the best of times, it was the worst of times."

Because it wasn't all bad, was it? In hindsight, at least.

It started as a rumour, a virus from China, then seeing Italians queuing two metres apart to get groceries, then stories of people dying in Europe.

It was something I was aware of but brushed off. I was in a newborn haze, a first-time mum having had a near-perfect pregnancy, with a little drama at the end (a breech baby and low amniotic fluid meant an unexpected C-section.) I was still recovering, both physically and mentally.

My pre-baby maternity leave had never happened, with my daughter arriving at 37 weeks, tiny but perfect and so loved. I had hospital visits from family and friends – in that respect, we were lucky, much luckier than those in hospital just a few weeks later.

The rumours quickly became more widespread, the news was full of stories and it started to become more real.

For my first Mother's Day, we met with friends for a walk in the sunshine, my daughter wrapped up to protect her. Huge smiles all around. But the announcement came that night. *You must stay at home.* The tears started. Suddenly, my maternity leave spent with my new baby, new friends, baby classes, family visits, everything... came crashing down. I sobbed to my partner that this was going to be my whole maternity leave. He assured me that it would surely be over soon.

I cried every single day. When my daughter did anything new it was for our eyes only. She was amazing and no one else would witness those 'firsts.' Daily messages were exchanged with new friends I'd met at antenatal classes, the ones we were meant to drink endless cups of tea with as we watched our newborn babies grow together. I'd been pregnant at the same time as one of my best friends, too. All the plans we'd made for the summer, spent together in paddling pools and beer gardens, disappeared. Suddenly, we were on Zoom calls, waving tiny baby hands and wondering if they would ever meet.

Daily walks with my husband and baby became something to look forward to, bumping into the same people every day and seeing the fear in their eyes, along with the loneliness, the monotony, the never-ending days and nights and the constant worry.

Through all of this, all the firsts and lasts and things that no one else would witness, I had my daughter. I saw everything. My husband saw everything. We witnessed every tiny thing our daughter did and we cherished it all. There was nothing to distract our little family bubble in this newly-terrifying world. Now, I think, what would I have missed with my daughter had I been rushing to meet friends or go to baby classes? Would her first smile have been at me or a stranger in a coffee shop? Would I have missed her first time crawling as I left her with a friend whilst I popped out? Would we have this perfect bond and the calmness in our lives, never needing anyone else?

So much was taken away from us as new mums and parents, but we were also given a gift: time together to enjoy each other without distraction or fear of judgement. We had the freedom to become a parent as we wanted to and to allow our babies to grow without any external influences.

When I reflect on it all, I feel sad, angry, neglected and alone, but I also feel loved, calm and so very, very happy. I watch my delightful little three-year-old running to me with utter joy on her face and I do wonder whether it really was the worst of times, or whether it might just have been the best.

ALLISON ISAAK

They sent you away. The only person in the world I was ever trying to get to. They sent you away. They took the baby from my arms and placed him in yours. You looked at me like it was the last look you would ever give me. I think I smiled because I knew our boy would be fine and you were going to be a great dad. I don't remember what happened next. I think I was too exhausted to be scared. I remember thinking, *if I die, at least I can finally get some sleep.*

But, I didn't die. I lost 900ml of blood and contracted sepsis, but I didn't die. I woke up and was placed in a wheelchair. I couldn't feel my legs yet as the epidural was still wearing off. They took me out of the room and put me onto a ward with five other mothers and their newborn babies and told you to go home. It was 4am. We both thought I was going to die less than three hours ago. I asked, "Can't he stay until morning?" They said no, and just like that, they sent you away.

Everything hurt. Every single part of my body ached. All I wanted was to be held by you. To be comforted by you. To be told that I was going to make it and that I was going to be OK, but I wasn't OK because they sent you away and left me with a baby that didn't feel like mine. We didn't know if he was going to be OK. He had sepsis, too. They had to give him antibiotics in the NICU so I had to take him there every day and night. I had to wake up every hour or two to feed my baby and set an alarm for 2am every night. Slowly, painfully, I would rise and then push his little bed through the hospital with tiny shuffle steps because everything hurt. It always woke him up. The injection of antibiotics into his tiny veins followed and then the cycle of crying and comforting would begin again.

You would've done it for me if you'd been there. You would've let me rest. You would've turned off the fluorescent lights before midnight. You wouldn't have talked so loudly on the phone or watched soap operas without headphones. You would've changed the sheets that I sweated through each night. You would've watched him so I could go to the toilet without worrying that every cry I heard was his cry. You would've let me take a shower so I could wash the dried blood off my body. But, they sent you away, and I was alone, so utterly alone and a new life depended on me but I felt too broken to be a mother.

Those five days felt like an eternity, but I made it home. I thought it would be fine once I was home, I was so happy to be back with you, but I still felt broken. I still felt alone. No one came to visit and no one held him except the two of us. I clung to you. I didn't know what else to do. I started having panic attacks whenever you left the house. You tried to go for a bike ride but I was alone again with the baby and the baby started crying and I couldn't do it. I knew I couldn't do it on my own and I called you to come home. So, you stopped going out. You stayed home. You lost friends. You lost yourself. I tried to tell you that I was OK but you didn't believe me. I didn't believe me, either.

I kept the baby alive and some days I even got dressed. I kept calling him 'the baby.' He still didn't feel like mine.

I want to do it over. I want you to stay with me this time, the whole way through. I want that magical moment with my baby that everyone talks about. Instead, I wanted to cry, I wanted to feel something but I felt nothing. I kept not believing that this child was mine and that he was going to survive. I didn't think I was ever going to be OK again.

They didn't need to send you away. It didn't save anyone's life. It only broke mine. You are still my world. You and our beautiful boy. He's really here and he's really mine. But, how many seasons came and went, before I felt it? How much time was lost to trauma and fear? If only you had been allowed to stay. I think I would've known so much sooner that I would be OK.

Allison Isaak, 35, lives in London with her husband, Nick, and her two-year-old son, London James. Originally from Canada, she met her husband, who is also Canadian, while teaching at an international school in Dhaka, Bangladesh. Their unconventional love story led them to the city of London in 2016 and they decided to name their son after the dynamic city they had come to fall in love with. She is a primary school teacher, music teacher, and singer-songwriter, performing under the stage name "Allison Conrad."
@allisonconradmusic

AMY SLATER-BELL

I hope you know, darling,
that none of this was your fault.

I hope you know, darling,
that the government 'rules' came up short.

I hope you know, darling,
that my tears and trauma weren't on you.

I hope you know, darling,
that we cherish you as much as it is possible to.

I hope you know, darling,
the terror and anxiety in my gut **were** tempered with my love.

I hope you know, darling,
that I would do it all again for you, should push come to shove.

I hope you know, darling,
that my body grew you, protected you and nourished you, the very best it could.

I hope you know, darling,
that the NICU heat and beeps kept you as safe as they said that they would.

I hope you know, darling,
how much our families longed to cuddle and kiss you throughout your first lonely year.

I truly hope you know, my darling,
how wonderful it is to have and hold you here.

With love,

Mama x

KATE OWEN

Trigger warning: Miscarriage

I have always hated hospitals. They are the landmarks of some of the worst moments of my life; places of 'goodbyes' that I thought were 'see you laters.' But, that day, the waiting room was full of women, bodies in bloom, soft light and silent anticipation. We had marked the date on the calendar in pencil, too anxious to commit to ink. I knew it should be a happy day, but I couldn't count on it.

"I am safe," I repeated like a mantra, "I am safe."

But still, the fear threatened to overwhelm me; not the thrill of fear you get on a roller-coaster but fear that you might not survive. Fight, flight, freeze. I always thought I would fight but in all the moments of my life where I have been truly afraid, I have frozen. I wanted to reach out to hold the hand of my husband, someone who was in this as deep as I was. But he wasn't there. COVID restrictions left him marooned in the car park, enduring the same dread as me, also alone. I imagined his fingers drumming the gear stick as he tried to distract from the echoes of the time before.

84 days. 12 weeks pregnant.

I should be happy, I was happy... This baby was so wanted we had celebrated it at every possible moment - the size of a sesame seed, a blueberry and a plum. I wanted to paint the nursery, read baby name books, cradle my stomach and feel the flutter of another heartbeat. But I couldn't let myself think of it, not yet. Because I had been here before - 84 days, 12 weeks pregnant... whilst the world patiently waited for the first lockdown to ease, I had been waiting for something else. The chance to see my baby, our baby, for the first time...

I am a pessimist. Something that bad luck and misfortune have taught me well. I had told my husband not to get excited, not until we had the scan. I told him the odds, I told him this might not be it. I tried to hold on to hope when the spotting started.

"I'm sure it's nothing," I told him.

We Googled it; it said, 'Nothing to worry about.' When it got heavier, we called the doctor.

"Nothing to worry about. We'll book you a check-up first thing in the morning. As long as you're not cramping I'm sure it's fine."

But then, inevitably, the cramping started. It didn't stop. That night, we lay in the dark, waiting for the morning to come so that we could get to the hospital. We both knew what was happening, we just couldn't say it aloud. I left my husband at the hospital entrance. COVID restrictions meant everyone had to go it alone. I expected this, I knew mothers who had gone through most of their labour without their partners. It was still hard to leave him. I squeezed his hand and he squeezed mine, but we couldn't delay any longer. I followed the green line on the floor in solitary silence.

The ward was almost abandoned and I was glad. I didn't want to see anyone else. I didn't want to be here. I was glad when they called my name, the waiting almost as painful as the cramping in my stomach. I climbed onto the bed. The sonogram screen was dark and I held my breath; hoping, bargaining with a god I didn't believe in that I would hear the big bang of a heartbeat. See some small spark in the dark. That the black screen would fracture with the white lines of my baby's bones. I waited, and I waited...

"I'm so sorry..." She paused. "You were pregnant but it wasn't viable. As you can see it is very small. It hasn't been developing for some time. I'm so sorry for your loss."

The shock hit me first. I felt dizzy from the force of it. Then there was a strange underwhelm like I had always known this was where I would end up. I stared at the screen, trying to take in every curve of the tiny baby, wanting to remember the first and last sight of my child. It was a goodbye without ever saying hello. I wasn't ready for it. After a minute, I thanked the sonographer. It felt strange but I didn't have any other words for them. I left the room and crumbled across the threshold. The nurse whispered from behind her mask, "I wish I could hug you but I'm not allowed..." It was a sweet sentiment but I wanted my husband to hold me. He wasn't allowed either. He was in the car, hoping against hope. I hated myself for it, but I texted him.

"Not good news..."

I knew my mouth couldn't form the words to explain to him what had taken place. The nurse handed me a letter, a greying sheet of A4 was all that I had to remember this baby.

That night it happened, like the falling of a shooting star, the end of it all. I spent hours lying on my bathroom floor trying not to pass out from the pain, retching as my abdomen contracted, dismantling me from the inside. My whole self was in danger of collapse. Eventually, I emerged from the bathroom to my husband's waiting arms and I cried into the sleeve of his shirt as he held me.

"It's over."

This time would be different, that was what we had told each other, over and over. It's what we had to believe. I just wished he was there to tell me again. I didn't want to be alone, if the worst happened I wouldn't be able to bear it on my own again. I lay back on the bed and pulled my top up, allowing the sonographer to press the wand into my belly. I held my breath, just like before...

"Could you relax? It's easier to see if you're relaxed..."

"Sorry," I replied and exhaled purposefully. She didn't know why I was so tense. She didn't know the fear, the freeze.

There was a long pause, silence and then, 'Bang...' The heartbeat. I could see the sparks of life bursting across the screen. It was like the beginning of the universe, each flicker of that tiny heart was the birth of a star, the start of a constellation. A galaxy of possibility inside me. I laughed, not loudly, just to myself. Lost in our own little universe. I squeezed my own hand in excitement but I wished it was his. He deserved to be there, this was the start of his new world, too.

Kate Owen is a TV Producer, mother and obstinately hopeful person. She started writing again in 2020, during the lockdown after more than a decade of writer's block. Her new life in the country, her husband and the birth of her daughter have become huge sources of inspiration. She is glad to have found her voice again and wants to tell honest, emotive and joyous stories about unwieldy women.

KAYLEIGH GISSING

Trigger warning: Lone birth

April 13th 2020 - the day we met.

I had dreamed of this day my entire life. I imagined both my mum and Michael (my partner) crying with joy at the sight of our son. I imagined my mum stroking my head and telling me how proud she was. I longed to see Michael hold our son in his arms and become a dad.

My reality was complete darkness.

I laboured my son into the world and I kept my eyes closed the whole time. My heart couldn't bear the sight of the people missing from the hospital room. I kept my eyes closed to stop my heart from aching.

I'm not sure anything could prepare anyone to give birth alone. I knew it was going to happen but I had no idea how I was going to prepare myself for such an experience.

Just before I went into labour my mum told me, "You can do anything - I know you can because you are my daughter." *I hope so,* I thought.

My waters had broken and it was time to head to the birthing unit. I left Michael in the car park. It felt so alien to be in so much pain and be walking away from the person I wanted and needed the most.

I was 7cm dilated and left in a room alone until I was ready to start pushing. The room felt huge: just me, my bump and the beeps from the machine. It was then that I decided I couldn't keep my eyes open, that the pain of being alone was too much to bear and so I would get through it with as little memory as I could at the end of it. The thought of remembering empty chairs and no hands to hold crippled me. My eyes squeezed shut. My goal was to get me and my baby home as quickly and safely as possible.

I was told that Michael could bring my hospital bag in and would be allowed to stay in the room with me, for a brief period, whilst I pushed. I held his hands so tight. Still, my eyes remained closed. The midwife tried to make conversation with me asking me the usual questions about my baby. Her calming voice and loving tone reminded me of my mum. I felt so angry I couldn't get my words out. I didn't want her, I wanted my mum.

"I don't want to talk or open my eyes, I just want to get home with my baby," I said. She said she understood and placed her hand on my leg. I think she knew.

Things moved at a quick pace and before I knew it I was being rushed for an emergency C-section. Michael had to leave. I was on my own again. I lay on the operating table, numb, my hands clasped tightly together. I was thinking about how sad it was that Michael wasn't going to see his baby be born.

I didn't open my eyes for a second.

Until... they placed his tiny cheek on mine.

The best moment of my life was our skin touching for the very first time, the midwife holding his tiny little face against mine. She explained he needed skin to skin but I couldn't do that until I was finished in surgery, so my precious boy was wheeled away to another room where his dad could meet him. A moment I would miss. My heart aches at that thought. Really, *really* aches.

My eyes squeezed shut again until we were reunited in the recovery ward. I was alone with our son. I lay in my bed, holding him, trying not to think of all the things we were missing out on. I was trying not to think about my sisters coming to visit, the baby gifts and newborn cuddles, but I did, and I cried a lot.

As soon as I could get out of my bed, I drew the curtains and kept them that way for the three days we were there. I didn't want to see the reality, hearing it was almost too much to bear. Women cried for their loved ones and made desperate 2am FaceTime calls to family for advice and words of support. Staff were stretched to the maximum. Not a single smile as they were all hidden behind masks. No visits. No hugs or kisses. Just me and my baby.

That was just the start of what was the most challenging time of my life.

Kayleigh Gissing, 33, from Barnet, lives with her partner, Michael, and their three-year-old son, Theodore. She works full-time as a Programme and project management officer. She spends almost all of her free time with family and friends. She enjoys true crime podcasts and drinking wine in the garden.

ANNA CARTER

This is where I'm admitted for the induction.
Alone.
Optimistic at first, with lots of 'I can do this' and positive vibes.

This is where things start to change. Painful examinations without him to hold my hand or tell me it's going to be okay. The pain becomes unbearable. I can't eat, the food stays on the tray untouched. A look of contempt from the woman who collects it.

This is where I'm constantly calling or texting him with updates as he's not allowed to be there. Not allowed to comfort me, rub my back or advocate for me. I have to make every decision on my own and I'm useless at making decisions at the best of times. My emotions are rocketing up and then plummeting down. I'm not sure I can do this on my own.

This is where I lock myself in the toilet, trying not to scream, afraid of startling or disturbing the other mums-to-be. There's a woman opposite me on the ward who is on her third pessary and she looks like she's dying. I'm terrified.

This is where they do a COVID test, despite the fact I'd already been in the hospital for a few hours.

This is where they eventually let me go and see your dad – in the hospital's car park. It's dark and chilly and I'm in agony. I feel like an inmate being teased with a tiny crumb of freedom. He's upset, feels helpless and doesn't want to leave me. He's terrified, too. I want to go with him. The pain becomes intolerable. Later, I beg for pethidine and the removal of the pessary. What follows is sweet, sweet, blissful slumber - a whole three hours.

This is where I'm told to call your dad to tell him to come back. It's time.
Time to go to the labour ward.
Things move fast now. Waters are broken. I'm feeling so much happier now that I have him with me. The relief of a partner. A teammate. Those positive vibes start to trickle back in.
With a supportive and kind midwife and your dad by my side, your journey Earth-side begins.
It isn't the birth I wanted. It's a traumatic experience for all of us.

This is where I'm spent, exhausted and broken.
You're here in all your wonderful newness. I struggle to take you in. You're really here! I did it. To be honest, I'm in shock.

We have a few precious hours of bonding, all three of us, but then it's time to go to the recovery ward.

"This is where Daddy leaves us."
Why is she saying it so breezily? I feel like something is being ripped from me. Your dad's face has a look of terror. We knew he wouldn't have been able to stay all day, but to not get the chance to settle us in, help me into bed or check we have everything we need? It just seemed so cruel after all we'd been through. Now he has to leave and go home without his partner and new baby.

This is where we're thrust into the unknown.
It's you and me, kid.
Together, alone.
We think it's only for one night. It's okay, I've got this.

This is where we're stuck for an additional two nights.
You won't wee. I get upset and frightened. I must be doing something wrong. I struggle with your latch. There aren't any breastfeeding support volunteers. It's deemed an unessential service.

This is where I buzz for help. Buzz. Buzz.
That bloody buzzing.
Most of the time someone comes. One night, no one does – staff are stretched to their limit.
I barely sleep. I'm swollen and bleeding. I've never felt so lonely. My phone is a lifeline. I'm worried I'll drain the battery.

This is where your dad only gets to visit for one hour a day.
It is not enough. It goes by too fast. He cuddles you and I lie next to you both, trying to rest but not wanting to miss a thing, it's too precious.

This is where I take two-minute showers (my hair is still a tangled mess with almost every kind of bodily fluid mangled in it) because there is no one to watch you whilst I'm gone. The staff say they'll keep an eye on you but I don't want to leave you for too long.
I'm sad that we can't have visitors. No grandparents to come and dote on you. No joyful aunties and uncles. We've been robbed of that.

This is where you eventually wee!
Everyone is relieved. I am elated. We can leave. We can actually leave.

This is where I pick you up, my little love. I cradle you in my arms and walk to the window of this place I called a prison to show you our city. Our home.

Somewhere down there, your dad is excitedly getting in the car to come to collect us. Freedom, at last!

This is where I silently pray to whoever or whatever is listening that we'll get to have visitors at home and that the government will not change the current guidelines.
That things will get better.

Anna Carter is a 36-year-old mum to a wonderful, spirited, nearly three-year-old daughter. Born and raised in Yorkshire, she lives there with her little family which includes her amazing partner and a needy tabby cat. Currently focusing on raising her daughter, she can also be found running community clothes swaps and having adventures by the sea or in the woods. Writing is a passion and a hobby which she would love to make a career of.
@a_carter_writes

ANNA GOODWIN

This wasn't how it was supposed to be.

It was meant to be a time of enjoyment, bonding and making friends with other mums, sharing my baby with friends and family, coffee and play dates, supporting each other after sleepless nights and finally finding a place to belong after waiting so long for it and always feeling like the spare part.

There was no way of knowing quite what was about to happen and the lasting effect it would have.

Years and years of waiting, praying and hoping that two lines would appear on a test, two miscarriages, various types of fertility treatment, medications, injections and then finally a successful round of IVF gave us the miracle we had been hoping for. Two faint lines on a cheap test from the fertility clinic.

There were months of anxiety filled with waiting and reassurance scans to check that everything was OK. It finally led to five long and traumatic days of contractions and eventually the birth of the missing piece of our puzzle. By the time he arrived in December 2019, we were in shock, in awe and traumatized by what had happened. Our little miracle was finally here.

Tongue tie, feeding issues, weight loss, problems with his neck from the difficult birth, colic and illness plagued the first three months. My mental health had already taken a hammering. I already felt incapable, isolated, alone, clueless, a failure and as if my baby didn't like me. He cried so much. I found it so hard to soothe him and felt so triggered by every cry. The shape of his tongue as he cried became permanently etched into my brain. Even three years on, seeing the shape of his tongue when he cries takes me straight back to that time. He was doing absolutely nothing wrong and it wasn't his fault at all. I just hadn't experienced babies that cried as much as he did.

By March 2020, two lines on a test meant something extremely different. I was terrified of seeing two lines on the little plastic test, that looked the same as the ones from the fertility clinic, in case that meant something awful was going to happen to me and my family.

The virus that had been mentioned in China just after our son was born was suddenly spreading near and far, something to now be feared and taken seriously as it could kill us or make us extremely ill. It felt like the world was shut off as lockdown began in the UK on Monday 23rd March 2020. Our 15-week-old son's experience of the outside world and his family immediately stopped. Our front door closed and we stayed safely inside, avoiding anything outside that might hurt our three-person bubble.

Formula, nappies, soap and toilet roll, along with food, became scarce overnight. It became cut-throat to try and find the things we needed for our son to keep him clean and fed. Limits were put on things like paracetamol and hand sanitiser so that people didn't stock-pile. There were huge gaps on the shelves in supermarkets, shops were closed and when online shopping did restart, stock was limited as the whole supply chain tried to adjust to a new way of life. Suddenly, getting clothes for a growing baby and the changing of the seasons became a new challenge to tackle and another thing to worry about. Our only visitors were the postman and the Evri courier.

The nightly briefings as the world battled to fight the virus became something to dread. More terrifying news, increasing deaths and repeated reminders of how deadly this airborne bug was. The messages of fear and avoiding people at all costs were burned into my brain. My anxiety, which had been triggered by my fertility journey and early motherhood, now had a new focus. The outside world became a scary, threatening and dangerous place.

What I didn't realise was that I was already living with a lower level of contamination OCD where I had developed coping behaviours to get me through triggering situations. It had started a long time ago and had gradually increased over a few years, but now it was about to smack me solidly in the face. Having a couple of sickness bugs within weeks of giving birth and then a global pandemic was just too much to cope with. I was terrified. Everything felt like a risk that needed to be calculated.

When I felt brave enough to try going out for a walk around the village, I realised it wasn't something to enjoy, but instead, a mission as I constantly crossed over the road and back again to avoid people. If there wasn't time to cross, I would hold my breath and try to push the pram as far away from people as possible so they didn't breathe on my precious boy. Babies attract attention so I was terrified of well-meaning people peering into his pram to see him or touch his face. It became safer and easier just to stay at home.

I spent months at home without going out. The only place I occasionally ventured to was for a walk around a field behind our house, but as my postnatal depression, anxiety and OCD got worse, everything felt harder and, at times, impossible.

I made my husband deal with post, parcels and online food shopping deliveries. Our hallway became a mail sorting depot. I wouldn't let him open anything until it had been quarantined in our house for at least three days. When he touched it, he needed to thoroughly wash his hands before he could come anywhere near us. Any food shopping that arrived had to be washed in soapy water or disinfected to make it safe. I would have refused to eat rather than touch unwashed food.

Occasionally, my husband had to pop to a shop for something, or worse, had to go into the office. Just the thought of it made me panic and become convinced someone would become ill. I struggled to sleep anyway as we had a young baby, but when I wasn't up feeding or settling him, I was lying awake with worry. When my husband got home, I would make him stand inside the front door and take all his clothes off before he could go any further. The washing machine door was wide open and he had to put the clothes in without touching anything else. He could then wash his hands and face and was finally able to regain some dignity and get some clothes on. Everything that had been out of the house felt contaminated and like it glowed with germs.

The week following was spent being hyper-vigilant, looking out for any signs or symptoms that might indicate one of us had caught COVID. I would only start to relax after the week had passed and I felt like we were in the clear. Any other interactions with the outside world would restart the clock again.

My days were spent at home looking after our son. We played together, explored his developing skills, joined online music classes and learnt new songs. Some days were unbelievably long and sometimes I had no idea what to do. I had no 'village' or new mum friends to ask and no break for myself to give me some space or decent time to sleep.

My husband worked from home from the start of the pandemic. Working in IT meant that he was busier than usual, working more hours to get the rest of the organization fully operational to work from home, even though that led to him feeling conflicted as he wanted to spend the extra time with his son. I felt lucky that he was at home with us as I can't imagine how much more isolated and desperate I would have felt without him around, even though he spent hours at his desk each day.

COVID, lockdown and isolation affected everyone in different ways. Friendships that I thought were strong seemed to nearly all disappear overnight as each person turned inwards and focused on their own situation. Ironically, despite feeling isolated and alone, I found it incredibly difficult to reach out to people as it felt easier to stick to where I felt safe, rather than reaching out for the social contact that I needed. I felt unable to complain or vent about my situation as the rest of the world was experiencing such difficult times, too. I wasn't having to work and home-school at the same time. I didn't have a child who was climbing the walls, missing the playground or their friends. It is only on reflection that I realise my feelings were justified and that having a baby is one of the most challenging points in life.

Even when restrictions started to lift, I found it too much to meet up with a group of ladies from antenatal Pilates, who now all had their babies. The thought of going swimming or trying a baby group felt too monumental to contemplate. Other people started to go and appeared to have no concerns or difficulties doing it. I felt like I was being left behind and that I was failing again.

I felt robbed of the maternity leave that I had waited more than a decade for, and never thought I would be lucky enough to have. This time I had heard so much about, from people who I knew with children, was likely to be a 'once-in-a-lifetime' experience, and I wanted to make the most of it. To be fair, they weren't wrong. It *was* a once-in-a-lifetime experience, as neither my husband nor I could imagine going through the baby years again. Our collective mental health just isn't up to it. It left a permanent scar, despite the amazing parts. I feel sad to think that we weren't able to enjoy it in the way we had hoped. Instead, we were sleep-deprived and locked away, hoping that we were doing our best.

My best friend Liz was incredible. Despite having her own personal circumstances to deal with, she was always so supportive, always checking in with us to see how things were going, always understanding of how I was feeling and always encouraging when I considered seeking professional help. Without her continual support, those times would have been even more bleak. She was one of the few people that I felt understood me despite being in different situations to each other. She has an incredible relationship with our son and I was, and will always be, so grateful to her.

As time went on, our son continued to develop and grow. He was my driver and the reason for carrying on and getting up each day. I can't imagine how the lockdowns and restrictions would have been without him. I know that he knew no better, but I can't help but feel desperately sad at all the experiences he missed out on in those early months and years, whether it was because of the pandemic, my state of health, or just generally because of how we coped. I can't help but wonder if it has had a lasting effect on him or his development. Would his personality or abilities be any different if the course of events were different? Would his interests be different if he had experienced other things much sooner? There is no way of knowing these things, but I know that he is the person he is meant to be. He has made me want to work on myself and seek help to deal with my anxiety and OCD. I don't want to limit his world even more than it has already been. I'm not embarrassed about what I have experienced and I will answer any questions he has when he is older. It doesn't define me, but it has made me realise that I am a lot stronger than I give myself credit for.

I feel grateful that, despite experiencing the hardest time of my life, I got to spend so much time with my son to bond with him and get to know each other. My husband was around for a lot more of our son's milestones compared to if he had been working in the office. He was there for the first laugh, rolling over, starting weaning, the first time he sat up unsupported on his own, and when he started cruising around the furniture. For all the hardship and heartbreak the pandemic brought, these were the positives to come from it.

Three years on from the first lockdown, our son is at nursery and is thriving. He gives us so much joy, laughter and everything in between. Face masks are no longer the norm and we are all getting used to the new way of living with COVID. I still have to work hard to keep my anxiety and OCD in check, particularly with nursery and other activities in the mix. I still get a pang of envy when I see new parents out for coffee together, talking about their babies and the latest challenge. I tell myself that I'm pleased for them that they will never have to endure the hell that we experienced. I wouldn't wish that on anyone.

Anna Goodwin, 42, from Bedfordshire, lives with her husband and their 3.5-year-old son, Jacob. She works part-time as a Systems and Project Officer. She loves reading, visiting Norfolk and being beside the sea.

AMY BALDERSTON

And in the blissfully unaware bubble of autumn 2019, we whispered YES, yes. Let's sack off that contraceptive pill and live life on the edge. We're ready, we're set. Let's go.

January. Dad turns yellow. Downhill fast. Rampant returns to home county. Gone in just over a week. High-functioning alcoholic. WE KNEW HE DRANK BUT NOT THIS. 62. Last breaths. Incomprehension. Shock. Numb. FURIOUS. Body blows of grief.

February. Funeral. A wedding. A blur. Snatches of memories but so little to grasp. Fog. Whispers about this mystery illness and lockdowns in countries far from ours. Capacity to absorb, blown.

Late March. Lockdown. Let's get a cat. I've always wanted one. That'll help. A rescue. Hopefully, gain some company and comfort.

Late April. Grief swamp. Incessant googling of physical impacts of grief on our body. 'Normal' reactions, emotions, why things can feel SO LOUD. Desperate moments of self-pity and loneliness. Nausea. This is TOO MUCH to process in the new world of lockdown. O sorry what, wait, could it? IS THIS FUCKING HORMONES?! What a spicy cocktail for our house of us two and a feral cat who won't sit on my knee. Pregnancy on top of grief. Good.

An early announcement - if this goes wrong and we're still locked down, not sure how to cope. COME JOIN US ON THIS RIDE. Probably best to shield, we haven't a bloody clue about the potential impact of this on you or your baby. Hide. Hide away. You're vulnerable. Fuck. Tell work, too.

June. The first scan. Mask on, terrified. Husband in the car. Let it be OK. It's already too much. No smiles with masks. Too scared to make eye contact. Distancing, distancing, distancing. Hand pat from the nurse, flinch. Searching eyes. Heartbeat. Image of an alien on a screen. Too scared to ask to record the sound for him. It's OK. We're OK. Run out. Reunited after the first of many anxiety-ridden hospital car park drop and waits. Fuck, we're bringing a baby into this shit. The reality of juggling this together/apart across car parks, corridors and walls settles murkily alongside the joy.

We're lucky. We're safe. We're OK. THE PRESSURE to keep this incessant babble of affirmations afloat. It could be worse. It is what it is. What joy in such a time. Hands clenched, grimacing smiles. Yes. Yes it is.

Suddenly, the weight does not stop there. The EXPECTATION that we will sail through this, there will be no hiccups. We will birth this perfect child like an offering of happiness, a distraction, a delight, a balsam for everyone in this battle against the invisible illness raging across our streets. The pressure to keep safe. To shield. To hide. To veer manically away from strangers in the street.

Work. Everything is postponed. Your days become two rather than three. Cut down. Guilty, grateful, glad for at least something.

A trip to the supermarket becomes a white-knuckle ride. Timed, considered, over-thought, planned for the precisely perfect moment the vulnerable can risk a public outing. A desperate thirst to PLEASE let me have something, anything normal and banal to bring balance to my days.

A walk up in the forest, a slip, a bump to bump. A screaming fear ringing in my ears. Not even this is safe. Foolish. STAY AT HOME. Save your own life. Save the baby. Hospital. Monitoring. All fine. A suitable punishment of bi-weekly blood tests to ensure we are OK. His blood is the baby's, and mine clashes. A bizarre comforting connection for him, shared blood. A reminder this is real.

The rules relax. The nation breathes out. We breathe in. The rules are different for us. Midwives comment - it just isn't worth it, is it? This becomes a sentence that haunts us with every small decision or justification made. Cut off, afloat, anxiety-ridden. Thirsty, desperate to understand, to build trust, to believe it is safe. But caught in those words that get repeated to us with every masked, flinching, lonely appointment or contact throughout.

The days grow colder, shorter. The relaxed summer days for some are now prised back as restrictions creep back in. A curious mix of fear and resentment for those who embraced and bent the rules for contact, joy, A PARTY. Empathy dwindling as reality slams. Another full lockdown. We are 32 weeks now.

Reduced movements, once, twice, always put off, a hesitation to ring, to ask for help. THE HEALTH SERVICE IS OVERWHELMED. Emergencies only, please. A horrendous moral battle for over-anxious guardians of a bump. Late admission onto the ward. Observations, observations. Freezing cold car parks for him. Waiting, waiting, holding. Relief, entangled in fear of the exposure from simply going in. We are sent home and on our way.

Burrowed deep into our cocoon now. Distanced deliveries to the doorstep, only brief contact. Everyone is suffering. There is a pandemic of empathy alongside the virus now. It is dancing between our relationships with others beyond our walls. We can't hold each other up anymore. The load too heavy, the lockdown too acute, the impact felt too deeply, widely. There are no hugs or hand pats from the ones you desperately miss or need the most, and we are all out of meaningful words. WE ARE FINE, DOING GREAT, ISN'T IT WONDERFUL? A JOY.

Christmas. A day before due date. Reduced movements once again three days before. We sit compliantly at home. Waiting. We hold. We see no one. We field gentle enquiries. We eat. Rest. Light the fire.

New Year's Eve. Midwife appointment. A week overdue. Raised blood pressure. Best go for your sweep in hospital, now. Not here. Pack your bag. Go now. Car park goodbye. The most anxious of all. The horror stories of partners being left out in the cold too long, for days, alone. THANK FUCK FOR PHONES.

A missed note to book an induction, three days before now. Admittance. A toe-curling, eye-watering sweep. A pessary. A room - a hideous mirror image of the one where we lost Dad. A part of me breaks down at this point and simply leaves. It is too much. I mentally go somewhere removed from my reality and I am not sure I come back for quite some time.

My husband is allowed in. Stay or leave, your choice, but we advise you go, it won't be tonight, get some rest. Feed that cat. YEAH I AM FINE, YOU GO, THEY KNOW BEST. We can only withstand so much on no sleep and I suspect you will need the energy. They will let you back in. We have made it, COVID-free. So many anxieties led to this day, this moment, the fear of being cut off, apart for the biggest moment of our conjoined lives. It's all going to be OK. Fireworks at midnight reflect off hospital walls.

One day becomes three. Inductions, pain relief, pulsating relief of the fucking tens machine. Upright, trying, really trying my best, until suddenly, I feel like I am not. New anxieties surface. Things are not quite right. Examinations. Epidural. Examinations. More. Time stills. A feeling of unease. Tired, overworked, overwrought consultant. She is done. So fucking done. She could not be more done. The midwife tries. I am distant, disconnected still, trying to trust in their actions. Until suddenly. NO. NO THANK YOU. This is not enough. We have come too far with too much to not feel quite right. A new consultant, the sweet relief.

A quick assessment. An onslaught of action. Emergency section. NOW. Calm faces. Panicked hands. People everywhere. My husband's eyes across the chaos. We're OK. A form. A rush to theatre. A scramble for the injection. A panic about the heart rate. I can't move. I can't help. Blue everywhere. The shakes. The kind eyes. A bloody loud SQUAWK. She is here. 8.40pm on 2nd January 2021.

Shakes. Tears. Bafflement. I think some relief. I am in shock. Physical and mental. We get a moment, perhaps forgotten. We take it. Is she Audrey, or Margot? Audrey Margot, Margot Audrey. Let's decide now. The first way. The same initials as my father, but the opposite way around. 3am. A sudden departure to the ward, husband must go. He nearly lost us both. Now pushed out into the cold.

The ward. Women and babies cry. Ask for help. Not always answered, and never in haste. She is here. Bundled. On my chest. I can't move. No feeling chest-down. Catheter in. Can't sit up. Alone. Mesmerised. Lonely. What world have we brought you into? She puts up her middle finger. Ah yes, I think. There she is.

Catheter out. Feeling back. FUCKING HELL THAT HURTS. Sit up. Stand up. Shower by 6am. Best if you move, best to carry on. Who will hold her while I wash? How do I wash? You'll figure it out. Can't stand up straight. Blood. Fear. Pain. Dress us both. Try to feed. Wait. Try again. Begin to share the news. We're here. We're OK. YES IT IS WONDERFUL ISN'T IT?

Early discharge. Fear in husband's eyes. It's OK. We need to come home. We can't be here anymore without you. Please don't touch me anymore. No more needles, checks, examinations. I just can't. Let us go. I am unravelling.

A baby seat. Soft gentle corners on icy roads. Home by 6pm. Dark. Cosy inside. We land on the sofa. We made it. We're here. FUCKING HELL.

Her first three months we survive as a three. No visitors. So little support. The fear of contact remains. Lockdown holds strong. No first holds. No hugs. No hand pats. But still, joy rolls in. We did it. She is here. We become less beholden day by day. We build. We smile. We light up. We begin. Two years on, an almost distant memory. The aftershocks recede. What a joy in such a time. Hands held, smiles unencumbered. Yes. Yes it is.

Amy Balderston, 36, from Otley lives with her main pal Chris and small pest Audrey, a two-year-old delight. She works part-time for an arts company as a general manager and in snatched wild moments within this juggle is an illustrator and homeware designer. She has increasing compulsions to write and holds a journal of heartbreak and joys exploring this. Away from work, when she isn't ardently drawing or firing up laser bae, she is often found trying to keep her feral toddler alive or scampering about the Yorkshire countryside, often simultaneously.
@ItsBalderston

ASHLEY ROSTRON

Boris came on the TV when we were just three weeks in,
"You must stay home and save lives," he said, my tears about to begin.

Baby in front of me lying on his mat,
his dad watching on from the couch where he sat.

I rocked and sobbed, convinced everyone would die.
What have we done to deserve this? I couldn't understand why.

For months to come - no loving embraces,
just us at home, no **heirs** or graces.

We made a good team, my husband and I,
but the toll it took, we cannot deny.

2020: the year my anxiety grew,
taking over my mind and not many people knew.

Surrounded by illness and the news on repeat,
no wonder first-time motherhood knocked me off my feet.

Convinced people wouldn't love him, for all bonds were missed,
dwelling on the fact **that he'd hardly been kissed.**

Trapped inside, allowed out for only one hour each day,
Daddy working upstairs so I'd try to keep the crying at bay.

Each time he grimaced, I'd think, *I know what that face means.*
"Please don't cry, Daddy's on Teams."

Persisting with breastfeeding even though it was rough,
determined to give him the antibodies to make his little body tough.

Garden visits with adoring looks from metres away,
our families desperate to touch him, but, the rules: we had to obey.

Throughout it all there was love in our home,
and for our boy, a type of love we'd never known.

Now, three years on, things are much better,
but no matter how much time passes I'll always be slightly bitter.

People try to give it a positive spin,
"At least you had that time home together, just you, your husband and him".

I smile, nod and let the comment go by,
but I feel a pang in my heart and, inside, I sigh.

Ashley Rostron, 34, originally from St Helens, now lives in Wigan with her husband Ian, little boy Tommy and ginger cavapoo called Rusty. She works full-time as a Quantity Surveyor and in her spare time loves to socialise with family and friends, exercise and eat out. After experiencing first-time motherhood in lockdown and finding it harder than she imagined she has set up a website and Instagram account to support women through conception, pregnancy and early motherhood. Ashley is loving toddler life and is thinking about trying for a second baby.
@xxapxx
@ar_bumpbirthbabybeyond

BETHAN MINTER

Trigger Warning: Suicidal ideation and attempt, traumatic birth.

Let me take you back to one of the darkest times of my life.

It was early November 2020 and I was standing in Barnetts Wood Nature Reserve, not far from my home. I was crying, tears streaming down my face and I was out of breath. It was dry, yet cold. I was overwhelmed with the taste of old pennies in my mouth from the over-exertion and having bitten the inside of my cheek. My fingers were linked through the wire fence I had desperately been trying to climb with no success, staring at the train tracks beyond. I knew that there would be a train soon, as the tracks were starting to buzz. I finally got a good grip on the fence, rammed my wellies into a wired wrung and pulled myself up. I neared the top of the fence. *I'm going to make it. It's going to be over.* From the footpath 100 or so meters away, my 13-week-old sleeping son woke with a little cry.

We had been out on a walk together, him in his sling, where he had fallen asleep. He looked so peaceful, perfect, and precious wrapped up in his teal fleece star suit and his hand-crocheted pumpkin hat I'd lovingly made him for Halloween a few weeks before. His little lips puckered with his tongue perched between them like he was trying to taste the air around him. We had reached the footpath by the train tracks when I looked down at his perfect sleeping little face, and, as I regularly am, I was filled with a wave of love for my precious baby. And as it often was, this wave was closely followed by a crashing tsunami of pain, shame, and failure. I was drowning.

I had failed my son. I had failed to bring him safely into the world. I had failed to bring him into a safe world. I had failed to breastfeed him. I had failed as a mother. He deserved so much better than me. I was ruining his life. He would be better off without me. He needed to be free of me, I needed to die. These thoughts had been my near-constant companions since August. Along with paralyzing night terrors, reliving what happened giving birth amid COVID restrictions. I saw the train tracks. I saw an escape.

I detached myself from the sling and wrapped my son tightly in my waterproof coat. I sent a picture to a friend of my sleeping son and tucked my phone into the swaddle, so he could be found. I laid the precious bundle on the footpath in clear view of the gate, praying someone would find him, and went to the fence.

Jump back to 13th March 2020. That morning I had my 20-week scan and found out I was having a boy. I excitedly went to lunch with my mum, who gifted me a blue dungaree set covered in whales for our baby. We ate our cake and talked about my plans for my maternity leave and the nursery. I didn't know I wouldn't see my mum again for three months. I didn't know she would be fighting for her life two weeks later and would take over a year to fully recover. I didn't know that I wouldn't get to do a single one of the plans we discussed. I went back to the office and I was accosted by my managers. They advised me that it would be my last day in the office for a while as being pregnant, I was classed as 'high risk.' Just days before, we had been chatting in the office about some illness hitting Europe from China. How we thought it might impact panto season come December if it was still around by then. We'd dismissed it as hysteria. So, I packed everything up that day to work from home for a few weeks. A week later, my industry crumbled as we were forced to close our doors without any government support or advice. A week after that the world stopped. I did not know that was the last time I would set foot in that office. Or that I would never return to that job again. Or that the industry I had worked in for 12 years would shrink dramatically. If you had told me these things as I left the office that day, jostling boxes of files, kit and a large laptop bag around my growing bump, I don't think I would've believed you.

June 2020. It was almost time to meet my first child and I was scared. Since March, everything had been over the phone. Reluctantly, the midwives were starting to see me in person, but I met a different one each time. None of them could tell me what to expect, what to do when it was time, or what was going on because they didn't know. I stood outside on the car park waiting to be called in, signs all around telling us to keep our distance from other mums and other patients. There was no shade, nowhere to sit, you could not use the toilets and they often ran late. Each week a policy changed, and every birth centre and hospital kept changing their rules on birth partners. After months of searching, we finally found a prenatal class that was going ahead, albeit sadly online. Along with other confused and nervous soon-to-be parents, we all gathered on Zoom once a week for a month. Sitting in silence, no mixing, just disembodied voices behind initials. It didn't feel real; these people didn't feel real. Where are the lifelong friends or playdate buddies made at these groups that other mums talk of? I've come to think that if they could have made us deliver our babies via Zoom, they would have.

The health visitor called to do a pre-birth house check, over the phone. How easy it could have been to lie. They would never have known if I didn't really have smoke alarms or if I actually lived in a crack den. How many people were missed?

Very few people knew that I was pregnant. I wasn't very big when people saw me last, I could just have gained a bit of weight. As I had almost lost my baby twice before Christmas, I hadn't made any big announcements like others do. But by this time, I was a fully-fledged waddling incubator. I struggled to fit behind the dining room table to work or to balance my laptop on my knees as there wasn't much lap left. No one asked how far along I was; no one tried to touch my bump; no one told me I was glowing or that I looked great... as I saw no one. My colleagues joked that I wasn't really pregnant at all, that I was just making it up to get a year off work. We all laughed.

A few weeks prior, my three best friends and I broke the rules and met in an empty car park for my birthday. We hadn't seen each other since the week before lockdown. We all cried but didn't hug. We all brought folding chairs with us and spaced ourselves two metres apart in a giant square across parking spaces. We took turns to sanitize our hands and get a cupcake from the centre of the space. We hadn't broken rules to see each other since we were 16, and we joked about how things had changed in the last 15 years. These women, my amazing soul sisters, were my rocks throughout all of it.

It was an insanely hot afternoon at the end of July 2020 when my son decided to start making his arrival. The birth was complicated and was badly affected by COVID hospital regulations and short staffing. Upon admission, I was denied my birth partner. I was then left at the end of the corridor and forgotten about. They admitted later that I was genuinely forgotten about. The pain relief did not last long, I could not find the light switch and was left in the dark, in pain and unable to move. My call button was not responded to, nor were my yells for help at footsteps past my door. I was left this way for 14 hours.

I was the only woman on the ward who did not have their birth partner. The hospital regulations had changed two weeks before but the ward nurse working that afternoon had been in quarantine since then and had not familiarised herself with the change of policy at the start of her shift, resulting in me being admitted alone with no one to support me. I was forgotten about and completely missed. Unlike everyone else on the ward, I didn't have anyone there to advocate for me. I was robbed.

Once I was finally taken to the labour ward, things did not get better. I was treated almost exclusively by unsupervised student nurses, due to COVID-related staffing issues. The daytime consultant refused to visit patients in person and was exclusively monitoring and advising on the care of mothers from a computer in their office. The trainee's inexperience meant my epidural failed and I contracted an infection.

They wanted to perform a C-section with my failed epidural, despite me telling them that it wasn't working. It took me screaming in fear before they listened and gave me a spinal block. Sadly, I had a bad reaction and started convulsing, whilst fully conscious. Instead of reassuring me or helping me, the anaesthesiologist held me down while they operated. I couldn't breathe. I felt all the warmth leave me. The room started to echo and go grey. My partner started yelling at him that I couldn't breathe. He shrugged and said, 'She'll be fine.' I was not fine. I thought I was dying. I've never felt so scared, invisible or worthless as I did at that moment.

I had to wait four hours to see or hold my baby. After the birth, my son and I had to stay in hospital for another five days, quarantined to our room. We were both pumped full of strong antibiotics and fighting multiple infections. My tiny son was regularly rushed away from me in the middle of the night by doctors. We ran out of supplies early on as we were only expecting to be there for three days, but my partner was not allowed to go home to get more things. We ended up having to break COVID rules to have parents drop us off food, clothing and essential baby items.

In the weeks that followed, no one held our baby. There was no trail of visitors or family through the door. We were alone.

In September 2020, at my son's nine-week review, the doctor cooed and doted on him as he batted his big blue eyes at her. She was all smiles until she unfolded his hands. I'd never heard the term 'seminal crease' before. The doctor says the hospital should have picked up on this, but like many things, they didn't. I didn't hear much after 'Downs syndrome.' It could be nothing, she said, but she referred us for more tests. What little light had started to come back in me was snuffed out.

We returned a few weeks later. I had to go alone. No one was allowed to support me. Our referral was denied by the local paediatrics team due to 'short staffing.' The doctor was given tests to run herself and they all came back clear. I fell apart. She asked me if I was sleeping. I said I wasn't. I told her about the nightmares. *Every night I wake on that operating table, listening to their panic, feeling like I'm dying. Or, I dream I'm trapped in the dark, screaming for help, desperately trying to find my baby, but I can't get to him.* She diagnosed me with PTSD and postnatal depression. My milk was drying up and I'd lost count of how many post-surgical infections and strong antibiotic prescriptions I'd had. I was referred to breastfeeding support groups... all of which were closed. I gave up.

At my son's 2.5-year health visitor review, in December 2022, I was asked, "How does your son compare to his peers?"

"His peers?" I asked.

"You know, your friends' children around the same age. Perhaps from his NCT group."

I fought bubbles of both anger and laughter as I told her we never met the other parents in our pre-natal course, I never got to meet other new mums and I do not have friends with children the same age. He does not have any peers.

Back to that November day when I was climbing a fence. From the footpath, my 13-week-old sleeping son woke with a little cry. I froze. My heart ached to comfort him. *He can find a much better mother than me.* I listened to his helpless and scared cries. Each wail was like a question. 'Where are you, Mummy?' 'Where am I?' Then, it clicked. He needed me. He really needed me. In that moment I couldn't go to the train tracks. I needed to hold my son. I jumped down, scooped up my wailing bundle tightly in my arms as a train thundered past, and ran. I ran as fast as I could away from the train tracks. I ran the whole way home. I didn't stop until I slammed our front door closed. I was ashamed I had got that close to not being here anymore. I promised I would become the mum he needed. I promised him. I promised myself.

In the months that followed, a lot changed. They doubled my medication and I started Zoom counselling with a therapist. I became a single parent. My son's father, my partner of seven years, struggled to cope as a lockdown father and grew tired of supporting me with PTSD and postnatal depression. He left on New Year's Day 2021, to be with someone else, when our son was five months old. Friends couldn't come to my house and support me as in-person emotional support and comfort were illegal. We ended up on a lot of walks where I had to bawl my eyes out publicly to keep to the rules. All the while, Boris and his cronies partied.

At just seven months post-partum, sleep-deprived and dosed to the eyeballs with antidepressants, I returned to full-time work. I was redeployed to the local COVID vaccination phone line, taking obscene verbal abuse from vaccine refusers. I did nothing except for working or parenting. I have never known loneliness and isolation like it. The cacophonous silence. All the while, Boris partied. The week my maternity leave ended, baby groups started to reopen. I felt robbed of a cohort of mothers, of support and comradery. To this day, unlike friends with non-lockdown children, I still don't have any mum friends of children the same age as my son.

Eventually, restrictions eased and I was permanently redeployed to another service. The desperate fight to save my career and my mental health and to survive as a single parent continues. My life will never be the same again. My vision of motherhood has been ruined. My days are getting brighter, but I will be scarred forever by what I went through. Will anyone believe us or truly understand what it was to be a lockdown mother? Do they even care?

Bethan Minter, 34, lives in Kent with her three-year-old son, Logan. Bethan works full-time in Community Arts Engagement and Producing in the Theatre Industry, and has done for 16 years. She does this whilst being a lone parent, thanks to her amazing, supportive family. She loves music, puppetry, theatre and making things.

CARLY ACRES

The first time that the pandemic and what was happening around the world really hit me, was when I went to a routine midwife appointment on my own. Everything had shut down, closed and stopped. The waiting room was empty and everything was cordoned off. Nobody could even share a smile. The outside world felt so cold and lonely. These appointments were supposed to feel exciting and reassuring, only now they felt frightening. Stepping into a building or even touching a door handle felt dangerous.

I was so lucky that my community midwife had the kindest eyes, the gentlest voice and the loveliest words of support. I needed her eyes to tell me the things her facial expressions no longer could. She allowed me to video call my partner and record our appointments so that he could hear our baby's heartbeat. The planning of what was to come now needed to be altered drastically as there was a very real chance that so much of my pregnancy and the birth of our baby would be faced alone, without him there, as COVID restrictions were tight. Just that fact alone triggered my deepest fears and provoked anxiety. Having lived and experienced trauma personally, the thought of examinations and physical contact from strangers became too much and my intrusive thoughts started to appear.

We had a few scares towards the end of my pregnancy with reduced foetal movements. This resulted in trips to the day unit where I needed to be monitored. Attending these appointments alone was, quite simply, awful. There was a constant battle between fight or flight going on inside, but overridden by the need to know that my baby was safe.

I had waited my whole life to be pregnant, it was something I had dreamed about since being a little girl. The yearning to be a mother ached deeply within me for most of my youth. This was supposed to be the most wonderful experience with each stage bringing more excitement. Only, it wasn't. I couldn't wait for my pregnancy to be over. I couldn't bear any more unknowns and uncertainty about where I would give birth and who could be with me. I needed my baby here right now, in my arms, so that I could shut us away from the world that was starting to feel apocalyptic. The irony was that she was going to be much safer inside of me for as long as possible.

Lockdown at this point felt as if it was going to be for the foreseeable future. We needed to find a 'new normal,' we were being told. Stay at home. Stay away from people. How could this ever be normal?

Weeks, then months, passed. Restrictions were loosened, then tightened, then loosened again. So much confusion, so much conflict.

My due date came and went. The next course of anxiety was about to start: induction. Something that, as a pregnant woman, you are already unsure of, but now you would need to experience that process alone. No birthing partner until fully established labour. Sheer terror. Again. We chose to let things happen naturally for as long as we were able. Luckily for me, I did go into labour and managed to stay at home for as long as possible. I kept telling myself I could get through another contraction. I needed to be somewhere I felt safe, with people who made me feel safe.

The time came to make my way to the hospital. I kept reminding myself that I needed to be in established labour. *Please let me be at that stage. I can't do this alone.* My examination at the hospital was borderline, I needed to be another centimetre dilated, but my midwife could see the anxiety in my eyes.

"Let's tell your partner to park the car and come in."

I burst into tears.

"Thank you, thank you, thank you," I said.

I was lucky, so very lucky. I gave birth to our beautiful daughter in the water, in the lovely birthing suite I had hoped I would. During the final stage of birth, I tore, significantly. I had lost a lot of blood and I needed to be taken to theatre immediately. My daughter was taken from me and given to my partner. I remember this feeling of blind panic. The intrusive thoughts started again. I couldn't hold my baby, I couldn't even see her and I was being wheeled through a corridor. My baby was in another room without me. *What if she cries? What if she's hungry? What if she thinks I've abandoned her? What if we now won't bond?* All you read about is that 'golden hour' and the importance of skin-to-skin. I felt like I'd already failed within the first hour of her life.

I was given a spinal block. I tried hard to stop my teeth from chattering from my excessive shaking. Once they started the surgery, I stared at the clock on the wall behind the nurse's head, counting each minute. Two hours passed and they told me I could go into recovery. I could hardly speak. I was exhausted, drained and scared. I just wanted my baby. The nurse brought her phone next to my head and showed me a photograph. It was my partner, with our daughter in his arms. She was dressed and fast asleep. I burst into tears. I think the nurses must have thought my tears were relief at knowing she was OK. They weren't. They were pain and sadness. I wanted to dress her, put her first nappy on and soothe her to sleep in my arms. I needed to be the person to do that. Isn't that what is supposed to happen when you have your baby? All these preconceived ideas were not happening the way I thought they would. They felt like failings.

I was taken into recovery. I lay there thinking, aren't you supposed to give birth, have tea and toast, get dressed, flap over the car seat straps and be on your way home by now? Instead, I was told I needed to go onto the ward to be monitored, so my partner had to say his goodbyes and head home without us. Fight or flight kicked in again. I had the urge to cry, scream and cling on to him. *Please don't leave.* He had to. He kissed us both on the forehead and made his way home. I felt sick. What was going to happen now? When could he come back? The posters were still saying no visitors were permitted onto wards. Was he now classed as a visitor?

We were swiftly taken downstairs and tucked into a corner of a busy ward. The lights were low as it was sometime in the early hours. Some mothers were sleeping and some were feeding. The newborn cry that fills the air makes you feel like you're on high alert, ready for the frontline. My baby girl was tucked under my arm, sleeping soundly. I lay there disorientated, anxious and frightened. A healthcare assistant entered the ward with an empty cot on wheels. She parked it near my bed, held out her arms, gesturing to take my baby.

"Time to sleep now," she said as she took her from me and placed her in the cot. "Sleep when baby sleeps, ring the bell if you need anything."

I could feel hot tears rolling down my cheeks. How could I sleep? I couldn't feel anything from the waist down, I could see a tube coming down the side of the bed into a bag. *That must be my catheter.* I looked under the sheet. So much blood. I wondered if it was old or fresh. I had messages of congratulations on my phone. I didn't want to read them. I felt homesick. I told my partner and my mum that I was OK and was going to get some sleep and that the baby was asleep soundly in the cot beside me, attaching a photo of her. That's what I was supposed to say, wasn't it? The reality was far from it. I couldn't reach my baby. The cot was not close enough to the bed. I pressed my buzzer some time ago and still no one is coming. *I'm so thirsty. I think I'm bleeding a lot. I have never felt so alone.*

The nurse eventually came, telling me how busy and short-staffed they were due to COVID. There it was, that word again that carried so much fear. The spinal block had started to wear off and I was aware that I was flooding through my maternity pad. I explained what I was feeling, she left the ward and returned with a clean sheet and a new maternity pad. She left it at the end of my bed and said, "Here you go." My baby started crying. She passed her to me and told me she probably needed feeding, then left the ward. How do I feed my baby? I can't remember how to latch her on, she's only fed from me once and that was straight after birth before I was taken to theatre. What do I do now?

The ward was getting noisier. New faces were coming in and out. I hoped there would be somebody coming soon who could help me, tell me what was going to happen next and help me change my blood-soaked pad and bedsheet. Time passed slowly, then I heard a voice that sort of sounded familiar.

"Good morning, congratulations on your baby girl." It was the midwife from the beginning of my labour. She had come back on shift and wanted to meet her. I burst into tears again. She hugged me, removed my catheter and helped me to the toilet. She sat with me and helped me change my baby's nappy and I attempted to feed her again. I will always be grateful for those moments of her time and kindness.

By lunchtime, we were allowed to go home. I was so glad to be home, to shower and feel the security of familiar surroundings. The first few days were tough, as predicted, with the lack of sleep and the difficulties I faced feeding her. I tried to reach out for support with breastfeeding but normal services and support groups were not running. There was no one to call when I was crying with pain, clutching a very hungry baby. Nowhere to turn. I was distressed and almost hysterical. I sat sobbing, feeling totally overwhelmed and alone again. My mum and my partner called the community midwife team, who explained how busy they were but that they would try to get someone out to visit me within a couple of hours. It was 12 hours after that phone call that I had a visit. I was diagnosed with severe mastitis in both breasts, I was completely engorged and she was concerned I was beginning to suffer with postnatal depression. I crumbled. Finally, an answer to why I was feeling the way I was. *Someone has heard me, seen me.* She stayed with me for hours, helping me to express, massaging, reassuring me I was doing a good job. She was amazing. She came to see me the next morning on her day off to check on me.

I felt so alone, with no clinics running to help with the early days of breastfeeding. This played a huge part in my postnatal depression. The first few months postpartum were some of the hardest months of my life. The pressure I felt to see family and friends so they could meet our baby was overwhelming. Even meeting outside at a distance, which we were allowed to do by this stage in the pandemic, felt so terrifying. We had been warned for so many months that we must stay away from others, and then we were told we didn't have to. It was an emotional rollercoaster on top of an already-overwhelming time as a new mother. When I look at photos of me holding my baby in the early days, I can see in my eyes the pain and sadness I was feeling. This wasn't how it was supposed to be or feel. The guilt is indescribable. I think I will always feel the guilt.

My daughter will be three this summer. To this day, I don't think I have fully come to terms with what it was like to be pregnant, give birth and become a mother during the pandemic. The more that comes out in the media about the corruption of our government just makes those wounds bigger and more painful. They will never know what they contributed to putting us through and the traumas some of us will have to live with for the rest of our lives.

I will be forever grateful for those few healthcare professionals and loved ones who got me through some of my hardest and darkest days.

And to my daughter, my beautiful darling girl. Thank you. Thank you for making me a mother and for flooding my heart with love. You were always the light in the darkness. I will forever be grateful for you.

Carly Acres, 35, from Cornwall, lives with her partner and their almost-three-year-old daughter, Daisy. She works part-time as a special needs teaching assistant.

CAROLINE ELLIS

The only good thing to come out of 2020 was Katrina Rose.

By Mother's Day 2020, I had just started to feel a little like myself again. I had undergone an emergency C-section in January, as the cord was wrapped twice around Katrina-Rose. I was looking forward to Mother's Day as a first-time mam. It was the beginning of lockdown and Boris had said we shouldn't visit our mams and have get-togethers, especially indoors. I drove to visit my mam and dad, I didn't know then but this would be the last time for 52 days. We sat in the garden and didn't go anywhere near each other. I cried as I drove home and so did my mam. It is not what I'd hoped for my first Mother's Day, especially as Katrina Rose was a miracle and was so wanted. She was the first grandchild on both sides.

Breastfeeding

My breastfeeding journey lasted 5 ½ months, a mixture of formula and breast. I went with the flow in the end. 'Go with the flow' is my dad's saying. Some days she loved just breast and others formula. I wasn't quite ready to stop but Katrina Rose was happy with the formula so I went with it.

Looking back on breastfeeding during lockdown, when out walking, there were no chairs to sit down on, as the council had removed them or taped them off. I started taking a picnic blanket with me, but my pelvic floor wasn't great so I had to plan walks closer to home, as toilets and cafés were closed. I felt trapped some days. I love being outdoors, so it was hard only being allowed to go out once for an hour a day. Occasionally, for my sanity, I stayed out longer and one day I even went out twice, feeling so guilty.

Masks, sanitiser and supermarkets

Wearing masks became the norm and Katrina Rose became used to seeing people wear them. We began washing our hands more and carrying hand sanitiser everywhere. The supermarket was a place that I went to weekly to get some 'me time,' wandering around the shop to get a bit of time away from home. I sometimes mixed it up a bit and went to different supermarkets. I would think about my week ahead. What could I make, bake or do with Katrina Rose? I cooked or baked every week with her, and she loves doing this together, even now, aged three.

Communicating differently

I connected regularly with close family and friends on WhatsApp video calls and did virtual quizzes with friends. It was good to connect but I was missing hugs, touch and closeness. Some people could see their families through windows, but the fines for travelling over half an hour scared me. My close family and friends lived over 30 minutes away and I didn't want to chance it. When restrictions eased, I was grateful we could be outside with people again, but it was bittersweet. Not being able to hug was so hard. I have a memory of walking with my mam and dad, and my mam tickling Katrina Rose with a long feather duster to make her laugh! We clapped and banged pots and pans in our street for the NHS and it was good to have connections with close neighbours. As a first-time mam, I missed out on the baby groups early on. I got to one before it went online. I didn't have mum friends that lived close by and lockdown played a big part in this.

Maternity leave, what maternity leave?

After six months, I returned to work for a few days and then had the summer off as restrictions were beginning to ease. This felt like my maternity leave was just starting. We didn't go on our summer holiday as planned as it still didn't feel safe to do so, but it felt good to be in a café or a restaurant again.

I felt I was cheated out of my maternity leave. I helped Pregnant Then Screwed in their plight to try and get the government to listen to those who had missed out on a normal maternity leave. When I see other mams on their maternity leave, since restrictions have been lifted, I can't help but feel sad and angry at the government that I missed out on all of that. It's not like we can get that time back.

COVID 2020!

I tested positive for COVID-19 in October and it made me so emotional. My husband, who I am now separated from, had it too and was very ill and bed-bound. This meant I had to cope with COVID and look after a baby by myself. I was grateful for her long afternoon naps so I could just rest. The tiredness was the worst, I was an active person beforehand but now I would get out of breath just walking up the stairs. Since having COVID I have had long COVID symptoms and lost my sense of smell.

First Christmas and birthday

My mam needed an operation after breast cancer and needed to self-isolate with my dad for two weeks because COVID was rife in the hospital. I felt so sad as they couldn't see their first grandchild over Christmas and on New Year's Day, her first birthday. They were upset, too. WhatsApp video calls were all we had. Sadly, it isn't the same as having connections with each other in the flesh. My mam and I are hoping to make memory books of lockdown with photographs, pictures and notes. There's a lot to put in and one scrapbook isn't going to be big enough.

Her first pair of shoes and delivery drivers

When Katrina Rose reached the exciting milestone of walking for the first time, I sent people videos as they could not witness this in real life. As shoe shops were closed, we had to wait until they opened again to get her feet measured for her first pair of shoes to walk in. We had most things we needed for having a baby but as she grew out of clothes and toys, I searched the internet to purchase them. I looked forward to the postie coming and we even made him a picture to say thank you.

COVID again - 2022

I had COVID again in January 2022 and this time Katrina Rose contracted it. Thankfully it was like a bad cold for her but she would sleep longer at nap time. I was grateful for this so I could rest. I was worn out, trying to juggle everything from running the home, working part-time and being the best mam for Katrina Rose. I just needed a break, help, and support.

Overcoming my traumas

In March 2022, I had a birth reflection appointment. This was a telephone conversation as they still weren't doing face-to-face appointments. The reflection helped a lot as I learnt things that I didn't know about my birth, and the chat helped me to process it. I also went to my GP and referred myself to talking therapies as a next step to get further help with my healing, and began my sessions in 2023. My healing journey is still ongoing and recent news around lockdowns and 'partygate' still triggers me. I am a single mam now as I left my husband last year. I am talking through these times as a new mam, and how these events made me feel, in my counselling. Lockdown didn't help my traumas and I hope professionals learn from their decisions and mistakes for the future. Crying is good and I have done a lot of that over the last few years, too.

I knew that my well-being and self-care needed to be made a priority, to be the best mam for Katrina Rose. I started doing more yoga by the sea and sea dips, finding other groups that did sea dips too. Meditation has also become an important part of my healing. The sea is my favourite calm place, I feel at home, safe and at peace. My close friends have been really supportive over this time, especially my two best friends Julie and Lynsey, and my work family who are extremely important to me. I have many good energisers in my life now and for that, I am truly grateful.

Unanswered questions

I felt I was abandoned when I needed my close family and friends the most but we couldn't see them. I couldn't understand if my baby yoga went online and my local Mumspace group, then why couldn't the health visitors? It was a sad and hard time for a new mam and I feel angry with the government and their decisions, especially after all the leaks since about them partying. I still have so many unanswered questions, but who is accountable?

Reflecting in 2023

I have become stronger since my traumas and experiences of becoming a mam. I look at Katrina Rose and think, 'You're definitely my 'mini-me." I say three things that I am grateful for each night. Tonight...

1. I am grateful that I became a mam.
2. I am grateful for a space to write down my thoughts about an unreal time when we mam's felt we were forgotten about.
3. I am grateful that I found this lockdown group to be able to share our hurt, feelings and be heard.

The other night, Katrina Rose told me, as we cooked tea together, "Mam you are brave, Mam you are mighty!"

Caroline, 44, from Durham, lives with her three-year-old daughter, Katrina Rose. She works part-time as a Learning Support Assistant and also a Forest School Leader. In her free time, she loves sea dipping, walking and meditating. She gets excited over afternoon tea, Take That, reading and enjoys having adventures with Katrina Rose.
@caroline_mam_thatter

CATHERINE GREGORY

Trigger warning: IVF

20th April 2020

To our future child,

We haven't met yet and I'm not sure when we will. We were ready for you two years ago when we bought a house in the suburbs with a big garden and an extra bedroom just for you. We've waited for you through two Christmases and two Mother's Days. We've felt the sad happiness of four of your aunties falling pregnant with babies of their own. We've looked for the signs: a twinge in my belly, a whisper of a line on a test, but we still haven't managed to find our way to you.

We thought we might meet you in December, after weeks of being poked, prodded and scanned, and an egg retrieval that couldn't have gone better. For the first time, your dad and I let ourselves think that this could be real; that in nine months we'd finally get to hold you. Then we got the phone call. All fifteen fertilised embryos - all fifteen of our chances to finally meet you - had deteriorated. The embryologist said they were developing abnormally, chaotically.

I've never liked the chaotic parts of myself: the constant tripping over my own feet, the clothing strewn over every surface and the thoughts that start racing as soon as my head hits the pillow. Since our failed round of IVF, I've harboured the completely unscientific worry that the chaos inside me can't be controlled. That it's in every cell of my being. That it caused our embryos to falter and fail.

Luckily, our doctors are more optimistic than I am and came up with a brilliant new plan to try again this month. But, chaos, this time in the form of a global pandemic, has once again scuppered our plans to meet you. Fertility treatments around the world have been stopped in their tracks. Millions of would-be moms and dads like us are wondering if they'll ever have a chance to meet their babies.

The thing is, we know we'll meet you one way or another. The "how" and "when" aren't certain, but one thing is: you will be so loved. Until then, we'll be waiting for you.

Love,

Your mom

Catherine is an American expat living in London with her husband, James, and her son, Teddy, who was a wonderful surprise during the pandemic. By day, Catherine leads impactful communications teams in the third sector. Most recently, she has successfully campaigned for better rights and entitlements around flexible working, parental leave, and childcare. In her spare time, she enjoys writing, running after her Hungarian rescue dog, and - most importantly - spending time with family and friends on both sides of the pond.

CLAIRE McNICOL

This poem is about our trip to A&E when my daughter was three months old. She had not been seen by anyone and her eczema was getting progressively worse.

Hold the mother not the baby,
but who is holding me?
No early intervention
has resulted in A&E.

She lies there smiling,
weeping skin upon her chest.
A string of consultants
but which one knows best?

A breastfeeding mother -
no food, no water, no phone.
It would be a crime to have my husband's support,
so here I am, all alone.

Unable to use the loo,
unable to think,
is this what the government want?
For new mothers to sink?

Hold the mother not the baby,
I thought we knew better.
I thought fathers were important
and that mental health mattered.

Empathy out the window,
common sense thrown away.
Hold the mother not the baby,
but who is holding me?

Claire McNicol, 35, from North Yorkshire lives with her husband, Hamish and two daughters, Cosima and Flora. She is an adult nurse and loves spending time with her family and being outdoors in the Yorkshire Moors.

CHLOE BROWN

Dear darling daughter,
The one who made me a mother.

You were born during unprecedented times. A lockdown baby. In a world dominated by fear and loss, you brought an abundance of joy and happiness. You proved the old adage that 'in the darkness, there is always light.'
You were my light.
You were with me when the whole world came to a grinding halt. A new life waiting to burst into the newly-quiet world; kicking and fluttering inside me. As the country plunged into lockdown and we were urged to 'stay home and save lives,' I patiently awaited your arrival. I stayed home. I paced the garden. I frantically cleaned the food shopping. I bulk-bought hand sanitiser. I watched too much news. I took the time to finish your nursery. I bathed in the sun. I felt you move and wriggle. I waited, hoping that once you arrived this would all be over.
I arrived at the hospital to be induced on Monday 13th April 2020. I said goodbye to your dad and walked through the big blue doors alone. I laboured for fourteen hours before your daddy was allowed to be with me and hold my hand. I was shuttled from room to room. I had to ask a nurse to attach my tens machine. I agreed to every intervention. I barely ate or drank anything. I didn't have anyone to encourage, soothe or advocate for me. But I did it. You were born on 14th April 2020 at 19:19. You unlocked an inner strength in me that I never knew I had. I felt so empowered. I couldn't believe I had birthed this little, squishy, perfect thing with a full head of jet-black hair!
And then - it was just you and me. Your father was forced to go home whilst we were wheeled to the postnatal ward. He was isolated from us when we needed him most. I can only imagine how stranded and disconnected he must have felt during this time of imposed separation. You were only a few hours old and I was newly stitched back together as we tried to navigate breastfeeding, sleeping and recovery. We relied on each other for survival. I was afraid to sleep in case something happened to you. I struggled to breastfeed. I was too scared to leave you, even to go to the toilet. I didn't shower. I was utterly exhausted. I was wounded. I was fragile. I poured all my energy into looking after you, but I needed someone to look after me, too. When we were eventually allowed home, I slept. A deep sleep that saved me from delirium.
You were first introduced to the world via Zoom calls and WhatsApp messages. When your Granny and Pa first met you, they stood six feet away in the garden wearing bandanas around their faces. I wheeled you out in your pram as they craned their necks to see your little face for the first time. Tears rolled down my cheeks. The exhaustion, the need to be embraced and the need to be parented, overwhelmed me. I just wanted my mum. I just wanted to be

told I was doing a good job. I wanted you to be held and doted upon. I wanted to be told how perfect you were and how lucky I was.

This lockdown became known as 'the first lockdown.' There were three in total. Much of your first year was spent in isolation. The days were long. It was often repetitive and mundane. The only way to escape the claustrophobia of the house was to go for a walk. I longed for a mum friend, a baby group, a visit to a coffee shop to sit and read a book whilst I breastfed (things which I had read about or seen on TV that had assured me would make 'mum life' more manageable.) I longed to make eye contact with a stranger, to exchange a knowing smile with another new mum, to share anecdotes about 'poonamis,' sleep deprivation and weaning. I wanted to find my 'tribe.'

All the support that had been promised to me whilst pregnant, vanished: the clinics, health visitor appointments, breastfeeding support groups, coffee mornings, baby sensory classes. Mums were ultimately forgotten about. We were expected to just get on. I will never forget the GP who was concerned about your weight at our six-week check-up appointment and insisted I track your weight, not realising that there was nowhere to go to do this. I had to fight to get you weighed at the GP clinic by a nurse who did not know what she or I should do with this information. Instead, I was left to worry about this constantly, with no help in sight. Once we left the hospital, that was it.

But, we did it. And, although it often felt lonely, I was never alone. You made me realise how strong and resilient I am. For every moment I felt like we missed out on, I know we made a million more memories just as precious. Because of you, I ultimately reflect upon that year as being truly magical.

Love always,

Mummy x

Chloe Brown, 30, lives with her husband and two daughters in Chester. She works as a teacher at a secondary school and enjoys practising yoga and reading in her spare time.

ELEANOR BAGNALL

As I write this, it is a few days after the anniversary of finding out I was pregnant, back in late March 2020. What better moment to write an account of my pregnant pandemic experience?

The feelings I have had over the last three years do not transpose into comfortable words. The noxious, visceral rushes of fear refuse to commit to a form. The dread that dwells and crawls within my lungs and heart will not be coaxed out to sit still willingly on any page. Neither can I smoke the feelings out of their holes, even just to describe them, which is why I have the same few phrases that I bleat over and over again: *No one understands what this was like for us. Why were they allowed to go to the pub when we couldn't have our partners with us? Did I miss the turning for the village that all the books mentioned?*

My lack of words is unsurprising. Mothering does not leave surplus hours in the day for self-reflection or expression. Women are not widely encouraged to feel or dwell on their anger. A microaggression itself, how society represses our female rage.

I, however, reject any 'watering down' of my feelings and I, in fact, view my anger as one of the many loud faces of my self-respect – it serves me well, as an internal, primitive prompt to remind me that all the bad things that ever happened to me were not OK and I don't have to accept any of them.

So, I will start there. With anger. Because injustice is really just anger, in one of its most concentrated forms. Because all of the things I have seen and experienced, all of the things that have been taken away from me and the other parents who were part of the 'pandemic mum club,' have made me angrier than I have ever felt in my whole life. Pregnancy hormones raged. Every time I had to walk in the road and cross over because someone else didn't socially distance from the pregnant lady on the pavement. As someone who has spent her whole working life not stepping aside for men in the street on principle (because most men walk like everyone will automatically get out of their way), it was hard to accept I was vulnerable and just had to quietly move out of the way. Going to scans by myself and forcing a resolve to be grateful that I was allowed to film the heartbeat for my partner waiting in the corridor. Going to hospital with stomach pains at six months pregnant and worrying at any moment that they would tell my terrified partner to go, leaving me while I vomited from the pain in my abdomen. Choosing a C-section, in part, to ensure his presence at the birth of his son for as long as possible. Crying in a shop at eight months pregnant because no one, not even the staff, were wearing masks, except around their necks like blue scarves, all while the shop radio ensured the customers that masks would be worn to stop the spread of Coronavirus. Hosting a Zoom baby shower, which was sweet, but ultimately rather forlorn. Being told by my midwife that no NHS antenatal groups were running broke my last hope of a link to other local pregnant women and sealed my fate for the next year.

After I gave birth, whenever I saw that a politician had broken a rule, I would think back on what I had been doing at that same time. Alone with my two-week-old baby, no idea what I was doing, thinking if I didn't stick to the guidance I might endanger someone else's life or my own.

I read that if you worry, you suffer twice. This made me realise the enormity of health anxiety: if you have it, you and everyone around you suffer indefinitely. My fear of contracting COVID stopped me from doing even the sliver of options available to me as a new mother. When you don't drive and are too scared to get on the tube or a bus (the nurse who gave me my whooping cough vaccine had told me not to because she caught COVID on a bus) and have to be near your home because there are no cafes open to change your baby and it is January 2021 and so cold outside, your world becomes the mile radius around your flat. It is so small. Knowing no one is coming to save you. All the quiet moments you need as a new parent are immediately extinguished by all the things you have to do that no one else can help with. Washing up, sterilising, writing down milestones before you forget, having a weekly shower, trying not to bite your partner's head off because you're both so tired and can't regulate emotions anymore.

There was no let-up and no support from friends or family. I won't deny that my heart was full of love during this period, for my beautiful little boy and my beloved partner, who was so worried about me and kept encouraging me to socialise, trying to reassure me that things would be OK. But, I just couldn't believe him. My rationality and perspective were both immobilised from being so isolated.

The lack of any classes entirely wrecked that first year of parenthood. Having no network of local mothers with new babies was like trying to learn a language with outdated textbooks and no classmates. It was like I had missed the first term at secondary school and now everyone already had their groups and were not accepting unsolicited friend requests. Every time I saw women walking in socially distanced twos and threes with their prams and slings, my heart sank. I felt like I had missed my chance to make friends when we were all sleep-deprived, talking about episiotomies and figuring out first baths and bottle-warming techniques. I felt I was letting my son down by my inability to connect with any other woman with a baby 'in real life.' I cried in the park on more than one occasion, feeling wretched in my loneliness and embarrassed that I couldn't make a single connection. My whole life, I had always been able to make friends easily but now, when it mattered the most, it seemed impossible.

Once restrictions eased, I enrolled us on baby classes. My son cried every time I took him. Some classes cost over £10 and I was spending half of them outside the room looking in whilst I tried to console my son and get him to interact with the music. After three months, when I finally broke down and wept with my son at the edge of the class, the woman running it took me to the side afterwards to tell me, "Lots of lockdown babies get overwhelmed." The empathy had come too late, though, and to this day I have never returned to a baby class.

The impact the lack of classes had on me remains even now. To this day I can't understand why there was no online antenatal class. I regret not paying for NCT, which I now see would have been a port in the storm, but I was 'Zoomed out' by that point and could not bear to see another screen. I was so tired of my pregnancy being something other people experienced online. Then, there were all the missed family meetings. No one met our son until he was nearly five months old. This weighs heavily on me, as my fears of contracting COVID, in part, prevented my son from meeting his great-grandfather before he died.

When I eventually caught COVID in 2023, it was no worse than a weary, dizzy sniff that lasted only a handful of days, however, I feel I had already contracted it in a thousand other ways. It was like my body had become immune to the actual disease, having become so accustomed to all the imagined outcomes of what might happen if I caught it and what would happen to my son and my partner. Fear of touching anything, washing my hands over and over again until they bled, leaving outside spaces if someone coughed, the panic that would seize me if I encountered a person who had been in contact with someone who had it and washing my son's hands and toys if they touched a 'bad' surface.

Another year passed, survival mode was eventually washed away and my body learned to respond to fear in different ways. I eventually came to find the desperate times darkly humorous and this was the coping mechanism that stuck. I also came to see that the vision of a village of mum friends was not going to be my reality, at least not yet. I made my peace with it and instead concentrated on making sure my son and I just had a lovely time no matter what we were doing.

Although some people who know me may not believe me, I am not wholly pessimistic and like to consider all sides. To that end, I will note that there were unforeseen benefits to the pandemic pregnancy. I had fortuitously quit smoking right before getting pregnant and not being able to step foot in a beer garden for over a year did wonders for my staying power. I remain smoke-free to this day, although it is terribly missed. I also filmed my family's reaction to the news I was pregnant on a video call which I probably wouldn't have thought to do otherwise. Hiding the pregnancy was the easiest thing in the world – I simply never dropped a Zoom call below the chest. I do wish that I had kept my pregnancy a complete secret from everyone except my partner and had produced my son at the end of the nine months as a surprise – it seemed like a once-in-a-lifetime opportunity for such a prank. Alas, my partner didn't go for it.

I'm afraid that none of the good things make a dent in the anger. The ripples from the good are lost in the distress from all the terrible waves of misfortune we all suffered. It is painful to see how short people's memories truly are when it comes to remembering how bad it got and that the people who helped the most are the ones who have been rewarded the least.

I do not envy the future history students who will be tasked with studying this depressing and confusing period of global history (although it may be preferable to studying Brexit or remembering who the Prime Minister was when the Queen died, which will be a tricky trivia question in years to come). I can only hope history never repeats itself, or if it does, that we are at least better prepared.

I will never forget what happened to us. It will live with me like another organ I have grown inside my body and will be witness to all the future happy times I have with my beloved little family.

Eleanor is a law graduate with a background in film production and regulation. She enjoys creating things, including being a presenter on the Legally Feminist podcast, and being outside. She and her partner are currently living in sin in London with their son and their cat.

ELIZABETH CLIFF

Too Much

It is too much to distil
A year of horror
Into a few simple lines
But I will try

Alone at scans
Alone
To be coerced into an induction I did not want
Alone in hospital for days
Alone on the first night as a mother
Trying to make sense of it all in the aftermath of birth trauma
Facing motherhood without a village

Ashamed
Of a physiological response to a pathological situation
Ashamed
Of struggling in unimaginably difficult circumstances

"It always seems impossible until it is done"
Somehow I got through it
Thanks to support from family and friends*
The year that broke me and made me.

*No lockdown rules were broken in the creation of this poem, not even for "work meetings."

Elizabeth Cliff lives in Lincolnshire with her husband and son George who is nearly three. She works part-time as a vet, part-time on the family farm and full-time as a mother. Her hobbies include cooking, photography, natural history and writing. In July 2020, she suffered a traumatic birth, exacerbated by lockdown restrictions. She subsequently developed post-traumatic stress disorder and came to terms with this through counselling.

MELISSA HASKINS

Pregnant and working in the NHS during a pandemic: homemade PPE, face masks, morning sickness, large scrubs to cover the bump, the fear of spread, the need to protect the unborn, being advised about the increasing risks of complications for those who were pregnant with COVID, no vaccines considered safe for us yet, COVID outbreak at work, time to go home, stay home, work from home.

Time to stay safe.

Family and friends never saw the bump. There were no baby showers. No shops open to try prams or to buy teeny tiny clothes from. Antenatal classes were through Zoom. No lasting connections.

Sunday evening and *Line of Duty* was nearly finished. I knew things weren't right. My cue to call the pregnancy assessment unit. *We think you should come in.* Alone, of course. A quiet, quick drive to the hospital, no traffic in sight, the lights all green. It was all too quick to comprehend what was happening. I felt a shiver knowing that this could be THE time. Not the excited drive I'd imagined. We travelled in silence. Aware that I'd soon be alone.

I was dropped at the hospital door, donning my face mask, carrying my hospital bag and taking the stairs to avoid sharing a lift. Alone and heavily pregnant. Admission for an induction was advised. I called my partner and told him to go home, there was no need to wait in the car any longer.

I got a room at 3am. My COVID swab results were still pending so I wasn't allowed to leave the room to use the bathroom and had to use a commode instead. I could hear the business-as-usual chats between staff but I was alone, in quarantine. Tears streaming.

The agonising wait. Hyper alert. Alone.

There were three other women in the induction suite, but with the restrictions, it meant closed curtains so no eyes met. There was a silent understanding of what was coming your way next, after hearing your unknown neighbour go through the uncomfortable process ahead of you. No hands to hold or ways of distraction, just labouring in a bay, alone. I could hear the local students coming home from the pub across the way to continue their evening. I smiled at their freedom.

I had the responsibility of monitoring the CTG as no room meant no one-to-one monitoring or remote monitoring.

"Just call the buzzer if the heart rate goes below 100."

Hyper alert. I couldn't rest as I monitored the beat, feeling her rhythm, noticing when it went faster or slower, for twelve hours. I felt like something changed, so I called for the midwife. I was told to call my partner in as soon as possible or he may be too late. A room, a midwife, gas and air, my partner finally there with a hug and hand. Time to push.

In the recovery room, we were lucky to all get some time together as I was not recovering as fast as they had hoped so couldn't go to the ward. Our first moments as a family of three. I watched her with my partner, knowing that soon I would be alone again... well, no longer alone as I now had my baby, but solo-parenting. Along with a body and mind that needed nurturing and time to heal, but with the strongest visceral feeling of the need to survive and protect.

I was on the postnatal ward with three other women and their babies. Our first night as parents, alone. Only 13 hours until visiting time - the one hour a day we could all be together. I wished my mam could visit.

She was a non-sleeper, cluster-feeder. I had not slept or showered in three days. My body hurt and felt strange. I begged a student to look after my baby whilst I tried to grab a piece of dignity and clean myself before my partner arrived.

The hours turned into many days and nights in hospital alone. Hormones, loneliness, imposter syndrome... *Am I good enough? What if..?* The texts and calls from well-wishers were mounting and becoming too much. No visitors meant no conversations to drown out the bad news given to your neighbour. Curtains are not soundproofed. Even when my baby finally slept, I couldn't.

Finally, it was time to go home. My partner's time to co-parent and our time to be a family. I had already been doing this alone and my brain had forever changed, something re-wired. I was wired. Hyper alert. I was not going to rest or feel at ease again for a very long time.

Only a 'virtual village' was allowed, so family introductions were over FaceTime. I loved my new little family but I needed my real village. There were no hugs. Hardly anyone held her when she was small. After one week at home, my partner went back to work. No baby classes, no cafes, no visitors, no weigh-ins and a letter instead of a health visitor review. Loneliness. A time I will never forget.

Melissa Haskins, 39, from Newcastle upon Tyne, lives with her fiancé and their two-year-old daughter, Isla. She works as a GP in the north east and is grateful to have re-found her singing voice now she's back in her local folk choir.

ELAINE GREGERSEN

Trigger warning: Baby loss, parenting a child with life-limiting disabilities

It's our first *Movement and Music* class. We're early, of course. The other mums and babies slowly join us and I frantically check and re-check the contents of our homemade sensory bag. I'm wearing the old grey maternity T-shirt I can't bear to throw away.

Do they see it? Am I going to be *that* mum? You know who I mean. The one everyone avoids looking at. The one who nervously mutters how they've forgotten the brightly coloured scarf and plastic water bottle shaker full of dried pasta. "She must have seen the reminders on social media," they'll whisper, as they sip from their branded coffee mugs.

Gene's sliding off my knee again. I put my hands under his chubby arms and heave him backwards. His bum scoots forward, undoing all my hard work. I feel the painful curve of his back as he slumps like a rag doll to one side.

We go around in a circle.

"I'm Gemma and this is Archie!" Gemma chirps. She doesn't look tired. I think I might hate Gemma.

"Archie was born at thirty-six weeks and we were on the unit for eleven days. Hardest time of our lives."

Everyone nods in solidarity.

"So, this is Poppy," says another mum. "Oh, and I'm Michelle. Nearly forgot about me! We were on the unit for five weeks."

More nodding and furrowing of the brows. Poppy is six months old and sits happily by her mum's side, wrapping her fingers through a rainbow of ribbons tied to a small wooden circle. She looks curiously at the strips of soft material as they twirl and curl around her.

The introductions continue. Connor was on the unit during Christmas. He was born at thirty weeks and is four months old now. Lacey-Ann (thirty-two weeks, seven days on the unit) wears a big stretchy bow on her bald head so that everyone knows she's a girl. She looks around and threatens to crawl off to find something more interesting than this chat. Fair enough, Lacey-Ann.

To our left, two small babies lie on their backs close to one another, legs kicking in the air. They can't be more than a few months old. A boy and a girl. Twins. Everyone looks and coos. Their mum reaches back for a moment to grab a bottle behind her. We are left mesmerized as the twins move their arms and legs in tandem; a beautifully synchronized dance.

We're the last to go.

"I'm Emma. And this little fella is Gene."

Some of the women make their child's hands move backwards and forwards in a stilted wave.

"Say hello to Gene," I hear Poppy's mum bark at her kid.

"Gene was born at twenty-four weeks, and…"

Oh God, *should I say it?*

"And, he was on the unit… Well, he was actually on two units… He was on the unit for one hundred and twenty-three days."

That's enough. I'll stop there. I can't bear the tilts of the head. The pity. The sadness. The relief they're not us.

We sing 'The Wheels on the Bus' and 'The Grand Old Duke of York.' We drape scarves around our children's faces and make ludicrously shrill noises of delight and surprise. I can't follow the actions to 'Wind The Bobbin Up' and Gene lolls dangerously to the left, limp and sagging.

"Come on, Geney," I whisper. "This is fun isn't it?" Gene looks off into the distance. His arms droop heavily by his sides.

Gene's dad, Andy, takes a photo of us with his mobile phone and I try to look upbeat and together, like a proper mum. One of the twins attempts to roll over and their mother rushes to move them back onto the mat with their sibling. The class comes to an end. We say our goodbyes. I wrap my arm tightly around Gene's tummy to steady him whilst I take his left hand and wave it back and forth, grinning and yelling, "Bye! Have a good day!"

I reach over to my laptop's mouse pad, use my index finger to move the cursor to the red 'leave' button, click on it, and close my laptop lid.

"How was it?" Andy asks as he comes back into the living room from our kitchen, munching on a slice of toast.

"Yeah, good," I lie.

I don't want to tell him that I spent most of the class confirming my fears that our son is very different to other children. Yes, he was born very early. Yes, he weighed 1lb 9oz. Yes, he nearly died multiple times. But what I'm seeing isn't simply delayed development. Gene doesn't roll. He doesn't sit. His eye contact is fleeting. There's no copying, pointing, waving. When I try to engage him in something I think he'll be interested in, he looks the other way as though I don't exist. The other premature babies were sitting and chattering and responding to the songs. Gene doesn't say 'mama' or 'dada'. Gene doesn't make any discernible sounds at all.

Four months of trauma from neonatal intensive care had stared back at me from the small square at the bottom of my laptop screen. It was etched upon my face. But I can't tell Andy that. He goes upstairs to the spare room, half-bitten toast in hand as he heads back to work. Gene and I are alone again.

"I think it's brilliant they're putting these virtual sessions on," I shout up the stairs. "But I'm not sure I'll go to the next one."

It's March 2020. Gene is nine months old. He came home from hospital carrying the aftermath of six surgeries and chronic lung disease. He is extremely clinically vulnerable - a phrase we have recently learned. That's the language we use now.

The man who delivers Gene's oxygen tanks leaves them outside the front door before ringing the bell. I put my thumb up from behind the window and he responds similarly. It's the closest to actual adult human contact I have, aside from Andy.

I do not have any mum friends nor have I ever been to a playgroup, soft play, baby yoga class or bouncy castle party with my son.

"Really want to get rid of that wallpaper!" I shout up the stairs again. I glare at the bright red flowery pattern all around me. Once the height of fashion in the '90s, the wallpaper is headache-inducing when surrounded by it every single day. But it makes no sense to strip it off now because we also need to remove the old fireplace and get new flooring. And no one can come into the house to do any of those things.

"What shall we do now?" I ask Gene. He is silent. He looks into the distance.

We go for our legally permitted walk around the block, passing the park with the thick chains on the gate and the warning sign to keep out.

*

When I first spotted the identical twin baby boys arrive in our cul-de-sac, I tiptoed cautiously toward our living room window and peeked through the gaps in the wooden blind. I see the twins in our street most days. They go for their lockdown walk too, in the double buggy pushed by their mum and, less often, by their dad. One morning, I see the dad carry a single boy on his shoulders. He holds his son's tiny gloved hands tight as they pound the pavement. The boy's green-hatted head bounces up and down in the fresh air.

Some days the mum looks tired and harassed. The glare of the spring sun makes her eyes squint as she pushes her kids past our window again.

Then, a pause. Months drift by. They disappear, and I am able to forget.

*

No one has said the words 'cerebral palsy' but I whisper it to myself in the dark. At 2am, when Gene's unable to sleep, I cradle his floppy body against mine. One hand is spread wide on his curved, warm back, feeling the crackles within his lungs. The other hand precariously balances my mobile phone as I turn down the brightness of the screen light and type words into the Google search bar with my thumb.

'baby can't sit'
'missed milestones'
'do babies with cerebral palsy smile?'

*

In the mornings, I dress Gene in rainbow-striped stretchy joggers and a long-sleeved top with a T-shirt over the top like he's heading to an indie disco.

He reaches and places a chubby hand on Andy's chest whilst we take selfies of all three of us on the sofa. Gene's face contorts into shock at the screen and we laugh at his hilarious expressions until we have to wipe tears away. When Andy is working at his desk upstairs, we go to visit. Gene sits on his dad's knee, looking around the room with a confused wonder and I greedily snap photos on my phone.

When Gene lies on the living room floor, I place a plush developmental toy I've bought from the internet near the top of his right arm. It's a Flip Flap Dragon, with crinkling wings, a bright yellow body and patterned feet. There's a white plastic clip to attach it to buggies and cots. Without looking at it, Gene finds the clip with his fingers and pulls the toy towards him. The clip falls into his mouth. He doesn't chew. It just sits there, in his mouth, whilst he remains like a statue. I gaze at this strange little human wondering what on earth is going on in his head. I rescue the clip from his mouth and he continues to look away from me. I talk incessantly to him. I don't know if he can hear.

One day, I blow bubbles made from washing liquid in the air as Gene lies in his usual position. A small one hits his face and he appears annoyed. He follows some with his eyes, unsure what is happening. He makes a 'mmmmm' noise out of his nose. Sometimes he goes completely still, on his back like a turtle, staring vacantly at nothing. Then he finds the inside of his mouth and chews it. I hear his body struggling to breathe clearly. And then - out of nowhere - he blows a raspberry. I race to capture it. I look around for someone to tell, for someone to see.

*

When Gene's asleep he looks just like his identical twin brother, Roman. Born a few minutes apart, they had lived tightly together inside me for just over five months before rupturing too early into the world. Roman was the first, but he was smaller, more fragile, less able to withstand infection and the devastating effects of prematurity. He might have still been alive for a fleeting moment when I first got the chance to hold him.

"You can go," I'd said silently in my mind, knowing he could hear me - that tiny, bruised and increasingly still creature I was embracing in my arms. "We'll be fine. You go," I told him as he slipped away.

They have the same face.

*

Andy says people don't think about us.

"I don't mean it horribly," he shouts across the kitchen when I'm washing bottles and teats and he's waiting for the kettle to boil. "They've got their own lives. Our shitty thing has happened and people move on."

At midnight tonight, it will be an entire year since my waters broke unexpectedly at twenty-four weeks. We are locked away. Other parts of the UK are opening up again, but our region remains in the highest level of lockdown. Tier 4. Maybe if I had been taking Gene into work, to lunches, to busy cafes with clinking cutlery and steaming pots of tea, things would be different. But we're still in the incubator; hidden away in quiet darkness, scared and alone. Elsewhere, in a garden party in central London, more than one hundred government employees are invited to 'make the most of the lovely weather' and 'bring your own booze.'

That evening, when I return from pushing Gene's buggy around the same old streets, I enter the living room and cry. Andy has ripped a massive chunk of wallpaper away from the wall. It rests on the floor, curling in on itself like it's dying.

"Why are you crying, you silly sausage?"

I don't know. Maybe the wallpaper coming off is a sign of moving on. A small note of progress. A nod to a future beyond all of this. I bury my head into Andy's oversized hoody whilst Gene makes gurgling noises in his buggy. As I do, I wonder if he'll ever sit. Or know who we are. Or call me 'mum.'

"I hate that wallpaper," I sniff. "Thank you."

*

A physiotherapist has arranged for Gene to have a specialist chair at home so that he can be strapped into a seated position with an advanced headrest to stop him from lolling to the side. I put him in the kitchen as I do the washing up with the radio on.

A friend has sent us a toy bee. It vibrates. Gene smiles.

Sometimes I smile and then he smiles and we are smiling together and there is nothing in the world apart from me and him.

I spoon blended food into his mouth as he looks away from me. I reposition his body to avoid sores. I lift and carry and lift and carry.

"You are going to be absolutely fine," I say to him, and to me. I will be his protector and his advocate.

My maternity leave is coming to an end. My grief remains. I am grieving for a baby that is dead. I am grieving for the uncomplicated life Gene won't experience. The people outside will stare and quietly comment. His familiar clicks and grunts and arm waving will be alien to them. Medical professionals will make me fill in forms and tell me he doesn't meet any milestones. We are safe here in this little world we have created inside our home.

There's a life I was meant to have, just out of reach. If I concentrate I can feel the boys crawling all over my legs, pushing and shoving each other. I hear them shout for a drink, or a biscuit, or some cereal. They would like cereal. Roman wouldn't be able to say Gene's name. He'd call him 'Eeen' and Andy and I would chuckle to each other at night as we hear him through the bedroom wall telling 'Eeen' off for taking his toy. We'd push them high on swings, and smile at strangers gawping at the two identical kids giggling next to each other as they soar in the sky.

The lockdown is lifting. I don't want to go out there.

Elaine Gregersen, 42, from Newcastle-upon-Tyne, lives with her husband, Mark, and their four-year-old surviving twin son. She is an award-winning Associate Professor of Law, National Teaching Fellow, and Law Teacher of the Year. Elaine and Mark host The Honeymoon Period podcast, a TV and film review show recorded from their living room sofa. She has just finished the first draft of her debut memoir about premature twins, the neonatal unit, and how pop culture saved her life.
@elainegwrites

KATHRYN BRANCH

My baby was born
In a global pandemic.
I feel powerful,
But it's lonely.

I walked into hospital,
Alone.
There's a pandemic,
Didn't you know?

I contracted,
Alone.
Surrounded by the pandemic
And masks.

I laboured through a pandemic,
Changed history,
The stories I'll tell.
But it's lonely.

I held her in my arms,
The world shrank,
The pandemic left the room.
I knew it would be back.

My baby was born in a pandemic,
And I long to go home.
But there will be no visitors,
It's so lonely.

I should be happy,
I *am* happy,
But I'm so alone.
The doors of the world are closed.

I will heal and feed,
Bleed and mend,
While the pandemic
Carries on.

My baby was born
In a pandemic.

I am powerful.
But alone.

Kathryn is a mum of two in the throes of early motherhood. She writes poetry documenting her journey, capturing the highs, lows and everything in between. Whilst she doesn't shy away from the messy and mundane, she openly celebrates the beauty and life-changing love she experiences on the motherhood rollercoaster. Her latest poetry has been featured in Gypsophila Magazine, Isabella & Us Positive Well Being Zine, Motherzing Magazine and They Call Us Zine.
@kathrynbranchpoetry

ELENA CHOW

I used to think that being in lockdown was the hardest part of being a lockdown mum, but now I've had a smidge of time to process, reflect and dust off the memories my brain tried to bury and file under 'miscellaneous,' I've since realised that lockdown was only the beginning of a much more complicated story.

"If this is your first time, leave your shoes outside the door and take a seat on a square," the lead singer boomed behind her hospital-grade mask. The squares outlining the perimeter of the church hall were taken by mama and baby duos already on the floor in varying states of anticipation: snacking, side-eyeing and sifting through their bag of allocated toys. I made a beeline for somewhere in the middle, balancing my son on my hip, his grip tight and eyebrows scrunched. The unfamiliarity of the setting had pacified his usual chaotic charm. The calm wouldn't last.

Once we settled in and the novelty of singing *Wheels on the Bus* with a room full of strangers lost its magic, as predicted, my son started banging to the beat of his own drum. Or, more accurately, going on a hunt for a miniature maraca three squares along (it was identical to the one in his hand, but where's the fun in playing with a specific set of sanitised instruments, when you could show off your new wobbly walk to a captive audience and steal another one?)

I hurried after him, hunched down so as not to disturb the medley of nursery rhymes happening at the front, breaking the unspoken rule that we shouldn't leave our zones. I instinctively smiled as I passed by the other mums, hoping that the warmth of my expression had travelled up to my eyes, our only window of communication.

When I finally caught up to him, he'd successfully completed his mission and had commandeered a maraca from an unsuspecting baby. I gave the mother my best *"What are they like, am I right?"* eye roll and exaggerated shake of the head. She didn't play along. Instead, she protected her baby's personal space with an outstretched arm and without breaking focus, continued miming the actions of the songs. She didn't acknowledge us, even as I pried the instrument out of my son's hand to the tune of a mini meltdown. It was as if we didn't exist outside of her bubble. I shrugged it off, assumed she must have really been into the music class and took us both back to our square for a hard reset.

However, my son wasn't done exploring just yet. Blissfully unaware that his energy didn't match those who liked to remain in their dedicated space, with their dedicated toys, he continued to work the room. I spent the next 45 minutes trying to keep up with him, wordlessly apologising to germ-fearing mums, their reactions ranging from polite but hostile head nods to physically recoiling.

As flustered as I was playing his shadow and as self-conscious as I felt with pairs of eyes tracking us around the room, I tried to not let it get to me. A smile permanently stretched underneath my hand-stitched, floral mask in an attempt to trick my brain into thinking that everything was totally fine.

See, Elena, your first mother and baby class is super fun, super-duper fun, in fact. Maybe not exactly as you'd imagined pre-pandemic as you caressed your watermelon bump and counted down the days to maternity leave, but worth the wait - and the annoyingly long waiting list - nonetheless!

I carried that wistful optimism right until the end. Before I headed out the door, I scanned the class, desperately hoping to lock eyes with a fellow lockdown mum who would sense my longing, and not only come over and ask if I was OK and if I needed help tucking all my emotions back into my coat pockets but would say the one thing I craved more than anything: "Do you wanna go for a coffee?"

Because *that*, right there, was the meet-cute scene that was on my 'first-time mum' storyboard. Along with a montage of meetups with mothers who lunch at noon, because they can, and go to obnoxious baby classes, because, why not? The mums who share their unfiltered moments mixed in with the odd self-deprecating joke to lighten the mood, who are full of the wise words you need to hear at the exact time you need to hear them. The mums who create a safe space where tears, tantrums and twilight feeds can co-exist in the same breath, without judgment. Did I mention, no one in my inner circle has kids? But that was OK because I was going to find my people, we were going to carve out this community, this 'village' that everyone bangs on about, together.

Only no one saw me looking. No one responded to my silent call for help, for IRL connection.

Disappointment came first, a drop-kick to the stomach. Then came the tears. I sniffed them back and rushed off home, where it was safe.

I never went back to the class.

At the time, I didn't question why tears were free-falling at the imaginary rejection of a mind-reading stranger. All that was clear to me was the class represented another thing that didn't live up to the motherhood experience BC (before COVID). After checking off pretty much every single 'baby's first milestone' in lockdown, quarantined in a flat with only one decent window overlooking a barbed wire fence, what's one more memory to add to the 'expectation vs reality' list, eh? In fact, I'd almost managed to erase this memory completely and all the ugly feelings that came along for the ride, like loneliness and the paranoia that told me I was doing everything wrong because my child didn't cling to me like a koala.

It wasn't until I was asked to think about what it *really* means to be a lockdown mum and *poof* this moment resurfaced. Suddenly, I couldn't get it out of my mind.

I started asking myself: Why did I react in that way? Why did I feel every glance so deeply, so personally? Why did that kind of connection with a stranger matter so much to me, when only a few weeks before I was finally reunited with my loved ones?

The answers hit the surface but didn't tell me anything I didn't already know. Clearly, months of isolation, of hoping and wanting, of dreaming that the 'normal' first-time mum experience was purely on pause during lockdown (and not fully obliterated beyond recognition) had coated the class in layers of complex emotions. A sneeze in the wrong pitch would have triggered me. It was only once I zoomed out that I realised it wasn't just my emotional state in the story that kept me replaying the footage of the class in my mind. It was the cues I got from all the other lockdown mums. Flinching at my son's touch. Positioning themselves in the furthest corners. Looking, singing, but never talking to one another.

Fear. Anxiety. Hesitation.

Maybe they weren't aware of what their eyes revealed the second I stepped into their personal space. But I felt it. It was as if I'd inadvertently stomped across landmines that were buried deep and what rumbled to the surface was different for everyone, from my desperate longing for connection and subsequent mini-meltdown, to a stranger's audible gasp at my son's over-friendly antics.

Suddenly, I could see the lockdown hangover in full 4K.

It doesn't matter that the world, fractured as it is, seems to have been haphazardly glued back together again. I carry lockdown motherhood in my bones, in my very essence. I wanted to write it off and pretend it didn't happen, keep putting one foot in front of the other and all that jazz, but my body and mind react whether I like it or not.

Even right now, as I sit here tapping out these words in my local library, watching two mums spooning yoghurt into their babies' mouths, catching up in between cooing and sips of coffee, I can't help but feel... really bloody jealous. This reflex announces itself, almost aggressively. Surprise! That sweet display of sisterhood is now a pity party for one, because lockdown stole from me and my family of three, in all sorts of ways, from unmet expectations (like not living out my maternity leave fantasies) to still-can't-talk-about-it-without-getting-frustrated memories.

Now, I've lost count of the number of times people post-lockdown have innocently exclaimed:

"I don't know how you did it all on your own with NO outside help! And with your first, as well. I CAN'T EVEN BEGIN TO IMAGINE!"

Maybe they think it's a way to tell me I'm brave, or that they're awarding me with a badge of honour that I didn't ask for and would much rather give back. Before the glass-shattering realisation that I'm still in the throes of a lockdown hangover, I would rattle off something along the lines of:

"I just took it day by day. I didn't know any better."

Not anymore. That doesn't cut it. I refuse to continue playing down what it's like to experience motherhood through the lens of lockdown, because by talking about it, not only do I bring colour back to that time in my life that my brain would rather forget, but those vignettes – from the darkest days to the mundane, to the surprisingly gleeful – still call the shots today. Consciously and unconsciously. And every time I swallow down the truth, I disconnect from my reality. Suddenly I'm right back there, at the end of the music class, crying because no one understands the racing thoughts in my mind.

So, I'm going to keep excavating. Keep questioning. Keep sharing the small stuff and the turning points. Keep reminding myself of what I experienced when knee-jerk reactions take me by surprise.

Because my lockdown chapter of motherhood has left an imprint that will last forever.

Elena Chow, 32, lives with her husband and son in North Yorkshire. By day, she runs copywriting studio Words by Elena, where she tells stories about everything from life coaching to top-secret skincare finds. By night, she tells stories that often involve talking dragons. When she's not clacking at the keyboard, you'll find her overcommitting to a stack of books from the library and hunting for the best kid-friendly coffee spots.
@words.by.elena

GEMMA LEE

I am a lockdown mumma who gave birth in July 2020 and it was the hardest thing I've ever been through. There is no easy way to explain the trauma and loneliness we faced but here is my story - raw, honest and real.

My husband and I discovered we were pregnant in November 2019 and although we were nervous and unaware of what was to come, the excitement set in!

I am very grateful I got to have my husband there for our 12 and 20-week scans and all went smoothly, but fast forward a few months **when COVID was around** and my pregnancy issues began. I was diagnosed with Gestational Diabetes quite late which meant all birth plans went out the window, not to mention trying to do a diet plan with food shortages. I needed extra scans to make sure my baby was measuring normally and I attended all of these alone, scared and anxious. I also had reduced midwife appointments **with no consistent midwife throughout, so it was missed that my baby was breech until 37 weeks. That gave me only two choices: either have a C-section or opt for a painful ECV where they flip the baby.** I went with an ECV which thankfully worked, however, it was one of the most painful and scary things I've endured and I had to do it alone while my husband waited in the car anxiously. I needed a friendly hand to hold and words of encouragement and it was **gut-wrenching** that I couldn't have this.

Due to my GD, I had to go via the induction route and I knew I would have to face this alone. I've never cried so hard as I did when I had to say goodbye to my husband, angry about all the things he would miss. The whole process was long, painful and ultimately failed. I was all alone in my most vulnerable state, sleep deprived, emotional and with no one to share this with. It broke me. I knew I had to get through it for my baby but I will never forget the darkness and isolation I felt. I still struggle with feelings of isolation because of this. After five days, I was moved to the labour ward and my husband could finally be there, hurray! I had a long and painful labour with a distressed baby so ended up with an emergency C-section.

I was so tired, nauseous and broken that it took me ten minutes to be able to hold my daughter, impacting the most special moment of my life. They also found I had sodium levels so low I was at risk of a stroke. Despite this, my husband still had to leave after a few hours so I was left alone again. I was kept in a 'limbo ward,' attached to a catheter, which made it impossible to be mobile, so after a few days I broke down and begged to go home. I couldn't handle it all alone for much longer. I was isolated, vulnerable and unable to care for my daughter as there were no visiting hours. All the midwives were amazing and happy to help with anything and I will forever be grateful for the humility they gave me.

When I was finally released and home I couldn't help the feeling of sadness at not being able to introduce Olivia to friends and family. My family is from Australia so all planned flights over were cancelled. My maternity leave was a lonely and isolating time, not able to make mum friends, go to sensory classes or grab lunches out. Instead, it was spent holed up inside as I was deemed 'extremely vulnerable' and put on the shielding list. The week I went back to work was when lockdown eased. I can't help but feel jealous when I see new mums out with their babies alongside friends and family or having the baby showers I never got to have. I still suffer from PTSD and am scared to try again, fearful something awful will happen and I will have to relive it all again.

When I get angry at everything that was taken away from me, I try to focus on the positives, like having a new appreciation for myself, my resilience and my strength. If I can get through that, I can get through anything.

Gemma, 34, is an Australian now living in Hampshire with her husband, Danny, and lockdown daughter, Olivia, who is now three. She works full-time as an e-commerce manager for a large retailer and her rare free time is spent crafting and gardening. She enjoys all things nature and has a dream of living in a remote part of Wales on a farm!

HANNAH DAVIES

It's hard to know where to start. Having a pandemic baby was hard. I found out I was pregnant on the Thursday morning before lockdown began on the Monday. We had discussed pausing trying for a baby if it hadn't happened that month due to all the COVID uncertainty, but, low and behold that little 'pregnant' sign came up on the test. We kept it to ourselves that day, although I was an emotional wreck at school (I am a primary school teacher.) We FaceTimed our parents that evening to tell them. I'd always dreamed of how I would tell them (and it had never been over the phone - but this was just the start of a very virtual motherhood!) I went into school the following morning and had to tell my headteacher. I was only 2-3 weeks, but it had been announced that pregnant people should shield and we didn't know what that meant, so I didn't want to do anything which would potentially cause harm. I told my year partner first and she gave me a celebratory hug about my pregnancy, the only one I ever received. My head sent me home immediately. I was devastated. I'd wanted to do the last day with my Year 6 class. I cried a lot that day. I cried a lot throughout all of this. I told everyone else about my pregnancy over FaceTime or Zoom calls. Not the announcements I had envisioned.

At the 12-week scan, my husband was not allowed to come in with me. He had to sit in the car and wait (along with the many other partners). This was hard. Looking back at our messages from that day:

'I love you so much. I am with you. Xxxxxx'
'One baby. All good. Measuring at 13 weeks. New due date 25th Nov. Do you want a pic now or when I'm there? I also got a little video. I love you. Xxxxx'

It all seems so removed. It should have been so special.

I am very much a people person, but for the first 12 weeks, I was alone and shielding, doing online teaching rather than being in school alongside my colleagues teaching the children of key workers. Although 'safe' at home, I found this incredibly challenging. I felt guilty. I felt lonely. I felt isolated. I felt anxious. I felt detached from the camaraderie that being in school brought. I felt worried for my friends and family members who worked in schools, hospitals and other frontline jobs.

Once pregnant people (pre-third trimester) were taken off the shielding list, I had hoped to get back into school to be with my class in their bubble, but my school were extra cautious and said as COVID was still such an unknown - especially to my unborn baby - they didn't want to risk me returning. This was incredibly supportive, but equally meant I continued to be anxious throughout my pregnancy. In Summer 2020, when others were more relaxed, we continued to be cautious.

By November 2020 we were back in a national lockdown. I spent my Fridays waiting for our hospital's Facebook live announcement to find out what the latest was regarding birth partners. So much was unknown. The day I went into labour (the day before my due date) we stayed at home for as long as possible as I knew I had to go in alone for an examination to see how far along I was. Only once I was in established labour would my husband be able to join me. He took a photo of me walking into the hospital alone while he sat waiting in the car and every time I see that photo I am transported back to how scared I was in that moment.

I was having back-to-back contractions. Thankfully, I was far enough along that my husband was allowed in. My labour was long and slightly traumatic with a haemorrhage, but other than everyone being in masks, I didn't feel like COVID impacted greatly on the birth itself. My beautiful little boy arrived safely and healthily into this strange and uncertain world, bang on his due date! I was lucky enough to be given a private room and the hospital staff were incredible. For the first time in nine months, I was in a bit of a bubble away from everything 'COVID!'

As my little boy was born in the morning, we were able to spend the day together, then I did that first night alone. We were sent home the following day but had to return a day later due to jaundice. Once again, my husband had to wait in the car while I waited alone in A&E with our little boy. I can't begin to imagine how hard this was for my husband. So much waiting and feeling helpless. We were admitted, but as it was the evening and past the allocated times, my husband wasn't allowed to come and help settle us in for the night. We spent two more nights in hospital and these were tough. My little one was put on a feeding plan. He never wanted to be put down and I began to feel my anxiety rising. I had so many questions about everything and didn't know if I was doing any of it right. The midwives were amazing, though, and I think I cried on every single one I met.

Once home, things didn't get much easier. My anxiety continued to grow. I was stressing over the unclear COVID rules and regulations about 'bubbles' as I wanted to keep everyone happy but didn't want to break, or even bend, any of the rules. Those following weeks and months were hard and I missed having my 'village' around me. Once my husband returned to work, my parents joined our 'bubble,' despite living over two hours away. After Christmas, we went into our third national lockdown. With my anxiety being what it was, I didn't want my parents to travel into London where cases were higher. I saw an advert where a breastfeeding mother was talking to her mother and I sobbed.

The first time my sister, who has Down's syndrome, got to meet her nephew was when he was four months old. We met outside, in the cold rain. We know now that the government parties were taking place at the same time. My other sister, who works in a school, didn't meet him until he was six months old.

Looking back on it all, I feel a great sense of loss and grief that both the pregnancy and the first year of our son's life was fairly consumed by COVID. Everything seemed to be timed badly. I feel sad that my entire pregnancy, postpartum and maternity leave were tinged with anxiety, worry, stress and abnormality - living day by day for the various announcements to see how they would affect us. I even feel jealous of others who didn't experience this. However, I have huge guilt for those feelings as I came out of it with a healthy, happy, funny, strong-willed, gorgeous and affectionate little boy and I know many people would do anything for that privilege.

I have cried a considerable amount writing this piece as I have looked back on various text messages sent and pictures taken during those difficult moments. The transition into motherhood has been a challenging journey. I know many of the ups and downs may well have happened regardless of COVID (this little one is not a sleeper) but the lack of a village - or rather, the village being a virtual one instead of a physical one - has definitely played its part. I am proud of myself and all those who battled through this journey and I know that one day, when we tell our small humans these stories, they will be proud, too.

Hannah Davies, 32, is a devoted mother and part-time primary school teacher. Living with her loving husband and their energetic two-and-a-half-year-old son, she cherishes family life. When not teaching, Hannah indulges in her passion for art and photography. She finds joy in spending quality time with friends and creating lasting memories. Hannah also loves visiting their families in Nottingham and Wales, embracing the warmth and connection of time together.

ALISHA SAMMS

The year was 2020
Postpartum depression took me in its reins in the midst of the pandemic
Six months of being a mom and now it had come to a screeching halt
Was this what my life would be like now?
Was this my version of mamahood?
All the things that were done before – stay and plays – now had restrictions forced upon them
One minute we were allowed outside and the next that privilege was snatched away
The masks
The isolation
The rules
I yearned to go out and experience this new journey, but it was like a ghost town with no one in view
Behind the window, I looked inside
That was all I could do
Until the rules were lifted
Whenever that would be
It was just a blur
Video and phone calls were all that could be made
Without physical interaction, it just wasn't the same
The government did its job by letting people miss out on milestone events while they were partying away
I just hope that everyone survived as well as they could, as the norm reappears, making up for lost time, back to the good old days.

Alisha, 34, is from Birmingham and is a mother to two boys (so far). She runs The Mamahood Space in her free time - a new initiative for mothers who need a space to talk and express themselves through art. It also aims to remove the isolation and loneliness that is sometimes found on the motherhood journey. She is a huge advocate for post-partum mental health, loves travelling, art and photography and her favourite colour is purple.
@themamahoodspace

FRANKIE TOWELL

The difficulty with writing a story about having a baby in lockdown is that stories are usually about things that happened. My lockdown story is mostly about things that didn't happen and the long, empty spaces they left behind. The people who never held our newborn, the family photos that weren't taken, the baby groups that were cancelled and the lifelong friendships with other new parents that weren't made. It's also a story about things that didn't happen but the fear of which hung over the last few months of my pregnancy like a patchy cloud, cheating us of the excitement and joy that we had envisaged for so long. Obviously, we were delighted to become parents and that shone through, but the happy glow was punctuated by moments of real anxiety and grief. People speak with the benefit of hindsight about 'draconian' measures, as though we knew much more about the virus back then than we actually did. The truth was that no one knew how dangerous it might be to pregnant women and newborn and unborn babies and the list of awful things that could happen seemed endless. They *did* happen to some people. We were extremely fortunate to avoid the worst, but the fear was real and so was the guilt. How did I get off so lightly? My maternity leave was quite normal in the respect that it passed in a monotonous haze of sleepless nights and nappy changing. People say that it's always like that, but when I tell them I'm afraid of having another child they say, *oh don't worry, it would never be like it was for you, again.*

I was in the GP surgery for my midwife appointment, on the day in March 2020 when things seemed to change. There had been a lot of talk about 'Coronavirus' (it wasn't COVID-19 yet). Posters had gone up all over the office encouraging people to wash their hands and stay away if they were ill. It had become normal to hear people yelling, "HYGIENE!" at each other across rooms in a mocking impression of the company director.

We were firing questions at the midwife, trying to ascertain how worried we should be and what were our shrinking list of options for the birth, all of which were met with the same helpless answer:

"We know no more than you. They haven't told us yet." We left in my husband's car, still discussing our spur-of-the-moment decision to switch to a home birth, and decided to drive home and check what the morning's announcement was before I headed back to work. I took my phone out of my bag and saw a barrage of missed calls from my manager and HR department. I called them both back. Boris had spoken, I was not to come in. They would drop off my computer, my work and anything else I had left in the office. My first thought was, "Shit. What's in my desk?" Images of my manager, a 40-something year old bloke, rifling through my top drawer and pulling out medication and spare tampons before an audience of apprentices flashed through my mind. And my work... it would have looked like a pile of random papers and drawings to anyone else, but there was method in the madness. They couldn't just shove it all pell-mell in the back of a car.

In the end, I was allowed to sneak back in at 6:30pm, when almost everyone had gone home, to pack it up myself. The few people working late gave me a wide berth, as though I was already infected. I knew they meant well but it made me feel as though I'd been fired for gross misconduct and was sneaking out the back door in disgrace. My flexible working request was rejected a year later so that ended up being my last day in the office. No leaving drinks, no card, no bringing the baby in to meet everyone. Just some more things that didn't happen.

One of the things I was afraid of was labouring alone. As my pregnancy approached the end of its forty-second week and I still hadn't got further than the odd contraction I became convinced that I would have to be induced. The restrictions meant that partners were not allowed in until the second stage of labour, so I knew if that happened I'd be on my own for most of it. I was terrified. I phoned my mum every day that week, needing to be talked down from an anxiety spiral, but it really wasn't words that I wanted from her.

She worked for the NHS, my mum. She was semi-retired then but had increased her hours to help them cope. The call had come and there was no way she wouldn't answer it. At one point she was talking about doing some swabbing at the test centres. I remember trying to talk her out of it, hoping I wasn't being too obvious. She was already over sixty and I thought it was too risky. They had younger people, and I needed her. I needed her to be safe and well and I needed her to be able to visit me and meet the baby and give me a break. But she was management level and insisted she couldn't ask her team to do something she wasn't prepared to do herself (take note, Boris.) She told me not to worry because she'd be in full protective gear, maybe even a HazMat suit! What could I say to that? I could hear how whiny, pathetic and selfish I sounded in the face of her heroic desire to lead from the front. I wanted to be proud. I *was* proud. But in the end, the NHS agreed with me and she worked from their almost-empty office or home, co-ordinating the response, and none of the things that had taken up so much space in my head actually came to pass. All the fear and the sadness I'd felt was misplaced, yet it didn't disappear.

I announced my daughter's birth to my parents via a text message. My husband offered to call them before he left the hospital but I said I'd do it. I thought it would be nice to have something to do while we were alone on the ward. But when it came to it, I found I couldn't. All the exhaustion and emotion had caught up with me and I was not up for the sustained conversation that a phone call would involve. I had just said goodbye to my husband at the ward doors and had to keep smiling as I watched him leave. I told him to get some food, have a shower and we'd be fine. I thought if I heard a familiar voice I wouldn't be able to keep it together any more. If someone is really there, you can hold their hand or smile. You can sit in comfortable silence while you all stare adoringly at the baby. A phone call is not like that. I couldn't talk my way through what had just happened and I couldn't put into words the beauty of Isabel's eyes. But, they knew my labour had started the day before so I couldn't keep them waiting. My dad had already sent about a hundred anxious messages. I sent them a photo, her name and her weight, and explained I'd been taken to hospital but would call them when I was discharged. I still feel guilty about that. They deserved to get more than a text. She deserved to be more than a text.

I still don't really know the full extent of the injuries I sustained giving birth. I know it was third degree, but only just, and there was some debate about whether I needed to go to hospital at all. When I got there, more phrases were thrown around, things like 'complex internal' but I wasn't really listening. After two and half hours in theatre, the surgeon came to say he was sorry this had happened to me, so I assume it must have been bad. I was worried about being away from my daughter for so long. I thought she'd wonder where I'd gone, maybe even feel abandoned. Adam promised he would hold her until I came back and he kept that promise. The midwives brought him a cup of tea that went cold because he wouldn't put her down to drink it.

After labour, 900ml blood loss and being alone on the ward, the exhaustion began to kick in. I don't know if I fell asleep or unconscious but at one point I remember lying there with my eyes closed and hearing a baby cry somewhere down the ward. It didn't stop and as I started to wake up I thought, 'someone should go and check on them. They might need help and some of us are trying to sleep.' I sort of came to... and realised the crying was actually right next to my head. It was my baby and I had no idea how long she had been screaming for me. After all of my husband's diligent care whilst I was in surgery I hadn't even woken up when she needed me. I didn't get back to sleep that night because she cried every time I tried to put her down. Eventually, a midwife came and rocked her while I hobbled to the toilet. I decided then that, come what may, I had to go home the next day. I wasn't in a fit state to be in sole charge of a baby.

In the morning a stern, Irish midwife came to discharge me. She radiated disapproval and put me in mind of a sister in a 1950s convent surveying all the unmarried girls who had 'got into trouble.' I was determined to pass whatever test she threw at me, so I said nothing when she wheeled my baby away at a brisk pace, leaving me to pick up all my bags and trudge painfully down the corridor several metres behind and nothing when she dropped a heavy door on me. I was convinced that any show of weakness on my part might result in another night alone, shattered with no help and another twenty-four hours before I could shower. Everyone on the ward was rushed off their feet, not just providing medical care, but performing all the mundane little tasks that would normally be left to the dads. I was a long way down their list of priorities by virtue of not having had a C-section. On the final stretch of the corridor, I could see my husband waiting at the end, one of a group of masked men with anxious eyes and empty car seats. They stood behind a yellow line on the ground, like an airport queue and could only watch as I made my agonisingly slow progress towards them. The temptation to lean on the wall, to just slide down it even, was strong but I thought, *if I can't make it to the door they won't let me leave.*

My daughter was already strapped into the car seat by the time I crossed the yellow line. My husband immediately took the bags out of my hands and supported me to the car. He must have said other things but the part I remember was, "I thought you'd be in a wheelchair!"

My work sent flowers after she was born. I hadn't been expecting it and was quite touched that someone had thought to do it, with everything else that was going on. Our head of HR called a couple of days later to check they'd been received, and proceeded to explain that she'd sent out two bunches: one to me and one to the wife of a colleague who had recently passed away. I sympathised with the awkwardness of selecting the right gift for such incongruent occasions, but I wished that she hadn't told me. Its much harder to enjoy your flowers once you know that an identical bunch is sitting in the house of a young widow.

They became a rather stark reminder that our celebration was taking place against a backdrop of so much grief, bringing home the reality of the situation in way nothing else quite had. What we'd worked hard to keep "out there" was suddenly intruding into our house, our bubble of happiness. In the end, I was quite glad when they started wilting and I could throw them away.

Reading this back, there are no major COVID-related dramas or traumas (besides the ones I created in my own head) and no heroism or glory in the way I behaved. So, I'll finish with the part that has a bit of everything, the one time when I did feel heroic and glorious. The birth.

She was born at home, in the pool in the end, just like we'd planned. Her dad had the pleasure of witnessing every gory and beautiful second of it. As she emerged, the midwife could see I was flagging and told me to put my hand there and feel her head. I said, 'Is that...hair?' as though hair was something I'd only read about in fairy tales. I hadn't quite believed in the baby before then. Intellectually, I knew she was there but my mind couldn't quite connect the wriggling swell of my stomach with the idea of another complete human with a head that had hair on it. She moved a bit further into the world and I saw her ear. The midwives exchanged puzzled murmurs on which way round her head was (sideways, it turned out, hence the injuries). The next second she was out, floating upwards into my arms. Her eyes were open already and she looked at me through the water. There was a moment of silence when I lifted her out before she screamed, totally outraged, then quietened as I clumsily shifted her closer to my body. We looked at each other for a while. I don't know what anyone else was saying or doing during that time, I hadn't even checked to see if I had a boy or a girl yet. Her dad was behind me, looking down at her over my shoulders. The midwife offered to take a photo, one of only a few that I have of all three of us together from the early weeks of her life. With everything that was going on around us at the time, and all that would follow once I tried and failed to stand up, that moment sits in a bubble for me, insulated from the rest. Quarantined, if you like. For a few moments, it wasn't a COVID birth. She wasn't a lockdown baby. It was just a birth, miraculous and commonplace as any other. The sun had pushed through the clouds and created a perfect little rainbow.

Francesca Towell, 33, lives with her husband and three-year-old daughter in her home town of Leicester. She works as a part-time CAD Technician, in spite of her literature degree, and in her limited spare time reads avidly and writes sporadically.

HANNAH BURGESS

11/12/2019
4 weeks

    Hey, you. It's future you, from 2023. After the longest two weeks in your life, you just found out this morning it worked. It actually worked. Yours and Kelly's first round of IVF. Three eggs collected, two fertilised, one implanted and it actually worked! I still pinch myself today about how lucky we were. I wouldn't usually check in but there are going to be some strange times ahead on both of your journeys to becoming mothers but all you need to know for now is that your baby will be perfect and everything will be OK. Enjoy how special the next few weeks are, keeping your wonderful secret.
X

16/03/2020
18 weeks

    Hey, you again! Those strange times I was talking about? Yes, this is the start of it. I know you've just seen the news and I know you and Kelly feel really terrified right now. The message is to isolate and stay away from others, so just do that for now and I'll check in again soon.
X

23/03/2020
19 weeks

    Hey, sorry, you again. You have just heard the news that the country is going into lockdown. You held your bump, terrified and unsure of what this means for our little family. You aren't going to stop feeling like that for a while. The next few months are going to be strange. You will have to stay at home and so will Kelly. Getting an online shop will be as challenging as getting Glastonbury tickets and you won't believe how many times you have to use the dishwasher or how much butter you actually eat. Check out some online pregnancy Pilates and yoga - you'll love it. Breathe. I'll message again soon. All my love, you.
X

3/04/2020
20 weeks

    Hi you, it's you. All of your NHS appointments have to be attended alone but the money you just spent on a private scan was more than worth it as it meant Kelly could be with you. 20 weeks and all is looking good. A happy moment amidst all of this solitude and loneliness. You both still changed all your clothes in the car park before you got in the car which is becoming a bit of a skill now your bump is bigger.
X

24/04/2020
23 weeks

    Hi, it's you again. Congratulations - you are an aunty! I know the happiness of that news is coupled with an overwhelming sadness that you won't be able to hold your niece straight away but one day soon you will meet her in the garden and she is perfect.
X

14/05/2020
26 weeks

    Hi you, it's you. I know you just got the call: Nana died. Thank God in all this madness the kindness of the staff shone through and they bent the rules. After months of Nana only seeing visitors out of the window, her children were there to hold her hand as she died. You won't attend her funeral but you will see it online. You will watch your brother sit alone, crying, with no one able to comfort him due to social distancing rules. Try to remember to call him and tell him to put some tissues in his pocket or he will make such a mess of his sleeve.
X

01/06/2020
29 weeks

    Hi you, it's you again. Big decisions made today. You let go of your dream of having a home birth. The local hospital has become a designated

COVID hospital and the idea of having to go in there frightens you to your core. You have made a strong and brave decision. *Spoiler alert* - the way things go you wouldn't have been able to have a home birth anyway so it's a good decision. Keep going with the hypnobirthing. Keep up with online yoga and think about packing the hospital bag soon.
X

10/06/2020
30 weeks

Hey you, you again. Someone called Grace messaged you on Peanut. Reply now! She will be the reason you survive your maternity leave alone in lockdown. Buy some good trainers or keep hinting to Kelly about getting you some for Christmas. You and Grace will walk miles together supporting each other in your motherhood journeys. She will be one of your only friends that can relate to becoming a mum in these unusual circumstances and you will need her as she needs you. Her daughter, Bonnie, will be your baby boy's first friend.
X

23/07/2020
36 weeks+3

Hi, it's me, just a quick one. Have a lovely meal with Kelly tonight and try to get to bed early.
X

24/07/2020 9:00
36+4 weeks
Battery 94%

So... your waters have gone. Kelly announcing that we would be financially OK if baby boy came now was the only prompt he needed to get going. The rules state you have to be 4cm dilated before Kelly can join you in the hospital but you could be at a pub with other friends. It doesn't make any sense! For now, stay at home for as long as you can and I'll be in touch to remind you of your affirmations:

'I am strong and I am safe.'

24/07/2020 15:00
Battery 68%

      You are doing amazingly. Keep breathing - I know the contractions are getting intense now but you will be at the hospital soon. You are going to get really sick soon - please try not to be sick on your phone this time!
      'My body was designed to do this like millions of others before me.'

24/07/2020 22:00
Battery 52%

      Hey, you - the contractions are really strong now, aren't they? Kelly's still not allowed in but you have been able to go out to the car park twice to see her. You don't feel safe out there though and can't relax. You are sitting in your own private room alone now, the contractions are getting stronger and closer together and it's harder to move. You are hooked up to a monitor so can't move around the room much either. All the bits you packed in the hospital bag are out of reach and pointless. No one can hook up the tens machine, no one can get hot water for your hot water bottle, the LED candles are staying in the box and the Bluetooth speaker is turned off and undiscoverable. It's getting dark now. It's just you, the sound of the hypnobirthing tracks through your phone and the rhythmic sound of baby boy's heart filling the room.
      Don't worry that you have been sick on your phone and it won't charge. Let Kelly know you will contact her when you can, she will be fine, don't worry. Just look after yourself and breathe.
      'I can do anything for a minute.'

25/07/2020 01:00
Battery 30%

      My love, you are doing so well! Keep playing the hypnobirthing tracks and focus on your breathing. At this point, you made the decision to send Kelly home from the car park. You have been examined and are 1cm now and you are doing so, so well.
      'Every difficult moment gets me one step closer to meeting my baby.'

25/07/2020 02:00
Battery 25%

It's getting harder now, isn't it? You will stop being sick soon, I promise, but it's painful and it's so hard without Kelly. Your battery is getting really low now and you'll need it to tell Kelly when she can come. Put it on aeroplane mode and keep listening to your playlists.

'*My labour is not too strong for me because it is me.*'

25/07/2020 03:00
Battery 20%

You are doing so well but you are tired. The midwife agreed to hold your hand for one contraction - it almost wasn't worth it. You've asked for morphine even though it wasn't in your plan. Please don't feel defeated. You are doing amazingly and if you can't have Kelly holding your hand you need some relief.

'*I make empowered choices that feel right for me and my baby.*'

25/7/2020 05:15
Battery 1%

We will never know what happened to us in the last two hours. You were given morphine, left half naked and no one checked on you. I know this as we attend a birth reflections session at the hospital and there is absolutely nothing in the notes for this time. You have never felt more vulnerable, neglected and frightened. You will think about this for a long time. It will influence your decision to have more children in the future and will make you want to speed up the next few hours so you never feel like that again.

The morphine has worn off now, the contractions are extremely strong and you have finally been examined and are 6cm! Well done! The midwife has said she won't leave you now and that means she won't contact Kelly for you. With your last 1% you just messaged '6cm come.' She will be here soon. Breathe, visualise, push, repeat.

'*I have got through 100% of my difficult moments.*'

25/07/2020 06:00

Over to you, Kelly, thank God you are here. Please give me some water and hold my hand.

25/07/2020 10:00
Battery 100%
3 hours old

    Hey, you. At 6:17 you gave birth to our Harry James with Kelly by your side. You bloody did it! You laboured alone for hours and hours. You dug deep and found a strength you never knew you had! I know you feel broken right now but you are a superhuman, a warrior and a Queen.
    You have just had to say goodbye to Kelly as she can't stay due to restrictions. You have been moved to a ward and you are just in awe of this gorgeous little boy. Adrenaline is an amazing thing, it's keeping you going even though you have been awake for over 24 hours. Hold tight - Kelly will be back at 2pm for an hour.
X

25/07/2020 15:00
8 hours old

    Kelly just left and I saw the heartache when they rang the bell to signal visiting hours were over, the tears you both shared and the ones that are still falling down your face. This is crazy, I still don't understand why you couldn't have her with you for longer. I know you feel like you won't be able to cope alone, but you will. It's going to be really hard but you can do it. I know the signal is intermittent and the WI-FI is shocking so contacting anyone is really difficult. I'll be here if you need me.
X

27/07/2020 12:00
2 days old

    Hey, you. A combination of the reality of being in hospital alone for three days, Harry having jaundice and trying to keep him happy underneath the UV lamps, feeding him every two hours, extreme isolation and loneliness, reflux and lack of sleep has led to a huge emotional breakdown to the ward sister. You have now been moved to a private room and they have told you that when Kelly arrives she has to make sure you sleep for two hours. That's one extra hour than you are allowed to have visitors for. Try and sleep. I know you don't want to because you want to share every detail with Kelly about what she has missed

and soak up the joy of watching her being Mama. Try to just get even a smidge of sleep, my love, as impossible as it seems. You will be home soon.
X

28/07/2020 15:00
3 days old

You are free! You have been released from what felt like a prison sentence. Harry is doing well and you are on your way home. The midwife's last words are playing round your head: "Take your baby home, lock the door and don't let anyone near him." It's going to be so hot over the next few days so you will be pleased you won't have to get dressed for visitors. I love you.
X

31/07/2020
6 days old

Harry hated his first bath, it was such a fail. How amazing is technology, though? Kelly's mum FaceTimed you and showed you how to bathe a baby using a doll in her sink. I promise you he will love every single bath from now on.
X

17/08/2020
3 weeks 2 days old

Your first visitor came today. It was Mum. You were so scared to let her in but you needed her to meet her grandson and you needed to cuddle your mum. It was a short visit and you didn't want her to leave. I think you hadn't realised how much you needed her and hadn't had a second to realise how hard it has been.
X

07/08/2020
6 weeks 2 days old

Hey, my love. Kelly returned to work today, so here we go. Maternity leave: just you and Harry. Your first baby class today, though, which is exciting!

You have to wear a mask and stay on your own mat - it's going to be strange but Grace will be there and you can go for lunch afterwards. A small taste of normality. Enjoy!

10/12/2020
4 months 2 weeks and 1 day old

  Hi, I'd ask how you are, but I know. This lockdown is much harder than you thought. The days are stretching and rolling into one blur. The challenge of not being able to see anyone is wearing thin. Mum has formed a support bubble with your sister to help her and you have never felt so alone. It's too scary to take Harry to the shops. Grace is isolating to try and see family at Christmas and Kelly is working long days from home with only a small lunch break. The loneliness is unbearable. The days are blurring into a haze of bottles, naps and walks alone. You are craving human contact and yearning for Harry to be able to sit next to another baby, to touch them without thinking it could be fatal. I know you are angry and I know you are hurting. I see the hair you have started to pull out. You will never know if you found this part of your motherhood so hard because of the isolation or because you always would have.

  I wish I could reach through the phone and just sit with you and hold your hand. Talking therapies have said you don't meet the threshold for support, they are oversubscribed and can't help you. You have been given an online programme to work through. You won't interact with it. I love you and you will come out the other side of this. Christmas will be different, but lovely. Hang in there.
X

23/01/2021
6 months old

  You had the vaccine today, a sign that there will be an end to this. I love you, keep going, pull on all your reserves. There is hope.
X

29/3/2021
8 months and 4 days old

Today was monumental. There is a 'roadmap' to easing lockdown restrictions. You met Grace at the park and you finally felt confident enough to let Harry touch the play equipment and then something wonderful happened. Harry touched Bonnie's hand. You stood back and sobbed with Grace's arm around you. Something that would have seemed so normal pre-COVID and a moment that will mark your healing.

There are a few months left of maternity leave and as things start to open back up and restrictions ease it will become so much easier. Your summer will be amazing and you will have a taste of what a normal maternity leave would have been like. I know this first year has been nothing like what you imagined and you have had to find an inner strength you never knew you had. You survived having a baby in a pandemic and you and Kelly have done everything to fiercely protect Harry. Harry will be sociable, chatty and meet all his milestones. You will have your second vaccine and booster and eventually in June 2022 you will all get COVID and you will all be fine. Harry will just have a bit of a runny nose. Regular testing will end and you won't have to wear a mask everywhere anymore. You will markedly feel this fog lift in a while and life will be incredible again. *Spoiler alert* - you are so happy now, Kelly is the best mama and partner and Harry is wonderful. You did it and even on the darkest days I think you always knew you could. I love you.

X

Hannah Burgess is 34 and lives with her partner and son in Brentwood. She has been a teacher for children with Special Educational Needs for over 10 years. She enjoys reading and writing for pleasure. On the weekend you will find her hunting for the Gruffalo on long country walks and with a glass of wine on the sofa at night.

GEMMA HAANK

Momentarily, it felt nice to be home. The familiarity of drinking tea from my own cup and letting myself cry without the risk of being seen.

"This must be the best day of your life," they said over the phone. It wasn't.

"Of course," I replied through the lump in my throat, telling them exactly what they wanted to hear. Inside, I was hollow. It would be four long months until they met him, 120 days where motherhood wouldn't feel like motherhood at all. More like my insides being completely gutted, and me, blindly caring for something that once belonged inside my body but no longer has a home there. And yet, doesn't really have a home outside, either.

At this point, what even is a home? What makes a home? How do I build a home without my 'village?' My newly-hollow insides eerily echoed the hollow outside. The empty streets, the locked-up shops, the bankrupt cafes, the deserted roads, the silence. I'd like to say that I looked forward with optimism that my baby wouldn't forever know only our faces, but the world had forgotten what optimism was.

I wondered why I got us dressed in the morning, but the action of doing so seemed to come as welcome relief: a normal task in an abnormal world. Each day looked like every other day with no distinction between time, weeks, months or even hours. Through the clouds, the house remained somewhat the same, except for the relentless cries of a newborn baby and his mother teetering between love and loneliness. The silence was only broken by muffled screams for help that would not be heard by anyone for months and months and months.

In my daydreams, the house smelled like coffee and there was a plate of crumbling hobnobs. There were gifts and flowers and people looking into his big brown eyes. *He's gorgeous. How are you? Let me hold the baby.* In reality, there was nothing left to do but stare bravery in the face, whisper lullabies and sway him to sleep. Just us, once again.

Through the night, I'd Google how to breastfeed. I'd Google 'why isn't he sleeping?' I'd hope for better feelings to flood over us and I'd imagine doing this in a world where our support group wasn't over WhatsApp. One where midwives and friends would reassure us, family would hug us and one where I didn't have to walk around in the rain praying he didn't need changing or feeding as there was nowhere to go.

If I try to remember when the house became a home, it's no coincidence that I can't recall. The truth is, those moments were entirely eclipsed by survival. Exacerbated by lack of medical care and human contact, sleep deprivation and the unknown. Our home felt less like a home and more like a hole in a world that was so unfamiliar.

Gemma Haank is originally from the UK but lives in Amsterdam with her husband and son. A nurse by background, Gemma now runs a Mama meet-up event company and spends her time helping new Mamas build communities. Sometimes you can find her writing and often you can find her running around after her toddler.

SARAH PICKERING

An overused phrase

These are unprecedented times, they suggest
As two lines appear on the pregnancy test.
Our rainbow baby, such exciting news
Overshadowed by something that we didn't choose.
Scared that this now makes me more vulnerable
To the COVID virus, which is new to us all.
Mixed information, how can we be sure?
Makes these early weeks more worrying than before.

These are unprecedented times, and still,
Going alone to our first scan makes me feel ill.
I'm aware of the reasons, but that doesn't offset
Not having my partner there when I'm upset.
Holding my hand and there for support
In case of bad news, like we had before.
Tears fall into my mask as I'm sending that text
To say everything's fine for now, 'til the next.

These are unprecedented times, have you heard?
Still attending appointments alone is absurd.
For months we've been careful, unsure of the risk
Stay home, they said. Save lives, apply the rule of six.
Virtual NCT classes, it's just not the same
Things would be so different if we did it again.
No baby shower, pretty Instagram shots
Browsing online for pushchairs, car seats and cots.

These are unprecedented times, so don't moan,
If you're faced with the prospect of induction alone.
We nervously approached our suggested due dates
Others drinking in pubs with five of their mates.
In the shops, there are people not wearing masks
Can't you see I'm heavily pregnant? Please don't be so daft!
Because if I catch COVID then go into labour,
I'll be on my own, so just do me a favour!

These are UNPRECEDENTED TIMES... we know!
Now the baby is born, and I'm here all alone.
Restrictions on visitors mean mothers are left
To fend for themselves, exhausted and bereft.

Calling for help, but nobody there
Staff so overworked, it's not that they don't care.
We're all trying our best in this situation
Praying one day there will be a vaccination.

These are UNPREC... please don't say it again!
Overwhelmed and exhausted, I don't know when
We last had a rest now the baby is here
Those newborn days long and so full of fear.
With no 'support bubble' to give us a pause
Meeting their grandchild from the outdoors.
No baby groups, no regular weigh-in
Feeling lonely, isolated and forgotten.

Whilst they were having parties and breaking the rules,
Remember that mothers had to do it all.
No one there to help us, though we kept going strong
But we won't forget what we lost, how it was all so wrong.
I hope we've learnt lessons if this happens again
That the wellbeing of mothers would be considered then.
Because I wouldn't want others to go through what we did,
When it's such an unprecedented time to have a kid.

Sarah Pickering is a 33-year-old mum to Francesca who was born in December 2020. She lives in Rochester, Kent with her daughter and husband. Her career for the past 11 years has been in transport planning, and her current role is based in London. When not working, she is usually with family and occasionally takes a break with a coffee (or gin & tonic!)

LYNSEY CARROLL

I will never know how different it could have been.

I often wonder what kind of parent I would have been if I hadn't given birth at the start of a global pandemic. Would I be the kind of mother who had mum friends and went to a weekly play group? Would motherhood have been less lonely? Would I breeze through all the nursery sicknesses without the debilitating health anxiety? How much more unburdened would I have felt not having to constantly worry about every little temperature or sniffle, every person we interacted with, every place we went? I like to imagine that I would have one or two close parent friends in the local community and that we would have supported each other and all been better parents because of it. Would I be so much more confident from all of the extra support? Or is this the parent I would have always been?

I often wonder what kind of child I would have if he wasn't born at the start of a global pandemic. Would he be more outgoing and sociable? Would he have closer connections with family members? Would he have had a playdate? Would he be less anxious to be separated from his parents? Or is this just part of who he is, the child I would have always had? How has all of this affected him? Of course, I would never have him any other way. I love him to the moon and stars and back just as he is and I always will. I hope one day I can tell him all about the time when he was born and the world stood still.

I often wonder what kind of wife, daughter and granddaughter I would have been if it wasn't for the global pandemic. Would my husband and I have argued less? Would it have made that first year easier? Would I have been able to be there for my parents more? The support I would have been able to give to them. The memories I could have made with my family. I like to imagine it would have made us all happier, less anxious, more connected. Would I have seen my grandfather more in his final years without being terrified of bringing sickness into his home? I still grieve the time I could have spent with him, and my son with his great-grandfather. The fear kept me away in his last years. I convinced myself I was keeping him safe. Maybe I was, but I still lost so much in the process.

I often wonder... but, it is important for me not to get lost in the depths of grieving for what could have been, and instead, to find a way through. To not let it overshadow what I have in the present. I want to let my wondering be a positive thing and to let it shape the person I want to be in the future as opposed to dwelling in resentment. I'm working on it.

Lynsey Carroll is 31 and comes from Airdrie in Scotland. She lives with her husband and three-year-old son, Harry. She has a PhD in Molecular Genetics and now works as a Regulatory Affairs Consultant with CS Life Sciences. Her greatest joy is spending time with her son and making him laugh. In her spare time, she enjoys baking sourdough bread and sweet treats, lying in her garden listening to the birds, reading a good book or watching medical TV dramas.

"How are you feeling?"

"I don't know. I really need a wee, but the antiemetics seem to be doing at least something today. I think I'm a bit scared. It's so stupid, we live together. If I have COVID, so do you. How are we any more risk to the staff together than alone?"

"We left the house ten minutes ago and you went to the toilet before we got in the car. Twice. How do you need to pee so badly already?"

"Because surprise, surprise. I'm pregnant!"

This was my 12-week scan in May 2020. As my fiancé drove me down to the hospital, he tried to keep things light-hearted. Making jokes about how my constant needing to pee was annoying before I was pregnant, and now we could barely walk or drive more than fifteen minutes away from a toilet before I'd start complaining. We also had the added bonus of needing to stop so I could throw up in a hedge. Seeing someone in the middle of the day throwing up in public is generally frowned upon (even if you're pregnant) but during a pandemic, it was more than just a social faux pas. It was probably one of the worst things you could do. As we pulled up to the hospital car park, I felt a wave of panic rush over me, making the nausea even worse. I was given a specific number to call to let them know I'd arrived. Engaged. I tried again. Engaged. Come on, third time lucky. It rang. I waited, legs shaking, for someone to pick up.

"Hello, maternity ward."

"Hi. I've got an ultrasound at 10:20. It's Myers. Just letting you know I'm outside in the car park."

"Okay, someone will call you back when it's time for you to come in."

They hung up. This was not how I expected my first scan to go. I ruffled the face mask in my hands, legs shaking, dreading the thought of having to put fabric over my face when I felt this sick. My fiancé grabbed my shaking leg.

"Hey," he said gently. "You're gonna be okay. You won't be waiting long, and then you'll be back and you can show me the pictures. Okay?" I nodded gently and squeezed his hand, giving the most convincing smile I could muster.

My phone buzzed. That was my cue. I picked up my water, maternity notes and face mask and walked across the car park. There were other women saying goodbye to their partners, gathering up their own notes and face masks. I put off putting on the mask for as long as possible, until I was at the entrance and ringing the buzzer. Breathe in... 1... 2... 3... And... Face mask on. The lack of fresh hair and my acrid breath was making me feel even sicker. As I walked through the hospital, the stale mix of breathing through a mask mingled with disinfectant just made everything worse. The room was spinning. Every time I moved my head a wave of nausea came over. Even the slightest movement and I thought I would throw up all over the waiting room floor. I clutched my notes tightly. Breathe in... 1... 2... 3... And out... 1... 2... 3... Breathe in... 1... 2... 3... And out... 1... 2... 3... Please don't be sick... Please don't be sick.

I'd been with my sister to her baby's first scan in 2017 and I remember the bustle of the waiting room. There were women talking to each other, with partners and parents sat holding their hands, telling them everything would be okay. This time it was very different. I was deposited in a vast waiting room. Three other women sat around me. Red tape and large signs were placed on every two seats: DO NOT SIT. There were signs everywhere, reminding you to maintain a distance of two metres and wear a mask at all times. I looked at the women across from me, all on their own, eyes visible above an array of different coloured face masks. Occasionally our eyes would lock and we would share a brief moment of unspoken understanding: *I'm scared, too.*

No partners, no parents, no brothers or sisters, no chatter and bustle in the waiting room. Just silence. Every now and then a nurse would walk past. This wasn't the constant hum of activity that hospitals used to be. It was like a ghost town, and we, the expectant mums, had been pulled into this lonely existence. I sat waiting, desperate for a wee, worrying how much longer I could hold on without darting off to the toilet, either to pee or to puke. It was anyone's guess which would hold out the longest. Finally, they called my name. I looked barely pregnant. I was skinny, with a minuscule pot belly, barely visible under a tight vest. All skin and bones. The reality was, everything made me sick and I could keep barely anything down. As I stood up, a wave of nausea came over me. Breathe in... 1... 2... 3... And out... 1... 2... 3... I took very slow steps toward the room, the midwife waiting patiently until I was near the door.

"How are you feeling?"

"Nervous. Sick. I wish my partner was here. And my mum."

"I know, darling, but it's for everyone's safety that we have as few people as possible."

For me, safety meant having someone to support me emotionally. Someone who could hold my hand and tell me that it was going to be okay. Someone who knew how difficult the last eight weeks, since finding out I was pregnant, had been. Instead, he was waiting in a car park outside and I was with a stranger I'd just met. I wasn't allowed to record in the ultrasound room. What should have been excitement shared between two soon-to-be parents was replaced with sadness that this was a moment we'd never share together, and never have the opportunity to get back. Tears pooled in my eyes as they turned on the screen and I watched this tiny, grainy image move around. The shape of a head, the outline of a toe, a tiny little arm. It was real. This was why I felt the most ill I'd ever felt. That was my baby, and I was truly alone in that moment.

I was growing this perfect little creature whose smile would eventually light up our entire house, whose curly hair I'd one day joyfully brush each morning, making each ringlet bounce up, who'd chase our cats through the house, desperate to stroke them, fascinated by yanking their tails, who would eagerly wait for his daddy to come home from work and who would feed me half of his biscuits. All of this was to come, but in this moment, when it all became real to me, a time when I was vulnerable and scared, I needed my family around me. It was just me and the baby, in a room with smiling, sympathetic strangers, trying their best to make it all okay, telling me stories about their own family and asking about mine. They did what they could, but it will never quite be enough to make up for the loneliness I felt, waiting to see if my baby was okay, wishing I had the one person who should go through this journey with me, sitting watching our baby wriggling around on the screen. The movie moment you're meant to share together.

Maria, 30, lives in Wiltshire with her husband, Dan, and their two-and-a-half-year-old son, Lucas. She works as a policy manager in Bristol and spends her free time crocheting Pokémon toys and painting. She began studying part-time for her masters in 2018 but had to suspend her studies due to suffering from hyperemesis gravidarum. She finally completed her MSc in International Security in September 2021, writing her dissertation during nap times while on maternity leave.

N. DESAI

Who am I?

I am the woman who had it all planned out, but had it taken away from me.

I am the woman who expected to smell the aroma of traditional food being cooked for me as I lay resting with my baby, but instead, was wiping down food parcels delivered to me.

I am the woman who imagined a house full of friends and family, but instead, spent my days alone with my baby.

I am the woman who wanted to hear the sound of the doorbell ringing and knocking on the door, but instead, I sat in silence.

I am the woman who was looking for guidance and help from the experts, but instead, I was left to figure it out alone.

I am the woman who will never know what it is like to have their first born in a busy ward filled with partners and visitors, with a house full of loved ones, drowning in cute hampers and outfits gifted to my baby.

I am the woman who feels cheated out of such a precious experience.

I am the woman who often cries at night when I think about my experience and how alone I felt, despite knowing that many new mums were experiencing exactly what I did.

Sadly, I am the woman who is scarred and who still feels hurt and angry.

However, I am also the woman who, through the tears and memories, is proud of what she achieved without any help, how far she has come and, more than anything, is encouraged by her own resilience and strength.

I am the woman who surprised herself.

It was the hardest thing I've ever had to do, but I've only become stronger because of it. So, as much as I hated you, COVID, I too am grateful.

N is a first-time mum to an energetic three-year-old daughter, who juggles nursery pick-ups, drop-offs, full-time work and all the other fun things around the house! She loves to travel and explore and although holidays are very different now, she continues to make the most of every opportunity to be able to get away. Also passionate about cooking, she uses every opportunity to cook and loves to get her daughter involved in the kitchen and loves that she is a foodie, too!

HANNAH PAGE

What do I want you to know about pregnancy, birth and postpartum in lockdown? This opportunity feels like a silver bullet for me to help other people understand the complexities of what I felt in the most terrifying, yet joyous, time of my life. 2020.

To find out you are pregnant with the most precious and loved miracle baby, and then within weeks, hear that the very air you are breathing could kill you both. That you cannot touch your own face, see the people that you love or leave your own house. My brain became consumed with fear, confusion, loneliness and anxiety at a time you would have assumed it would be filled with love, celebrations, daydreams and baby shopping.

How can I explain how terrifying it was to be shielding, having to go alone into a hospital, where there was definitely COVID, to check on my tiny baby? To check they were OK, whilst simultaneously putting them at risk. To do that alone, with no hand to hold, without my husband to share in the magic of seeing our baby moving, seeing the four chambers of their heart and hearing it beating. How can I explain that instead of greeting my husband with photos and a hug, I was too terrified to touch him before I had showered and changed clothes, in case I passed COVID to him from being in the hospital? I spent a lot of time daydreaming about this tiny human and what things I needed to prepare for their arrival but the things that I wanted were out of stock because of COVID, and then when I did manage to order something, instead of excitedly opening it, it would sit in quarantine and I'd be terrified of touching it.

I tried so hard to be resilient. What things could I do to keep calm and build some support for us? We joined virtual NCT classes to try and make some new parent friends and took a hypnobirthing course via Zoom. We kept in contact with our loved ones via FaceTime and presented my bump to them on a screen. Would anyone understand the grief of no one getting to touch my growing bump and feel my baby kick?

As his arrival grew closer, the world started opening up more. People could socialise and the 'eat out to help out' scheme had started, but I still had to shield. I would spend my days in the lead-up to the birth checking the hospital policy over and over again, emailing the head of midwifery, PALS, the local MP, the BBC and AIMS trying to find out why my husband could go to the pub but couldn't be there to hold my hand whilst I was going to give birth to our son.

So, instead of getting excited together, the terror of being alone and in pain, with no advocate, gripped me. It took such a hold, despite all the positive affirmations, meditations and essential oils. I was terrified when all I had dreamed about was to be excited.

* * *

I am alone. I am alone, bouncing on a ball in a waiting room, with no hand to hold. I am timing my own contractions and comforting myself, messaging my husband when I can. Desperate for more than a few messages to help me through.

Of course, 'thanks' to the 4cm rule, my husband is allowed to join me. The relief makes me crumble. After a traumatic birth, ending in emergency surgery, he is forced to leave us alone in the corner of a dark ward. I lie there and try not to die. Sepsis, kidney failure and blood loss. My son's tiny body, which also had sepsis and jaundice, is left out of my reach. The next five days are torture. Both of us are battling to get better and no one is here to help us, bar the two hours of visiting that my husband is allowed. Thank God for those hours. There isn't enough staff to help us and I am not well enough to do a good job of looking after my poorly newborn baby, as I can barely look after myself. I long for someone to be there with me, holding me and telling me everything is going to be OK. To help me to hold my son and make sure he is OK, too. What if, in my morphine haze, something happens to him? I am not in a fit state to look after him. And yet, that is our reality.

**

The sheer relief of getting home, away from COVID and back into comfort, was quickly muted by my inability to look after myself. I realised how poorly I was. This beautiful boy that we had longed for was here. I'm sure it was his soft warmth that he shared with me, that helped me to heal. It was those tender moments together that made me feel like everything would be OK again soon. But when?

With more restrictions happening (lockdown, tiers, cancelled Christmas) we soon realised we would be alone, for now. What we didn't realise was *how* alone we would be. We didn't realise that the GP would not see our poorly baby who wasn't eating and sleeping, that he wouldn't be weighed by a health visitor, or that the support group for new mums that Homestart set up for us would be stopped by the police and we'd be told to go home, despite the guidance saying it was allowed. Never did we imagine that no one would be allowed in our house to hold our baby and help us get some sleep, cook us a meal or do the washing. So, we stayed inside all day, every day, for six months. We got to see our amazing little boy grow and change, learn to roll and sit, and try his first foods, all without anyone else ever feeling the warmth and weight of his quickly changing body. We could only share his first smiles and giggles with people through the screen of a phone. The only baby groups he knew about were virtual. He had never been next to another baby. We would walk around in the same circles over and over again. How was that our reality?

**

Finally, it was over. We were allowed to go outside, allowed to be close to one another, allowed to touch. But it wasn't all over. It was all in my head.

Every surface, every breath, God forbid, a cough. How could I take my precious baby outside and expose him to the risk of catching COVID? Expose him to the risks that come with being close to other people? How do I even take a baby outside? How do I make a bottle or change his nappy outside of the house? The excitement of freedom was quickly overtaken by more fear. I wanted to share him, to live, but at what cost?

He was the light in it all. He was the one who smiled and laughed and enjoyed seeing other humans. His hands were the ones that stretched out to reach others, to grab life and to live. He was the one that helped me overcome some of my fears and start living again. I do not want to hold him back or put my fears into him, so I hide them the best that I can. I take a deep breath and tell myself we're safe, hoping that he simply enjoys the people he loves, the people he should have been with from the beginning.

It still plagues me now, the PTSD and the OCD that I am working hard to overcome. The fear of the air, the surfaces, germs, death and even the people I love. From 17 weeks pregnant until he was six months old, I was in isolation, trying my best to enjoy what I could and trying to be proactive whilst coping with so much stress, anxiety, and fear. How do I move on?

How do I handle the grief of everything I had imagined, that never got to happen?

How do I move past the guilt that I couldn't just enjoy my pregnancy and the birth of my beautiful boy?

How do I move past the fear that the stress and anxiety I felt may have impacted his newly formed brain?

How do I put aside the anger of 'partygate' and the strict restrictions now being explained away as 'guidance?' That 'guidance' broke me. It changed me and it stole so much from us.

Our son is the light in the dark, the happiness, the calm and the absolute pure joy. It was my privilege to carry him into this world and it is my duty to not let what happened to me, plague him. So that is why I tell my story, for him, so it's heard, so I feel that I matter and I can move on. We can move forward and enjoy what we have now: our wonderful, happy, and healthy little adventurer who makes us laugh and gives the best hugs. We love you so much, Leo!

I hope that no other woman is ever put through this level of torture again. No one should be forced to be alone in their most vulnerable moments.

Hannah Page, 37, lives in Warfield, with her husband, Jon, and nearly three-year-old, Leo. They all love being outside and enjoy a bit of family gardening time on the weekends. Hannah is a former teacher, charity worker and volunteer, who loves being around people, so COVID was hard!

RACHEL GALLOWAY

Trigger warning: Miscarriage

On the 1st of March 2020, I miscarried, at home, in my bathroom. I laboured and lost the most wanted dream at almost 11 weeks. It was traumatic, painful and surreal. I had been in and out of my local Early Pregnancy Unit and was aware that it was likely I'd lost my baby, but it was still a shock. A visceral, bloody, brutal shock that can only be truly understood if you've experienced it, something I wouldn't wish for anyone. After four days at home, some time at EPU and home again with a pamphlet, I went back to work. Not for long – I'm a school teacher and only a few weeks later every school in the country would be closed for the foreseeable future.

I don't think it really hit me until lockdown began.

After a year of trying to conceive, my husband and I could not have been happier when we saw those pink lines. I know that we are not unique in our struggle with fertility and our subsequent loss but something I truly struggled with was the sudden onslaught of silence that the pandemic placed on everything. With no follow-up care to speak of, as the world was put on hold, I struggled with my mental health at home, alone.

Even more so, once I fell pregnant again in June 2020.

To say I was terrified was an understatement. I did not allow myself to believe it for two whole days, hiding the test from my husband, in plain sight, until I felt ready to reflect together. At seven weeks, we had a scare where I woke up bleeding heavily. I was rushed into EPU and they informed me the heartbeat was strong, the baby was safe, there was a hematoma but nowhere near the baby and sac. I clung to my husband's hand the entire time, clawing at his skin in fear before realising the news was good. I recognised the same sonographer from before, delivering wonderful news this time, instead of tragic. She quietly said she remembered us and was so happy it was good news this time, but to leave the room separately as she shouldn't have let my husband into the department.

My 'booking appointment' at nine weeks was over the phone, something I had previously done face to face, with my husband's hand in mine, at the midwives office. Now, I had to relay my family history, fertility woes and even my weight, over the phone. I just accepted it, swallowed it, as we all did at the time, as the "new normal."

My 12-week scan letter explicitly stated I was to come alone. Once it was determined I had hypertension and had to be placed on medication immediately, I was told to attend repeat appointments alone. I heard my baby's heartbeat for the first time, alone. I asked if I was allowed to audio record it for my husband who was waiting in the car park. I only met with my community midwife once throughout my entire high-risk pregnancy. My sister, now at the halfway point, has met hers four times already. I went for my sweep alone.

My waters broke at home whilst my husband and I were sitting on the couch. I was told to come into triage immediately, alone. I was kept in for monitoring, alone. My husband parked his car in a spot where he could see me from the hospital room window whilst we spoke on the phone for three hours. My labour was ramping up fast. I was handed co-codamol and sent home, quietly told, "Best to be in the house doing most of it yourself, at least your husband can be with you there."

He drove me the six-minute journey home where I sat on my birthing ball for all of four minutes before calling them back to tell them my contractions were now seconds apart. He still wasn't allowed in with me until a midwife was able to examine me, a further hour later, behind a mask, unmedicated, alone, afraid and in agony. When they realised I was fully dilated and the baby was back to back, he was finally allowed in.

After a complicated labour that resulted in an emergency C-section, our rainbow baby, miracle daughter and tiny perfect human, Lily, was born. On the 1ˢᵗ of March, 2021, exactly one year after I miscarried. A true blessing sent to us at precisely the right moment.

My husband was sent home two hours after she was born and was told he couldn't return until later that day, and only for a three-hour slot. In our delirious haze, we chose 12 until 3pm and I waved him off, drunk in love and likely the cocktail of drugs I was on.

When I look back now, it is absolute madness that my husband wasn't allowed longer with us both. We had only just come out of theatre an hour before he left. My daughter's first real latch happened when he was at home. Her meconium nappies occurred whilst he was at home. I was expected to get up and get on with it for the first 48 hours of Lily's life, whilst having just been cut open and stitched back up again. I was to wear a mask throughout my two-day stay. My husband left at 3pm on Tuesday and I didn't see him again until noon on Wednesday, alone on a ward with the occasional other Mum and newborn, equally alone behind their masks and individual "COVID-safe" curtains. I still double-take now when a friend talks of their mum or in-laws visiting them in the hospital. It feels such an alien concept to me considering the father of my daughter was only with her for brief windows during the first two days of her life.

When we finally got home, the lack of flurry really caught me off guard. No visitors or well-wishers were allowed in our home so there were many doorstep deliveries and tears shed at windows, but no regular helping hands or revolving doors of family and friends. Instead, it was me, my husband, our brand-new baby girl and the daily checks from the midwife. There was also one emergency stint at triage, where I was told the only reason I was allowed my husband by my side was because I was a breastfeeding mum still establishing. I pondered – if I were a formula mum, would I have been expected to fend for myself four days after major surgery? We were given nowhere to place Lily. She had to lie in our aching arms for almost five hours, apparently due to COVID safety measures.

Looking back now, it's such an odd experience to consider we had 'meet and greets' with our girl over FaceTime and we just accepted this. Lockdown restrictions began to lift in the Spring of 2021. How bizarre, that we were excited to move into "tier two" with the new "rule of six" (in outdoor spaces only) which allowed people to meet Lily in our garden or on benches. Many family members didn't meet her until she was four months old. Some never held her until her first birthday. I reflect on this now with incredulity and think of the many baby classes, newborn experiences and even just simple help that we did not get and never will. In many ways it really was just us, alone in our house, figuring it all out. Terrifying, wonderful, amazing, insular, lonely. I listen to the government's pathetic excuses now regarding the parties - the lies, the media spin - and wish we'd broken far more rules than we did, as petty as that sounds.

In the grand scheme of things, we did not face the worst experiences that some new parents did during that awful time. But, it is a bitter pill to swallow, to consider that the first six months of our daughter's life were restricted and my long-awaited, desperately wanted maternity leave looked nothing like I'd imagined. Christmas Day 2020 was one of the only times our very close family of eight got together. The saddest part of all is that my sisters and best friends barely saw me pregnant. My now-pregnant sister touched my bump only once to feel tiny little kicks. Now, I see her at least once a week and can't help but rub her growing belly, eager to feel any tiny flutters, surrounded now by our family of nine. I think about all these little instances that I missed and might never experience again and I feel robbed.

I wouldn't change our timeline as it led us to our girl, but I do lament those lost months. Those lonely days. No one expects to face one of the most human experiences, alone. That's the inhumane part.

I hope my daughter knows how loved she was, is and always will be. I hope I was enough for her.

Rachel Galloway, 33, from Motherwell lives with her husband and their two-year-old daughter, Lily. She is an English teacher with a passion for empowering young people through literature and personal writing. She loves to travel, taste worldwide cuisine and read as many books as possible throughout every school holiday.

CHERI ANGHARAD LEWIS

    Who knew
that I'd still be attending maternity appointments alone
while thousands crowded football matches and festivals?

    Who knew
that sitting alone in a waiting room would lead to a beautifully crocheted
'anxiety blanket'
that I would go on to cocoon you safely in?

    Who knew
that I'd be terrified to do the food shop in case I brought home COVID,
yet I'd be expected to care for COVID-positive patients at work?

    Who knew
that I would be so upset about not having a baby shower or work leaving party
when I slunk out through the back door into maternity leave?

    Who knew
that I'd have to choose between my husband and my mother being with me in labour,
while Boris and his cronies had a fucking party?!

    Who knew
that I'd have to do a COVID swab in between vomiting,
just to be admitted onto the ward?

    Who knew
that I would meet you behind a face mask,
in a room crowded with over 20 people?

    Who knew
that even a year later, I would be so triggered by a colleague's 'special
treatment' of two birth partners,
yet myself, and thousands of others, struggled through?

    Who knew
that I'd feel completely abandoned when we had no breastfeeding support
when I could get on a flight with hundreds of strangers and jet off to high-risk
countries?

      Who knew
that being pregnant in a pandemic would give me such inordinate anxiety,
to shake my core and ruin so much of those early days of your life?

      Who knew
the extent of the jealousy and rage I would feel
hearing of my friends' experiences unmarred by disproportionate restrictions?

      Who knew
that we would be so robbed - of our sanity, of toilet roll, of formula milk, of pasta,
of support, of sisterhood... of normality?

Cheri Angharad Lewis, 32, lives with her husband, Deano, and their son, Frankie, who is 18 months old. She works full-time as a midwife in the NHS, however, motherhood has reignited her lifelong love of writing. She started writing as a form of therapy during early motherhood and has continued to do so wherever she can steal those little moments of peace!

CHLOE PRIVETT

It's 2020, the year I became a mum.
The start of motherhood, a life full of fun.
I awaited your arrival, nine months grown in my tum.
I tried to keep you safe, but who knew what was to come?

Suddenly, the words flash... STAY AT HOME.
What does that mean?
Can I travel to hospital?
Can I see my midwife?
Can my family visit?
Can my birth partner be in tow?
Nobody knows.

Emails ping, NCT classes are cancelled.
Phone rings, water births are no longer an option.
COVID testing must be done before entering hospital.
Masks must be worn after baby is born.
Hand sanitising is a new routine daily.

My baby boy is put into my arms.
The most special day.
Just four hours later, my husband cannot stay.
"Strict hours," the staff say.
"He's allowed to come back to collect you... in two days."
My birth experience has been taken away.

We are finally home
with our new bundle of joy,
soaking up our newborn bubble.
But, my husband is a key worker,
so back to work he goes. No hope for furlough.
Leaving me on my own.
Some days I feel alone.
I try to keep connected, FaceTiming family on my phone.

COVID is everywhere, you cannot escape it.
News stories, radio stations, daily press conferences.
What has this world become?
What will the future be for my little one?

There is so much sadness, worry and fear.
I've got what I've always wanted right here,

But I can't help but feel sorrow,
Family are missing out,
Videos are all they have of his milestones.

But, despite this crazy world
We made the best memories.
We became more grateful
and without doubt it brought us closer together.
One thing's for sure, we'll certainly never forget it.

Chloe Privett, 30, from Southampton lives with her husband, Aaron, and their two boys, Finley, 3 and Oliver, 1. Chloe's always loved writing poetry in her spare time and lately has been on a health kick to be a healthier and fitter version of herself, in body and mind. From a non-runner to signing herself up for 10k races. She's a big believer in supporting and encouraging others. @chloepriv93

KERRY LOCKYER

I originally wanted to dedicate this to my daughter, born in May 2020, into a world I didn't understand and am glad she won't remember. As I started writing, it became clear just how angry and resentful I was about my experience and the inhumane birth restrictions at the time. It didn't fit to dedicate such fury to someone so innocent and beautiful. After all, little Orla was my lighthouse in a storm of 50-foot waves which battered my emotions and left permanent scars - mental and physical. She was the only thing that got me through.

So, I dedicate my piece to every woman who gave birth under COVID-19 restrictions. It took a strength that most of us didn't realise we had which is why it is so important to document what we went through.

At the time it felt silly, trivial even, to moan about going into labour without a birth partner when we were reminded daily of how many thousands of people were dying of COVID. However, the pandemic made us mums realise more than ever that the trauma of giving birth and the importance of maternal mental health should never have been underestimated. Maybe we could have put up with the restrictions for the greater good, but when pubs reopened and maternity wards stayed shut, when the Government partied whilst we screamed alone in agony, the collective anger of mothers was not going to stay suppressed for long. I'm proud to be part of this collection alongside some incredible mums.

Alone walking into the maternity unit, after hugging my husband goodbye, with a naive optimism that I'd see him again later that day. Looking back, I'm glad I had no idea what was to come. I wouldn't have been brave enough to get out of the car if I did.

Alone when I was induced and sat for hours whilst my baby decided to stay firmly put. Books, music and box sets my only company; Sharon Horgan and Rob Delaney my alternative birth partners. I'm still strangely grateful to them.

Alone when my daughter did not respond well to the unwelcome kick-start of drugs, which sent her heart rate skyrocketing and a concerned midwife suggesting an immediate C-section.

Alone when a busy consultant insisted I was fine and gave me anti-contraction drugs to slow my already non-existent labour down and calm my stressed baby.

Alone during a 48-hour cycle of drugs to start me off, followed by my daughter's dangerously high heart rate, back to anti-contraction medication to stop everything and so on. All whilst strapped to a monitor in a bed with curtains drawn and nobody to talk to.

Alone as I was told to "relax and breathe" for the copious internal exams and sweeps, one so particularly savage I had to have gas and air. All for 1cm progress over 48 hours.

Alone as a trainee midwife held my hand as I cried from exhaustion and fear of another impending sweep, the only human touch I had during my time on the labour ward.

Alone when after a gruelling 48 hours, my first contractions suddenly rushed over me, taking my breath away and forcing me on my knees.

Alone as I tried to control the pain through breathing and humming, pacing my curtained cubicle, feeling desperately isolated on a packed labour ward.

Alone as I was offered pethidine. In my overwhelmed state I couldn't remember if I planned to take this drug. With nobody to ask and desperately needing something to help my pain, I took it anyway.

Alone as the effects of pethidine took over and I immediately regretted it. Trapped in a drowsy, half-asleep loop, snapped awake by the sharp pain of a contraction, attempting groggy breathing techniques and back into a heavy half-consciousness. I rode this out for over an hour, but it felt like an eternity.

Alone as the drugs wore off and the full reality of a contraction made me scream like a farm yard animal.

Alone as the midwife came rushing over to check I was dilated enough to warrant gas and air. She smiled at me from the foot of the bed like I'd won first place in a crappy raffle. I couldn't share in her joy - my legs akimbo, counting my breaths and focusing on the sterile hospital ceiling to remain calm. "Quickly, please," was all I could get out.

Alone as the rush of relief hit every inch of my body and I greedily sucked down as much gas and air as I could. I called my husband; I was in active labour - we were finally about to have our baby and I was finally not going to be alone anymore.

High as a midwife wheeled me to the lift and I shouted something incoherent about gas and air being a conspiracy theory and the reason they let you get to the point of despair before giving you the wonder drug, was because the reprieve felt more euphoric when it finally came. Telling one nurse "you must be Catholic, too," as the lift door shut.

Euphoric as the midwife in the lift laughed at my drug-induced babble until she looked at the floor and stopped smiling – my waters had broken all over the floor.

Tearful when I saw my husband in the corridor. I was so happy to see him, yet I had endured so much alone, I felt like I didn't have the headspace to let him in. Everything was too impossible to explain.

Crushed when another consultant looked at my notes and called more doctors into my room to check over my daughter's monitor readings.

Terrified when she hit the emergency button and said they needed to get our baby out immediately with an emergency C-section.

Shame that I should have trusted my instincts and the first midwife, who recognised something was seriously wrong two nights before, and made a fuss sooner.

Shaking from the cocktail of drugs pumped into my body without the proper time to absorb them.

Scared at the look on my husband's face as he took in the situation with a clear head.

Relief as we heard the doctor say she was out and OK.

Joy at hearing her first bird-like scream.

Tears as my husband brought her over for me to hold her; with her perfectly squished and swollen face.

Alone again when my husband had to leave us after a total of three hours in the hospital. I felt so desperate for him because at least I was with our baby.

Purpose to be finally looking after the daughter I had spent nearly three days in despair bringing into the world.

Happy and oblivious to the next stage of parenthood, which would involve an infected C-section scar, nipple thrush, breastfeeding agony, a tongue-tie and exhaustion beyond belief, but at least I wasn't **alone.**

Kerry Lockyer lives in Watford with her husband, Neil, and 'threenager' daughter, Orla. She is a TV Producer who, in her spare time, remembers to text her friends back and buy Babybels. She loves live music, but in recent years has swapped festivals for Disney soundtracks, which she secretly enjoys more than her daughter.

KATE BROCK

Today, like every day, I tell myself I'll ignore my phone. I vow not to get lost doom-scrolling in its depths, to stare into my baby's eyes for longer, to drink him in. *It goes so quickly! They're not little for long!* But I want to press fast-forward. I want him to grow and soar and leave these dark days behind, to emerge three or four years down the line, whole and undamaged, healthy and victorious.

He should be babbling more by now, says my mum, and I think, well, why would he when there's only me to stare at, day after day? I mean, I'm doing my best here. I stare back, I coo and I narrate our days; I put on bravura solo performances of nursery rhymes, singing and signing along to Mr Tumble, we go outside and look at trees and flowers and cars and scudding clouds, sometimes I'll meet a friend for the exquisite luxury of a takeout coffee, we walk or push our prams in parallel and I sanitise mine and his hands approximately every five seconds, and I try to smile at him a lot, I really do. I write my litany of Things to Be Grateful For every night and I try not to offload too much on my hard-working, economically viable husband about how horrendous the birth and subsequent hospital stay was. How it's torn something deep down inside of me that was once happy and whole and good.

And yes, yes, I know - there are so many others worse off than me. I'm reminded of this a lot. I know there are people dying alone, people working their fingers to the bone and living apart from their families all for the greater good. I am, in comparison, hashtag blessed. Yet here I am, sulking that no one can hold my delicious baby, no one can revel in his loveliness with me, in the triumph of him. Such a trivial thing, I know. I am so stupid, my new-mum brain so addled, I actually forgot for a second that people were dying, whoops! I'll attempt to stifle this sorrow, or at least contain it - make it softer, quieter, politer and more palatable because people are dying.

My mum is right, as usual: he's not babbling enough. His speech is delayed, they will tell me, months and months later; some of the sounds he makes are atypical. *Probably because he's a lockdown baby,* the health visitor shrugs.

It's going to be very interesting to follow all these lockdown babies to see how they develop and turn out! I hear this a lot, too. As if these babies are purely an academic exercise. As if there aren't real lives involved.

So interesting, yes! I want to screw-drive my fingers into the eyes of people who say this. My child isn't a sociological experiment. There are life chances at stake here.

After the baby was born I would send these manically chirpy voice notes to people, because typing something out took forever with one hand while the other was constantly clutching him to my breast. I'd always begin with *Sorry, I know these notes are a bit cringe and everything but they're so much easier at the moment* and *hey how's your pandemic going* and *tell me about child-free life in the real world* and *sorry it's taken me so long to get back to you I've just been really busy cleaning and clothing and sustaining new life during a global apocalypse, hahaha.* They were probably relieved when the messages dried up altogether. My WhatsApp is now a desolate wasteland of long-abandoned, fragmentary conversations. *OK, so you're terrible at replying,* says a friend who's had her wedding twice-postponed due to COVID, and I realise I don't care one single bit. There's not a shred of compassion for her in me, nope, not a shred. No one asks me how I'm doing now. I skulk at the fringes of the groups.

Other fun to navigate: the sea of newsletters I'd signed up to back when I was anticipating some sort of vaguely normal, even enjoyable maternity leave. I wind up spitting at the screen, at the mass of lazy, cruelly irrelevant, completely obsolete content that oozes into my inbox as the weeks tick by. No, don't send emails about the joys of going to baby classes or Baby's First Dentist Visit when none of that is an option for us. Update your e-shots, you arseholes. But then, what would you write? We're making this up as we go along, us mothers in lockdown. Our milestones look very different.

You learn to avoid the pavements at certain times of day, or certain stretches of path altogether, like the narrow bits where you end up having Mexican standoffs between your buggy and that one really irascible pensioner in a mobility scooter. No one comes to peer gleefully over the side of the pram, no one comments on my sweet baby or admires his lovingly hand-knitted cardigans. No germ-ridden fingers reach out to stroke his soft hamster cheeks, and I don't want them to, of course, not now, not ever.

And oh, how I do.

I read everything I can get my hands on. I hunger to experience new motherhood vicariously through the words of others who didn't have to spend it shut away from the world. Mostly memoirs and novels rather than parenting books (hasn't the parenting rule book just been ripped up, anyway?) These books are a solace, but they make me ache too: a powerful rant about how public spaces aren't designed for parents has me nodding in recognition but also seething with envy. A writer bemoans the behaviour of customers in her local so-called breastfeeding-friendly café, and all I can think is: bitch, at least you get to take your baby to a café.

My bitterness is making me egomaniacal.

I don't know how to live through these days.

I wanted to live them well. I wanted to take pleasure in them. Cherish this time that everyone's telling me I'll never get back, these days that *go so fast, oh they go so fast, you want to enjoy them while you can.* And I do want to enjoy them, to enjoy my baby. I just want some sort of a life, rather than this twilight-zone existence. I wake up each day and remember that we live in this warped dystopia, and I feel shocked all over again, like an idiot. It's like being back on the postnatal ward, hobbling to the toilets for the first time, a bright rose of blood blooming on my lower back. Blindsided by the rawness of it all, this new reality.

Stuff starts to reopen, but we hang back. I have asthma, and he had an unknown infection when he was born, and I am scared. Later, when his speech delay is confirmed, I will look back and castigate myself for this, for not socialising him sooner, for not going to Rhymetime and those longed-for baby groups as soon as possible. What untold damage have I wreaked upon him now, I wonder, through my own fear and ignorance?

At night, when I feed the baby to sleep, I recite whatever scraps of poetry I can remember. I can never make it through the whole of *Dover Beach*, no chance, but I think I understand the darkling plain: it's here, we're standing right on it.

Omigod lighten up, people say. *You forget the good times,* says my husband. And they're all right: never mind the unfolding wonder of my new baby, the days are also punctuated by moments of humour, silly things and in-jokes that make us smile. Like asking each other, when stress is mounting, if we want to 'do a line' (of Dairy Milk, that is) or my mum's crush on Chris Witty, or the way we briefly panicked over a neighbour seemingly hovering around in dramatic, head-to-toe PPE. Perhaps some deadly new strain had emerged just down the road? Nope, the guy just kept bees. And I try to home in on these moments, I do. Part of me is longing to mellow, to thaw. To let the deep well of bile and fear that lies hidden inside me dry up and be gone for good.

And yet, part of me clings on ever more tightly to the bitterness. The anger and sadness that this is how motherhood started for me and so many others; that so much was taken away, so soon, and we won't get it back. There is no replaying his babyhood. If we dare to feel sorry for ourselves, us new mothers, we are quickly silenced. But our pain needs memorialising, too.

Kate is in her late thirties and is a travel copywriter by day and an aspiring fiction writer by night. She lives with her husband and two young sons in Oxford but is really a stealth northerner, forever pining for the North York Moors.
Twitter: @brockyspen
Instagram: @katefbrock

JENNIFER WEBBER

I only went out for nipple cream.

As we prepared to welcome our first baby, we travelled through the exciting milestones you expect to achieve. Handover of work and projects, obligatory out-of-office on, lists of stuff to get ready for the baby's arrival and a few lovely catch-ups planned with family and friends before our world got tipped upside down. If only we knew...

Breaking news on repeat. Some awful virus from Asia has popped up in the Alps. It's spreading like wildfire across Italy and Europe. Pregnant people are classified as vulnerable. Do not mix! What is this virus? What does it mean for our unborn baby?

Finally, our special time arrived, labour had started! We arrived at hospital on Monday 23rd March 2020 and settled into the labour ward. Little did we know how lucky we were to have gone in on that day. Our darling boy arrived on Tuesday 24th March, the first day of lockdown, an event we barely noted. Our baby was healthy, but I was not, so we stayed in overnight. My husband came to visit us the following day and was begrudgingly allowed into the building by security, only to be told when arriving onto the ward that this would be his last visit and it would only be for an hour. He was told all this before he even held his son.

'A pandemic,'
'Country-wide lockdown,'
'A patient tested positive,'
'There's been another death,' were phrases we could all hear from our post-natal prison. The days rolled into nights in a disorientating blur and my health was not improving. By day four, the medicine was finally working, and off home we went to start our life as three. Time to transform!

There was no home check-up, so we headed to a pop-up post-natal midwife unit. My husband had to stay in the car. Checks complete, we headed to a supermarket as I needed a few essentials such as nipple cream, nursing bras and sanitary pads. As we pulled up in the car, my husband handed me gloves and a mask and sent me in alone. *Weird*, I thought. *Why has he passed me these medical things and why are they staying in the car?* But the baby was asleep so I didn't think much more of it.

When I got into the supermarket I approached a sales assistant to ask where the nursing bras were. She scurried away from me like I was covered in a disease. *Weird*, I thought, again. *Maybe she didn't hear me?* I found the clothing section, grabbed a pair of bras and a tube of nipple cream and approached the checkout, only to see Perspex screens up and crosses on the floor. Suddenly, I noticed everyone had a mask on. *What the hell is going on?* It was like a movie set for some sort of zombie apocalypse film! I paid for my things and ran out of the shop in tears, confused, scared, a shell. It was a moment I will never forget, just like I'll never forget the birth of our babies.

The day my world was tipped upside down was the day I walked into a shop as a fresh, smitten, new mum to proudly buy my nipple cream. I came out anxious, terrified of this invisible killer, too scared to allow our families to meet or hold our baby, obeying the government mandate.

The day I bought my first tube of nipple cream will never be forgotten.

Jen Webber, 34, from Chelmsford, lives with her husband, three-year-old son, Douglas, nine-month-old, Margot, and their large lovable labrador, Wallace. She is a part-time Planning Manager currently on maternity leave. She enjoys spending time with her family, going to the gym, walking their dog and a very chilled rosé with lashings of ice.
@_jenwebber

JASMINE BUNDOCK

My sweet baby Arthur,
You are my first baby, my first Son.
You are my Son-shine, my reason for living, breathing, I'm so glad you are mine.
You pulled me from the darkness and brought me to the light.
You are my pandemic baby, although you're now almost three. You'll always be that sweet, little pandemic baby to me.

A cold November morning, two blue lines appeared. We really couldn't wait for Summer 2020 to be near.
You burst into our lives on the hottest day of the year, your loud and angry cry was the best thing we could hear.
Not long after you entered, Daddy had to leave, he wanted to hold you so badly but was told that just couldn't be.
He tried to fight the system, he was ready to go to war, but he was threatened, pushed aside and warned to say no more.
So then, it was just me and you, I stayed up through the night. I couldn't take my eyes off you, I had to keep checking you were alright.
We made it to the morning and through the nightly plight, finally, we went home together to start life
As a family of three.
You, Daddy and me.

Your grandparents came to see you, even though we weren't sure they could.
The photos are hard to look at, as everyone wore masks.
You can't see how much they're beaming at you, my little sweetheart.
The months rolled on and seasons changed and still, we stayed at home.
We entered lockdown number two and I spent all my time with you.
Your first Christmas was spent at home, just Daddy, you and me. Shortly after this, we entered lockdown number three.

So, by the time we were able to leave the house, you were nine whole months old. I really wish someone could have told...
Told me what was coming, how your first year would pan out. I never saw this coming, I never thought about
The things we'd miss out on, experiences snatched away, precious time with family that we'll never have again.

But as we near your third birthday, there's never been a doubt. You were the best pandemic gift; one I couldn't live without.
So this is for you, my sweet boy, my historic summer babe. The pandemic could have broken me, but you helped me find a way.

A way to find the little things, the little things in life. The things that add up to big things and really make everything feel right.

Arthur, you are my Son-shine, the wind, the earth, the sea. My darling little pandemic boy, you truly, wholly, saved me.

Jasmine Bundock, 31, lives in Kent with her husband and two young sons, Arthur and Ralph. She works part-time in financial services admin and is on the board of directors of her local nursery. She is part of the local Maternity Voices Partnership and volunteers as a champion for Make Birth Better. She is passionate about improving maternity services in East Kent. When not at home, you will find her on the North Cornwall coast, enjoying long walks along the beach with her family.

LEANNE BOWEN-BRENNAN

Trigger warning: Miscarriage

For Tabetha, my greatest gift.

When I think back to 2020, I don't think about missed holidays, missed events, working from home, hand washing or face masks. I think about 31st December. I carry a certain kind of grief about that day. It's with me all the time. An inexplicable grief. A weight on my chest that will never lift.

Blood is terrifying when you're pregnant, but my worst fears came true that day. I ended up sitting in A&E in severe pain, a mask stuck to my face that was soaked with my tears. The entire waiting room just stared at me. My mum had to wait in the car park and the most my husband could do was wait for updates because he couldn't get out of work. Whilst people were moaning that their New Year plans couldn't go ahead, I was miscarrying. Alone.

After a lengthy wait in A&E, I was sent to the Early Pregnancy Unit. I had a horrendous internal exam.

"Your cervix is still closed but this is almost certainly a miscarriage."

The doctor wasn't awful, but I don't think he looked at me for what I was: a heartbroken woman on her own.

"You can have another one."

After two years of trying, we had just started our fertility treatment journey, so 'just having another one' didn't seem possible. Regardless, was that appropriate to say? Exhausted and distraught, there was nobody to stand up for me. I couldn't find the words.

I was admitted onto the ward because there were concerns of an ectopic pregnancy. I don't think I slept that night. I saw the New Year in on my own.

The next morning, I had a scan, alone. No ectopic pregnancy. No signs of a viable pregnancy. Empty sac. I knew that was coming but it didn't make it any easier to hear on my own. I sat on the bed and sobbed. Looking back, I feel for the sonographer. They were not allowed to comfort me. It really was a helpless situation.

Then, I had to tell my husband. There are no words to describe that feeling and it is something I should not have had to do. He should have been there with me.

Later that afternoon, finally at home, I passed what a medical professional calls an embryo. I call them my baby.

Leanne Bowen-Brennan, 34, from Swindon lives with her husband Lee, 19-month-old daughter Tabetha and four rescue cats. She works for a charity in their Payroll department. In her spare time, you'll find her buying more plants for her garden, reading smutty books and drinking a lot of coffee.

LAURA GOOCH

Patched with love

Your life's been a jigsaw.

Times and places,
relationships,
faces.
But my heart feels the spaces
that shouldn't be there.

There's a missing piece where
first cuddles should go.
From friends and from family
when the government said no.

There's a gaping hole where
your sister should've been,
in the hospital, with you,
not meeting on a screen.

There's a grandma-shaped piece
that's the biggest loss yet.
A relationship promised
that has since gone unmet.

There's a visit to work
and going on planes,
there's meeting your cousins
and day trips on trains.

There are mum groups and mat leave
and parties and hugs.
Every piece of the jigsaw that's missing,
it tugs.

At first glance, the picture seems
bright and unbroken.
But I've thought long and hard
of the memories unspoken.

My husband sent home
while I stayed on the ward,

hands squeezing goodbye,
our heartbreak ignored.

My time in the hospital,
alone and afraid.
Of our short time together,
how I wished he could stay.

The news, with the death toll
rising each day.
New lockdown announcements;
more hiding away.

The masks and the rules,
the fear and the dread.
The gaps in the narrative
on a loop in my head.

I've seen only voids.
Too many to fill.
My fingers ran over
the fractures until
the edges were worn,
smooth and distorted.
All attempts at normality
cruelly thwarted.

Those chasms, so clear
since the day you were born.
I've been left with the
urge to do nothing but mourn.

What a couple of years!
They all joke, as I sigh.
Look at her now,
how the good times fly!

Yes, she's a toddler.
You missed out on it all.
We missed out on things, too.
And the tears
       start
          to
             fall.

Yes, she's a joy.
And we love her to pieces.
But some fragments are sharp
and that's not where my peace is.

Only now, I am learning.
The grief will subside.
The dark times retreating,
my fears pushed aside.

I'm realising slowly
that the jigsaw's not real.
The gaps don't reflect
all the love that I feel.

It's more like a quilt -
a patchwork of feeling.
We've been through hard times
and some left me reeling.

But we've loved you since day one
and that's never changed.
Though the world all around us
seemed desperate and strange.

For the past couple of years,
we've been mending the rips.
The threads of our family,
sewing up every split.

Patched up with love,
Compassion and kindness.
The good times,
the bad times -
together, they bind us.

Laura Gooch, 39, is a part-time communications account manager and mother of two daughters - the youngest of which was born in the first lockdown in 2020. Laura loves soul music, strong tea and savage banter, and lives in sunny Eastbourne with her lovely husband and two gorgeous girls.

RACHEL JEAN BIRCH

I had in my mind an idea of what pregnancy and early motherhood would be like. It was shaped from others' experiences, often filtered and photoshopped, as most of our world now is. Perhaps it was too romantic, idealistic and unrealistic. Or, is it because no one tells you what it's like, *really* like, until you become a parent? How utterly exhausting and exhilarating it all is, Insta vs Reality? Was my ignorance what made it all such a shock? Or was it actually the added layer of lockdown and a global pandemic?

I still dream of what my journey would have been like if the pandemic hadn't happened. We could've married in 2020, gone on a long-haul honeymoon to a paradise-esque resort and then began the process of starting a family. What could have followed were shopping trips for baby things and maternity clothes, baby showers with my girlfriends and lunch with my parents and siblings who could see my growing bump. I would have had my partner at the first scan and shared the excitement of seeing and hearing our baby. Attending the 12-week scan alone is a trauma that brings me to tears every time I think about it. I imagine how the birth would have been easier, with more choice and support.

That wasn't Mother Nature's plan for me. Putting the wedding and all of our life plans aside, we decided to give baby-making a go. Conception was surprisingly easy, given my endometriosis diagnosis, the doctor's prognosis of a likely difficult road and the potential of IVF. Second cycle lucky and those two blue lines showed up strong on the test before I'd even finished my morning pee! My pregnancy happened above the camera line of my Zoom calls, so most of my colleagues didn't know I was pregnant. My best friend of ten years was pregnant at the same time, and at no point during our pregnancies did we see each other's changing bodies in the flesh. Such a monumental change came and went without us being able to share it like we have done with everything else in our lives for more than a decade. That was really hard.

41 weeks and it was time. At 2am, I called my mum and dad to tell them my labour had started. Powerless to help, my mum stayed awake and occupied herself by baking an incredible birthday cake for her first ever grandson - woodland creatures, a sparkly cake topper and all!

I was terrified of giving birth, mainly the threat of having to do it alone. I wanted to stay away from the hospital for longer but the pain was too intense. I was one of the lucky ones as they let my husband stay with me. I swear I would have given birth in the car park if they hadn't.

They gave me a PCR test between my contractions and tried to make me wear a mask. I took it off. My dream of a water birth almost didn't happen because they were short-staffed, but my husband rolled up his sleeves and helped prepare it. I'm a Piscean, so water is my peaceful place. It brought me some calm momentarily but the waves of contractions started coming every two minutes. I felt too hot, I felt sick, it was too much and I wanted to get out. I didn't know what to do next. I opted for the epidural, even though I felt so pressured to go without, because of the shame that comes with not birthing 'naturally.' The relief was a weight lifted. I could think, I could breathe, I could see the monitor peaking with every strong contraction and I felt thankful that I didn't have to endure it any more.

Seventeen hours after my labour pain started, I gave birth to our son. The little horror was facing in the wrong direction so they had to drag him out with the salad spoons. The moment they lifted my baby from my womb and onto my chest felt magical, distinct, untouchable and untainted by all of the chaos, disappointment and stress that had led up to that point. It was pure ecstasy, joy and love in an instant. For that tiny moment, the world stood still and all was as it was always meant to be.

For the fourth trimester, we had to be our own village. It would be three and a half months before being able to introduce our son to my parents, by then, no longer a newborn. I was only able to share his start in life and my new life as a mother through video calls. There are days when I despise technology and others where I thank my lucky stars for the ability to share special moments with loved ones.

Our story does have a happy ending. Our son is happy, healthy and thriving. He's rarely poorly and has travelled with us to five countries in the two years he's been on this earth. My now-husband and I did get to have our wedding in the end, although we had to extend the guestlist to eight more children who were born since the invitations were first sent out!

Whilst going through pregnancy, childbirth and redundancy during a pandemic were the worst years of my life, I can't help but wonder if that's what was the making of my family today. Would we still be this strong, this connected? Would my incredibly amazing son be the same awesome little character, had circumstances been different?

No thanks, I'll keep the birth I had. It's mine and it can't be changed or exchanged. I'll mentally filter away the hard parts that upset me, and release the pain, fear and frustration that got stuck in the corners and crevices of my body as I grew my son. I'm learning to live peacefully with the way it happened and not fear the next pregnancy (if we're lucky enough to see another two blue lines on the stick.)

Our son just celebrated his second birthday. Born on the International Day of Happiness and the first day of Spring. He's a Piscean, just like his mama. There were 359 days of pandemic lockdowns and restrictions between Boris' announcement and the day I gave birth. Since then, I've had 741 of the best days of my life raising our son.

Rachel Jean Birch, 35, lives in Newcastle and Catalonia with her husband, Adrià, and two-year-old son, Joel. She is a full-time Creative Producer and is co-founder and co-director of Moving Art Management. She is a trained dancer, book worm and travel lover. @racheljbirch

RAJVINDER SHERGILL

Trigger Warning: Traumatic birth, lone birth

You should be careful what you wish for. Those words became true, for me. I always used to tell my husband I'd never want him to see me giving birth. I got my wish in the worst possible way on 11th December 2020 when I gave birth to our beautiful son, Dylan, alone. This is my story of giving birth during the pandemic.

The Birth

The midwife has run out of the cubicle muttering something about aromatherapy. She knows I'm terrified of being here alone as my husband is going to be sent home shortly, once I've been induced. This doesn't make sense to me. He's just been in this small induction bay with me anyway. What's the harm in letting him stay when we have all just breathed the same air? She comes back in and shoves pieces of paper with various things spritzed on them under my nose. I fight the urge to laugh out loud. She explains how to see my contractions on the monitor I'm hooked up to, and how to see my baby's heartbeat. Once I've been induced, I am having contractions within minutes, but I'm told I'm a long way off yet. They tell me they will examine me in 24 hours to see if I'm in active labour. When I question what will happen if it starts earlier, I'm told confidently by every midwife I encounter that it won't, that it usually takes at least 24 hours and if it doesn't happen, I'll have a day's break where they take the pessary out and then try again on the third day. I'm exhausted just thinking about this, I hope it doesn't come to that.

The monitor shows I have had constant contractions. The pain is constant and I feel my waters break at 9pm. I pull the buzzer and a midwife comes in and tells me I have just wet myself. I tell her I'm in labour and the baby is coming, and she leaves the cubicle and comes back with another midwife. She also seems to be under the impression I have wet myself. I'm panicking inside now; they don't believe me. I pull my underwear down in desperation and exclaim, "This is my waters breaking! It's completely different to the look of urine!"

The midwives tell me they need to put the pessary back into my cervix and I start to cry, wondering if this is necessary now that my waters have broken. One of them hands me the gas and air and talks me through how to use it as they get the pessary back into place. I ask for pain relief between sweating profusely and breathing through the pain. I'm given pethidine and anti-sickness medication which only helps me sleep for a few hours through the torture.

I wake at around 3am desperately feeling that something is not right. Why aren't they examining me to see if I'm in active labour yet? My husband would then be allowed in and could be here for the labour. I'm grateful he can't see me like this, though, as I can't even breathe or speak. I'm in the worst agony possible and I have given up. I think I am going to die from the pain. I tell my midwife, between frantic breaths, that I'm in labour now, I know I am. I ask her if I can use the gas and air yet, but she tells me it's only for when you're in labour. I can't believe what I'm hearing. I want to scream but I can't muster up the energy. Instead, I simply tell her that I feel like I'm going to die. She laughs and tells me that I'm not going to die. The last words I tell her are that I'm going to the toilet.

I sit on the toilet for the whole hour between 5 and 6am. I just think I need to go. Unfortunately, that feeling is my baby's head tearing its way through my body and into the world. The pads from the tens machine attached to my back have started to come off as I'm sweating profusely. My whole body is shaking from the pain. There isn't a time throughout my whole labour where I scream in agony. I just breathe. I remind myself that so many midwives have told me I'm not in labour. I have lost trust in my body and my gut instinct. Finally, the pain stops at 6:05am. I hear a loud bang in the toilet basin and I know it has happened, that I've finally given birth.

I don't remember much from this moment as I am running on adrenaline, but I look down and I see he is unresponsive and blue. What follows, are screams I have never heard come out of my mouth before, and what feels like the longest wait for the midwife to come in.

The midwife runs into the toilet and exclaims, "Oh, you have had your baby on the toilet!" *What a genius*, I tell myself. We walk to my bed, placenta between my legs as the midwife holds my baby and reassures me he's fine. I take a photo and send it to my husband, telling him I'm so sorry he's finding out like this. I call him and tell him briefly what happened. He's on his way and I'm so relieved. If he had been here, he would have advocated for me and this whole thing would never have happened, that much I am sure of.

The doctor is yelling at the midwife who I was under the care of. I'm absolutely terrified as I watch the whole thing unfold in front of me. She is really going for it, telling her that skin-to-skin wasn't more important than getting him checked over first. She is firing questions at her.

"Have you even checked him over, considering the way he was delivered?"

I can tell she is embarrassing the midwife. She turns to me and sees the look on my face. I must be wide-eyed and open-mouthed as she quickly walks towards me, puts my hand in hers and looks me straight in the eyes.

"I am going to make sure your son is OK, I promise."

I immediately relax and nod gratefully. I'm still trying to process what's happened to me in the last 24 hours, but there's no time for that, my son needs me.

Post-natal ward

Following having stitches in theatre for my third-degree tear, I am taken to the postnatal ward. It takes them two days and mixed-up blood results to realise I need two bags worth of blood transfusion. They tell me if I feel unwell in the first 15 minutes once it is started, to alert them as it could mean I'm having an adverse reaction. I ask if someone could help me feed Dylan as he is due a feed and my arm isn't free due to where the drip is placed. A midwife arrives and says she will do it, but suddenly, she has to rush off. Before I know it, he is plonked straight on top of me while the blood transfusion starts. So, I am left with a hungry newborn while I have to wait and see if my body will accept the blood transfusion I need.

It's not all bad. I meet a complete angel; a midwife support worker who comes to me during the night feeds to help me if I need it. She swaddles Dylan into the blanket, only his head visible, and he looks like a little snowman. She is the only helpful person I come across on the postnatal ward. Without her, my whole story would be filled with sadness. These little snippets of good things, or good people, have helped me to not completely give up or have a mental breakdown.

Home

I'm frantically texting my husband from the toilet. I took my phone in just in case the first bowel movement was difficult. I was relaxed about it and joked to him it would probably take me 20 minutes to get out four days' worth (grim, I know) but I'm sitting on the toilet and finding myself sweating profusely. I can't breathe and the pain is sickening. I tell him to call an ambulance as something isn't right, but we are told it will take four hours. I can feel I'm desperate to go and it's stuck, it's the worst feeling in the world. I crawl to our bedroom and I'm on all fours, crying. He calls his mum and dad urgently to look after our son who we only just brought home two hours ago. As soon as my in-laws arrive, I'm on the way to the hospital again. I am in an insane amount of pain and slip my trainers on rather than put them on properly. I'll never forget the walk to the ward from the car park. I am doubled over in pain, completely unable to walk straight. My husband is terrified. I'm trying to fight through the pain, but I can't, and the panic is all-consuming as it's reminding me of my birth. I'm sent to an emergency ward within the labour ward and given a suppository to clear out my system, which eventually helps hours down the line. I'm met with midwives telling me I should have brought my son with me as the first days and weeks we should be together as it strengthens our bond. I bite my tongue until hours later when I am admitted into a side room and a senior midwife comes to check on me. When she utters the same words to me, I scream at her between tears.

"DO YOU THINK I WANT TO BE HERE ON MY OWN??? THIS IS NOT HOW I IMAGINED MY FIRST DAY BACK AT HOME TO BE WITH MY SON!! THIS IS NO PLACE FOR MY CHILD AND IF HE CATCHES SOMETHING HERE INCLUDING COVID I'LL NEVER FORGIVE MYSELF! WOULD YOU BRING YOUR NEWBORN IN HERE GIVEN THE CURRENT SITUATION?? I CAN'T EVEN LOOK AFTER MYSELF AS I'VE BEEN IN SO MUCH GOD DAMN PAIN!! HOW AM I SUPPOSED TO LOOK AFTER MY BABY?!"

She immediately stops talking, pulls me into a tight hug and tells me, "Fuck COVID, I don't care, you need this." We talk about my birth for a while, which I am still unable to process. She gives me the number for PALS and recommends I complain about my birth experience, telling me it should never have happened. As she leaves the room, I get a text from my husband who tells me he hopes I get a good night's sleep. I find myself laughing hysterically at this. It's 4am, and it's taken me five hours to go to the toilet and clear out my system. I attempt to get some rest, but my mind is on getting myself home to my family.

The debrief

It's taken a whole year for me to get to this point of being able to talk with the hospital about what happened to me that day. My husband and I are here with a senior midwife having a debrief about my birth. I still don't feel like I'm ready to hear what my notes say or hear any defence for her staff. As we talk about what happened, I am hysterical. My husband attempts to calm me down but I am sobbing like a child and can't hear a word anyone is saying to me.

She tells me the pandemic was a testing time and put the whole department under pressure. They didn't have enough staff and couldn't work safely. She explains that, because of this, they delivered poor care, including to myself. She tells me she is 'beyond sorry.' She advises me she will have an informal chat with my midwife so that she learns from this experience. She tells me that I should have been offered an examination when my midwife last saw me and before I went to the toilet. That, apparently, would have been the turning point, as they would have seen I was in active labour. They would have called my husband and used warm compresses on me in an attempt to stop me from sustaining a third-degree tear. I am relieved to hear the word 'sorry' for the first time and I tell her that's all I wanted. I make the decision to stop reliving it, as it is draining and exhausting, and choose not to make a formal complaint to PALS.

Therapy

"You've seen my descent, now watch my rising" - Rumi

September 2021.

A family member has just given birth and had a positive experience in hospital. Her husband was there throughout, right until the end, and to my knowledge, for some time after she gave birth. I find myself in a horrible state of self-pity and feel like a victim. I realise my first thought isn't that I'm happy for them, but instead, it's a feeling of grief for the experience I did not have.

I spend days reeling about the whole thing. I realise this isn't how I want to feel. Of course, I'm happy for them but the fact that my first thoughts are a comparison of both our experiences followed by resentment towards my own experience rings alarm bells. That night, I make the referral for therapy.

I finally get a diagnosis of post-traumatic stress disorder due to my birth trauma. My heart truly breaks for this version of me because although I'm not 100% myself even now, I really was a shell of myself. I truly lost myself during the pandemic. It almost ended my marriage. My husband had the patience of a saint. How he put up with my screaming, threats of self-harm and panic attacks, I'll never know. I know there were many times he was truly frightened and felt helpless. I can't imagine being the other person watching a loved one suffer mentally the way in which I did. But we survived, and I'm so amazed and relieved that we did.

Raj Shergill, 33, from Derby lives with her husband and their almost-three-year-old son, Dylan. She is a registered nurse, determined to make a positive impact on the lives of everyone she meets. In her spare time, you'll find her reading self-help books, doing Pilates, or cooking up a storm in the kitchen. @pregnantinthepandemic

LAURIE GOLDIE

Little Red Book

Her Little Red Book is blank
Almost - they wrote her name but spelt it wrong
I added the "a" onto the end myself
CHI number still missing, I don't know that one
"Your health visitor will complete that"
But the health visitor **never came**

She did only once, apron and mask
I don't know what her smile looked like
But I remember her hands
Sanitising the scales and ripping off blue roll
As I placed the baby on myself
Two dots in the Red Book, one for height, one for weight
She was smaller than average
That was eight months ago

I don't think I had postnatal depression but I was never given the test
"We'll do it over the phone," she said
But the phone call never came
"Weaning - I'll send you an information pack"
But the weaning pack never came
"She'll be on the move soon - I'll send out some child locks"
But the child locks never came

We cried alone, we weaned alone
We secured our cupboards and stairs alone
No baby groups or clinics, library still shut
I wonder what percentile she is now, what line she's following
She has teeth now, coming in big and strong
But the dentist keeps reminding us to stay away
They don't know she exists yet
Or that I was pregnant and entitled to free dental care until my child is one
Another three months

Her world is this house and her world is us
A cocoon of safety in a disaster zone
She sees smiles via eyes only
Mouths remain mysterious
Private parts
I laboured with a mask on

She was delivered by masks and visors
No visitors, health or otherwise
I hope her life never feels as empty
As the pages of her Little Red Book

Laurie Goldie, 35, lives in Glasgow with her husband Chris; her kids Logan (6) and Breagha (2); and her needy rescue dog, Iris. In real life, she works full-time delivering anti-stigma public education work for a national charity. In her other life, she writes poetry about motherhood; social justice; feminism; family life and dog poo, among other important topics.
@thegoldiehawn

SAMANTHA TAVENDER

Our son, Theodore, is about to turn three years old. Time feels like it's flown by, with crystal clear memories that fill my heart with pure joy and amazement, but other parts of the last three years feel like they exist outside of my own reality. As if they happened to someone else entirely or as part of some sort of grainy, blurry film.

Like many expectant parents during the initial lockdown in 2020, my mental health and anxiety were at an all-time low. The main thing that sticks in my mind is the fear caused by the uncertainty. So many things happened at once. Suddenly, both my husband and I lost our main sources of income (we were both self-employed and the restrictions meant we could no longer work.) We were living away from home in the USA. Navigating a new healthcare system is complex enough without the added strain of restrictions and rules. We were about to have a baby but had no idea what would happen if any of us got COVID or even if my husband would be allowed in with me during delivery. I cried for hours worrying about the possibility of being alone while giving birth. Well-meaning friends tried to be reassuring, but if I'm honest, they just didn't get it or understand why I felt the way I did. The uncertainty led me to make decisions about my maternity care that I would not have normally made, which still haunt me today, as I grapple with PTSD caused by a traumatic birth and medical negligence. Like many others, we kept calm and carried on, obeying restrictions and introducing our son to family via videos and photos.

The months that followed contain some of my most precious and treasured memories - all-day cuddles on the sofa between feeds, the three of us going on walks to the beach, the waves lapping at our feet while I gazed adoringly at my husband and son. But they were also some of the hardest times and I honestly don't know how we coped. Being in the USA with no maternity leave and a reduced income because of the pandemic, I went back to work full-time just four weeks after giving birth. I was teaching online, wearing Theo in a sling, turning the camera off whilst breastfeeding and continuing to teach – but what other choice did I have? It was just the three of us and there were days amidst the hourly wake-up calls and colic that I felt like a zombie and our only routine was eat, not sleep, repeat.

In October 2020, we made the decision to come back to the UK permanently, to be closer to family. At nearly six months old, it was the first time our families had been able to see Theo in the flesh. We arrived at Heathrow on November 1ˢᵗ 2020, four days before the second lockdown. It was during this second lockdown that things escalated quickly, and my husband's health took a turn. We had an uncertain Christmas and once again the panic and fear escalated alongside talks of a new variant.

In January 2021, my Husband Jaemes was diagnosed with cancer. He had to go alone to be told the news. I found out afterwards when he called me on the phone as he sat in the car. In our most difficult time, we could not see family or friends for the support that we needed – this is the part that hurts the most. We had a week between the news and seeing the consultant for an update on treatment and prognosis, during which we would take Theo in the pram and go on our daily walks. Before this, we had chatted about the mundane, exhausting, overwhelming existence of the fourth trimester; now we spoke about what we would do if Jaemes died, whilst still trying to remain positive and hoping for the best. I tried to put on a brave, confident face to be supportive but inside I was falling apart piece by piece. Each bedtime, I would go upstairs on my own, read Theo his stories, feed him to sleep and then sob. I feared the practicalities of being a single parent and my heart felt like it was being shattered imagining a life without Jaemes by my side. I couldn't breathe thinking about the idea of Theo growing up without his dad. In February, Jaemes had a complex and lengthy surgery which successfully removed the tumour in his chest. It was the size of a pint glass and had wrapped itself in the pericardial sac of his heart. There were complications, but it had gone well. On the day of the surgery, Theo and I went on our daily walk alone while I waited for a phone call from the hospital. Due to the restrictions, I had not been able to go with Jaemes, I was not able to be there by his side when he needed it the most and he spent a lengthy hospital stay with no visitors. Solo parenting was tough as a full-time working mother, but solo parenting while also caring for your husband recovering from major surgery and then going through cancer treatment was mentally and physically exhausting.

As I went through the motions of day-to-day life, trying to just get through each day, I had no idea of the toll everything had taken on me, until one day, I turned to Jaemes and said,

"I just wish I could be hit by a train; I don't want to die but I don't want to be conscious anymore."

It was shortly after that I recognised the gravity of the situation and spoke to my GP, was diagnosed with post-natal depression and prescribed anti-depressants. Eventually, things got easier and Jaemes was declared cancer-free in September 2022. We both still deal with the aftermath of it all, even now.

None of the experiences we had in that first year and a half of Theo's life would have been easy for any parent, but they were compounded by restrictions and failings of our government at the time. I am filled with a white-hot rage when I think of the days I spent crying, scared, isolated, and overwhelmed when all I wanted was some help with childcare, a hug from my mum, to sit and drink a brew with my sister, and have a glass of wine and a big old ugly cry with friends, but I couldn't and didn't. Yet, at the same time, our

Prime Minister, Boris Johnson, and his pals were doing the very same, profiting off dodgy contracts and conducting extramarital affairs in the office. The lack of social and practical support put us into a delayed state of limbo. It is only now, as we start to process what we all went through, that we recognise the impact the trauma has had on our family. I understood the need for the restrictions, it saved lives and reduced the spread of COVID, but it was one rule for us and one rule for them, and for that, I am furious. I also truly believe that, while doing the right thing and obeying the rules was for the greater good of society, it doesn't take away from the pain and suffering it caused on an individual level. Both of those feelings can coexist, and that's okay. However you felt during that time is okay, however you coped during that time is okay, and however you feel now in the wake of it all is okay.

Samantha Tavender is 33 and lives in Huddersfield with her husband, Jaemes, and son Theodore. Samantha is a lecturer in occupational therapy, and in between juggling family life, work and a PhD, likes to spend time with friends and family and exploring new places.

LEANNE LOWIS

To my darling daughter,

This is my love letter to you. People might think that is a strange thing to call this but my love for you is more encompassing, enduring and pure than any other love I have known. I have fought so many internal struggles as I want to be the best version of myself so I can be the best role model for you throughout life. I want you to know I am your constant and I will be here through the highs and lows, the celebrations and the commiserations and whatever life throws at our little family we will get through it together and come out stronger.

Finding out I was pregnant with you was the biggest shock of my life. I had wanted it for so long but was too scared to admit that to myself for fear of failing you in so many ways. When I told your dad, he was infectiously joyful and we cautiously got excited for the future to come.

When we saw you on the screen at the first scan, I was in awe and I carried around the scan pictures of you, showing them with pride to anyone who would look. Soon after this moment, our life changed, but not in the way we were expecting. The whole world came to a halt. I was told I was 'clinically vulnerable' and should stay at home as much as possible. Going from working in an office to working at home by myself was a shock to the system and I've never felt so isolated as I did on that first day. Unfortunately, this feeling has stayed with me in various ways over the years since. Your dad was told he should shield due to him having had a kidney transplant, so suddenly our world became insular and we felt in an impossible situation of putting our health and family at risk every time we left our bubble.

Every dog walk, every line I stood in (two metres apart from everyone else) and when working in my home office, although I felt a range of emotions, I knew I was never alone as I had you with me. I would put the world to rights, sing to you and tell you all about your furry brother and sister.

Every scan and midwife appointment after the first, I attended alone. The joy of getting to hear your heartbeat or see your little face was always tinged with sadness that your daddy wasn't with me to experience it.

When it came to the birth, there was so much emotion involved. From the induction where I spent a lot of time alone in a faceless room waiting for the swell of contractions, to the birthing suite and the lightning-quick reaction my body had to the oxytocin drip, I felt exhausted. The hours passed and I was so thankful that I could have your dad by my side being my constant, my calm in the storm and my advocate when I was unable to do so for myself.

After you were born, you had to be taken to NICU to have a cannula fitted, and as everyone dispersed from the room and as the silence set in, the enormity of the last few hours overflowed along with tears. Before long, you were back in the room and your dad had to leave. My heart broke a little. As quickly as we'd become our little family, we were being split up again. I had no idea what to do. I realised I'd researched the pregnancy and labour but not how to be your mum. That night, I didn't sleep for fear of missing a vital clue that you needed something.

For the next week, we had to stay in hospital whilst you fought the infection. We would get windows of time where your daddy could visit and we soaked up every moment, from deciding your name and many other 'firsts' we had to do on a hospital ward rather than in our home. We moved rooms more times than I could count, only saw nurses when observations and medication were needed and heard numerous false promises of being able to go home. All my instincts were telling me to leave but I knew we had to stay. To this day, it is hard to think of this time as I am so angry and upset about all the experiences we lost out on and the lack of support given to us. This tornado of feelings comes with so much guilt about feeling this way toward our wonderful NHS. There is a lot of this time I struggle to remember and that makes me sad as I feel I should have been soaking up every moment of this journey that I will do only once with you.

When the day finally came to take you home it felt like our life could truly begin, but so many 'firsts' had to be delayed, like your grandparents and family being unable to hold you for fear of passing on COVID to you, as so little was known about what effect it would have. We couldn't meet my friends or coworkers who were desperate to see more than a photo. We missed out on coffees with other mums to compare stories, to help me feel less alone. In fact, there were no mum-friends to share stories with as there had been no opportunity to make them. I couldn't learn from your granny and nanny about how to do things like swaddle you or that magic move to bring up wind. They were now conversations over the phone, trying to provide me with reassurance through my tears of sadness and frustration. I had experienced the most seismic change in my life and I had never felt so alone.

Throughout all of this, I sunk into a deep depression and my anxiety was sky-high. At my lowest, the one thing that shone brighter than ever was my love for you. I wanted to do better, and be better, for you. I wanted you to be proud of me, so I got help. I admitted my antidepressants were no longer helping, had open and honest conversations with doctors and fought for access to help. I knew I had to do it for you, my darling girl. I got support from a charity called Bluebell and it saved my life. Everything was so dark, apart from that light of my love for you, but with their support, from one-to-one chats with my "bluebell buddy" to our weekly support group over Zoom, colour slowly returned to my life.

Every stage had its challenges and I still find it difficult to process that period of time without an onslaught of emotion. But, one thing I know is, I would not have gotten through it without you and your daddy by my side. So whether it be going for our walks together, feeding the ducks, snuggling up reading a book together, hearing you call me mummy mama or you randomly bursting out into the Hokey Cokey... Spending time with you is my favourite thing to do. I can't wait to see what our next chapter will bring, but one thing is for sure, it will be so much brighter now I have you.

So, my darling girl, if you ever read this, please do not feel sad or guilty. I have felt enough of these things for us all. Please take the positives, the strength, the love and the light you have brought to my life. For you, my little one, are the magic in my life that I never knew I needed. You are fearless and will take on this world with that cheeky little laugh. I, for one, cannot wait to see what you achieve and I will never quite believe how I got so lucky to be yours.

You are my sunshine.

Lots of love, your mummy mama

Leanne Lowis, 37, from Clevedon, lives with her husband, her almost three-year-old daughter, Olivia, and her two dogs. She works as a part time-administrator for a recruitment agency and in her spare time she enjoys exploring the West Country with her family and reading thrillers with a cup of Yorkshire tea.

LAUREN CLARK

'2-3 weeks,'
it said on the stick
Scared and excited
I just hoped I wasn't sick

The thoughts began
Of the places we'd go
With a growing belly
Not yet starting to show

We started to imagine
Sharing my bump with our mates
A babymoon in France
And going on dates

Before us two
would become a three
There were plenty of things
to do and see

As though the world heard us
Getting ahead of ourselves
The pandemic set in
We put our dreams on a shelf

Week after week
We stayed inside
We watched the news
We clapped, we cried

12 weeks, 20 weeks,
Growth scans in between
Doing it alone
just felt really mean

FaceTime in the car park
A video here and there
All the scans he missed
That seemed really unfair

My tummy grew bigger
But only I could see
The wonderful changes
Happening in me

The contractions started
In the middle of the night
I was induced alone
I turned on the light

What are these feelings?
These twitches, this tightening?
I wanted him with me
Alone was frightening

More time passed
I pressed the alarm
I needed that midwife
Who was patient and calm

An assistant told me she was on her break
"Shall I get her?"
"No"
Maybe I'd made a mistake?

I went into labour
With no one there
To hold my hand
Or play with my hair

"Can I call my husband?"
I frequently asked
"Wait a bit longer,
Until more time has passed"

Many more hours
Went by in a haze
You finally arrived
I was totally dazed

Placed on my chest
For a minute or two
Then I went down to theatre
And had to leave you

Safe in Daddy's arms
Until I returned
Wheeled down to the ward
He couldn't stay, we learned

At 4am
He was told to go home
We stayed in our ward
Tired and alone

With the curtain pulled tight
Around us, we lay
Waiting for Daddy
To come back the next day

Willing the hours
To go by in a flash
As soon as we could
We made the mad dash

Out of the hospital ward
This time as a three
Ready to begin
Our family

Smiling at nurses
So they'd think we were okay
We hadn't a clue
I just didn't want to stay

We took you home
You taught us so much
You only knew
Mine and Daddy's touch

Into this world
Of hand gel and masks
And scrubbing our shopping
And menial tasks

With rainbows on windows
No planes in the sky
We'd take a quick walk
And have a good cry

It was the best and the worst
It was everything between
We now have these memories
Of the things we've seen

When you're a bit older
We'll share our stories
Of how people came together
When pushed apart by the Tories

You'll look back at Boris
And all that went on
And wonder how someone
Could get it so wrong

But these are the tales
Of when you were born
So forgive us, if in photos
We appear forlorn

We were solely trying
To muddle through
So, my sweet baby boy
This poem's for you.

Lauren Clark initially trained as an actress and has since developed other creative skills such as knitting, sewing, teaching and, most recently, turning her hand to pottery. She enjoys cooking, coffee, reading and wandering new places. Originally from London, she now lives in Kent with her husband and son, where they try to visit the seaside as often as possible.

SARAH BOYD

Numbers were everywhere during lockdown. Daily death tolls, infection rates, isolation days required, testing rates, hospital beds filled... It seemed there were constant counts on our television screens, computer screens, phone alerts and radio interruptions.

Alone in an empty hospital bay in October 2020, I was keeping my own counts, too. I was catapulted from a nurse, enforcing the rules and counting the seconds of hand washing, to counting the days I spent alone on the antenatal ward. The day the consultant said to me, "You must stay now, until he is born," I felt like the floor fell out from underneath me. I disintegrated into a mess of sadness, fear and hopelessness, with no loved ones to hold my hand and reassure me. Instead, a group of professionals giving sympathetic smiles as they pulled my curtain around and walked to the next patient. Another count - a quick calculation in my head, *that's three weeks until he is going to be delivered. Three weeks. 21 days. Sentenced, alone, in a hospital bay.*

In that 21 days I didn't hold my two year old daughter, tuck her into bed, smell her hair or kiss her toddler cheeks. For 21 days, I couldn't see my husband and child. I'd never left my daughter for more than a day or two. 21 days seemed like a cruel punishment. She didn't understand FaceTime and would just wander away, unaware of how desperate I was to see her face and hear her voice. My husband often had to turn the phone away because I couldn't hold back my sobs.

Whenever my husband would bring me more supplies to the hospital, I'd sit on the edge of the bed, praying this would be the time the staff weren't watching and I could sneak out for a cuddle. I just needed someone to wrap their arms around me and tell me it would be OK. The staff were just doing their jobs and following the rules that the government had set. In a twist of fate, the same rules I'd observed on my own ward with such vigilance. They would stand and watch and make sure I stayed a distance from my husband. *No contact, please.* The door would click shut again and I'd watch through hot, heavy tears as my world walked away.

I desperately needed to hold my little girl and be her mum, not a grainy image on FaceTime blowing kisses at bedtime. I snuck out one day to the hospital car park where my precious girl was strapped in her car seat.

"Mammy!" she beamed. "Are you coming home?"

"No, baby, I'm not."

Her face crumpled and so did my heart. As I write this now, some two years later, the tears still fall, the pain still real.

After 21 days, my perfect lockdown baby was brought into the world, albeit a strange and uncertain one. I had a planned caesarean due to my medical issues and I found myself overcome by fear moments before going to theatre. I walked with a member of the theatre staff down the corridors, my legs like jelly, and entered the operating theatre, alone. *'Hold still,'* you're advised as the enormous needle enters your spine. I held still but my mind was racing - was my husband going to make it in time? He hadn't been allowed to wait in the hospital and was now rushing to get there.

He did make it, and was present for the birth of our son. The time he was allowed to stay afterwards was brief, a few moments with us behind a mask while paperwork was finalised and last observations were checked. I was wheeled swiftly to the postnatal ward and he was left walking behind. I had to remind the staff to stop and let him say goodbye to his son before the doors clicked behind me once more.

Another count. This time five days. Five days I spent alone on a busy postnatal ward. I was so exhausted I began hallucinating. The baby wouldn't be put down and I had no partner to help. I was sitting upright in bed some 24 hours after his birth and remember looking at the curtain I'd pulled around our bed. The curtain melted away and suddenly I was looking at an old-fashioned nightingale ward, watching the hustle and bustle of people passing by. It was as clear as day but my mind felt muddled, unsure if I was dreaming. I blinked again and the curtain was back. That's the first time in my life I've ever hallucinated. There was another point where a student midwife was asking me some questions and my head snapped forward. I'd fallen asleep mid-conversation. I hadn't mastered one-handed breastfeeding and often my hot meals were taken away before I'd had the chance to eat them. The location of my ward meant there was nowhere that my family could go to wave up at me, a simple thing that might have pulled me out of the abyss.

In those first few hours, a staff member came to check on me. Upon finding my son still nestled on my chest, she said abruptly,

"Oh. Haven't you put him down yet?"

No, I hadn't. I'd waited almost nine months for this, gone through numerous hospital admissions and a global pandemic, now I had him safe in my arms I wasn't letting him go. For the last 21 days, it had been just us.

It was later I found out that one of the infamous Downing Street parties took place during this time, while I was in the darkest and most lonely time I have ever experienced, unable to fulfil my most basic needs, because there were rules to be followed and lives to protect.

I called my husband one evening, in the depths of despair. Through heaving sobs of exhaustion I said I couldn't do it anymore. I told him to bring formula because the feeding support was non-existent and I felt anxious that he wasn't feeding. He did as I asked and a brown paper bag arrived via a health care assistant. It was Christmas time and the bag was emblazoned with *'Give a little love.'* And that's exactly what that bag did. It was like receiving a care package on a desert island. He'd sent nipple creams and shields because he knew my heart was set on breastfeeding, a formula starter pack because he didn't want to dismiss my wishes, food, drink and a little cupcake in a box that read *love*. It meant so much. In what world could a cupcake feel like a hand hold /

hug / hair stroke all at once? Maybe because I knew it was as close as I'd get to the human interaction I desperately needed.

Every day that passed felt like groundhog day. The same monotonous routine. Minimal interaction from anyone other than my husband's phone calls. No sleep, no washing, no support. I often sat and wondered if this hopelessness is what prisoners feel. Extreme in retrospect, I agree, but I was being kept from my home and my loved ones under basic conditions and with every meal time dictated to me. There were no conversations, so I had no idea when the end was for me. I had no idea why I was still an inpatient or what they were waiting for.

And now another count was running. My daughter's birthday was fast approaching. Her birth was traumatic and it took me a long time (and some counselling support) to work through my PTSD, and now I found myself trapped in a literal trigger point with no support allowed.

In the end, I self-discharged. A kind midwife took pity on me and explained that they couldn't *make* me stay. I signed a form to say I acknowledged the huge risks to myself by leaving. I frantically wrapped my baby up and packed, afraid if I wasn't quick enough they might change their minds. The post-caesarean hobble to the doors felt like my life depended on it. I walked out of those double doors, into my husband's arms and broke down. It was midnight, going into my daughter's birthday.

There was no 'going home outfit' carefully planned and no picture of my husband carrying the car seat down the hospital corridor. It felt as though we left under a cloud, my anxious, overly tired brain convinced people were judging us, the risks on that form niggling on my mind. I will never regret leaving that night. I don't think I could've lasted any longer. I needed my daughter, my husband, my own bed... I needed support that strangers couldn't give.

The experience lived with us for a long time afterwards. My daughter favoured my husband, which I found heart-breaking. I felt robbed of the last month of just me and her, before the new baby arrived. If we had a doctor's appointment she would get upset and say 'Mammy please come back,' because the last time I went for a check-up I didn't come back. I pined for the relationship we had, mourned it almost, as there'd been a clear shift. She had a new constant and that was her dad. While I was so grateful she was with her loving family, it felt like the last few years with her had been jaded by the 26 days that I spent away. 26 missed bedtimes. 26 missed early morning wakeups. 26 missed nap time cuddles. 26 days of emotional torture because the health care system were trying to keep everyone safe whilst the leaders were flouting those same rules. It's alleged there were 17 gatherings or parties held during the lockdowns and I wasn't allowed to give my two year old daughter a cuddle for 26 days.

It's almost three years later now, a count that feels like a lifetime ago. I am forever grateful for my two wonderful children, but the heartache that I endured (and my husband, who was helpless to my pleas for support as well as being separated from his newborn son) are feelings that neither of us can forget. The birth and newborn days were not what we expected or hoped for and not a time we remember fondly.

We will, however, always be grateful that, unlike so many, we emerged from the pandemic with our health intact and a new member of the family. And grateful to the NHS who were just doing their job in keeping us safe.

Sarah Boyd, 34, lives with her husband and two children on the North East Coast. She works full time as a nurse and in her free time you will usually find her soaking up the fresh air with her children on the beach.

KATY BENTLEY

Emergency buzzers, talk of delivery suites. Alone and confused, I'm only 32 weeks. It happens too fast, too soon, I'm so scared. I push the thoughts of 'what if' to the back of my head.

'Congratulations,' they say, 'I'm sure she's doing just great.' All I can think is: *What's your survival rate?* Neonatal monitors and alarms, the endless beeps. But my baby classes promised golden hour was so sweet?

Body broken, exhausted, I'm in total shock. You start life in an incubator, not home safe in your cot. 'You can hold her,' staff say, 'but just not quite yet.' *Was it something I did?* Feelings of guilt and regret.

'It's time to go, Mum, you need some rest.' How can I leave you behind in your medical nest? Tubes and wires, the sight breaks my heart, my little bird born too soon, our world torn apart.

On my slow walk back to the ward, I hold on to my tummy. *You should still be in there*, I whisper; *I've failed as your mummy.*

Kind nurses and doctors become my lifeline and tribe. I beg them, "please just keep her alive." The hours turn to days yet, still, we are here. Will we ever get home? My thoughts fill with fear.

The days turn to weeks, I drag myself out of bed, thoughts of tube feeds constantly swirl in my head. COVID restrictions, isolated, alone. The walk down empty hospital corridors, yet again, on my own.

Your first feed, first bath, the first time in clothes. Kind nurses snap photos, a forced smile through the mask on my nose. Just one parent allowed, your dad and I work it in shifts. Our first steps into parenthood, how did it end up like this?

The moment finally comes, you are ready for home. I should be happy, but I'm scared I can't parent alone. No monitors, no nurses - how will I cope? Yet again, I just have to cling onto hope.

Medical check-ups by Zoom, are you both doing OK? Hiding my PTSD, *we're great*, I hear myself say. My anxiety high, all sleep is absent. Every time my eyes close, I'm back to your birth in an instant.

Maternity leave, just you and I, the silence, it deafens. They say it takes a village to raise you, but Boris, he took them. The days blend into one, just our little bubble, but my mental health, I can feel it starting to crumble.

The lockdown lifts, but home bound we stay. 'She's vulnerable, no germs,' medical professionals say. A trickle of visitors come to our home. Until now, nurses' gloved hands are the only touch you've known.

You see faces, warm cuddles for the very first time. 'How's Mum?' they ask. *Oh I'm doing just fine.* I lie easily, hiding the depth of depression. No rush of pure love, my body always riddled with tension.

Birth and prematurity - I faced it alone. Flung into motherhood too soon, the total unknown. The anger, guilt, grief - it comes in waves every day. Every moment that passes, I struggle to keep it at bay.

The months plod along, the darkness slowly starts to lift. As my bond to you grows, I edge away from the postpartum cliff. The realisation, my girl, you're my shining light. Your first moments, born in a pandemic, fighting for life.

"You both did it," they say, it was one hell of a ride. I'm changed to my core, I can't believe we survived. You will now be my only, too scared to face it again. A premature pandemic mummy defines my motherhood experience from start to end.

Katy Bentley, 34, from Northern Ireland lives with her husband and their three-year-old daughter, Isabelle. She works full-time as a Civil Servant and is passionate about raising awareness of premature birth, through sharing her own personal story and connecting with other parents who have had their own neonatal experience. In her down time she enjoys drinking very strong coffee (and the occasional glass of wine or two) and often wonders how it's been almost three years of navigating the crazy and joyous path that is parenthood.

ESTELLE MOON

Dear Noodles,

Today is Mothering Sunday. Your soft, carefree curls bounce between the soap bubbles whilst you giggle beneath the spring sun.

We didn't know.

"No visitors," commands the midwife as she closes the heavy, grey door. Noodles, you are a day old and we are trying to get your blood sugar back to normal with glucose pouches. As the curtain is pulled around our hospital bed, the woman opposite picks up her third phone call whilst soothing her bundle of newness.

We didn't know.

As we drive home, I feel each turn of the wheel deep in my broken, torn womb. The radio allows the waves of confusion in. *China? Boris? Masks? Staying home?* Your little cries drown out the noise and we wish for our own sheets and the smell of your brother's hair.

We didn't know.

The armchair holds us close, we feel its support as you suckle onto me whilst I eat chocolate and drink pints of orange squash. Boris, the hair, the desk. "You must stay home." No going out, no family to help us, no baby groups, no walking with friends in the park with our prams.

We didn't know.

We didn't know this was coming, that this would be our fate, that they would take us from our families in the midst of the newborn bubble which needed such care, support and love. Your health visitor never came, Noodles. The visits with arms filled with flowers and ready-made meals never came in our first days together.

We were at sea, floating on our raft, not knowing which direction we would float, how high the waves would build and if we could land on dry land.

Estelle Moon, 40, from Bromley lives with her husband and their two children, Louie, 7, and Nancy, 3. She works as a primary school teacher and her happy place is with a crochet hook in her hand. She runs StellaMoonCraft, making personalised knitwear and loves anything colourful and bright. @stellamooncraft

JO COATES

I had my baby as the world went into lockdown and it very nearly broke me.

I'd like to think I'm not one for big dramatics but I think my story (and my friends and family) will tell you otherwise. My husband and I got married abroad with two hurricanes as unwelcome visitors. We shared our honeymoon with a cyclone. So, I guess, on the rule of three, it feels fitting that we'd have a baby just as the world went into lockdown. In fact, we left hospital on the day the world stopped. People were being told to stay indoors while I was begging the nurses to let me leave the hospital.

Just the three of us. Unsteady. Winging it. Slightly broken. Definitely terrified. Thrust into unchartered territory with a juicy-thighed, hairy babe to raise. But with no collective 'village' able to help.

Three years on and the thought of it all can still bring me to tears. It has done so now, as the words flow from my fingers. I can be floored by a memory. The overwhelming sense of vulnerability. The way my husband had to prop me up constantly, physically from the emergency caesarean and mentally throughout the fourth trimester. I'm not sure I've ever felt lower.

My midwife saw it all. She demanded that my mum came round for a cuddle the night I was out of hospital. It's possibly the best hug I've ever had. Pyjama-clad, just-in milk leaking and tears streaking my face, I melted into the comforting arms of the one person who's always been there to hold my hand. Even though the restrictions meant we shouldn't have.

She didn't hug my son. I showered after touching her. The pandemic was fresh and scary and I was petrified that something would happen to me and I'd be separated from him. That was the closest she got for some months.

Our parents met their grandson through our bedroom window, pressing palms against the glass as we presented him through the double glazing. Everyone left with tears in their eyes. Essentials were dropped off by friends and family at the doorstep: nappies, painkillers, toilet roll... Necessary things that had become hard to get. We scheduled Zoom calls to introduce him to the wider family. We'd stay on the call far longer than needed, staring at each other, not knowing what else to say.

While I still find all of that hard to sit with, I also don't know any different. I've nothing to compare my newborn story against. I'd not done it before and I likely won't do it again, and with that, it brings some clarity to what I've learnt about myself. It has shaped me. It has broken me down and given me the opportunity to rebuild myself. I'm gentler with myself. I'm more compassionate with myself. And I'm really fucking proud of myself. Because, despite having the rug pulled from under my feet, I've raised a beautiful, curious, chatty kid. I see mine and my husband's best qualities reflected back at me daily. Part of that has to be due to all the time we got to spend just the three of us.

My husband got six months at home versus the standard two weeks paternity leave. He was there, right beside me, every single minute of every single day. I wouldn't have got through it without him.

Lockdown gave me precious family time. It gave me time to work on breastfeeding and nailing the perfect latch. It gave my body time to heal from major abdominal surgery. It meant I could live in my PJs for as many days or weeks I wanted. It gave me a phone full of precious photos and videos.

Lockdown took so much. But it also gave me a lot.

The scars will heal in time.

Jo Coates is a thirty-something, midi-skirt and fugly-shoe obsessive, navigating life with a fearless toddler. By day, she works as a Content and Social Media Manager and by night, writes brutally honest thoughts on motherhood, IBS, anxiety and the things that bring her joy.
@jocoatesy

SHELLEY SMITH

I gave birth to twins on 1st April 2020 by elective C-section. The team in theatre took such good care of me and my beautiful babies. It was a straightforward birth and we were all healthy, thank goodness. We were told a few days before that my partner wasn't allowed to be there at all. That changed to him being allowed into the recovery room next door as one of the nurses in theatre took a lot of photos for him - I will always be grateful to her for that. The hospital was chaotic as a result of the new guidelines. No one knew where anyone was meant to be or what was going on and everyone was stressed and anxious about COVID, understandably. While I was in recovery, we were pretty much abandoned and my partner had to run out to find a midwife to come and help us. I'm positive my maternity care is the reason I couldn't breastfeed – both the lack of support before and immediately after the birth and the stress of such a chaotic environment.

My partner was sent home after a few hours. One of the midwives kindly found us an empty recovery room so we got a bit longer together. Then, my babies and I were put in a private room (standard with twins, I believe). I had to press a buzzer every time I needed anything and wait for someone to have time to come and see me. I couldn't lift them out of their cot. I could feel that I was bleeding but couldn't move or see what was happening. I was delirious from the lack of sleep, the painkillers wearing off, I couldn't breastfeed and I honestly didn't know which way was up! I determinedly checked myself out within 48 hours, still in a lot of pain. The midwife who checked me out remarked on how calm I seemed. I felt like I was in a peaceful little oasis, staring at my babies while the world went crazy around me... a neglected and painful oasis, but a calm one, at least.

My wonderful sister took us home from the hospital in her car (we didn't drive at the time so she isolated her whole family for two weeks solely for this purpose.) After that, it fell to my amazing partner to care for me and our two new babies 24/7. We were first-time parents so it was full-on for both of us. We'd originally planned for my parents and sister to stay with us in shifts, so to go from the idea of lots of support to the reality of none at all was pretty scary.

The midwives and nurses who looked after my babies and I were great, and even the cleaners and kitchen staff in the hospital were very sweet and caring. It was just so clear that everyone was struggling without partners on the ward, and the new hastily made-up guidelines. My son was born with a tongue tie that would usually just get snipped straight away, apparently, but that counted as an elective procedure which was no longer allowed, so we had to pay for someone to do it privately at home. Zoom calls with a health visitor were patchy and useless. I didn't get any follow-up care at all.

Trying, and failing, to breastfeed and being too scared to leave the house were my lowest points. I think my partner will take a while to come to terms with the intensity of their birth and the first few weeks and months, and

I'm struggling to come to terms with how to reconcile the whole period - simultaneously both the absolute best moments of my life and the absolute worst.

Shelley Smith, 45, moved during lockdown from Brighton to the beautiful South Wales Valleys. She lives with her toddler twins and partner, and works as a freelance copywriter. Shelley spends most weekends with her family exploring the coast, mountains, valleys (and play parks) of their lush new home. In her spare time, she picks up books she doesn't find time to read, starts creative projects she probably won't finish and drinks coffee after it's gone cold.

KIRSTY HEADFORD

I am strong when I decide to birth my baby at home, safe.
I am sad when I'm told it's best I go into hospital in case there aren't enough midwives.
I am brave when I decide not to go into work, as we don't know the risks yet and I'm not safe there.
I am stressed when I may have to start my maternity leave early to 'stay home and save lives.'
I am happy I get to have my antenatal appointments.
I am scared when I see them in full hazmat suits whilst assessing me.
I am hopeful that this will be over soon.
I am disappointed when my partner can't come with me onto the labour ward.
I am pleased I can bring my belongings with me.
I am frustrated when they say I need to be checked for COVID-19 and they swab me whilst I'm contracting.
I am glad I have my own space and they have allowed me to a bed as the pain is getting worse.
I am upset I am labouring alone.
I am proud that I've remembered the breathing techniques I've been learning.
I am nervous my partner won't arrive before the baby comes.
I am excited as I start to feel my baby boy move down, ready to be born.
I am angry that my partner can't come in yet.
I am grateful that the midwives come when I call for them, eventually.
I am worried when they say they are short staffed and are very busy.
I am firm when I tell them that my baby is coming quickly.
I am concerned my partner won't make it in time.
I am relieved when my partner is allowed in, mask and all.
I am numb when he's told he has a one-hour limit once baby is born.
I am delighted when someone comes in to help with feeding.
I am saddened when they can't come close enough to help.
I am ecstatic when we can go home the next day to meet big brother Stanley.
I am lonely as I learn that lockdown has cancelled life as we know it.
I am positive as I try to keep busy in the house and garden and spend time with my beautiful boys.
I am struggling as baby groups and family visits are banned.
I am strong as I dig deep, knowing we are in this for the long haul.
June 2020 - the happiest and scariest time that I won't ever forget - the time when my second son, Walter, was born.

Kirsty Headford, 35, from Sheffield, lives with her partner and two little boys aged 7 and 3. She works part-time as an Early Years teacher. When she isn't working or chasing after her two very active boys she enjoys reading, drinking tea/coffee (anything with caffeine!) baking and going on family trips out. @kirsty_mumof2boys

CAITLIN LANGDON

When I look back on the world you were brought into,
I can't help but wonder how different you would be

Would you be as wary of new people
if we hadn't veered off the path to avoid people coming our way
on our daily walk?

Would you still cry at the confetti falling through the air
if we hadn't had so few occasions to celebrate
in such frivolous ways?

Would you be more adventurous
if leaving the house hadn't felt like an act of bravery
in the first months of your life?

Would your smile be different if you had seen
the different smiles looking down at you
instead of covered by a mask?
but
I can't imagine a smile more beautiful than yours

Would you hold my hand in a different way
if the hands meeting you for the first time
had not been fearfully sanitised to keep you safe?
but
I can't imagine a hand that fits mine more perfectly than yours

Would your laugh sound different
if you had heard more laughs in person
instead of through a jittery FaceTime call?
but
I can't imagine a better-sounding giggle than yours

When I look back on the world you were brought into,
there's a lot that I would change
but

I can't imagine a better you,
than the you created by that world

Caitlin lives in Derby with her husband, son, who was born in July 2020, and daughter, who was born in July 2022. Having a second baby out of COVID times highlighted just what we missed out on in 2020. Caitlin has recently started embroidery to try and unwind. It is yet to be seen whether this is possible whilst raising two young children!

CLAIRE MARTIN-QUIRK

Mother's Day 22.03.2020.

"It's a girl," my husband said.

Exhausted, I cried with joy. For a moment I believed that the hardest part was over, blissfully disconnected from the world outside. We named her Sienna. We'd been warned by midwives and doctors that no one should touch our newborn baby, family and friends should meet her via video call and we should shield her until it was safe. I fiercely wanted to protect her, nothing was more important than that. *Maybe this would just be for a few days? A couple of weeks, at most?*

The day after her birth, we brought her back to our empty, quiet house. We sat amongst tubs of formula and boxes of nappies, ordered with urgency when rumblings of a deadly virus and supply chain issues had started to spread the week before. The same week that my husband had been made redundant from his job working in the theatre industry, and the same week that I stood on my parents' driveway and cried, anxious about what was to come. We switched on the TV as our baby lay peacefully in her Moses basket. The announcement came – a 'lockdown' had been ordered.

In that moment, I had never felt more vulnerable and alone. My lifelong dream of introducing my brand new baby to my family and friends was snatched away in an instant. This human I had grown, given birth to and was already so proud of, couldn't be shared or cuddled by the ones my husband and I loved the most. We were going to have to cope all on our own; first-time parents in a world that felt like it was falling apart.

The weeks rumbled on quietly. I juggled managing my bridal business that I had worked hard to build, trying to keep it alive and reassure customers that their orders would be safe, whilst trying to reassure myself, too.

Furlough. Stay Home Save Lives. Zooms calls. Clap for the NHS.

The days bled into the nights. Newborn clothes were packed away whilst I cried. No one had met her, yet she had grown and changed so much. Glimpses through our car window on our parents' driveways were the only ways we could introduce our baby, with tears in our eyes. My mum held up a painting of the city, Siena, to the glass.

A lump that had been found in my husband's neck had to be removed, almost two months into the first lockdown. The hospital told him to isolate when he got home. Sienna and I had nowhere else to go, of course. Perhaps this was an opportunity for my family to meet her. It was an emotional tug of war, pulling our new little family apart, but the opportunity for Sienna to meet some of her grandparents and aunties was drawing me in. We did it and took the risk. Walking through their front door, they all greeted Sienna and I broke down.

"Finally."

Sienna and I spent a precious week with my family. They bonded with her, bathed her and helped soothe her, and I felt like I could finally breathe again. It was hard for us all to articulate how we felt during this stage of the pandemic, or at any stage for that matter. During a chat with my dad that week, I said, "It wasn't meant to be this way." I'd been robbed of my experience as a new mother. I'd been abandoned by healthcare professionals who were meant to support me, check that my baby was OK and that I was, too. Because I wasn't. At times, I felt like I was hanging on by a thread.

The weeks and months went by.

Traffic light systems. Road maps. Isolation. Support bubbles.

Countless times I was told, "She won't remember it."

But I will, I would think.

Eventually, being able to form a 'support bubble' provided a lifeline. My sister and my new nephew met with Sienna and I twice a week. We lived through every ounce of progress, disappointment and backwards step together. Rules loosened. We could finally meet inside, but just six of us, two metres apart. On a couple of occasions, I felt brave and safe enough to offer my friends a cuddle with Sienna.

"You can hold her if you'd like?"

The offer was declined.

"No, I won't. Just in case."

I know it shouldn't have done, but it felt like rejection. How could my friends and family bond with our baby if they'd never touched her, been close enough to look into her eyes and smell her baby smell?

We reached Sienna's first Christmas. The country was hopeful that we'd be able to spend it with loved ones, making up for the most terrible year. Shops were open, small groups continued to mix inside, people ordered turkeys and made plans. Sadly, it wasn't meant to be, as at the last minute, the government decided that families uniting would be detrimental to the spread of the virus. A memory that I will always cherish, and feel desperately sad about in equal measure, is my mum wheeling my elderly grandma outside onto their driveway. We put Sienna on her knee. It was the first time they'd touched. We all stood there on the driveway, in the cold, unable to go inside. Four generations came together and were being pulled apart by COVID.

The final lockdown lasted a painful three months, with restrictions in place until the 29th March. All I wanted to do was to celebrate our daughter's first birthday with everyone who cared about her, but it wasn't meant to be. Another disappointment and another special moment snatched away.

Spring brought hope and some stability. I fell pregnant with Sienna's brother. When telling loved ones our news from a 'safe distance,' it dawned on me that I hadn't touched a single friend since bringing Sienna into the world, and here I was, carrying another child and still not able to celebrate with a hug.

Seeing people experience things that I didn't get to experience, doing things I didn't get to do and feeling feelings that I didn't get to feel, is triggering and causes emotions to surface. Despite everything that happened, most of the time, I am at peace with it now. My experience has made me stronger, more independent and more grateful than ever before. My bond with Sienna, and with my son, Xavier, who was born in December 2021 when some restrictions were still in place, is unbreakable and we make the most of every day that we have together. I may not be exactly the same 'me' as I was before March 2020, but being Sienna and Xavier's mum has redefined my life purpose and brings me all of the happiness that I have ever dreamed of. The pandemic was just a small part of our journey and the best is yet to come.

Claire Martin-Quirk, 33, from Kent, lives with her husband, Inigo, and two children Sienna, who is three and Xavier who is one, and their dogs, Lola and Luna. Her background is in fashion and bridal wear, and she is currently freelancing in Social Media Management and in Bridal Styling on weekends. Aside from spending as much time with her children as possible and working part-time, she loves catching up with friends and family and a spot of retail therapy!

CHARLOTTE MORGAN

The Island

It takes a village
they say

But there is no village
on the tiny island that is our new parenthood

It is just me, and him, and this miracle of new life
The island had looked so beautiful from afar
It was breathtaking to behold

But living there is another matter

On the island, there is no shelter from the elements
The sun is blistering
In the heat, a mirage of the mother I am supposed to be
taunts me from a distance
Dark and desperate thoughts are carried on the wind
not good enough, it begins to scream
Insects gnaw at my skin
Opening old wounds
Creating new ones
I am at the centre of my own personal storm

On the island, I am broken
But no one sees me shatter
Not the passing ships
Nor the sister islands dotted on the horizon
Not even the stars; they twinkle with indifference

It feels like the island is at the very end of the earth
I've never felt so alone

The storm gathers strength
Giant waves swallow us and sweep us from the shore
carrying us into oblivion
It's all we can do
just to hold on
to each other

One day, we feel land beneath our feet again
The water sparkles and the sand feels soft in between my toes
We let go of each other
to gather up our shattered selves
I close my eyes and feel the warmth of the sun on my skin
A sweet breeze plays across my face
I hear the sound of crashing waves
and the music of her laughter

I open my eyes
The island looks much the same
We are forever changed

Charlotte Morgan, 31, lives in London with her husband, Jack, and her two-year-old daughter, Imogen. Charlotte is a science communication professional, currently working in patient involvement. In between parenting and working, she loves writing and reading poetry, dinners with friends, live music, not-frequent-enough date nights with Jack, and watching rom-coms. @notanothrmillennial

NATALIE COOMBER

My darling boy,

This is the story of your start, a lockdown baby, a pandemic pregnancy, forever a statistic, a time that you won't remember but a time that I will and a time that no one should forget.

Every burst of joy was levelled by a cloud of sorrow. The joy of the positive pregnancy tests was countered with the surreal situation of holding it up to a screen smaller than my hand to show Nanny, Grandad and Grandma that they would be grandparents again.

That first scan was longer than expected and Daddy wasn't with me. Not allowed. Too high of a risk. I lay there alone with a full bladder, the ultrasound wand searching and probing, searching and probing, and then there you were, your little heartbeat filling the room. I looked for Dad but it was just me, a stranger and an empty chair. I wasn't allowed to record it. I raced out to him, gripping a strip of photographs that we had to pay for. That still feels like an insult. We shared them on Zoom and FaceTime, showing you to our family: this glorious bundle of new cells.

We had a brief moment of light when we could meet in Nanny and Grandad's garden. You were still a secret, then, to many and I whispered the joy of you into your cousin's ear, confident a three-month-old wouldn't tell, saying *it's alright matey your bestie's in my tummy and they can't wait to play with you.*

I attended every appointment alone, knowing if the unthinkable happened, I'd be the one telling your daddy with no one there for me. Reduced movement appointments, watching the ticker tape, clicking the clicker. Sitting in the hot waiting room, mask on, bumps of every size on chairs two metres apart. The walk back to the car, keeping to one side of the corridor, the rustle of PPE from those that passed and the sting of too much sanitiser on my skin.

The first time your daddy saw you and heard you was on a private scan. He gripped my hand so hard! Apparently, it was safe for him to be there if you paid for it.

Antenatal classes were all virtual. That strange feeling of loss was there again. How could I form bonds and go for coffee with that nice-looking couple who lived 500 miles away? Where were our play dates, your first tiny buddies? There were 45 mini faces and mini bumps. I muted and sometimes hid, camera off. Notes upon notes were made on induction, labour, how to bath a baby, layers, temperature control, dark rooms, white noise, breastfeeding, foot to foot, sleep bags, clear sleep space, informed choice, that first nappy change... lists and lists and lists.

We thought, in October 2020, that we were on the home straight. Restrictions were lifting and Christmas looked promising. I was driving back to the office and I heard it on the radio: numbers are rising, back to restrictions for those who were vulnerable, which included the pregnant. I spoke to my boss, the responsibility weighing heavy to protect you along with the worry that I'd have to start maternity leave early. I was told to work from home and not to worry. No 'support bubbles' for us, Nanny and Grandad were already taken, so we did as we were told - we stayed home. We had a Zoom baby shower, which was lovely but not quite the same.

When my waters broke, up to the hospital I went, institutionalised to doing it alone, saying to your daddy, *don't worry, stay home, you can't come in anyway, I'll let you know what's happening.* Driving in, I was trying to remember the rules. *When can my husband be there? When does he get to cross the threshold and then when is he booted out again?* After the compulsory COVID test, I was told there were four women ahead of me. I asked, already knowing the answer,

"Can my husband come in?"

The tight smile, the sorry in their eyes.

"No, not yet."

I made the decision to go home and come back in the morning. I think that's why, even now at your grand old age of two years and three months, I forget to consult your daddy and I just make decisions. It was trained into me when you were the size of a pea in my tummy and I have never stopped since, not thinking of the impact that this has on your dad. I was a one-woman warrior then, it was all on me, but it's important to remember how excluded fathers felt, and may still feel, because of the restrictions and that ripple effect we feel even now. That mindset of perseverance and protection that I had to adapt so that we could get through COVID has never gone.

We went to the ward and the wonderful midwife hid us at the end with Daddy. She drew the curtain around, insinuating for us to be quiet and we could get away with it. We waited for ten hours for a space on the labour ward, surrounded by women waiting, like me, women losing their babies, women in for the long-term and being monitored closely, but they were alone. I will never forget the woman in the cubicle next to me. She was contracting too early, only in her second trimester. She needed a scan and it was taking hours because it wasn't available. I don't know what happened to her or her baby, I just know it shouldn't have been happening.

Your entrance to the world wasn't straightforward. Quite simply, you got stuck. That big head they'd told me about proved to be tricky, so we were bumped along to theatre, where several masked strangers introduced themselves. I thought, 'I'm not sending you a Christmas card - get this baby out!' On 24th December 2020, out you came, delivered by a smiling (I assume) lady with a brightly coloured headscarf.

I was moved onto a ward with instructions of 'don't try and stand.' Your daddy was gone. Just me and you, kid, in an empty ward - you, two feet away in your see-through cot and me, prone on the bed. My legs were dead from the spinal block, the catheter was in the way and my IV canular was flapping around out of my hand. I physically couldn't reach you.

My biggest regret is that I couldn't breastfeed you. We tried for days and fell back on formula. When I called the midwife for help, I was told, 'Just pump,' and the phone was put down. Clearly too many calls from too many mums desperate for help. I pumped for hours and we got next to nothing out. There was no one to tell me what was normal. Maybe that was normal but there was no one to say that was the case and you were screaming and screaming. Your daddy turned it off.

"Stop, it's not meant to be like this," he said.

The decision was taken from me and I was so grateful yet guilty. You thrived on formula but it doesn't change feeling like I let you down.

We were discharged at 5.45 am on Christmas Day. We continued as a team of three, sneaking Nanny and Grandad through the back gate so they could see you in person, but no touching, not for months.

We called to register your birth but were told to call back in a few weeks. They couldn't offer us anything, as they were too busy registering deaths.

We relied on apps and screens instead of people. That first year may have been easier if it was the other way around.

We made our own 'normal' and recorded everything to send to our families and friends so they didn't miss out and to keep us connected.

Those first months were so hard with the obvious: lack of sleep, cold coffee, etc. We were there to look after you but there was no one there to look after us. When I felt blind with exhaustion, I would think how a nice dose of appendicitis would be if it meant a few days' break, or maybe a slip on the stairs, just for some respite. I needed to speak to someone but there were no clinics, no calls and no one checking in. I had no idea if you were tracking as you should have been growth-wise so I ordered home scales to weigh you. I started to obsess over it, a new worry to internalise and churn myself up over.

The legacy of the pandemic lived on in the first two years of your life, with trips to A&E for temperatures that we couldn't control because the GP wouldn't see us. Still only one parent allowed in the waiting room for 6-10 hours, to be given a prescription for tonsillitis that we should never have had to go to hospital for.

You will be an only child and that also feels like a failure. A lot of people we know are on their second baby now since you were born and I am in awe of them. I envy them for having the strength to do it again. I wonder what it would be like to experience it restriction-free but I can't do it again. It nearly broke me.

After what we went through, you are my focus and my world. This time we are now in feels like how it should have been from the start: annual passes to farms, Happy Meals as a treat, coffee and juice dates and meeting friends with no worries. I want to embrace it all with you. I've grieved your unborn siblings but seeing you buck the predictions of COVID babies is a joy. You're meant to be unsocialised, unsure in crowds and unable to deal with strangers or new situations. But you, my love, give the middle finger to all of that and throw yourself into everything with the joy of a toddler. Seeing that pushes all else to the back of my mind (until the next trigger of a breast pump advert on social media or a pregnancy announcement) but you, my sweetheart, are enough.

It's important that you know how you and your future classmates and friends got here and what your parents went through. Like I said, you won't remember, but I will never forget and neither should anyone else.

Love Mummy xxx

Natalie Coomber, 37, lives with her husband, James, 2.5-year-old son, Noah, and Cinders the cat. She happily multi-tasks full-time work as a Personal Assistant in the lettings industry, with gardening in her little slice of Kent and learning all the words to The Gruffalo. If she does have a spare moment, you're likely to find her sitting in the garden with a book or reorganising a cupboard with her label maker in tow.
@mrsnatcoomber

IONA MAXWELL

Maternity Stay

Stay still
Don't move
Your hand or arm
He's finally asleep, he's calm
For now, but how quickly things can change
When ten minutes ago he was red with rage

Stay home
At ten and then at two
Or how will he learn to sleep if you
Are not consistent with his naps?
'It'll free you up'
But I feel trapped

Stay calm
And breathe
Put on a smile
Even if it's been a while
Since you washed your hair or changed your clothes
Or went to the loo for once on your own

Stay strong
They say
Through the sleepless nights
'It'll be over before you know it,' indeed it might
But right now the hours pass so slowly
Holding him in the dark, I love him so wholly
So why are there tears streaming down my cheeks?
They mix with his hot breath, it's been weeks
Since I slept a stretch longer than two hours
Just 'sleep when he sleeps,' advise the powers
That be - But how can I when he
Will only fall asleep on me?

That first day we met you
Four AM
Then began the overwhelm
Taking your first breath, breath-taking
There are nights I think I must be breaking
Can you die from lack of sleep?

My Google searches become more bleak
The touch of your skin, your giggling squeak,
I'll never be whole if you're not with me
Your fat little hands wrap around my heart
Back to work but not really apart

Stay still
Stay home
Stay calm
Stay strong
Always feeling I'm doing it wrong
Please stay this little as long as you can
I'll throw away the sleep training plan
Stay on my chest as your eyes close
Your tear-stained cheeks and your soft little nose
I wouldn't have it any other way
It's not maternity leave, but maternity stay

Iona Maxwell, 32, lives in Exeter with her husband and nearly two-year-old son, Kitto. She works as a junior doctor in the local hospital - training to be a GP - and when not at work you'll find her on the beach or exploring Dartmoor.

ELLEN CLAYTON

It is the start of a new year, but the fear of 2020 has followed us into January. Boris is boldly claiming schools are safe to return tomorrow. My husband and I talk ourselves in circles - is it safe to send our children to school? What about our unborn child, are we risking their health and my health, if we let our kids mix in large classrooms? The anxiety is threatening to swallow me whole and I wish I could see my mum or my sisters. They are at the other end of the phone but it's not the same.

Eventually, the decision feels clear. Nothing is worth the risk of COVID coming into our household, me needing extended periods of hospitalisation, birthing alone or our baby being needlessly exposed to this virus which has dominated the world for the past year. I compose an email to the headteacher, hoping she understands our position. Within minutes I receive a reassuring reply and it's as if a weight has been lifted: my shoulders drop a few centimetres and my chest loosens a little. I place my hand on my ever-expanding bump, feel my baby kick against my palm and exhale, slowly.

Within 24 hours, Boris enacts one of his infamous U-turns and closes all schools again. It is a depressing déjà vu, a colder reprisal of March. This lockdown holds none of the guilty relief of the first, no opportunity to relish time together or enjoy the rarity of taking our feet off the accelerator of life. How naive we were; how optimistic that things would blow over quickly. There are glimmers of hope with vaccines being rolled out to the oldest and most vulnerable in our society, but January feels heavy with dread and isolation.

I scour the updated guidelines around families, sending my mum a passage with jubilation: "Families with children under one can form a bubble with one other household." It becomes a beacon for us all: the knowledge that sometime in April, as spring takes hold, my parents will be allowed inside our home to meet our new baby.

The days tick by in a blur of home-schooling and half-hearted video calls to our parents. At the appointments I attend, masked up and tense, my midwife keeps measuring my blood pressure as high and my baby as big. I am sent to the hospital for a prolonged period of blood pressure checks and multiple growth scans. I wait, in my mask, alone, wishing my husband could be by my side. Every time, it's concluded that my blood pressure is fine. The stress of the midwife appointments at the GP surgery, with the one-way system and sanitiser stations, are manifesting in my body.

At my third growth scan, I am nervous, wondering if this will be the time I am told my baby is big and the time my plans for a water birth get pulled from under my feet. It feels unfair that I get to see the features of our unborn child, so much bigger and clearer than the 20-week scan, while my partner waits at home. He doesn't get to see the profile which convinces me that our third child will look just like our second born, the nose an exact replica of his at birth.

He's not a witness to the laughter in the sonographer's voice as he says, "Look, your baby has lots of hair!" All of this, I experience alone.

A few weeks before my due date, our boiler breaks. I am horrified that we'll need to let a stranger into our home and the experience unfolds even more unpleasantly than I'd expected. In he comes, coughing away with no mask on. He boasts about his anti-vaccine stance, claims that COVID is a big hoax and that its danger is exaggerated. My husband tries, and fails, to shut the conversation down while I sit in another room, shaking with anger. If this bastard has given us COVID, destroyed all our careful plans and ruined our chances of both being present at our child's birth, I vow to report him to the council for unsafe COVID practices.

At night, I lay in bed listening to hypnobirthing meditations. My hips ache and I am finding the last weeks of this pregnancy physically and emotionally depleting. I repeat affirmations to myself, trying to quieten my mind and lock out all of the doubts. *What if I have to birth alone? Am I strong enough?* I tell myself I will be but in reality, I fear I will crumble.

We inch closer to my due date and we are testing ourselves daily, determined for there to be no nasty surprises when the hospital tests us. Each negative test is a sigh of relief.

When at last, after days of stop-and-start contractions, I am in established labour, I wait on the assessment ward to find out my husband's COVID result. When I receive the text that he's negative and will be joining me in a birthing suite shortly, it's as if every cell in my body lets out the breath I've been holding in for months. *This is it,* I think. This is the moment we've waited for, here at last, and we will do it together despite the pandemic which has upended and destroyed so much. From that minute on, I pivot from fear to hope and a slow, steady, upward trajectory begins.

Ellen Clayton is a poet from Suffolk, England. Her poetry has been published in various online and print publications, including Capsule Stories and The Hyacinth Review. Her debut chapbook, Home Baked, was published in April 2022 by Bent Key Publishing. Ellen has performed poetry at the Soho Theatre and the East Anglian Storytelling Festival and her work has been featured on BBC Upload. More of her writing can be found on Instagram @ellen_writes_poems

GENEVIEVE BEECH

mother-becoming*
in the blanket of that night
i let my girl-heart out,
its muffled murmurs, its soft
unfolding sounds;
i let it go completely.

under the pastel moon, i bruised
my way to a beginning –
half-bloomed, resurfacing,
i knew of ruin;
you unearthed a new season in me.

to the blue of the bedcurtains,
in this ward ripe with birth-song,
i offered up a newcomer –
a honeyed, breathing thing –
to offset the deaths on the screen.

the animal of you small,
beheld in first blush –
the sound of your wanting,
the shadowed hush –
where colour used to be.

i felt the tumble of you cling
in the morning light,
i shed the tubes and socks and hospital gown,
but my mask was on too tight
to remove completely.

*mother-becoming is a term coined by and in: Dana Raphael (ed.) Being Female: Reproduction, Power and Change (De Gruyter Mouton, 1975), p. 66.

My selves: Writer, mother, editor and librarian / Location: Bristol / Current project: Motherlore Magazine, a creative writing and literary motherhood magazine / Instagram: @motherloremagazine

HARRIET CLAY

The idea of completely letting go was tempting. We've all felt it, that sinister, slow manner in which depression starts to suck you down and then holds you there in the dark. Then suddenly, you're held so far down that you can't remember what breathing freely feels like anymore. But this went deeper than depression, this was that 'rock bottom' people speak about, where you are so broken, beyond the tears and self-indulgent pity, that you wonder what the point of doing anything is. I think I was held in that thought for close to a year, staring daily at the bottom of the void but somehow staying just above it.

Some days I'd wash myself, other days I hardly saw the point in moving from my bed, and the chasm grew bigger and the bottom drew that bit closer. *Maybe it would be easier if I just let go, stopped fighting and dropped into that nothingness.* To be nothing, to do nothing, to care about nothing seemed so tempting.

Yet, even in the darkest recesses of my mind, this tiny little light no more than a glint, a whisper, a thread so fine that clung to life, forced me to care, made me want to do things, made me want to be someone. If not for me, for her.

I could lose myself, but she couldn't lose me. She needed me. Relied on me. I couldn't let go and that made it that much more unbearable. To have that weight of expectation on me. Because, to her, I was perfect. To her, I was someone, the only one that mattered. Her mother.

I always wanted to be a mom, the sort of want society implants in your head from a young age. I married and then I was pregnant and then I thought I'd have everything I ever wanted. How do you say, "I don't want this," when you're holding a perfect baby? Nobody would understand why, after years of begging for this thing you thought you so desperately wanted, you ended up feeling trapped and deceived by society.

Being handed my baby gave me a sinking feeling and as she cried in my arms, instead of a rush of love I felt as if a blindfold had been ripped off and the stark reality of what life was really about slapped me in the face. I was plunged into an ice-cold pool of sweat and anxiety. This is what life was now, day in, day out, this monotony of the same awful world. Forever inescapable.

Leaving the hospital, it got worse. Things I used to love doing, like going for a walk, now played like a relentless episode of 1000 ways to die. I imagined dropping my baby, stumbling over her, crushing her, suffocating her or falling down the stairs with her. My baby, the one I wanted, created, carried safe and protected for nine months was crudely and barbarically born into this world full of evil, full of dangers, full of everything my rose-tinted glasses had kept hidden from me, now so close, so real and in touching distance of this pure, innocent thing: my baby Elizabeth.

And then the pandemic started. She was ten weeks old.

Much like a nightmare that gets worse and worse, so too did my journey into motherhood, as a cloak of melancholic desperation took hold. Locked in and locked away from the world that was so brutal. Alone with my baby and my racing mind.

One night, after clearing the quarantined mail from the hallway, I turned on the TV. I was obsessed with watching the news, fixated on the darkest of times. Unexpectedly, I felt a glimmer of light, so close to being snuffed out I didn't know it was still in me. It started when I saw nurses on the front line wrapped up in protective bubble gear, challenging the adversity they faced. Weirdly, seeing them be so brave gave me hope. It was a small moment, distinct, where I realised I couldn't run away from my dark secret. My postpartum anxiety was something real, something I had to face up to as it was about to consume me. If nurses could go into work to fight a disease they knew little to nothing about, then I could open my laptop and seek help.

Slowly, after a CBT therapy course I learned how to live with my condition. The pandemic gave me time at home to find the joy and simple pleasures of growing my own food, spending time drawing and taking photographs. As this light and hope grew, so did Elizabeth. Despite the challenges and all that the world was facing she grew stronger, bigger and ready to take it on. Seeing her strength brought out a newfound resolve in me. It drew me slowly out of the dark void until the bottom looked unimaginably far away. Each day I made a choice to live, to love and to face those fears. Maybe now, I am like a Kintsugi vase, made beautiful by my flaws. By baring them for the world to see, others might be lifted out of the dark void that becoming a mother can feel like.

Harriet Clay, 35, lives with her husband, Richard, and daughter, Elizabeth, in leafy South London where she teaches English. The lockdown experience inspired her to become a mental health first aider at her school and between running a student newspaper and raising a toddler she loves to write children's books.
@hattiebat

AMANDA ANTHONY

What you least expect, when you're expecting.

My birthday celebrations in March 2020.
Pancakes stacked high, my bump wanted plenty.
I finished my work, put my phone on vibrate,
my laptop was moved to make space for my plate.
A makeshift home desk in the heart of our kitchen,
little did we know this was just the beginning.

We were ill, our toddler had been sent home poorly -
a dry cough, temperature, his voice spoke sorely.
My midwife was caring, yet mindful, and said,
"It's best to stay home and perhaps stay in bed."
So we did, before lockdown, we all stayed at home,
the clock began ticking for us home alone.

How long would this last before we'd be normal again?
We missed birthdays, new babies and seeing old friends.
Slowly, the reality hit that this was big.
For Bojo's announcement; I sat upstairs like a kid.
It was all too much, our baby growing inside
whilst the world was crumbling in chaos outside.

Then, complications, new risks and I felt so low,
more scans, yet this time, I was in there alone.
The sonographer was quiet, the screen dark and grey,
so quiet, yet my mind felt so loud as I lay.
Waiting to hear what the outcome would be,
then, "Sit outside my love, over there in chair three."

I sat and waited, my mask felt so tight,
keep a metre apart, sit still, stay in sight.
I was called in, I sat down, the silence was deafening,
my husband was outside in the car, alone, wondering.
The scan had shown issues, there were risks to deliver,
this could even be fatal for us both... I shivered.

Isolated, helpless, I felt I'd lost all power.
Afterwards, my consultant said to go home and shower.
Don't risk taking anything home to those you love.
So, I'd stand there under the water and scrub and scrub.

The days turned to weeks, the nights never ended.

Anxiety and panic whilst reality was suspended.
Those nights spent awake won't be forgotten, like scars,
partly healed, yet there will forever be a mark.

Focus was consumed by our toddler each day,
innocent fun, so much joy as we played.
Yet, this time, when we were supposed to settle and nest,
we were told to bleach shopping and boil-wash new vests.
Vans and loudhailers would drive down the streets,
"You're in a high-risk area, stay inside," they'd repeat.

Treasured Zoom calls with family, missing their hugs each day,
they tried to reassure us, *it will all be OK.*
They gave up so much, asked to shield and stay home,
so they could bubble for our toddler, care for him when we phoned
when it was time. Our bags packed, a trip in the car.
Our first time on the road in weeks felt so far.

The rest is a little bit of a blur,
lots of masks, door security, there were passwords, I'm sure.
"To enter you need a secret phrase,"
my poor husband heard me shout down the phone in a daze.
Between contractions, the midwife held my phone to my ear,
"You can come in now, baby, it's OK, I'm in here."

Then the time came and she entered this world,
my husband's delight declaring, "It's a girl."
The hottest day of the year, in sweltering heat,
our girl had arrived for us all to meet.
What then came after is hard to share.
Trauma cuts deep, I was so unaware
of the impact it would have on my life, even now.
It's a process and I'm thankful I'm here to say how.

Injections, surgery, a spinal, vomiting,
tests, shock, transfusions, touch and go... I'm left wondering
why, after all this, mums are often left alone?
I felt so grateful my husband could stay, rather than being sent home.

To NHS midwives, doctors, consultants, porters
and all other staff, I feel it's so important
to thank you for everything you did and still do,
without you, I wouldn't be here... it's true.
We stood out to clap, you deserved so much more,

risking your lives to help others, selfless acts so pure.

And from the darkness came light, our new baby was here,
I won't forget what you did, you brought hope out of fear.

Amanda Anthony is a mum of two living with her husband and family in Manchester. Having enjoyed a career in BBC Children's television for over a decade, it was this and her pregnancy and birth experiences in lockdown that encouraged the start of a new family venture. Bumbleberry Park launched in 2022 and is a new children's brand for gifts that gift back, where a donation is made to Tommy's baby charity for every sale. Amanda loves hot chocolate, walks on the beach and whenever there is music playing, she will be dancing. @bumbleberrypark

CARLY PARTRIDGE TONDEUR

Tears roll.

The announcement we all knew was coming but didn't want to hear.

Lockdown.

Holding my six-month-old, peacefully sleeping in my arms. I needed to protect him. I needed to keep him safe.

We tried to stay strong but my mind and body were already exhausted through lack of sleep and postnatal depression.

We tried to find the positive. At least he will be getting more time with us: his parents. Hours, days, weeks and months of our sole focus and attention. More time as a family. Some quiet in the storm of life. The thought that he would never remember this.

But it wasn't that, was it? No matter how much I tried to stay positive by switching off the news, avoiding all the conspiracy theories on social media, the daily walks, the online baby groups and the Zoom quizzes... The fear was overwhelming.

'What ifs' became every thought in my head:
What if he gets ill?
What if this cough is COVID?
What if I end up in hospital?
What if one of us dies?
What if this affects him for the rest of his life?
What if he only knows faces wearing masks?
What if he doesn't get to see his grandparents again?
What if our society begins to crumble?
What if this never ends?
Is this the new normal?

I felt so angry about everything. Angry that the virus would change our lives forever. Angry that my maternity leave had been stolen. Angry that my baby had been kept away from people during such an important part of his development. Angry that he screamed any time he saw any faces but ours. Angry that no one saw him when he first started babbling, sitting, eating and crawling.

But gradually, the light started trickling in. The walks with friends. Being able to get some 'cakeaway' (takeaway cake) from my favourite café. The countless National Trust visits. The first cuddles with grandparents after months and months. The baby groups reopening. His first day at nursery. Things started to feel more bearable.

Now, looking back, it is a haze. I couldn't tell you the dates of when we were in and out of lockdown, what tier we were in or what the rules were. I can tell you about the loneliness, staring at four walls with a young baby and moving him to another room to give him some different visual stimulation. I can tell you about the grief, the sadness and the depression.

But, I can also tell you about the strength that I found to carry on. The strength I saw in the people around me. The small blessings we had each day. How happy a box of cakes left on the doorstep by a family member made me (even though we froze them before eating in case they were infected.) The strength of my little boy, who, even though he was completely socially isolated for such a large part of his life, is now a happy and thriving three-year-old.

Tears roll.

Tears, this time, looking back at the sadness and fear but also reflecting on how strong I became and what I achieved, even when the world completely stopped around us.

Carly Partridge Tondeur, 34, from Somerset lives with her husband and two children in Sussex. She is a Mental Health Nurse, currently working in nurse education. In her spare time, Carly loves spending time outdoors with her family, especially splashing in puddles with her toddler and starting (not necessarily finishing) a variety of craft projects.

NATALIE SHARPE

I was fortunate enough to be granted NHS-funded IVF before the pandemic hit. I fell pregnant on our first attempt in September 2019 after a tough few years of struggling with infertility and associated declining mental health. When the first lockdown was imposed, I was seven months pregnant. I kept myself safe at home and did not set foot in a supermarket in the months before my son was born, for fear of what the virus might do to myself or my longed-for baby. My husband was my only companion for months and would go out to buy all of our essentials – a task which, ordinarily, I would have done. I only left the house for a daily walk in nature and to go to antenatal checks.

Initially, some of these checks were conducted over the telephone, however, as I got closer to the end of my pregnancy I was invited to be seen at a nearby medical centre by a midwife until delivery. Rather than having continuity of care with my assigned midwife, I would be seen by any midwife who was available on that day.

At my 39-week appointment, I was informed that my blood pressure was slightly elevated, but even more worryingly, that my bump measurement had dropped 2cm in size compared to the previous week. Friends tried to reassure me that this could be a variation of normal, but I couldn't shift a feeling of unease. The midwife referred me for a growth scan and said it could take up to five days to be seen. This was communicated to me when alone in the medical centre as my husband, Matthew, was made to wait outside in the car. This would become a recurring theme in my birth journey. Previous growth scans that had originally been arranged due to it being an IVF pregnancy had been called off thanks to the pandemic. When I was eventually scanned, they had nothing to compare it to.

The following morning, due to reduced movements and my continued worry regarding the reduced bump size, I decided to call and attend the maternity day unit to put my mind at rest. They were extremely efficient considering the circumstances and saw me on the same day. They checked mine and my baby's vitals and squeezed me in for a growth scan, where the baby was measuring on track for his gestational age. However, they discovered an issue during the Doppler scan of the umbilical cord – the blood wasn't flowing through to the baby as it should be. They checked six times. Again, I was alone as I was told this information whilst my husband waited for hours in the car park. Being a first-time mum, I had no idea what to expect in this situation. I am also scared of hospitals and medical intervention, so to say that this was worrying for me is an understatement. All of this, against the backdrop of conceiving a child after infertility, felt like an impossible situation. Anyone who has walked the road of pregnancy after infertility or loss will know just how hard it is to believe that everything will turn out OK in the end.

The consultant suggested an induction and said that otherwise she "couldn't guarantee what might happen" to the baby. This wasn't a route I wanted to go down, mostly to avoid a prolonged hospital stay, but we felt we had no choice. So, the next morning, carrying my suitcase, the baby's bag and my pillow alone, I walked into the eerily quiet hospital, not a clue where to go as maternity ward tours and face-to-face appointments had been called off. My only support system over the past few months, my husband, waved me off at the door, as we both had tears in our eyes. The hospital was like a ghost town. Nobody could be seen walking the usually busy corridor, the coffee shop was closed and a strict no-visitor policy was in place.

Being alone on the induction ward was the next hurdle I was to face. The midwives kept their distance behind masks and I had my very first COVID test. I tried my best to relax and settle in, however, once the pain of the pessary kicked in and others on my ward started having adverse reactions to the synthetic hormones, I felt scared and alone. I suffer from emetophobia: a fear of vomiting. I felt trapped with no one to confide in when I was panicking about all the women around me vomiting. The sound, smell and sight of two women opposite me being sick made me feel everything but relaxed. Unsurprisingly, all my contractions came to a halt.

The next morning, after a struggle to get reassuring readings, I was scared and tearful, so they finally agreed to allow my husband to be with me. Over the next hour, I endured two failed attempts to rupture my membranes, so was started on the hormone drip which led to the baby's heart rate dropping and failing to recover quickly. Several doctors rushed into my room, just like you see on the TV, and declared it was time to send me for an emergency C-section.

I had struggled to gel with my midwife, partly because I found it hard to connect with her through masks and social distancing, but mostly because she didn't seem at ease with the situation, which in turn made me feel on edge. As she pulled the surgical stockings up onto my legs, she looked me in the eyes and said,

"Natalie, has anyone told you that as soon as you have had the C-section, your husband will have to go straight home?"

I broke down inconsolably. How was that fair? That, after he had only just arrived at the hospital, after being on my own for over a day, having fought so hard to get to this moment on our IVF and infertility journey, I now had to go through the first moments of motherhood, alone?

It felt inhumane. Alone, with no visitors and no birth partner once the child had been successfully extracted from my womb, was not how I had imagined becoming a parent would begin. Because of this, I initially refused the emergency C-section, and as the baby's heart rate had stabilised somewhat, the consultant agreed to let me try and continue with the induction and vaginal birth.

The midwife took this opportunity to take her lunch break and reset herself. To this day, I still feel guilty for having expressed so much raw emotion to her. I was simply angry at the system for taking away the little piece of support

I had left - my husband. It was heartbreaking for everyone involved and the pain the midwives felt in communicating these strict measures was palpable.

We continued with another 12 hours of the hormone drip. Eventually, the pain, restriction of movement and being nil by mouth became unbearable, and upon examination, I was still only 3-4cm dilated. I agreed with the doctors to proceed with an emergency C-section.

I was wheeled down the corridor into the operating theatre, still contracting and in agony. The trainee anaesthetist attempted to insert the spinal block, and she failed to do this six times. Each time I felt a 'buzzing' sensation down my spine and my heart rate rocketed with panic. I believed I was going to be left paralysed. For the 45 minutes or so this was going on, Matthew was helpless, forced to wait outside and not knowing what was going on. Luckily, the consultant anaesthetist arrived just in time from the other side of the hospital and successfully administered the spinal block on his first attempt. I was fortunate to have narrowly avoided the general anaesthetic and both Matthew and I missing my child's birth entirely.

As soon as I was stitched up and left theatre, my husband was ushered down the corridor and sent home. It felt wrong. The care I received in recovery helped in not having him there - they really were angels - but it felt so strange that my husband wasn't allowed to meet his child and that my baby was dressed for the first time by a total stranger.

Once I was moved to the postnatal ward, the care I received took a nosedive. The midwives and maternity care assistants were under immense pressure. Needed a sip of water? Dropped your phone? Needed the toilet? A baby crying out of reach who needed to be picked up? With no visitors allowed, every single waking need of the new mothers and babies had to be attended to by them.

Alone with my thoughts, I felt immense pressure to recover quickly to get myself and my new baby back home with his father. There was a strict zero-visitor policy on the postnatal ward. On day three, when I was hoping to be discharged before plans changed, my mood and ability to cope with the ongoing isolation took a turn for the worse. My son had jaundice and I was struggling to keep my blood pressure under control, so the doctors wanted to keep us in longer. Eventually, following hands-on lactation support and a prescription for beta blockers, we were discharged just before midnight. My deep desire to escape that environment and for my husband to meet his child took over any rational thoughts to receive more care and support from medical professionals on the ward.

When home, the care and attention I received from my health visitor, Siobhan, saved me and helped to rescue my confidence in breastfeeding and my ability to be a mother. Unfortunately, that care did not come soon enough and I was admitted back onto the labour ward due to high blood pressure. On top of adjusting to life with a new baby and recovering from major surgery, I believe it was anxiety that caused my blood pressure to spike and I was fearful of what might happen to me if I stayed home.

Not wanting to separate my child from my husband again, I left my breastfed newborn baby at home with his dad whilst I went to the hospital. Leaving my son at home and separating us as a new breastfeeding dyad went against every maternal instinct inside my body. Subsequently, I suffered a massive panic attack. After a few hours of monitoring and an increased dose on my prescription, the doctors agreed to let me go home.

What I really needed was support and care. New mothers giving birth in lockdown were robbed of a community. I feel that with more support at home from healthcare workers, family and friends in those first few days, my situation could have been avoided.

After two rounds of NHS-funded CBT for postnatal PTSD, and many sessions with a private hypnotherapist, I am starting to see an improvement in how I feel when I talk about my birth experience. However, it is not the birthing experience and maternity leave that any woman should have had.

Luckily, the government started to listen and 'support bubbles' for those with babies were introduced. Even then, the general community around us did not seem to understand the need for bubbles for those with newborn babies. On two occasions, a police car turned up at my in-laws' house, following reports from neighbours that they had been breaking lockdown rules by having visitors over. New mothers struggling with their mental health during a pandemic didn't need the police to control when their parents could support them with day-to-day tasks during that critical time.

When I think back to my birth experience and look ahead to the future, as we try and bring a sibling into the world for my son, I have mixed feelings. Whilst I know that the same situation will likely not occur again, there are aspects of my experience that continue to haunt me. I grieve for the experiences he and I missed out on in those early months and years. Luckily, it did not take away from the incredible bond we share; in fact, I believe it made us stronger. But, my experience will shape how I approach birth, medical intervention and new parenthood in the future, should we be so lucky to get there again.

Natalie Sharpe, 35, from Northamptonshire lives with her husband, Matthew, her three-year-old son, Milo, and her faithful westie, Poppy. At the time of writing, she is currently pregnant with her second IVF baby. She works as Head of Marketing & Commercial Development for a promotional merchandise supplier and in her spare time supports new mothers by volunteering for a local breastfeeding charity. Outside of work, she will mostly be found chasing after her little boy at a country park, as well as squeezing in some time for yoga and swimming.
@baddienatnat

REBECCA JONES

All alone,
It was the middle of the night,
With no one in sight.

All alone,
No one to help carry my bags up to the labour ward.

I pause,
I hold onto a wall while a contraction takes over,
Tears rolling down my face as I struggle to walk,
All alone.

My husband left in the car to wait,
Only it's almost too late.

I make it to the maternity ward,
Welcomed with a physical examination I didn't want to take.

Calling down the hall,
Where is the husband?
As I lay alone,
Birthing my child during lockdown law.

Too soon; it's time to say goodbye,
As I'm wheeled up to the ward with my newborn in arms,
all our bags by my side.

No visitors allowed.
All alone,
Where's my village?
Not allowed in.

Breastfeeding groups, baby groups, Mum groups closed.
All alone.

Mental health service don't get in touch,
Support from the government; none.

All alone,
During lockdown law.

Rebecca Jones, 33, from South Wales lives with her husband and two children; Oliver, 4, and Willow, 3. She runs Nourished Motherhood, supporting mothers and mothers-to-be to feel their best through the trimesters and postpartum. When she has a spare moment, you will find her by the sea, or on her yoga mat.
@nourished_motherhood__

JULIA COOPER

From our third-storey flat, we looked out over tanned families playing and barbecuing in their gardens. Texts from the NHS told me that if I wanted to go outside, I should sit by a window instead. I'd never felt such a burning desire to stand on grass. To grow plants. To connect with nature.

Instead, your mother *became* nature.

It was the most inappropriately technicolour, fragrant, beautiful spring, as if she hadn't got the memo. Trees blossomed excitedly, as I did while carrying you. The blossom and your existence willed me on.

You and I walked the same streets every day, dodging neighbours yet getting to know their gardens intimately. Even now, though we've moved twice, I could draw you a map of where the fig tree, the wisteria and the pink Spanish bluebells were.

As you grew from grape to strawberry to orange, so did the realisation that this would not all be over by the time you'd arrive.

After the 20-week scan, I met your dad in the street outside the hospital. You were a girl. I wish he could have seen you moving and growing inside me. I remember that ultrasound, lying on the bed, mask on, gazing in wonder at your perfect spine. I made that! How did I make that? I am so grateful you were healthy and I didn't have to bear the burden of bad news, as so many other women did.

And then, we left London. Not able to say goodbye to anyone, we drove our life up deserted motorways. After months of Groundhog Day, that drive felt like emancipation. Thank you for being there with us.

I can't write about your birth. I'm not ready. I think both of us knew it was safer for you to stay inside. You went two weeks past your due date and no amount of long walks could encourage you otherwise, as that's all we'd been doing all year.

You were born. You were perfect. People tell me I *gave* birth to you, but I'm still not sure I believe it.

I am so glad you're here. I love you and I am so proud of you and I never want you to think otherwise. I'm working on holding and shaping our shared story, so that when you're older and we talk about 2020, I will be strong and happy and help you feel that way, too.

Julia Cooper, 34, lives in the Peak District with her husband Sam and 2.5-year-old daughter, Agnes. She works as a Graphics & Communications Coordinator for an architecture practice. In 2022, Julia successfully campaigned to change the law after a man photographed her breastfeeding without her consent. Julia is an accomplished tap dancer and performs regularly across the country.

KIRSTY WOODS

We circle the Arch of Remembrance, the war memorial in the park. It is a war of attrition, trying to get you to nap. Your little head bobs up and down, the little grey rabbit ears on your hat flapping gently. There is too much to interest you, your senses assaulted from every angle with noise and colour and pattern. So, we stop our walk around the park at the memorial and I just circle. Around and around. Wood pigeons are cooing in the trees. The high-pitched call of a bird I cannot name. I pause to let you listen before carrying on, steadily circling this monument of sacrifices. Gradually, your muttering and grizzling quietens and your little grey head rests gently on my chest. You are asleep. The battle won. I stop to rest on a bench but you, as if sensing my surrender to tiredness, start to stir, ready to wake again. So I carry on walking, circling the memorial, as if pulled into orbit by a gravitational force I can't resist.

'Remember in gratitude,' the engraving above the arch reads. 'All who served and strove and those who patiently endured.'

There is no comparison of course, no true similarities between the battles fought and the losses suffered by these men whose unspoken names are celebrated by this monument. Nor of those who continue, to this day, to fight in wars across the globe. I am not so arrogant to assume that there is. But I feel a kind of comfort in the presence of this giant arch of rock. It is a visual symbol of this very idea of 'patient endurance.' It seems to acknowledge battles of a different kind, albeit without pomp and ceremony.

It is guarded by iron railings and topped with brass finials. The gates into it are locked. It is sacrosanct, entirely separate and untouchable but right now its energy is palpable. I have walked past it so many times on walks like today and barely registered it, save for its size and the fact it seems to be a magnet for personal trainers and yoga fanatics to work out on the path which leads up to it. Yet, today, for some reason, it calls me in. I circle again, stopping frequently to look up and read the inscriptions as if seeing it for the first time.

'I will not cease from mental fight, nor shall my sword sleep in my hand.' *Jerusalem* rings out in my head. I remember myself in another park, in another lifetime. In my twenties, last night of the proms, soaked in rain, watered liberally with beer and nourished by the rousing chorus of my girlfriends around me. I sang the words then but did not appreciate their gravity. How very distant that person feels now. How very ignorant she was of what lay ahead. Good things and bad.

Government rhetoric throughout this pandemic has called upon the metaphor of war. Whether it's really an apt or appropriate analogy to draw upon is up for debate, of course, but there is no denying that this situation has presented us all with daily battles of our own kind. This certainly feels like a kind of war and there have, undoubtedly, been losses. We have all been enlisted to fight with small, everyday sacrifices and means of attack. We have been asked to show resilience. To think of others as comrades needing our protection.

I am heading back to my battle ground now. You have woken up. Your little cheeks pink from the cold but giving the smallest smile as I kiss them. We stop circling and start to walk back home. I wonder what war will lay ahead of us between here and bedtime. I don't want to feel this way about it.

'I want to enjoy my children, not endure them,' I told my husband the other day.

'Pithy,' he said. But there it is. That's how it feels. Each day, a battle, my little allies sometimes feeling like the enemy. My thoughts and feelings of inadequacy torturing me. A bombardment of guilt. Each day the battle lines are drawn, the advancing battalion of three small people who weaken my defences steadily with repeated requests for snacks and TV and attention at all costs. Repeated skirmishes between your elder brother and sister as they fight over toys and territory. Each day I feel the weapons at my disposal are less effective at countering the barrage. I will not cease from mental fight nor shall my sword sleep in my hand. It will not sleep, but it is blunted, nonetheless. My body is weary. My skin is literally scarred with the scratches and bites and pinches where you have tried to seek comfort from teething gums. My mind feels shell-shocked.

I want to serve and strive. To endure this situation with the quiet patience that surely a good mother should feel. I want to stand strong and proud like the limestone of the war memorial in the park. But sometimes I wonder how much longer this struggle will last and just how much fight I have left in me. This writing is my memorial to this time. A testimony of the struggles that I, like thousands and thousands of mothers, have faced over this past year. It is my own anthem of remembrance and I hope that, one day, I will feel I can sing it out loud, a chorus as rousing as that girl singing *Jerusalem* in the park twenty years ago.

Kirsty Woods, 42, lives with her husband and three young children in Leicestershire. She is a part-time children's bookseller for an independent bookshop and full-time dreamer of a life more full of creative endeavours. In snatched moments between sorting endless piles of laundry, despairing at the discarded crumbs under her sofa, and repeated pleas to her children to stop jumping on the bed, she loves to garden, write, paint and make linoprints. She dreams of one day being a 'proper artist and writer.' Kirsty is extremely proud to be part of this anthology which gives voice to the experiences of so many mothers during a truly strange and unique period of history.
@homelovingk
@birdandbuddesigns

SARAH HOWARD

"I would have loved to not be disturbed by visitors when my baby was tiny."

It's not the same when your mum could get stopped by the police for visiting you when you are at your most vulnerable and need her more than ever.

"Wasn't it nice to have that newborn bubble as a family?"

It's not the same when that bubble is not a choice, but forced upon you, with no visitors or support at all, for months.

"You can't do much with a newborn anyway."

It's not the same when you are forbidden from leaving your home to take your baby outside and get a change of scenery.

"I didn't find health visitors helpful."

It's not the same when you desperately want to have your baby weighed for reassurance that he is getting enough food, but you get a phone call instead.

"I think they have lactation consultants online now."

It's not the same when every book or post you read says the best thing you can do to improve your baby's latch is to get face-to-face support, and none of that is allowed.

"Little babies don't benefit from baby classes anyway."

It's not the same when you're trying to calm a crying baby as the online Baby Yoga buffers and crashes.

"I didn't do much on maternity leave."

It's not the same when the maternity leave you dreamt of, swapping stories with new friends across cosy café tables, is instead spent wrapping your baby in layers to keep them warm on socially-distanced walks in the rain.

Middle-of-the-night feeds aren't the same when instead of worrying about sleep deprivation, you are worrying about when you will next be allowed to see your friends.

Long, lazy newborn days aren't the same when you know that in a few hours, the latest press conference will tell you if any of your family will be able to meet your baby soon or not, or when you will be able to take your baby somewhere other than for a walk round the park.

Taking photos of first smiles, first baths and first milestones aren't the same when you ache inside, knowing that none of those closest to you will ever see your baby this tiny for themselves.

It's not the same.

Sarah Howard, 34, is originally from the Wirral and now lives in Sheffield with her husband and two sons, three-year-old Freddie and baby Charlie. She is a history teacher and lover of yoga, going out with friends and adventures with her family. You will often find her at a soft play trying to drink a hot cup of tea.

EMILY LOUISE WALKER-LAKHANI

This can't be right. It's not how it's meant to be! A lockdown? A pandemic? I'm having a baby! Why me?

I watched it roll in like a storm on the horizon. Dark, unknown clouds looming closer.

Watching the Downing Street briefings every day at 4pm. Every Thursday, 7pm, clapping for the NHS.

One day it hit me. Survival mode. Mama bear. Lioness. It was no longer the lead-up to a baby you see others go through. No baby shower, no goodbye to my colleagues, no shopping with my mum. It was appointments alone. Online orders. Zoom calls.

It was now: plan, protect and prioritise.

Stay home, stay safe, save lives.

Midwife appointments moved to the car and car park. At first, a phone call, then the measuring of bump and checking the heartbeat. In and out. Alone.

I had a bleed at 37 weeks. I had to go into hospital overnight and have tests galore. My husband stayed in the car park, unable to be with me, and I had no idea what the machines meant. I will never forget the baby in a trolley in the corridor or the woman epically losing her waters like in the movies. I lay there wondering if I was going to leave with a baby! Rubbing my tummy, I repeated, "I've got you and you've got me."

This was it!

I spent the night contracting. As we were told birthing partners were only allowed when in active labour, my only focus was to stay at home for as long as possible so my husband could be at the hospital with me.

Stay home, stay safe, save lives.

I tried my bloody hardest.

Imprinted on my memory, I will never forget leaving my husband at the door and walking away from him, in labour. I felt like I was gliding down the longest corridor that felt like a mile, hot in my dressing gown, with the smell of hospital chemicals, dimmed lights of the night and the weight of a baby. Instructed to stop halfway to wash my hands, I sang, 'Happy Birthday.' I didn't want the watching midwives to judge me. *She's unable to wash her hands correctly.*

I can't remember how long I was labouring by myself. I just remember telling myself to focus and stay safe.

"I've got you and you've got me."

Hurrah! I was 4cm and my husband could come in.

Three midwives and a lot of pushing later, I just knew she wasn't moving. We needed to go to theatre. Forceps or C-section? Prepping for theatre, we were separated again.

"I've got you and you've got me."

Getting my spinal, the contractions were fierce. I gripped onto my midwife's arm, unable to move, screaming through gritted teeth. Three pushes, an episiotomy and a tear later, my meconium-covered baby came into the world with the help of forceps on 3rd May 2020 at 10.09pm. She was blinking beautiful. I was high as a kite and puking.

"You're a daddy!"

My mission complete.

Two hours together.

Then, alone again. But this time, not really.

"I've got you, and you've got me."

Faceless silhouettes wheeled me into a bay, gave me a buzzer and left. I was in a room of five other new mums and their babies. Curtains were drawn and I lay in a starchy bed, unable to move due to the anaesthetic. Just me and a trolley with one tiny baby swaddled up inside a lavender blanket, Perspex walls surrounding her. She woke up with delicate cries that barely pierced the night. I couldn't reach her. I couldn't pick her up. I couldn't feed her. I was the only person she had and I let her down at just a few hours old. Too weak from blood loss. A faceless figure arrived and fed my baby her first feed. No smiling face or warmth, no Mama singing softly. Her first feed was with a stranger head to toe in plastic PPE.

Medical professionals, on their rare visits, stayed at the bottom of the bed and wouldn't come near us. I had just had a baby and should have been glowing with pride. Instead, I felt dirty, contagious and alone.

Every time I stood up, urine would fall out of me. Uncontrollably. Each time I would gingerly remove my pyjamas, the pad and white netted freebie pants. As visitors were not allowed there was no delivery of clean clothes or celebratory balloons. I rotated my piss-stained pyjamas between me and the radiator. I quickly ran out of pads and pants, so for the second time, went to seek more. I stopped someone in the corridor and shyly asked for some more. I burst into tears. The plastic-covered woman ushered me into a store cupboard and asked if everything was OK. It wasn't. I explained I couldn't hold my wee and told her about how I felt.

She hugged me.

She broke the rules.

She held a new mum in a pandemic and offered a small gesture of humanity and support.

I wasn't contagious to her. I was vulnerable, scared, alone and in pain.

I am so sorry I didn't ask your name. I couldn't see your face. But that moment meant everything to me.

Thank you.

Home. Thursday, 7pm. I stepped onto the street holding my baby. I was Kate Middleton! My road applauding and cheering for me! I had a baby. Here's the celebration. Clap for the NHS. Raise your glasses higher and clap a little harder. Look what they helped me do.

Recovery was hard. Bleeding, sweating, leaking and weeing. We had one visit, one weigh-in. The baby didn't lose weight, so that was it, just us, no support. I raised my concerns over my stitches but a doctor wouldn't see me. A video call. A fucking video call to check my stitches. Lying on my bed, with my legs wide open, my husband held his phone as a torch whilst the doctor was on the other end of my phone on a video call. "Can you get closer please?" How degrading. I felt worthless. This was postpartum care during the pandemic. Hubby with a torch between your legs trying to focus on your flaps. My stitches had opened, I could barely walk up the stairs and this was the medical care I received.

We took our own family portrait wearing matching rainbow t-shirts to show our thanks to the NHS. Little did we know, on this same day was an infamous Downing Street party. The very people who made the rules that affected us so much, that influenced and impacted this experience and took so much away, were partying and mocking us as we posed and thanked armies of people for their tireless efforts.

Car window visits between feeds. I felt well and ready enough to show her to the world. People peered in at her like she was a zoo animal.

Lioness. Mama bear. Defend.

"I've got you and you've got me."

Such conflicting emotions.

I didn't have to share her. She was mine to protect.

Stay home, stay safe, save lives.

I didn't have to pass her around like an object or watch people take photos with her like a trophy.

What glorious, private family time. Just the three of us, giving us the ability to navigate our way through the fog in our own time and space. Time and space to recover, ease the leaks, manage the hormones and bond.

The lockdown stole so much from me, more than can be explained in words. It gave me so much, too.

Emily Louise Walker-Lakhani, lockdown mama. That title is mine and I wear it with pride.

Aella Rae Walker Lakhani, my lockdown baby.

I've got you and you've got me.

Emily Walker-Lakhani, from Leicestershire, lives with her husband and two daughters, Aella 3, and Kora, 19 months. Whilst completing her studies to become a counsellor, she works part-time at the University of Leicester. By day she loves crafting, baking and gardening with the kids and in the evening you'll find her crocheting, reading and watching TV.

REBECCA DAVENPORT

Some moments in our lives are tied together as inextricably as rain is to a rainbow. For me, pregnancy, postpartum and pandemic are three of those moments. This is the story of the days that are etched as permanently on my mind as the stretch marks on my skin.

I've just found out I'm pregnant. I ring my husband glowing with excitement. We eat pasta for tea like the whole world isn't about to turn upside down. We go to see my parents, and his, to tell them. We are so full of potential. It's 28th January 2020.

There is a magpie in my kitchen. I've just walked through the door from work and somehow, there is a magpie in my kitchen. One of my cats must have brought it in but it's still very much alive, squawking and marching around on the windowsill like it owns the place. I manage to let it out of the front door and later remark to my husband (who isn't my husband yet) that's surely the weirdest event that the year can bring. It's 6th February 2020.

"I think you should sit down to watch this," my husband says to me. The news has been getting odder and scarier for days now but this next moment is pivotal. This next moment is the clear separation of my life into before and after. I bet you have one, too.
I watch in disbelief as Boris Johnson says that we - the pregnant - are now like the elderly, the very young, the vulnerable. The *vulnerable*. The clinically vulnerable. I feel emotionally vulnerable. It's 16th March 2020.

I still go into work the next day and am sent home. Before I leave, I sit in the staff room, trying to get my head around this bizarre feeling. I go for a walk with my mum and her dog, acutely aware that this is the last time I will see them for a while. 12 weeks, he said on the briefing last night. I'll be 25 weeks pregnant in 12 weeks. It's 17th March 2020.

I have my scan today. My 12 week scan. I've had a text message telling me I must attend alone. I am literally sick with nerves. I don't want to do this on my own. I am terrified, running bad news scenarios through my head all day. There is crime scene tape on the chairs in the antenatal clinic so we don't sit next to each other. It feels a crime to be out in public right now, though this is one of the rare circumstances that it's not.
The gel is cold on my stomach. The sonographer is mercifully kind and says instantly, "there's your baby!" It's profound and I feel a confusing mixture of thankfulness and sorrow that my husband isn't allowed to be here. It's 27th March 2020.

The weather is irksomely perfect today. This was meant to be my wedding day. Instead, my not-husband and I spend it in the garden. We get flowers through the post from my mum and dad, whom I haven't seen for weeks. I can't believe how long a week lasts for now. It's 5th April 2020.

I make a rainbow out of coloured card and stick it on the window in what will be the nursery. It makes me feel better and worse simultaneously. It's 25th April 2020.

My anomaly scan is today. This time, the sonographer warns me not to face her while I'm being scanned, so I don't breathe on her. I am given the tiniest glimpse of my baby on screen. I ask her to tell me if I am having a boy or a girl. "It's most likely a girl," she says. A girl. A daughter.
We tell my mum and dad-in law from the bottom of their garden.
We tell my mum and dad on a video call.
No one hugs us to congratulate us. No one can. It's 19th May 2020.

People are returning to my workplace today - it's a primary school so some of them never really left. The children will soon follow. It's been about 15 weeks since I saw my parents in person and the only human who has felt my baby move, other than me, is my boyfriend. I want my mum to be able to feel her too. It's 8th June 2020.

'Super Saturday,' they're calling it. I can barely enter a supermarket, never mind a pub. Going out to socialise feels like a fantasy from a story book. I wonder what antenatal classes would have been like. We are supposed to get married (again) next month. When I agreed to this rescheduling it was illegal to leave the house for over an hour. It's 4th July 2020.

We finally get married. It's felt like an absolute battle to get here but we've done it. A tiny wedding. It feels both brave and foolish to see other people, even from six feet away. It's a beautiful day though, in every sense of the word. It's 9th August 2020.

My waters break at 8pm. I go to hospital and come home again. I return at about 1am. Thankfully, restrictions have 'eased' enough that my mum can join my husband as my birthing partner. I still labour alone for three hours, though. It's 21st September 2020.
My daughter is born. I hold her, feeling like the building could burn down around us and I wouldn't notice. I am finally meeting this person who has been my constant companion throughout all of this. My daughter.
But then it's insisted that my husband leaves and we go to the postnatal ward. Even though all the other women there are in a similar situation, I want to leave. There's no place like home, but I'm Dorothy without her ruby red

slippers. I fight to be discharged. Eventually I fumble trying to put my tiny baby into a car seat by myself. I didn't think I was going to have to do this.

The bliss of finally lying in my own bed with my husband and our newborn is incomparable. It's 22nd September 2020.

My dad meets my daughter whilst wearing a mask. My grandma meets my daughter whilst wearing a mask. Everyone does everything whilst wearing a mask. It's 23rd September 2020.

We spend the morning lying on the bed together and for the first time since her birth, I'm not worrying about trying to still live my life as before. I am learning about this little person who is adjusting to life outside me, as I adjust to ever-changing news outside our house. I love her so much and this is so intense, but today is a good day. It's 1st October 2020.

Johnson's announced a second lockdown which is coming into effect today. Trying to keep up with the constant changes and back-pedalling is almost as exhausting as looking after my newborn daughter. We wanted to take our little girl to meet some of her wider family in person but we can't now. It's so disappointing and difficult. It's 5th November 2020.

I am as low as I have ever been. I am sleep-deprived and, outside of my wonderful husband and family, I'm support-deprived as well. My health visitor never comes to see me as she has COVID and the appointment is not rescheduled. I don't know a single other person who also has a newborn. Guess those cancelled antenatal classes would have been good for that. I don't know how other mothers do this. It's 19th November 2020.

My daughter naps in her cot for the first time. I have held on as tightly as I can for the last two weeks and this moment where she is peaceful suddenly stands out to me. I am getting better. It's 5th December 2020.

As the year closes, my spirits begin to lift. My baby is sleeping for more than two hours at a time and we have survived this so far. We have each other and I am slowly, slowly managing the multitudes of motherhood. I can start to imagine a future that **doesn't include wearing a face mask.**

It's been the best, worst year of my life. It's 31st December 2020.

Rebecca Davenport, 29, lives in Manchester with her husband, Stuart, and daughter, Ella, who was born in 2020. Rebecca is a teaching assistant, always has a book on the go and loves to document her life through words and images; she combines these passions by scrapbooking. Her favourite biscuits are custard creams and she is happiest in her garden.

JO MATTHEWS

When I wake to feed my daughter
Lockdown 2020

The light-filled days are simpler now
they shine in raging technicolour
life stripped bare to the bloom
       but was it always this bright?

and we watch stacked in our concrete
boxes, from our balconies and from
our newly washed windows
       and we watch it alone.

I march out my prayers along
pastel-chalked pavements
of hopscotch and hope
       swerve and smile at strangers

see blossom swirl, hear the hush
of the trees, watch white birds catch
the light of the shining sky
       old worries sent up in the sway

spend a moment to notice how the leaves
dance against my white kitchen wall
hear a wood-pigeon call, send love
       from the safety of my screen

but when I wake to feed my daughter

in the inky undulation of the night
I think about the certain wreckage
of it, the stubborn march of it, the
> too-soon tears of the bereaved

the mass graves and mask-marked faces
lungs watered in liquid, last breaths
no loved ones can witness
> and I wonder whether grief

will weave its way to my backdoor
as life as we know it sinks like a stone
can we rebuild in bricks and mortar
> or will it be blood and bone?

and I long for the open hills
at the back of my childhood home
and I long to show my mum the
> mother I have become

to lay my head in her lap and
feel her stroke my hair like she did
waiting again for her to say
> it will all be ok; *it will all be ok.*

Originally from Oxford, Jo Matthews is a freelance writer and copywriter now living in Amsterdam, the Netherlands with her partner and two small daughters. She has had her work published by The Times, Popshot Magazine, The Fish Anthology, The Rappahannock Review, Prairie Fire and Acumen, among others, and is currently working on her first chapbook. Jo has completed workshops and courses with Breadloaf (USA), Arvon (UK) and the International Writers Collective (Netherlands.) She is fascinated by the power of words to transform and transcend the perplexing and often messy experience of being human.

- **Late 2019** – My fiancé, Kofi, and I decided we'd start trying to conceive after our trip to Barbados in March/April 2020 (a trip that never happened.) This was a very exciting for me as I'd always wanted to become a mama.
- **18th June 2020** – I took a test as my period was late and WE WERE PREGNANT! We didn't really know what to do, think or say. We just grinned at each other. All my thoughts and emotions were flying about, just a completely muddle mind!
- I was working from home following the COVID restrictions that had been put in place and all was great. I didn't really think too much of it other than it being strange. We were advised that we'd all be lone working a week at a time in the office, to avoid potentially spreading the virus. To begin with, my thoughts turned to how boring this would be, rather than how vulnerable I was.
- **17th July 2020** – We had a telephone appointment with a midwife where she filled out our details to form the 'green folder notes.' Not how I expected our first appointment to be, but the midwife was informative and made us both feel at ease. We booked in for me to have my first appointment and it then dawned on me that I'd have to do it alone, without Kofi. And wearing a mask. It was not how I ever expected being pregnant and going to appointments to be.
- **21st July 2020** - I had my first bloods appointment and collected my notes from the hospital, alone. I was anxious, sitting in the waiting room with other expectant mothers. None of us spoke. It was surreal. I could almost hear my heartbeat in my head.
- **4th August 2020** – Our 12-week scan came and all was fine. It felt surreal being there on my own, watching this baby squirm on the screen. I couldn't quite comprehend that baby was inside of me and was ours! I asked if I could video call Kofi so he could see but was told no. I didn't feel I could question or challenge this decision, so I just left it. Why couldn't my fiancé experience this as well? This was his baby as much as mine.
- Going to our community midwife appointments on my own just became my normal. I tried to not get anxious or worked up, but I always had that thought in my mind of, 'What if it's bad news and I'm on my own? What if there's no heartbeat? Kofi would be at least an hour away at work!' Thank our lucky stars this never happened, but those first

intrusive thoughts had already started to kick in. So, I'd record the heartbeat sounds on my phone to play back to him.

- **28th Sept 2020** - Our 20-week scan came around and I had thoughts again of, 'What if it's bad news?' The restrictions in place were completely pointless. I was going into a place where there would have been COVID patients, wearing a thin mask that was supposed to protect me and my unborn baby, without being tested before entering. Thankfully, all was OK and I called Kofi straight away.
- The thought that racked my brain daily was, 'I should be sharing this milestone in my life with my nearest and dearest.' Still to this day, some people don't even know I've been pregnant as they didn't see me for so long.
- **28th Oct 2020** - We were fortunate and managed to book a private 4D scan in our local town. I wanted to do this purely so Kofi could see our baby on a screen and not just a picture. Why should he not be able to be part of these appointments? How was this fair on him or all of the other dads out there?
- **Late Dec 2020** - I attended our 32-week community midwife appointment and was advised my bump was measuring small, so I'd need to attend a growth scan. She assured me this was probably normal but she just wanted me to be checked out. I didn't feel scared or nervous about having such scans - I felt grateful that my baby and I were being looked after in such uncertain times - but I couldn't feel OK with having to do it all on my own for no apparent reason.
- The consultant talked about me being induced, which I wasn't so keen about. I wanted to leave our baby to enter the whole on their own! However, at almost 39 weeks, the growth scan showed that our baby had stopped growing. I was booked in to be induced the following day. It was supposed to be my last working day before having a week's maternity leave. No such luck! That evening, I had mixed emotions. I knew we'd be meeting our baby imminently, but also, I'd have to be in the hospital on my own until I was in 'active labour.' I couldn't fathom this - this surely wasn't how the birth of babies happened, was it?
- The next day, Kofi dropped me off at the hospital. I think I was in a little bit of a daydream. I didn't feel much - I knew no different. He wasn't allowed in with me, so I buzzed on the intercom, was let in and booked into the induction ward. As soon as those doors closed, all I could think was, *when will I see him again?* He wasn't allowed back in until I was able to go down and have my waters broken - this didn't happen until two days later. The induction ward was very quiet. We

were all checked into our bays and monitored every four hours. The pessary and first gel they administered didn't work, and after the second gel, I could feel very minor period pains. I asked to be checked and I was advised that I'd started to dilate. I felt pretty calm considering, but I knew this was it. Where was Kofi?

- Whilst on the induction ward, we had to wear masks if we left our bay area. There were no visitors allowed whatsoever. I caught the eye of a young woman across from me and we started conversing. From there on we talked all day and into the night. I needed the comfort of speaking to someone to stop me from feeling so alone. We also started talking to another young woman within our bay area on her way back from the toilet – and we all still speak now. In the end, we all had boys within a day of each other. They were my saviours both on the ward and postnatally. They felt like my friends, that friendly face you seek out in a busy place. With no visitors, I heavily relied on them to keep me sane.

- **7th Feb 2021** - By lunchtime, I was called to go down to have my waters broken. I was finally able to call Kofi to tell him to come in and then the process would begin. I'd not seen him for 48 hours. I really wanted a water birth, but at the time the pool was being used so we were allocated a delivery room. Things were getting real, but I still didn't feel nervous.

- The process of my waters being broken wasn't nice, a little uncomfortable and strange – but I coped. My contractions started and I was dealing with the surges for a while. I used gas and air for a while, but I didn't like that much. I remembered my hypnobirthing tools I'd learnt and had dim lighting, relaxing music and was just left to it. I managed to do this for about 16 hours, after which I was super tired and had no energy. I wanted to be able to sleep, or at least rest, so I requested an epidural. This was super painful and took some time to put in as my contractions kept on coming fast. But once in, within 10 minutes it kicked in and I was able to have a much-needed sleep.

- When I woke, I was checked again and was dilated further but still not 10 centimetres. The midwives noticed the baby's resting heart rate wouldn't come down, and that the baby was back-to-back. They advised me that we were going to theatre as they needed to get the baby out. Panic set in. I was adamant I didn't want a C-section. I was advised that they would try with forceps or ventouse, and if baby didn't come within three tries then a section would be needed.

- I was hooked up to the necessary drugs and then advised they were going to try and turn the baby and use forceps. My midwife was feeling my tummy for contractions and telling me to push. I had no idea if I was actually pushing or just doing the motion as I couldn't feel a thing. My baby was coming – I was scared about giving birth, but I couldn't feel it. With my first contraction, our baby's head was born. On the second contraction, our baby was born at 11:41am.
- I thought I'd feel an immediate rush of love, but I almost felt numb – was that just from the medication or did I emotionally feel it? I didn't know, I was confused.
- Kofi announced we had a boy. I wanted to have skin-to-skin and a few other things I'd got in my plan, but there was an issue with the cord and his breathing. He didn't cry, so they worked on him and he did a little whimper. I held him briefly and was then advised he needed some extra help, so was taken straight to NICU. Kofi was torn between being with me and our new baby boy. I asked him to go with the baby and make sure he was OK. This all seemed pretty normal to me – but then the time came for me to go up to the post-natal ward on my own and I immediately felt alone and isolated. I had no baby to care for. That was the last I saw of Kofi until he collected us to go home, five days later. It dawned on me that I was with all these new mums who had their babies with them, and I had no baby. It was like this until night three.
- In that time, our baby had to have a lumbar puncture test for possible meningitis, a cannula to administer IV antibiotics for an infection and a NG tube for feeding. I was distraught at this as I was desperate to breastfeed but was getting no milk. I had a midwife come and visit me with a breast pump, but I was just left to it. I had no idea what to do. I was lucky that one of the midwife care assistants on the ward (a family friend) was on shift that night and came to help. Amongst my many distraught tears, she spent about an hour with me and helped get things going. I was so grateful for her help!
- To go and see our baby I had to be taken down to NICU as it was too far to walk, having just gone through what I had, BUT Kofi and I couldn't be in there at the same time. I couldn't comprehend this – how could he come in from the outside into a unit where there were VERY vulnerable babies, without being tested? Yet, I, who had been tested, couldn't be down there at the same time as him? I just couldn't understand how that was fair. It wasn't, but we were powerless.
- I did feel that all the midwives on the post-natal ward did the best they could in a tough situation. Having such restrictions in place meant they

were extremely stretched and, at times, I had to ask for help for the same thing multiple times.
- Days passed and I was advised that our baby had jaundice and needed phototherapy treatment. He came up to me on the third night post-birth, with a blue light. We were given a side room because of this and although it was nice as I could concentrate on just the two of us, I also felt even more isolated and cut off from the world as soon as the door closed. I was glad to have my baby with me but it made me really sad that Kofi wasn't able to see him until we left the hospital. Because of this, Kofi was given squares of material to wear under his t-shirt, so that the patches would be left with our baby to still smell his daddy.
- My emotions were running wild. I was completely on my own with no support whatsoever. I was getting more and more anxious that Kofi hadn't seen our baby much. I made him come by my side window at points throughout the week so I could show him our baby. It was not how I wanted our first days together to be.
- I was finally allowed to go home one week after I'd been dropped off. I couldn't wait to leave the hospital and have my fiancé back for some support and help.
- I am not traumatised by my birth and actually feel positive about it. I was upset that my mum and family weren't able to come and visit and I wasn't able to show off our baby to them. My mum was in a 'bubble' with my younger sister and not allowed to come into our home. However, I was desperate for her to meet her new grandson so she self-isolated for 10 days before visiting. I had to have my mum there to help me!
- I also wanted Kofi's mum to meet her new grandchild, but she lives in Norfolk and because of the tier restrictions in place at the time, we were unable to visit her. It wasn't until our baby was seven weeks old that we could take him to visit his grandma. I cried sad and happy tears.

Rebecca Bartlett, 41, from Letchworth - Hertfordshire lives with her fiancé and their almost-three-year-old son, Markus. She works part-time in Property Management for a local Estate Agents. In her spare time likes to keep fit and try her hand at baking. Although a qualified hairdresser, she is currently studying for her Level 1 in British Sign Language. When she has any moments of downtime, you'll find her with a cuppa in hand accompanied by a biscuit or two.
@_rb2

DIMPLE MISTRY

Trigger warning: Birth injury, fourth-degree tear

I gave birth to my first child, a girl, on the 17th October 2020.

I had the most incredible pregnancy and start to the labour with my husband beside me. I had practised mindful breathing and used the techniques I had learned throughout the labour. I guess lockdown gave me the chance to have a relaxed pregnancy and all the time in the world to enjoy it.

I came into hospital on the morning of the 17th and was taken into a side room to have a scan with my partner. They confirmed everything looked good and that I could make my way to a room with a pool to potentially have the water birth I wanted. The midwives said they could see the baby's head and if I was ready, I could push. Nothing happened. Time passed, they took me out of the pool to examine me and realised I was only 6cm dilated and as I had used up so much energy I should be moved to the labour unit.

This was the moment I had new midwives and was told that I had to remain on the bed. The doctor came in and examined me multiple times. The new midwives suggested I agree to a syntocinon drip so my body could rest but everything slowed down from that point, so an instrumental birth was suggested. But, after more time passed, I was 10cm dilated and the baby was just not coming out. The doctor came in with a team of people and instruments. He used the suction cup, attempted it twice and then went on to use the forceps.

Pop, she came out. He told me I'd had a bad tear and that I'd have to be taken to surgery to be repaired. I was taken away from my husband and daughter.

After the surgery, I was told it was a fourth-degree tear. I was taken onto a recovery ward where I was met by my husband and newborn. My husband was distressed, telling me that the nurses in NICU said my daughter was hungry and needed feeding. I had no idea what to do. We had to speak to multiple people before any staff came around and showed me how to feed my baby. Then my husband had to leave and I was all alone with my daughter.

None of the staff were able to tell me any information about fourth-degree tears or what I went through and how to look after myself going forward. I was in hospital for three days, all alone with my newborn, and was distraught.

The morning after I'd returned home, I was passing faeces through my vagina. I mentioned this to the midwife who visited me at home. She suggested I go to the hospital immediately. I returned to the hospital, alone with my baby daughter and was examined and sent for an MRI scan. They discovered a fistula and I was told the only thing they could do was give me a stoma. I had to hand my daughter over to my husband and I stayed in hospital alone. I was given an ileostomy. I was still waking up every two hours post-surgery to pump milk for my daughter. I was in hospital for an entire week, alone, after life-changing surgery. Not able to feel like a mother or a wife and instead just a patient - all alone.

I was sent home one week later with no continuity of care from the maternity unit. I received no information on pelvic health or tears before the birth. I was offered no specialist support after and had to go private to make sure I looked after myself. I heard nothing from the hospital due to the pressure they were under from the lockdown. It was almost three months before I had my first appointment and I had to attend that alone. My entire recovery took well over a year.

I wish there was a support system in place at the hospital providing continuity of care and the potential of contact with others who had experienced the same situation. I did my own research and joined various support pages. I felt alone and it was only when I found a fourth-degree tear Facebook page and reached out to these women that I began to understand that there were others out there. My biggest saviour was hearing other women's experiences and using their knowledge for my treatment. The other women on social media were my saving grace - allowing me to feel less alone at times where I was completely alone in hospital.

Being in lockdown allowed me the time I needed to heal and grieve the changes my life was facing once I was home. It allowed me to have the privacy I needed at home. What it didn't allow me to have, was my life and love with me throughout the experience. My husband and newborn daughter were all I needed by my side but I was denied that. In all the times I thought I was going to die in hospital, all I could think was that it would happen when I was alone, I would never get the chance to grow old with my husband or see my daughter grow and live her life. For all the hospital appointments, for all the surgery, for all the post-op days - I was left completely alone and scared.

> Everything I went through was uncomfortable
> Everything I went through was lonely
> Everything I went through was hard
> Everything I went through was exhausting
> Everything I went through was uncertain
> But having my daughter was breath-taking
> Having my daughter was special
> Having my daughter was wonderful
> Having my daughter was selfless

Dimple Mistry, 34, from Hertfordshire, lives with her husband and two-year-old daughter, Isla. She works full-time as a video verification editor at a national newspaper and in her spare time loves taking pictures of delicious food to post on her Instagram.
@girleatsw0rld

EMMELINE BAGLEY

I know I am so lucky; you are a happy, healthy, sociable little girl and we have so many other photos. Things could have been so much worse and, of course, they were for many. But when I think of that missing photo it makes me sad.

The 'leaving hospital' picture, the one in the entrance, proud parents holding the car seat, excited and terrified to be starting the journey home. I imagine the ward staff waving them off just out of shot, maybe a proud grandparent taking the photo.

We didn't have that. We had dark, cold, midnight and the back entrance of the hospital. You and I were helped into the lift by a health care assistant, down to where your daddy was waiting with the car, impatient to see you for the first time since he had to leave just a couple of hours after you were born.

The only other people around were two police officers restraining a man wearing a spit hood.

May 2020. Welcome to the outside world.

That missing photo reminds me of what we went through. The extra anxiety, the isolated walks and the food left on the doorstep. There were no visitors on the ward. I went through three days of induction on my own, the midwife looking shocked when it failed and I let out two months' worth of bottled up anxiety and tears. Then, I was on my own with you on the ward, post C-section haze, unable to move properly and terrified of going to sleep. New mothers all around; all of us alone. Desperate to go home.

There were no tiny newborn cuddles with grandparents, and when we eventually dared to risk it you gazed up at faces in masks. Each time I worried it would be the risk I'd regret taking forever.

You met all our friends from two metres away. If only we'd lived on Downing Street we could have passed you around with the cheese and wine.

Maternity leave was spent walking in all weather, sometimes on our own, sometimes with another lockdown mum and baby. You were wrapped up and oblivious to the alternate world where we were sitting in a warm coffee shop. I got really good at breastfeeding while sitting on the ground in a windy park and you got used to having your nappy changed in the pram or the boot of the car.

The memories are getting more and more distant. Sometimes we talk incredulously about the steps we took to stay safe, or someone asks if we did any baby groups and it takes me a minute to remember why we didn't. Mostly we just say *thank goodness for you*, because how would we have coped with lockdown without your tiny presence to keep us going?

Just occasionally, though, I see someone's 'leaving hospital' picture and remember what we missed.

Emmeline Bagley, 41, from East Sussex, lives with her husband and three-year old daughter. She is an Occupational Therapist and works in mental health.

HAYLEY ANDERSON

There's an elusive intimacy, connection and support that dwells in the spaces between mama baby groups, visitors, cafes and fearless physical closeness. A special social bond that fuses people together in early mothering. I notice it in the lives of those becoming mothers now and I see it so clearly because I was denied it so definitely. For a long time I was hyper-vigilant seeing groups of new parents meeting up without fear, as if it posed some sort of threat to me. That is lessening over time but the grief of missing that myself still flows.

I find myself thinking a lot about how I can't get that first important year or my maternity leave back again. I can't 'do over' the care, support and connection that should happen in those early, tender times. I can't magic it back or recreate it now. Gosh, I have really tried, though! Something is lost. There's a gaping hole in my experience of becoming a mother. A hole that should have been filled with hugs, helping hands, kind words, friendly faces and cups of tea made for me; where arms and hands were free to touch.

I thought I'd had a false start in motherhood. It felt like I was left stuck at the blocks for that first year. Once restrictions lifted, I was still unable to move, stuck in a learned behaviour that had taught me that isolation is just how motherhood is. I'd become way too good at coping and doing it all alone. Coming out of lockdown, I was a frazzled, self-reliant, hyper-independent robot mother. I worry that lockdown taught me how to mother without support too well. I worry it disconnected my impulse to reach out and believe that help is there.

I have spent a lot of time and energy connecting the lack of support and care through that first year with many of the challenges I face now as a mother. Lockdown and it's after effects still impact my ability to form and maintain connections I can rely on for support. My social mother muscles are still learning what to do and the story of being unsupported and isolated lingers in my present day experience.

Lockdown impacted how my family bonded with my daughter, it placed a burden on my partnership and gave me a bumpy start to motherhood.

I don't like how my continual blaming of lockdown makes me sound like I'm blaming the world out there instead of owning and healing from my experience. Yet, it is true that I *was* a victim of lockdown. Postpartum is one of the most vulnerable times of our lives where we need support and a community around us. It is healthy for me to keep looping back to talk about it and if I'm traumatized, as someone who had just had their first baby, then that is understandable. Getting through lockdown with a new baby was pure survival. Until recently, I rejected the labels 'lockdown baby' and 'COVID mum,' but now I find myself welcoming them in with open arms. I want it known and understood. It helps me claim my experience as real, valid and something that fundamentally shaped who I am.

Nausea sways in my stomach when I think of times locked down as a new mum. When it began she was five weeks old. Despite all the trauma-release work and talking therapy I have invested in privately, what happened still impacts me today and how I navigate mothering and relationships.

At first, I welcomed the prolonged cocoon with my baby. My attention on her meant I wasn't consumed with pandemic realities out there. I didn't follow the news. It was bliss for a time. There was immense relief at no longer trying to publicly breastfeed a colic-y baby. People told me of the online course they were doing, the garden project they could finally do, the amazing TV series they were binging... I couldn't relate to any of it because caring for my baby was my lockdown reality. I did baby every day and every night. Baby, baby, baby. On we went each day between bed, sofa and garden... Out for a walk at nap times and back to the sofa and bed.

I leaned into my little love and practised soaking in the small things: the smell of her head, her sweet little suckles as she slept, her soft, wispy hair, first giggles and tiny hands and feet. Her body was always close to mine and that was an immense comfort. We were afforded the luxury of constant touch with one another and so we remained as one for closer and longer than we might have done in a world operating 'business as usual.' That was our gift, amongst the harshness of it all: uncomplicated, uninterrupted time together.

I remember our daily nap walks so well; seeing the same trees every day and noticing the tiny signs of the long, changing seasons. I carried with me that familiar lockdown feeling of both total wholeness and total loneliness all at once as I walked around with my precious babe on my chest. Every day I craved company along the same lonely lanes. It changed me.

One particular nap walk stuck in my mind. An older woman was coming the other way, I looked up at her and thought, 'she's probably a mother, she will get it, she will see me. Maybe she'll even say hi and acknowledge this inhumane madness.' But she didn't give me the slightest nod of acknowledgement. Instead, a quick glance and a wide berth, circling at least a full three metres around me. I felt empty, in a moment of such desperate longing for someone to *see* me, to hold me against all the odds and all the rules.

I was denied the six-week check-up, mama baby groups, health visitor home visits and family visits. I remember the relationships that were ruptured during the pressure of the whole thing, the bubbles I tried to form that got formed elsewhere. It seemed there wasn't many people who wanted a baby as part of their lockdown experience. We, of course, had no choice but to dive into baby life head first.

Two months into lockdown and I had almost entirely stopped sleeping. I gave up on trying to get back to sleep through the night. I couldn't. So I survived lockdown days on 3-4 hours of sleep. Time blurred and high levels of anxiety set in. He was struggling because I was struggling and I just couldn't find myself in it all. My inability to cope or sleep or be calm was ever-present and the isolated pressure started to build in our home. A new scary edge appeared inside me alongside a belief that I was a terrible mother who was doing *every single thing* wrong. I had become a big ball of anxiety, despair, rage and grief. I developed a compulsive obsession with the timing and lengths of my daughter's nap times. I planned wake times and sleep times down to the minute. When her sleep didn't match the plan, my world came crashing down and I couldn't cope. I would be beside myself over one imperfect nap. I see now how I attempted to create a perfect structure to avoid facing the difficulty of my everyday reality. I coped through each sleep-deprived day by ticking off each perfect nap we achieved.

I did endless nap walks and worked every day to try to keep the tumbling, spiraling thoughts of self-doubt and despair at bay. These naptime coping mechanisms, accompanied by a constant stream of bolstering voice notes from friends, guided meditations and breathwork kept daily panic attacks at bay. I was somehow managing with strict structures and routines, but I wasn't well.

Something in me broke during that first year. I was like a rope pulled too tight for too long, snapping one thread at a time until I was thin and worn. Not being seen as someone struggling was deeply painful for me. There was just no one there to see how bad things had become.

One sleepless night, I left the house in total despair. I walked the quiet, empty, dark roads alone and wondered where I should take my lost self. I didn't want to go back home but where could I go? Where do I take the enormous task of surviving this unrelenting beast of a time? It all felt too big for me. For a split second, I imagined handing myself in at the police station for being so utterly lost inside, for being an awful mother and for being too weak to cope. This was my scariest lockdown moment by far. I wanted it all over. I believed my baby would be better off without me and I was desperate for some instant relief from the weight and responsibility of it all.

I see now how going to that edge in myself awakened something new in me. After rejecting the police station idea, I ran back to my lockdown nest to find her tiny face still sleeping sweetly. Her smell enveloped my heart and welcomed me back to doing my best. I wept on the floor and got back to it.

Spontaneous, exhausted sobbing became the new normal. When I'm really run down I tend to get styes on my eyes, usually only one at a time. During lockdown, I had three huge styes on my eyes that weren't going away. I was a picture of stress. During a telephone appointment with my GP he asked me how often I was crying. I said 3-5 times a day.

Humans evolved to bring up children in villages - not on our own for months at a time under social restrictions. My body simply wasn't equipped for the reality of lockdown with a baby.

During another sleepless night, I was messaging a good friend who was also awake. It turned out we were both living out lockdown unhappily. She arrived at our house the next day and we formed a 'bubble' for three months.

She helped with the babe like a lockdown angel who enabled my return to a place of coping. It still wasn't easy for me beyond this point but that marked in the sand where it went from survival mode to manageable and, sometimes, even enjoyable. My story is proof that in-person connection and support is an essential basic need for new mothers. It is all I needed and it scares me to think what could've happened to us if we hadn't formed that bubble. I believe it saved me and our little family from breaking beyond repair. A friendly face, a listening ear, another set of arms for the babe, a friend in the kitchen to see that somewhere, beneath the demands of isolated mothering, I was, in fact, still there.

It was locked-down life that shaped the new mother I was and the mother I am now. I worry about this but I've also come to see and feel the power of it. Growing into my role as Mother in isolation was a unique and momentous shaping that was also inhumane, brutal and ruthless.

I have carried with me an unshifting sense of a chapter missing from my journey into motherhood; a gap in my experience, a space I cannot fill, needs that can't be met in hindsight. There was a giant loss sitting in the backdrop of those locked-down mothering days and it was there for so long after, too. Somewhere along the way, I noticed this giant loss and I learned to tend to it. I welcome it in now as an honoured guest. I want to sit in close and listen to its stories and I write something of them here now. Because, it taught me how to be with loss and loneliness, with the expected or denied. I know now that grief can be a friend who lives so close to love. I know that rage and depression are a part of grief and I've learnt how to move through them, how to scream into pillows and weep into rivers, to move it and shake it and dance it all out. It taught me how to mother slowly and in my own way. I learnt how to love myself and my daughter through moments, upon moments, upon moments and more. This giant loss reminds me to ask for help. That it's OK to be broken, to not be able to cope or to feel overwhelmed mothering alone. We know now, this giant loss and I, that the mother in me was shaped by an unrelenting storm. Like any young tree thrust around by the harshest of weather, I sent thicker, stronger roots down deeper than I otherwise would have. Whatever struggle I have and whatever life presents, I know I can draw love and strength from these giant mother roots.

Hayley Anderson, 39 from South Devon lives with her partner and their three-year-old daughter. She is a stay-at-home mama, working part-time as a birth story listener, sensory herbalist and natural family planning educator. Her work guides women towards healthy fertility cycles and matriarchal post-birth experiences and offers a held space for birth stories to be witnessed and honoured for the power and significance they carry. You will find Hayley tending her medicinal herb garden in the company of bumblebees or cycling her daughter anywhere and everywhere in all west country weathers!
*@_hayley__anderson_*

RACHEL GALE

Oh, hello. I'm not sure anyone that hasn't lived through a worldwide pandemic with a very small human to look after will ever fully understand this, but I'd like to give it a shot. So, here is the inside of my brain, on paper, talking about my experience of being a new mum in lockdown.

I had a baby, Clementine, in October 2019. She's really cute and all but I had a tough end to my pregnancy, a pretty horrendous delivery and ended up being treated for PTSD, post-natal depression and post-natal anxiety. Clementine was also diagnosed with a severe milk allergy, leading to her inability to feed well. So, that was all fun.

So, I had this beautiful little mini-me, and then? A bloody pandemic happened. Right? Mad. We all know that this was an utterly bonkers time to be living and that as grown-ups, parents, caregivers, employers and employees, we had to adapt like never before. Boris Johnson stood at his little perch and told us not to leave our houses or be in contact with any other humans. We entered a lockdown, for what would be, what? Days? Weeks? Wrong, MONTHS. (Apart from Bojo who continued to have lovely parties, but that's not the point here.)

Now, what I would never do is undermine anyone's experience of having a baby between March 2020 and, well... now. I think that came with a huge number of challenges and you're all bloody heroes. Those who had to juggle homeschooling or working from home with children... Bloody hell, no wonder we're still a bit broken and knackered from it. You're all super-parents and I have so much respect to you for surviving this time. But, I wanted to talk about the 'forgotten babies.'

The babies that were born in 2019, those babies (and mums) that initially had their 'village' to support them in the early days, they had their baby groups, their bounce and rhymes, their music classes, their exercise classes, y'know... all that jazz. Not to mention a bunch of family and friends who were always desperate to help out because babies are flipping cute! Then, suddenly, they were stranded on their little island with no one.

Those living alone were allowed to bubble, those with slightly younger babies were allowed to bubble, but not you.

The newborn stage comes with loads of challenges but at that point, I had my village and even some 'me' time every now and then. I could meet a friend for a coffee when I needed a time out from full-time mumming. But then the babies get bigger; they start rolling, sitting, crawling, climbing and developing their own little personalities (Clementine is a sass queen and I love her so much for it but my goodness it's hard work!) They need to learn to wean, but your support from your health visitor isn't there anymore, your mum friends can't see you in real life so can't offer support in the same way, they can't watch the baby for five minutes whilst you go and have a little cry in the toilet or take the baby for a quick stroll around the park whilst you gather your thoughts or calm down. They learn to walk; they learn to run. They learn that there is something outside of just hanging out in a living room with their mum, singing wheels on the bus 400 times daily. They want to be outside, with people – we all do. But they can't be.

They want to be on the go, all the time, their brains are developing and need constant stimulation, not to mention they need to see other children and learn to develop relationships. You're at home, you're one person. You can't give it to them. They can't see their families. They cry when they see their grandparents in real life because they're not on a screen and that's their new normal. It's bloody heartbreaking. Clementine cried some mornings when I put her down, she had never been like that before. She cried when I put her in her pram when we were out because she was desperate to run around in a park, but they were closed. She cried when I fed her because she is a fussy eater and there were no weaning/nutritional support groups to help with this and the NHS is buggered so they don't have time for us. She cried, I cried, we all cried.

This was not the time we expected with our children. I broke the rules and bubbled before it was allowed. So rebellious, but frankly, without my mum, I think I would have had a breakdown.

Know what else I did? I went out TWICE a day. Wild, right? I took Clementine for a walk and then I went for a run, by myself. Absolute rebel. Lock her in jail and throw away the key. I spent a lot of time feeling angry, REALLY angry about how lockdown went for new mums and I still feel like I defend myself even now, whilst seeing the impact that this strange time had on my daughter. She's in speech therapy now, probably because she wasn't exposed to conversation in a normal way. The saddest thing? When we were eventually able to meet people, Clementine was terrified of men. So scared, she would just sit and cry. I guess she hadn't seen any men, aside from her dad, for some really important months of her development.

This generation of children had a very strange start to their lives and I hope that there will be no lasting impact on them, but my god, SO DID THEIR PARENTS. I am still cross, I still feel as though I missed out on my daughter's important start to life, on a maternity leave that I spent growing into my new role as Mum. But, most importantly, I'm still sad and angry for my daughter, and I wanted to share that with you all.

Rachel Gale lives with her husband, cat, and three-year-old daughter, Clementine. Aside from being a mum, Rachel also works full time as a bookshop manager, helps run big book festivals, and even has her own book instagram page @mummyreadswithclementine. Books and motherhood are two of Rachel's biggest passions so combining the two into a piece about motherhood was important to her. Unsurprisingly, during her downtime, she can often be found with her nose in a book... with a large cup of coffee (or glass of wine).

KAYLEIGH STANNARD

On the 23rd of March,
'Stay at home,' he said.
34 weeks pregnant,
many tears were shed.
Pregnant women vulnerable,
nothing made sense,
watching the news every day,
sat in suspense.

Scared for our lives,
my baby and me,
a life-changing moment,
two to become three.
I needed a hug,
I needed my mum,
But who knew when
that time would come?

Your due day approached,
I wanted you here,
a mix of excitement
and a little fear.
The world seemed safer
with you inside,
so much uncertainty,
waiting for you to arrive.
Appointments and scans
on my own,
concerns about your growth,
a fear of birthing alone.

On the 16th April,
'Just three more weeks,'
we stayed at home
practising hypnobirthing techniques.
Meetings on Zoom,
this felt abnormal,
little did we know
this would be our 'new normal.'

A time of excitement
filled with concern,

from woman to mother,
with a lot to learn.
Every announcement a blow,
with no end in sight,
you kept me going,
my guiding light.

The 29th of April,
the day you were born,
the best day of life,
a new baby to adore.
Just hours later,
Daddy had to leave,
unable to stay,
after all we'd achieved.

Mustn't leave the room,
the ward just us,
no family to visit,
Nor make a fuss.
I lay with you,
tried to get some rest,
I smelled your head
laid upon my chest.
Kangaroo cuddles,
I scrolled on my phone,
navigating this new life,
my new role, alone.

This was just the beginning,
little did we know,
no family around us
to watch you grow.
We stood outside,
the Thursday clap,
rainbows in the windows,
hours on WhatsApp.
They say it takes a village,
That wasn't to be.
All we wanted
was for you to meet family.

My girl gang, my mamas,
you understood,

when no one else
ever really could.
New mum, post-partum,
you helped me through,
I hope you know
I'm grateful to you.

I'll tell the tale,
of COVID-19,
introducing my baby
via a screen.
It's not how I imagined
this time would be,
grateful for the memories,
you, Daddy and me.
A time the world stood still,
no end in sight,
in the midst of darkness:
my love, my light.

Kayleigh Stannard, 34, is originally from West Sussex but has relocated to Solihull where she lives with her fiancé, three-year-old Jaxon and little brother Zachary. She is a self-proclaimed foodie with a passion for health and wellness, leading to a career as a Registered Nutritional Therapist. She is a family girl, who enjoys travel, yoga and music, with a love for Glastonbury festival. Whatever the weather, you will always find her under a fluffy blanket! @naturallyyou_nutrition

VICTORIA NICHOLLS

This wasn't how it was supposed to be.

I wanted to be a mum for as long as I can remember and after two years of trying it was finally my time. I was so excited and had all these ideas of what the first year with my baby would be like. Friends and family visiting, baby classes, going out for coffee and lunch, family days out, holidays... then COVID happened.

I went into hospital the day that lockdown was announced in the UK. I spent six hours in triage, alone, due to concerns about my son's heart rate. At one point, the emergency alarm was pulled. Doctors and nurses seemed to come from everywhere. People buzzed around me doing various things as I lay there crying, thinking I was going to be rushed into theatre to have my baby while my husband sat in the car park. There was one nurse whose only job at the time seemed to be to hold my hand and try to console me.

Thankfully, they managed to stabilise my son's heart rate and although I still ended up having an emergency C-section, it was a couple of days later and his dad was present. We were fortunate, being so early into the lockdown, that once I was transferred to the labour ward they allowed my husband to stay with me and I wasn't made to wear a mask.

Leaving hospital was surreal. The corridors were empty and there were security guards at every entrance. It had been reported on the news that someone had died from COVID at our hospital. I couldn't get out of there quick enough. Driving home, the roads were eerily quiet.

The reality of lockdown hit me when we came home to an empty house – no balloons or banners and no family to greet us. My parents met their new grandson through the window, my in-laws met him via Zoom and my niece and nephew stood on the doorstep, desperate to get a closer glimpse of their new cousin, whilst my brother and sister-in-law urged them to keep well back. We have no photos of our son during the first few months of his life with anyone other than us.

The thing I found hardest to deal with was having no professional support. My son was only 5lb 9oz when he was born and I was recovering from a C-section. We saw a midwife in a deserted clinic when my son was a few days old for his first and only weigh-in and heel-prick test. At the same time, the midwife checked my wound but that was the only time either of us were seen. Thereafter, it was impersonal phone calls with faceless people who sounded like they were reading a script. They didn't know me and I didn't know them. There was no rapport between us and I could have told them anything as nothing was ever followed up or checked.

My husband ended up buying a set of baby weighing scales on the internet just so we could monitor our son's weight and check that he was gaining because no one else seemed to be interested. No one checked whether I was coping OK or needed anything. There was no reassurance or support. I still struggle to understand why midwives and health visitors stopped seeing new mums and their babies. If doctors, nurses and paramedics could wear PPE and see people - why were we forgotten?

The baby blues hit within the first few days of being home, as they usually do for new mums. I was tired, sore, worried he wouldn't thrive, worried I wasn't a good enough mum as well as being worried about a global pandemic and the possibility of us and our loved ones getting sick, or worse. Other than my husband, who was also still trying to learn what being a parent entailed, I had no one there to help or reassure me. My mum and friends did the best they could and were always at the other end of the phone, but it wasn't the same and wasn't what I had envisaged.

I talked to my mum numerous times a day, sometimes fretting, sometimes wanting advice and sometimes just crying. She would listen to me cry, tell me to get it out of my system and try to soothe me. It shouldn't have been over the phone. At that moment, even though I was a grown woman and now a mum myself, I needed my mum. I needed a cuddle and looking after.

When my son was about 2.5 weeks old I got a chest infection. I was beside myself worrying that I had somehow caught COVID and was going to pass it on to my baby, even though I hadn't left the house. I couldn't get a doctor's appointment but was sent to a hub about 20 minutes away from where I live. The only problem was, I had a massive wound across my stomach meaning I couldn't drive and by this point my husband was back at work. Thankfully, he was in a job that enabled him to work from home and had an understanding boss which meant he was still able to help when he could. I don't know what I would have done had he been a key worker. There were times I couldn't even hold our son because I felt so rough or couldn't get my breath properly.

I had never been a particularly anxious person but it is definitely something that appeared quickly during lockdown, particularly health anxiety, and is something that continues to affect me today. I was petrified of one of us catching COVID. I truly believed that if I caught it I would die. I would think, *I've waited all this time to become a mum and now I'm going to catch this and will never see him grow up.* Every time my husband so much as cleared his throat he got the Spanish Inquisition from me about whether he was feeling OK. Even to this day, whenever my son is unwell, I worry and become anxious about it. Some people might say that's just what being a mum is like, but I believe the pandemic and being locked in a house with no outside support exacerbated this.

After a couple of months of being at home, I still hadn't left the house. Even though I was sick of being stuck indoors and we were allowed to have an hour of exercise a day, I couldn't face it. I was too scared. My husband did all the shopping in between working and looking after us. I was neurotic every time he went out, telling him to be careful and nagging him to wash and anti-bac his hands the minute he walked through the door and to not go near our son until he had done so. I did eventually summon up the courage to go out walking with my son in the pram and that became my daily routine – pounding the pavements and walking around the local park just to get out of the house.

When I was pregnant, all my friends that were already mums spoke about going to baby classes, going for coffee afterwards and making new friends. One friend told me that getting out of the house and speaking to other adults is what kept her sane. That didn't exist for me. I tried to do baby sensory classes online, rummaging around the house looking for foil and lights and tying ribbons to the inside of an umbrella to try and stimulate my son's senses. I was worried that lockdown would affect him and his development because at such a young age he was missing out on so much. I paid to attend classes to learn about weaning because all the resources that should have been available to me via the health visitor and local clinic no longer were.

I always knew that I would have to return to work at the end of my maternity leave and that my son would have to go to nursery. I also knew that there were waiting lists for nurseries so when my son was only about three months old I started looking into places for him. Due to lockdown, all the nurseries were closed and I was unable to go and visit any of them, but all were telling me they had limited spaces and waiting lists for when I was due to return to work. How can any parent be expected to choose where to leave their baby for ten hours a day, without seeing the environment they were going to be in, or meeting the people who would be looking after them? But that's what we had to do. When the day arrived for him to start, we weren't allowed into the nursery to drop him off. We just had to hand him over at the front door – my 11-month-old who had only been with his dad and I since he was born just got handed over to someone he didn't know on a doorstep. It broke my heart.

The lockdown rules impacted nursery quite a lot. Every time a child got a temperature they had to get a PCR test. Have you ever tried holding a one-year-old and sticking a swab up their nose? I can still remember how he screamed. It was awful and traumatic for all involved. One afternoon, before the vaccinations had been introduced, I got a phone call from the nursery telling me that three members of their staff had tested positive and to come and collect my son because they were closing. I burst into tears. I was petrified that my son was going to get ill. The rules at the time were that my son had to isolate and I watched him like a hawk, continuously taking his temperature, much to his annoyance!

At the end of 2020, we had a slight glimmer of hope in the shape of a normal Christmas. I clung on to that with everything I had. I was desperate for my son's first Christmas to be normal and to be able to make some proper family memories. That was cruelly taken away from us just a couple of days before. I was devastated and sobbed for hours following the announcement. It also caused family arguments, the effect of which is still felt today.

There are so many negatives to lockdown but there was one big positive, which I am grateful for. Working from home meant my husband got to spend far more time with our son than he would have done had he been in the office. Although we couldn't go anywhere or do anything, we had our own little bubble. We had no one to help us so we had to fathom things out ourselves. I won't lie, it was bloody hard, and at times being stuck in a house together for months on end with a baby really tested our relationship! But, we got through it.

I understand why lockdown had to happen, but things should have been handled differently for new mums and their babies. It is only with hindsight that I realise just how much it impacted my mental health. I felt exhausted, overwhelmed, scared and isolated. I will always be angry about the lack of support and help I had as a new mum, especially from healthcare professionals. I will always be sad about the things we missed out on. We'll never be able to get those moments back and the memories of those early weeks and months will always be tinged with sadness and fear. But, there's also a little piece of me that's proud. I did it. There were days where I felt like we would be living in lockdown forever, but I survived. My husband and I navigated those early days, weeks and months of parenthood without any of the support we should have had, but we got there. We now have a happy, cheeky, clever, loving little boy who thankfully will never remember the chaos that was going on in the world when he was born.

Victoria Nicholls, 38, from Essex, lives with her husband Richard and three-year-old son, James. She works part-time as a paralegal at a London law firm. In her spare time, she enjoys reading, shopping and spending time with her family.

REBECCA SAYCE

E,

Today I saw you for the first time. I must admit, I was terrified, but that's not uncommon any more. For the past two months, I have been at the forefront of the pandemic as a journalist, delivering the news in excruciating detail for all those eager for updates. It's been impossible to switch off and embrace blissful ignorance as the world comes crashing down around us. Every day is bright red breaking banners and a rush to file copy with a snappy headline delivering yet more worrying updates. But you, you have been a little glimmer of hope through all of the darkness. A baked bean-sized miracle. Some breaking news that doesn't fill me with dread. You won't know what a pandemic is - and why should you? But with the way things are unfolding, I'm sure it will become a common part of your vocabulary. First words - mom, dad, dog, and COVID. Your father had to wait outside while I started at the ceiling, praying to see the flickering of your heartbeat. And there you were, in all of your embryonic glory. Our future. I'm sure he will see you soon. I hope he will see you soon.

Love, M.

*

E,

It was wonderful to see you again today. You looked very different from the last time I saw you floating around on the big screen like the weirdest film I had ever watched. You have four limbs now, a bulbous head (just like your father, but don't tell him that) and a strong, thumping heart that echoed around the room. The sonographer told me when I could expect you to arrive - just in time for Christmas! And what a present you will be. Your father had to wait outside again. He didn't want to, I promise, but this is how the world is right now. Lonely. Fractured. Broken. We haven't seen your grandparents or your aunts and uncles in three months now. We miss them so much. They can't wait to meet you either, whenever that will be. This milestone made everything feel that much more real. Twelve weeks. It feels safer to start buying clothes and toys ready for your arrival, it's heartbreaking that we can't do that anywhere but online right now. I have looked forward to browsing the shelves for your essentials, now reduced to the click of a mouse while the country is at a standstill.

Love, M.

*

E,

I felt you wriggle for the first time today. It's fabulous to know you are doing well. I can't wait until we can share these moments with your father. He has missed out on so much already. He's never seen you dance in the darkness of my womb on the hospital screens, never heard the medical jargon that tells us everything about you, never had to stare at the pastel walls and pamphlets opening you up to a world of breastfeeding, gestational diabetes and episiotomies. Don't look up the last one, trust me. As we get closer each and every day, I worry that he feels a gulf grow between the two of you. On a lighter note, all of this time in lockdown has meant we have made so much progress on your nursery. You're going to love it. It's my favourite colour and your father built all of the furniture. Things like this bring us closer together when there is so much division in the world. It brings us closer to you.

Love, M.

*

E,

Today, I met our midwife for the first time. Well, our fourth midwife, to be exact. The pandemic has meant healthcare services have been brought to their knees and it isn't just service users suffering. But don't worry, you will be safe in her hands during the coming months, if it even is her hands, but let's not focus on that. The constant changing of hands has been unbearable. Speaking of hands, I felt the touch of someone other than your father today for the first time in five months. The midwife felt my bump to see how you are growing. And I flinched. It brought a tear to my eye - will you ever experience the power of a handshake? The joy of hugging a friend? See a stranger's whole face and not just their eyes? The midwife told me she's unsure whether your father will be present for the duration of your birth and that shattered us both. The idea of him missing even a second of your arrival fills me with fear and dread. I have never done this before and I need support. We both will.

Love, M

*

E,

The news is out! You are a girl. We are having a daughter. Your father finally got to see you - that was him sobbing loudly as you popped up in front of us, I'm sure you heard even through litres of amniotic fluid. Everything feels so much more real. We know your name. I feel like I know what you will look like. A carbon copy of me, with brunette bangs just like Matilda. Or maybe you'll be the spitting image of your father. I've never been good at predicting these things. With so much promise for the future comes the crippling realisation of our reality. It has been six months since we entered this 'new normal,' whatever normal means anymore. As each hour passes, I feel the world I once knew slipping further and further away, and I mourn the future I wished you'd have. Will you have to walk to your lessons at school while maintaining a metre distance from your friends? Will you ever see a classroom or will learning from home still be in place? So many uncertainties and so much worry.

Love, M

*

E,

I'm sure you heard lots of strange voices today. Lockdown restrictions have started to ease, which means we have been able to see our family - your family - outside, at a distance. It took all of our self-restraint not to run across the garden and embrace them in the tightest bear hug, but we have to keep you safe. And not just you. Family friends, colleagues and people we grew up with and loved are no longer with us. Gone in the blink of an eye after falling to the pandemic. As if there wasn't enough to worry about in pregnancy already - what I'm eating, counting your kicks, studying discharge - I'm now ever-paranoid about the slightest cough or temperature. But, today was magical. I will never take for granted the laugh of a loved one, a corny joke or an anecdote we've heard over a thousand times. These moments are so precious and it took this pandemic for me to truly see the value of these things we are so lucky to experience. I can't wait for you to experience them, too.

Love, M

*

E,

We're three-quarters of the way there now... But we're back under lock and key. The only thing with more twists and turns than pregnancy are the decisions our government makes. We had to cancel your baby shower. No big pastel-coloured cake. No precious moments with loved ones feeling you wriggle. No cheesy party games. But, we still celebrated you. The most fantastic thing to come out of this terrible time is the way it has brought people together against all odds. Friends and family across the globe have found ways to maintain their relationships even when they can't see each other face to face. We took your party online. I hope you loved the quiz and everyone's guesses about your birth. I hope the 10lb birth weight guess isn't right! Soon, we will find out. In a weird way, though this is never what we planned, your party felt so special. Despite everything happening in the world, the people in our lives took the time to celebrate this glimmer of good news on the horizon. That is love, right there. And what's more, there won't be many who can say they have had a party like yours, that's for sure.

Love, M

*

E,

Today was the final straw. With the constant unpredictability of care and the toing and froing on whether your father will be able to be present when you enter this world, we made the final push to birth you at home. That's right, you'll be born in the place you will be raised with your furry and feathery brothers and sisters. Throughout lockdown we've seen a rise in home births and I'm sure hospital restrictions have a part to play. Mothers left to experience contractions alone. Fathers left in the dark as their child is born. Long nights caring for a newborn with only a brief window for visitors. Home birth is something we had considered from the moment we saw those two blue lines, but the pandemic has solidified our decision to welcome you in the comfort of our abode. We have experienced pushback. We heard the words 'high risk,' 'transfer,' 'lack of progression' and eventually 'induction' over and over, but we know what is right for us. For you. The strain on hospitals due to the pandemic is shocking, and we feel more comfortable staying in the place we've spent so much time in during lockdown. We have your birth pool ready to go - I wonder if you'll love the water as much as I do. The birth affirmations are on the bookcase. An apothecary of essential oils lay in wait in the corner. It's just a waiting game now. And we have little time left.

Love, M

*

E,

Today I said goodbye to the newsroom. For the last time. Not just for the 365 days I had planned. The pandemic has taken so much away from people, jobs being a common loss for many. While it opens up a world of opportunities, the fear I feel has manifested into a lead weight in my chest. What if there is no work for me after you arrive? What if I'm out of the game too long and no one wants me? What if news never recovers from the dreaded C-word? It's a world of unknowns, much like the journey we are on. Though, right now, it doesn't feel like there is a miracle at the end.

Love, M.

*

E,

Come on now, girly. I'll keep this short and sweet. Your eviction notice has been served. You've kept us waiting a week over your expected due date and quite frankly this fashionably late malarkey is becoming tiresome. I imagined the start of maternity leave would be full of crafts, household chores and naps. But lockdown has meant we have had a lot of free time on our hands. We have rearranged your nursery eight times, tidied the kitchen four times and considered cleaning the loft twice. Your time is up, little miss. We're getting bored!

Love, M.

*

E,

My darling E. This will be my last letter to you. You are here and you are more perfect than we ever could have imagined. Ten fingers, ten toes, beautiful blue eyes and that enormous head we've joked about since you were just a jellybean. You barrelled into this world after three long days of labour - you sure know how to make a dramatic entrance - in the pool in our living room. Your father helped deliver you into the world, with the midwives of course, and cut your cord as you roared into the night. We locked eyes under the sparkling fairy lights and the dread and disorder of the last nine months melted away. While the world may be in complete disarray outside, as I lay on our sofa while you enjoyed your first feed, ours felt complete. You were a product of chaos but you've brought a calm and content to our lives that we never knew existed. I never would have imagined a love so fierce and raw could be born from a time of such despair, and here you are. The future is still so uncertain. While the world begins to feel like it once did, I feel forever changed by our experience of the pandemic. Can we ever truly live with COVID? Only time will tell. Whatever the future holds, it feels a lot brighter with you around. Our E. Our Edith.

Love, M

*

E,

It has been two years since our last correspondence. I said my last letter would be exactly that, but recent developments in our lives implored me to write to you again. It has been a wild 730 days. So many firsts - first words, first laugh, first steps. So many tears of joy and despair in the hazy, early days of little sleep. So much laughter as your fiery personality has grown. You have blossomed from the most inquisitive little newborn into a sassy, intelligent, loving, hilarious toddler that brightens every single room you enter. But that's not all. You're a big sister now. I write this letter as I watch your newborn sister sleep, and I can hear you snoring away next door. As I listen to her heavy breathing as she slumbers, I can't help but be reminded of you at the same age and compare you both. I feel angry for how your newborn days unfolded. For everything that was taken away from you, time that you, and we, will never get back. When I first wrote to you, I was trying my hardest to see the bright side of our situation, to remain positive and make the best of a bad batch. But after my pregnancy with your sister, I am furious. Today we had friends and family gather to meet your sister for the first time. For you, it was four months before you could meet our loved ones. Yesterday, we went to the farm and ate some breakfast together and next week we will go to play group. For you, we were housebound. We didn't get to grab a coffee with other moms on maternity leave after sensory play. You didn't get to interact with children your own age. I am back to work again. I'm glad the worries I shared with you never came to fruition. Every day, a new revelation of how the government handled COVID comes to light. I feel consumed with rage over how your life was shaped by the fickle attitudes of those who will never know you exist, or care, for that matter. Precious time with those who love you that we can never make up. Chances to aid your social development that we have no idea what the effects will be. We have already met children terrified of others after being kept inside for so long during lockdown, and I wonder if that will trickle down to you, despite you being so young. Your father could attend every scan and appointment for your sister, whereas he missed so much with you. You would never know that now, with how close you both are - two peas in a pod - but it shatters my heart to remember how excluded he felt in those early months. And we were lucky. Lucky that you were born at home and we were not subject to the stringent hospital restrictions that traumatised so many parents through the pandemic. I'm angry for you, and everything you lost, but I am angry for them, too. For every pregnancy touched by the pandemic. For the first-time moms who had to navigate this terrifying time in isolation. For those screaming for their partner as they crossed their fingers and toes that they had reached 4cm so they didn't have to labour alone anymore. For those told, 'I'm sorry, there's no heartbeat,' while alone. We were failed. You were failed. While you are a happy and content child - and always have been, you really are sunshine incarnate - it does not change the fact that the pandemic cost you, and all those born alongside you, so much. And for that, I will always mourn. But I hope, dearly, we have learned from this time and take the little glimmers of happiness that arose. The days of uninterrupted bonding time as a new family, the lack of outside pressure to present you to the world, time to catch my bearings and get to grips with this dramatic life change. These are the things I cling onto as I watch you grow. The unique chance to have been so fully enveloped in your early days. Can we ever truly live with COVID? Even now, two years on, we do not know. But one thing I do know is the future feels a lot brighter with you - and your sister - around.

Love, M

Rebecca Sayce, 28, is a freelance journalist from Wolverhampton specialising in film and TV, particularly horror. She lives with her husband and two daughters, two-and-a-half-year-old Edith and seven-month-old Winona, not to mention their menagerie of dogs, parrots, and chickens. When she isn't keeping the family in check, you can find Rebecca tending to her plants, inside or outdoors, or dancing round the house to noughties emo.

KIMBERLEY CORNWELL

It still feels like yesterday, your warm skin on mine,
9th Feb 2021, 6:49am was the time.
I looked at your face, then froze for a minute,
I can't believe you're here; we actually made it!

Wheeled out of theatre; your dad beaming with pride
But not allowed to stay, I could tell it hurt him inside,
A kiss on our forehead then ushered to go home,
Just you and me, boy, we're now all alone.

With medics in masks, hand sanitiser on display,
No visitors allowed, yet we had to stay.
I tried to enjoy the moments of just us two,
But couldn't shake a feeling, could it have been baby blues?

Back at home, everyone couldn't wait to meet you,
Are we all prepared? Masks, sanitisers and tissue!
See, having a baby is a hard thing to do,
But imagine throwing in a pandemic, too!

Appointments were restricted to patients only,
What should have felt exciting, instead, felt lonely.
Scan photos to show you were real,
Government restrictions without a care for how we'd feel.

Yet, while they all partied, we tried to protect,
One thing that was rising: mental health neglect.
Postnatal depression, something I'd suffered,
My baby needed me, yet I needed to be mothered.

So, inside our little bubble, my mother came to stay,
My father made us our meals while your daddy worked away.
A knock at the door, our health visitor arrived,
Julie, her name, doing her job with pride.

She took care of us both and checked everything was fine,
She said it would get easier, it would just take some time.
I listened to her words, oh, she was so very right
I started to relax and enjoy motherhood, I could finally see the light.

Now two years on, life back as we once knew.
Although hard, together we got through.

My lockdown baby, side by side.
Conceived and born, through the COVID pandemic, we survived.

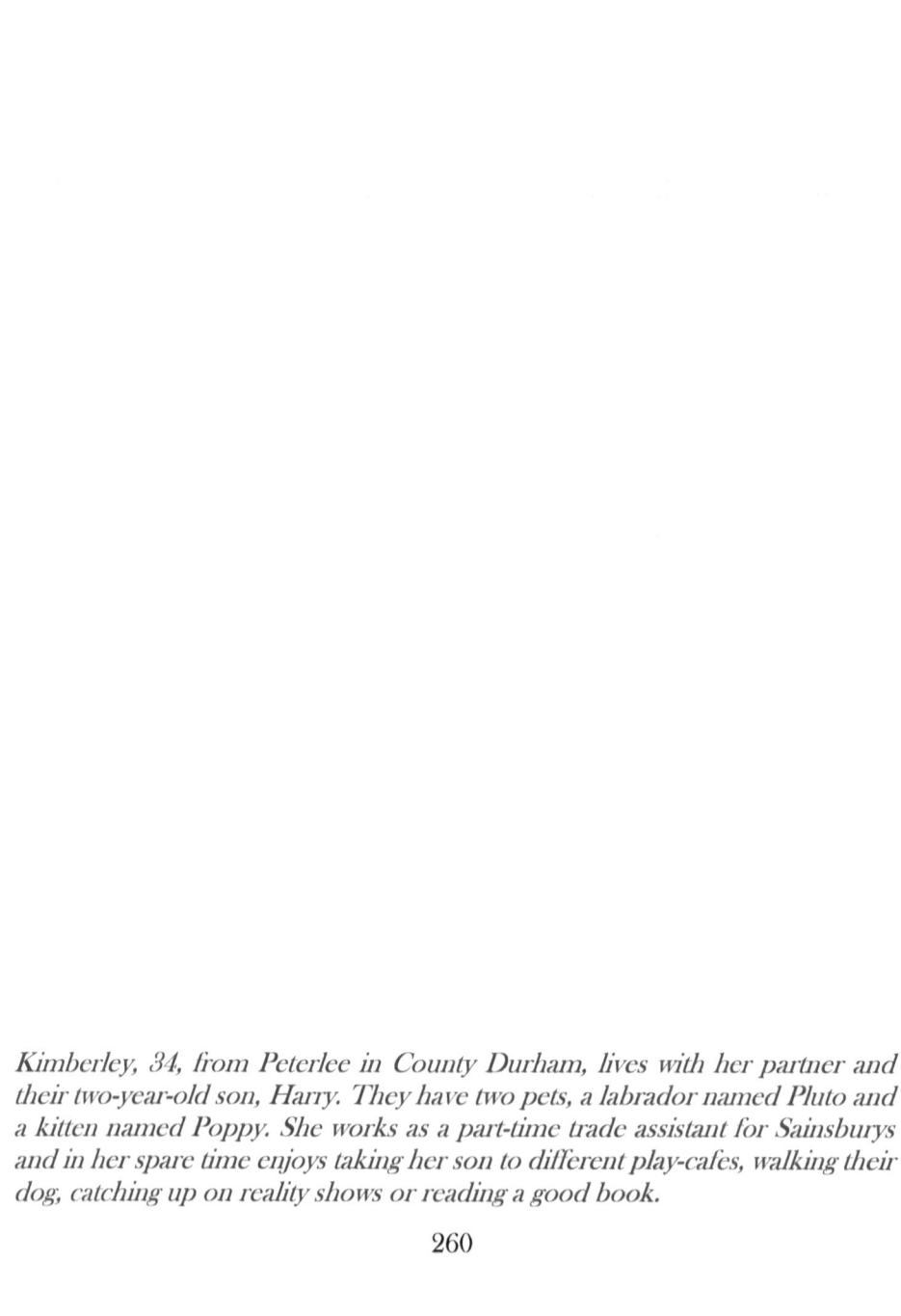

Kimberley, 34, from Peterlee in County Durham, lives with her partner and their two-year-old son, Harry. They have two pets, a labrador named Pluto and a kitten named Poppy. She works as a part-time trade assistant for Sainsburys and in her spare time enjoys taking her son to different play-cafes, walking their dog, catching up on reality shows or reading a good book.

TONI GREENWAY

Bubble

Happy times once again
My baby in my arms surrounded by friends
Family come and share the love
This beautiful gift given from above.
Stop
Stay away
Stop
No more help
No more shared joy
Just a window to look through and pray.
Pray for the day I can hug again
Pray for the day I can share my beautiful baby
Not be afraid for someone to touch her.
Not be afraid of losing a life.
Just a toddler, a baby, Daddy and me.
Our own bubble filled with love and glee.
But a sad Nan, Aunt, Uncle, Grandad, left behind
Going out of their minds.
When will she hug her granddaughter?
Will she know her face, her voice away from the screen?
When can we burst this bubble and love once more?
Not wave and talk from behind a door!
When will she see a smiling face, not a blue mask?
See another baby, meet another mum and laugh.
Just needing to escape and have that support, love, a friend.
The unknown, when will this bubble end?

Will my little birdie be okay?
Know how to interact and play?
Will she cry when someone else gives her a hug?
Will she die from this unknown bug?
Outside our own bubble
Will it cause her so much trouble?

A first birthday and Christmas all alone.
Only wishes through a phone
Hurry up and burst and let her see
That there's more to life than her sister, Dad and me!

Toni Greenway, 35, from Hayes, lives with her husband, Adam, their six-year-old daughter, Lois, three-year-old daughter, Robyn, and the newest addition, son Alfie, nine months old. She works part-time as a Primary School teacher. Any free time she does get, you'll find her playing netball or socialising with her fabulous friends.

HAYLEY CARNE

I had always sat on the fence and was somewhat ambivalent when I thought about having a baby. I enjoyed my life and had everything I thought I wanted; amazing friends and family, hobbies, holidays and day trips filling my spare time outside of a job I enjoyed. But, your dad was definitely keen to be a dad and when I really thought about it I decided that as I didn't have any strong reasons *not* to have a baby, I was happy to see what happened and if things didn't happen for us then that would be OK. Being in my mid-thirties by this point I was also aware that nothing was guaranteed and my time to be a mum may have already passed.

After almost a year of people (some, I knew and others, strangers) greeting me with their baby bumps, I was referred for an ultrasound to check everything was OK. Unbeknown to me, but spotted quickly by the sonographer, was the tiny bundle of cells that would grow and develop over the next few months into you, my precious little daughter. At that moment everything seemed to stop. I drove to work alone, in silence, processing what I had just been told before sharing the news with anyone, even your dad. This was now happening and what we had been trying for was, all being well, actually going to happen.

Carrying you with me everywhere I went and feeling you wriggle around was a feeling I will never forget and will always cherish. It was a time when you and I were inseparable and I had you all to myself and I loved it, though I could have done without your feet being wedged up under my ribs in the evenings when I wanted to recline in comfort! It was probably the first time in my life that I felt completely comfortable with my body and was amazed by what it was doing all on its own without any training or instruction. It was making a new person, it was making you.

Anyone who knows me knows that I am a planner and I like to be prepared. After researching and planning for a home water birth, booking the birthing pool, arranging the 36-week midwife home visit and following the hypnobirthing techniques I had studied, my waters broke on the morning we hit the 34-week mark in February 2020. Little did I know that from this point on, so much of what was to come was not going to be what I expected. I didn't get the water birth or home birth that I had desperately wanted but I brought you safely into the world and for me, that was the most important part.

You were taken to the neonatal ward for some additional care. Your dad went with you, and I was looked after by the midwives who provided the notorious jam on toast seemingly given to all women after giving birth in the UK. The midwife and I were chatting about anything and everything and she mentioned that the staff were all due to have their mask fit testing that afternoon in case 'that coronavirus' that we had been seeing on the news, causing lockdowns and spreading across other parts of the world, came to the UK. What happened only a matter of weeks later was still a surprise to us all.

You spent the next two weeks in the neonatal unit whilst your dad and I shuttled back and forth from home. We would spend all day with you whilst you were still developing the ability to maintain your body temperature or to breastfeed. We lived on sandwiches and snacks at the hospital before coming home and starting the night shift where I would wake every three hours to express breastmilk to give you in your feeding tube the following day. Even for such a short period of time (in the grand scheme of things) this was emotionally draining and going home without our baby every day was not what I expected.

You were finally discharged from hospital under the care of the outreach team. You could finally meet your grandparents who had been unable to visit you whilst you were in hospital.

Whilst I hadn't had the start to maternity leave that I had planned and essentially left work one Friday and didn't return for many months, I felt as if we had weathered a minor storm and were now able to start looking forward to our new life as a family of three. Sadly, as will be written about for many years to come, 2020 was anything but normal and became more about survival.

The coronavirus that *might* come to the UK that I chatted breezily with my midwife about in my postpartum haze, was here and it was running wild in the community. We went into lockdown when you were only seven weeks old. The number of predicted deaths from COVID seemed unbelievable and completely surreal, like the storyline from a film. The eventual toll of the pandemic would be felt by everyone, some of whom will be forever bonded, and others forever torn apart.

Overnight, everything we knew had changed and we were living in near-total isolation from everyone, in a new world different from what anyone had ever contemplated or experienced before. Looking back now, only a few years down the line, it doesn't feel like it really happened and at the same time, it is still such a raw and painful time to remember.

I had never felt so alone, overwhelmed and isolated. I had you, my beautiful daughter, who I adored more than anything and I had your dad, but all the support from family and friends evaporated instantly. As every three weeks passed and we watched yet another update about the restrictions placed upon us, the hopes of anything like the maternity leave that I had expected to have, began to disappear.

They are right when they say 'It takes a village to raise a child,' and after missing our NCT classes due to your unexpected early arrival, I certainly felt like we were the sole inhabitants of an island trying to make it through each day (and what felt like the never-ending nights.)

I did meet a group of five other new mums as part of an online community group (which had originally been planned for face-to-face activities) and to those mums I will forever be grateful for being my 'people' and for helping to get me through those tough times. Our 24-hour WhatsApp group was a lifeline for me as I navigated some of those early weeks and months of having a newborn. So much has passed, but the emotions make it feel like it happened only yesterday. I am not sure many mums who experienced reduced antenatal care, birth restrictions, the postpartum period or raising a child in the pandemic have begun to process their emotions yet.

All of the 'firsts' were experienced with just the three of us, or with grandparents and other family members viewing through a screen or at a distance. The first time you rolled over, your first laugh, your first tooth, your first steps, our first Mother's Day, your first Christmas and your first birthday were all experienced away from our families and friends. We followed the rules, whether these applied to the whole of the UK or the part of the UK we lived in. It didn't matter how ludicrous or non-sensical some of them were, we followed them to protect people and prevent the spread of the disease. Ultimately, as time would reveal, the rules were only for 'the little people,' as those in government who made those rules partied throughout lockdowns with flagrant disregard for anyone else and what they were losing and sacrificing by obeying the rules. The visceral anger I feel towards those people is something I won't ever forget or accept.

The grief of what I hoped for and expected to experience in comparison to what I got during the pandemic is something I have certainly not fully come to terms with. I know I didn't have it as bad as some other people (which I have been reminded of on numerous occasions) but I am learning that my feelings are valid and knowing that others had it worse than you does not discredit how you felt.

Even now, when I see pregnant bellies and new mums, I feel happy for them to be having a baby outside of a pandemic but also a deep sense of sadness and jealousy for what I won't get again. My time for having another baby has likely passed. I am not ready and if I ever get to the point where I might be ready then age and the extortionate cost of childcare in the UK would likely be prohibitive.

Whatever you think when reading this, I don't want you to think that everything was negative and that it was all a complete disaster day in and day out. Yes, sometimes I would cry when out walking alone, clocking up my 10km a day because there was nothing else to do with my time. There were no coffee dates, lunch dates, baby classes, swimming lessons, play dates or other village-building activities. I certainly sobbed when I handed you over on your first day at nursery to a stranger in the car park as we weren't allowed to go inside or help you settle in, despite you having barely been out of our arms for the first year of your life. Our weekly trip to the supermarket was as sociable as some of those pandemic months got. But, I had you, the most important person in my life and it was you who gave me the purpose, motivation and incentive to keep going through those long and seemingly never-ending days and nights.

From that teeny cluster of cells to the tiny baby in the neonatal unit, to the little mini-me you are now. You have brought more love into my life than I can express and, for you, I will always be grateful. I am a mum because of you and although I may not always be the best, I promise I will always try my best for you. As we say every night before you go to bed, I love you *this* much and *that* much and nothing will ever stop me from loving you.

To all the other lockdown mums, a collective of women who experienced such monumental uncertainty, challenges and change during those COVID years, we will forever be bonded. We survived through unprecedented times which were certainly not what I expected.

Hayley Carne, 41, from Welwyn Garden City lives with her husband and three-year-old daughter, Mia. She is a lecturer in Veterinary Nursing, who plans one day to finally commit and get a family dog (but isn't quite there yet). In her spare time, she trains in Olympic weightlifting whilst trying to get through her long podcast playlist, drinks far too much tea and can't commit to watching anything beyond 9pm as she will undoubtedly fall asleep.

NICOLE FOX

Daddy first saw you
At 12 weeks and who knew
That would be the last time
He would be by my side

All future appointments would be on my own
A mask over my mouth and nose
Taking my temperature each time
Making sure I did obey and abide

Fearing birthing alone, wanting James by my side
Despite my anxiety, this was to be denied
Calling up private hospitals just to see
If they would allow James there, we couldn't afford the fees

From March 2020, working from home
No one saw me pregnant or watched my belly grow
Virtual baby showers, no parties for me
To keep you safe was the most important thing

Trips to the supermarket and so many walks
Oh my gosh, please make it stop
Essential shops only, such utter crap
What a way to ensure that we all felt trapped

Booked our babymoons and ready to go
Oh wait, they're all cancelled, we've never felt so low
Unable to celebrate our last days as two
Before we welcomed you

We wanted to celebrate you, my dear little one
From wanting two babies, we became one-and-done
It was so hard to raise you, and we never thought it would be
But that's what a pandemic did, it nearly killed me

Those worries and the stress
When you moved slightly less
Alone and sitting strapped to the machine
Hoping to hear your speedy heartbeat

I breathed a sigh of relief when I heard it, though
Despite feeling terribly alone

Filled with anxiety, sadness and uncertainty
The happiest time in my life, this should be

I had a contraction, I definitely felt that!
All alone, panicking, I made sure James packed the bag
We had to drop Baxter off to Mum's
And focus on you, my dear little one

It was not long until I entered the birth centre
Alone, of course, what's new? I surrender
Contractions one after another
They checked me and soon I would be a mother

James joined and we went up to the room
Eight hours later, you joined us, I was over the moon
I couldn't believe after everything we'd been through
You were finally here and I didn't know what to do

When I looked down at you
I knew it was true
Love at first sight
Despite my plight

Alone, afraid and isolated
When we should have been celebrated
Growing a small baby
Without the village or family

But right then and there
As I held you when bare
I felt so much fright
To care for you alone for the night

James went home
All on his own
And left me be
With the little baby

Postpartum was harder than I thought it would be
No one to visit, talk to or see
I'll never forget how low I felt
No help to deal with the cards I was dealt

I felt so low trying to be the best mummy

To the best little baby who would look up to me
I would cry and all of the time
Think about ending the pain and taking my life

No one to talk to or to offload my pain
I wasn't sure I would be able to be me again
You were there, my little one, I had to pull through
And be the mummy you deserved, the only one you knew

In the future, I would be known as a lockdown mother
Little did I know there would be so many others
All those restrictions during the pandemic
Inside my mind, will forever stick

I cannot believe I went through what I did
We really tried our best, I'm telling you, kid
Your mummy and daddy, we really love you so
Coming through COVID like we did, we are the unsung heroes

Nicole Fox, 32, is a CBCD - Canadian-born confused Desi - born in Canada to Indian parents but never actually lived in India. She lives with her husband, almost three-year-old and their dog. Nicole used to work as a City of London banker but has taken time out from the relentless rat race to focus on herself and her family. When she is not tackling the never-ending to-do list or experiencing a night of broken sleep, Nicole can be found in front of the TV bingeing her favourite shows.

CLAIRE UNWIN

2020 will forever go down as the year that totally flipped the world on its head in so many beautiful and fucked up ways. At the start of the year, I was in the third year of a relationship and thinking about nothing but weekends, holidays and CrossFit. By the end of it, I was pregnant, single and living alone during a global pandemic. Three years on, as I write this, I'm still full of disbelief that so much happened in one year. Everyone has a defining moment and, for me, this year was full of them.

When the first lockdown restrictions came into play it was a welcome change. As a marketing lead accustomed to remote working, I could now undertake this full-time and finally get on top of the washing. I think a lot of people were guilty of being naïve in those first stages and seeing the situation as a novelty. I remember not grasping the situation in full or understanding the gravity of COVID-19 until the first lockdown got extended and the government started announcing health warnings and regulations. My boyfriend and I had been together for nearly three years at this point and had lived separately. Once the rules on bubbles and visits became stricter we decided to take the plunge and move in together. Never at this point were we discussing the future or becoming parents.

As we moved through the months we soon realised that our relationship wasn't cut out for the long term. Living together had exposed cracks and highlighted our incompatibility. You will always truly learn who someone is when living with them. In September, I had a 'funny spell' one night and found myself dizzy and propped up against the toilet bowl. I instinctively knew something was amiss and the next day I took a pregnancy test. I was faced with two blue lines and the role of motherhood opened up before me. I had always wanted children but knew I wanted them in a secure family setting. Despite the seemingly good news, my partner packed his things and moved back in with his mother. I was one month pregnant, working full-time and now left with the task of emptying and moving out of the three-bedroom house we had shared. The pregnancy and parenthood to follow would be unassisted, as the father of my child cut all communication from us and made his intentions clear - he wasn't going to support us. At the time I couldn't focus on the heartbreak of the split, let alone process the thought of him not being present in his future child's life. I had to compartmentalise and focus on getting myself set up again from scratch.

Thankfully, I had a good support network who helped me move into my current home, however, I never anticipated just how lonely the rest of my pregnancy would be. On top of processing a breakup and the abandonment by my ex, I was now living alone, trying to get my head around becoming a mum whilst faced with the uncertainty of lockdown rules. From the offset, for all midwife appointments, hospital visits or emergency scans it was just me, myself and I. This amplified my anxiety and feelings of abandonment. It was so incredibly lonely attending what should have been an exciting occasion on my own, and then having to share that news with friends and family via WhatsApp.

On one occasion, I had to go to the hospital for an emergency scan, as Little Miss had stopped rocking the boat as usual. I sat in the waiting area: a cold, lifeless room full of expecting mothers with masks on, distanced at two metres apart. There was no casual chat or asking others how far along they were. Instead, it felt like a room to be processed. No partners were allowed access to the obstetrics ward and had to sit separately in another room. Walking in, you'd be faced with partners embracing and kissing. "Call me as soon as you're finished." This made me feel sad that I didn't have a partner to share this scary moment with or confide in, followed by immense sadness for the partners who did want to be there but couldn't be. The pandemic restrictions were taking away connections to the unborn child and the opportunity to bond.

Once I'd been admitted onto the ward, I got tied up to the heart rate monitor machine and commenced the hour-long process of laying around while Little Miss got monitored. I tried to get comfortable and regulate myself but I kept having moments of overwhelm. Whenever there was a moment I felt panicked, I'd see a spike on the machine. Right in front of my eyes, I was witnessing the direct impact my stress was having on my unborn daughter. A physical manifestation of the stress and weight I had been carrying alone throughout the pregnancy. I decided there and then that I needed to be stronger for her.

Looking back, I feel almost resentful at the opportunities missed to share my pregnancy with others and to saviour my last few months child-free. I know we're not supposed to say that and don't get me wrong, I adore my daughter – but, during the biggest hardship I have ever faced I was having to navigate lockdown rules and could not reach out to my friends. I needed the chance to talk this over face-to-face. I needed therapy to help process the abandonment by my ex. My pregnancy felt tainted with carrying the weight of everything by myself.

When I had Harper in the hospital I had to stay in for a few nights because of issues with her feeding. As any new mum will tell you, this newborn period is intense and riddled with anxiety. All I wanted was my mum with me to show me how to feed my baby for the first time and to give me the bit of respite I needed, so that I had more energy to put towards learning to breastfeed. Instead, visitor restrictions meant a lot of time was spent alone on the ward, in a confused haze and full of aches from labour. I feel lucky my mum could visit, even though for only two hours a day, but I had to take the opportunity to prioritise sleep over emotional support.

I am aware that if I had Harper earlier then there would have been a lot more restrictions. It brings me to tears thinking of the mothers who had to go through labour and birth separate from their partners. I feel lucky that my journey to motherhood wasn't robbed of a birth partner, but I still felt robbed of meaningful connection and support. During the abandonment by my partner, I have never before had to tackle such hardship. This was exacerbated by virtual midwife calls and lone visits to hospital. Confirming the gender of my baby, alone. Receiving the positive news that everything was OK, alone. It's a time to be nurtured and cared for, but I was truly alone.

You look back and see that this shapes you and I believe on some level this shaped me to be a more resilient and independent parent. What happened wasn't within my control. Harper will read about the pandemic when she's older and undoubtedly ask about what life was like, and I'll tell her, *"Babe, it was absolutely batshit, but we are who we are today because of it."*

I am forever grateful for the friends who supported me from afar. Going through this challenging period alone only highlighted who truly has my corner, and I am bloody lucky to have so many great people in my life.

Harper wouldn't be here if it wasn't for COVID, plain and simple. Yes, maybe I would've gone on to have another child in an alternate timeline, but I believe my daughter was the result of a perfect blend of extraordinary circumstances. I'll forever be proud of how we've tackled the world together. It was, and continues to be, a challenging journey. You're my stars and moon, Harper June, and I'm proud of us x

Claire Unwin, 33, from Chesterfield is an independent mama who currently lives with her two-year-old daughter, Harper June, and rascal cat Chai Bean. She works part-time as a Marketing Manager for her local hospice and in her spare time likes to introduce her daughter to the great outdoors and make the best of being on the doorstep of the great Peak District. In her downtime, she likes to work out and drink Yorkshire tea.

ALEX RANDLE

Quack and *Duck* were your first words. You knew their sounds and faces better than family.

Eyes glinted at you from two metres away, distant 'hello's muffled through masks, gloved hands waved and everything smelled of sanitiser.

The sofa swallowed me whole. I missed the scaffolding of mother love being erected around the bare bones of my body. I slumped. The poles would stem from my ancestors, made up of other exhausted mums. These would be bolted together with honesty, cups of tea and belly-aching laughter. I felt so lonely, yet I was never alone.

We found all we needed in each other's gaze. I'd lose myself between your lashes, diving deep into your mahogany marble eyes during and between feeds. Your podgy fingers clasped my necklace tight, tugged my earrings and grasped my bottom lip - and with that, you opened a magical portal. Our hearts enveloped each other and we created the most wonderful cocoon.

Our cocoon lifted us from the sofa and transported us to the pond. All by the power of cheeky grins, muddy palms and make-believe. You gave me the gift of life during lockdown. Our cocoon sustained me.

The cocoon we built is indestructible. I am not sure I ever want to leave it. Some day - you will.

Alex Randle, 34, lives in Hoddesdon with 15-month-old Tomilola, 3.5-year-old Gbemi, husband, and long-suffering smooth collie, Drax. Managing cross-sector school partnerships 9-5 and managing a hectic home life 5-9 (am and pm) leaves some wiggle room for long dog walks and cross stitch. Passionate about improving education for all, reading and writing.
Twitter: WaysWith_ Words
Instagram: @a_s_randle

SARAH PEGRAM

"It'll be over by the time she comes,"
They say.
Just keep positive and don't get swept away
by the news and the worry and the constant sanitising of everything.
It will be okay.

I kiss your daddy goodbye and shuffle to reception.
Now my back is turned, my eyes fill with tears.
The crushing, heaving weight as I let out a sob.
I never imagined I'd be alone here.
The receptionist says, "It'll be okay," from behind her mask.
Nothing about this is okay.
I have to be brave
The bravest I've ever been.

Message my family to say I'm alright,
hiding behind a picture of hospital dinner.
I don't want them to worry
but panic builds inside me as I hear screams
and agony from the cubicle next to me.
I can't do this.

It's the eighteenth of June and your daddy arrives at 4am.
He is my safe space.
This is my favourite part.
For a while, it's almost... normal?
The world and the fucking virus
just stops
as I laugh between contractions
and the excitement builds.
I can't wait to meet you,
my little one.

The hours pass and my body starts to lag.
Nine centimetres.
I'm pushing through the agony,
praying you'll arrive any second so we can go home with Daddy.
You're stuck in my pelvis and everything becomes a blur.
Doctors and nurses rushing,
"I'm sorry," I whimper,
knowing surgery means
separation.

We hear your cry
and there you are, my darling,
all pasty and squidgy and magic,
a mop of dark hair just like mine.
I've never fallen in love so hard.

The rush of you is interrupted as my body goes cold
and I can feel my life draining away.
I keep my eyes fixed on you,
snug in your daddy's arms,
telling myself not to fall asleep.
I have to be brave
The bravest I've ever been.

I guess they'd call it a success,
Mother and baby alive,
but they wheel us away to a room all alone
and your daddy has to go home.
Every hour feels like eternity as you cry in the cot next to me.
It breaks my heart as I frantically press the buzzer
over and over and over
and forever later someone in a mask and gloves and apron
finally appears and puts you in my arms
and I swear you smile a real smile.

All I can do is study your face,
the dried milk on your chin
and how bright your eyes seem in the dusky light.
Getting lost in you, sweetheart,
is the safest, cosiest place we could be.

Loneliness keeps coming in waves,
too afraid to sleep,
so exhausted I could sleep a year.
There's pain and I can't move alone.
I need your daddy here.
This is not what I imagined,
depression is flooding in
as I stare at these four walls.
We are alone and no one is coming.
I have to be brave
The bravest I've ever been.

Weeks and months pass.
The world outside our flat door still feels dangerous.
As people start to meet and drink and pretend it's all fine,
The sofa is our home
The sofa is safe
Cuddling day and night,
you, milky sweet and content.

I want to share you with the world,
I really do,
but the fear has been drilled into me
and the weight of guilt is crushingly heavy
when I tell them I can't let them touch my baby.
I'm terrified they might kill you.
I have to be brave
The bravest I've ever been.

I wonder if they'll resent me?
First grandchild born and they can't hold
your tiny, precious little body
or breathe you in completely,
but you are my life and soul and heart
and I have to protect you no matter the cost,
or the hurt or the longing or the agony.
I have to be brave
The bravest I've ever been.

Sarah Pegram, 35, lives in Staffordshire with her partner, Matthew, their three-year-old daughter, Lumen, and Enid the cat. The family are patiently awaiting the arrival of baby number two, due January 2024. Sarah is currently a stay-at-home parent and enjoys spending her days adventuring with Lumen. In her spare time, Sarah can be found working on embroidery or crochet projects, usually with a cup of tea nearby (which has gone cold).

RACHAEL FIELD

When I first came to write this piece I knew exactly what I wanted to say and the parts of my story I wanted to focus on. As I let myself go back and relive the experience of pregnancy, birth and postpartum in lockdown, I realised there were things that I hadn't processed or worked through, and some things I was unaware needed to come to the surface. I discovered that I was grieving again, in real-time, as I wrote. My daughter is now two years old but I still feel angry that I spent pretty much the first year of her life isolated and alone.

This is where I'm going to start: the area of my life where I've seen the biggest change and where I feel that lockdown had the biggest impact. This was compounded for me by being in a new town - we moved right before lockdown and finding out we were pregnant - therefore I hadn't even had the chance to build a village before I was told I couldn't have one. In Scotland, our local lockdown began four weeks after my daughter was born in October 2020 and led right up to the Christmas lockdown.

I was coping, and not coping, all on my own. Motherhood is lonely enough without lockdown and so the pandemic amplified that loneliness. I would have given anything for in-person peer support, particularly with breastfeeding, and above all I was so desperate for friends. Friends that understood how I was feeling, friends that would just 'get it.'

Sometimes there are still moments where grief comes knocking. Only one of these friends truly experienced, like myself, the full impact of early motherhood in lockdown and they occasionally send a text about missing the newborn days in cafes when babies slept and you got coffee. I can't help that it makes me sad because I never had that.

We're now expecting our second baby. It's something we've been wanting for a while so, of course, there is excitement and anticipation, but for me, there is also sadness. Thinking about the first time around is a little overwhelming. We were robbed of the first scan together, hearing the heartbeat for the first time together and our daughter meeting her daddy for the first time without being able to fully see his face. I keep thinking about these details as we begin our journey all over again. We will get to have firsts with this pregnancy but they will never take back what we lost. The first of the firsts didn't look the same for us and that still hurts. I remember lying on the bed whilst having my first scan and feeling disconnected from the whole experience, thinking, *this isn't how this is meant to go, where's my husband?*

I sometimes feel like I am walking into the unknown with this pregnancy because I genuinely don't know what to expect. All I've ever known is a pandemic pregnancy. This was one of my coping mechanisms through lockdown. I would tell people, 'At least I don't know any different,' as if that would somehow make it all better. It didn't make it better. I hated the masks at appointments and not being able to see people's faces as I got diagnosis after diagnosis. I hated that my husband had to wait outside for scans and many clinics as I attended alone. I hated that he had to hear the heartbeat for the first time on a WhatsApp voice note. It really hurt.

I had a difficult pregnancy with bad sickness throughout and a third trimester dominated by gestational diabetes, cholestasis and hypertension that developed into pre-eclampsia during labour. My life was dominated by taking pills and twice-weekly clinic visits as well as a short hospital stay at 33 weeks. In some ways, being furloughed made these things easier to deal with and I do have to acknowledge that it was a huge blessing to avoid sick pay or early maternity leave because of that. In writing this, I realise that I became so focused on dealing with the diagnoses and the traumatic birth that I never dealt with how lockdown made me feel and the impact it had. Writing this, and grieving all over again, has been the best thing I could have done. If I hadn't, I might never have realised that I was still holding those feelings so deeply.

I hope, that as this new pregnancy progresses, the times when grief comes knocking become less and the feelings of excitement and joy begin to prevail. I hope that sharing this pregnancy in person with my friends and family doesn't come with a tinge of sadness, and having people who can come and clean my house and hold my baby during the postpartum experience will feel like the biggest relief rather than being overshadowed by anger. I want to heal from this experience, give myself grace and accept that grief usually only gets smaller as we heal, but at the same time, might never go away.

Rachael Field is 32 and lives in East Kilbride, near Glasgow, with her husband, two-and-a-half-year-old daughter, Isla, and soon-to-be Baby 2. She works full-time as a stay-at-home parent and is very interested in the Montessori method and implementing this at home. On the side, she has a very part-time Harris Tweed business and loves to champion small Scottish businesses as well as the Gaelic language. When not in the midst of parenting she is a huge cinephile, avid novel reader and has recently taken up embroidery art.
@fieldnotesbook

SAMMY KATE MAGGS

Best buried

It wasn't the right time to tell our story then, so I buried it.
I hid the facts.
I hid the fear, the tears, the pain.
I showed the world how brave I was, how strong.
But now it's time to dig it up, to tackle it anew,
to explain the story after you were born.

One month in, the usual sleepless nights.
Overdoing things in an attempt to show I was coping. I was fine.
My body had other ideas.

I found myself removed from you.
Taken back to where you took your first breath.
This time alone and bleeding.
Pumping milk in the darkness.
Forced to make painful decisions all by myself.
Given science I didn't understand. I still don't.

Masked faces showing no empathy.
No warm hugs. No warmth.
Quiet corridors and hushed anxieties.
Exchanging breast milk through a cracked door.
Touch forbidden.
A trickled tear falls.

All alone.
Hormones raging. Breasts aching.
Yearning to be back with you.
To smell you, to feel you.
Will you remember me?

Four trips in all. Each with growing restrictions.
Less love. Less care. More science.
And then to make a decision. Alone.
Under the knife again, removing parts of me that made you.
Gone.

And after all that, did they check on me?
Did they ask me how I was?

No.

But then, other people were dying. Losing loved ones. The world in crisis. An inevitable slip to the bottom of the pile.

Praised for being brave.
At least I was alive, I'd say. At least I was back with you.

So, I buried it all.
In the battered capsule of that time.

Sammy Maggs, 38, is from Wales but now lives in Reading with her husband and two sons (five and three years old.) She currently works part-time as a freelance social media manager for a support group for mums and birthing people. She also volunteers at her son's school in their food bank and as a reader. She loves listening to podcasts about parenting and food, usually while nursing a flask of coffee and a pastry!
@sammykate84

ALICE ANN TURNER

Pregnancy in a pandemic is the hardest and loneliest thing I've ever experienced. Being a parent is not something I ever thought I wanted to be. In fact, I spent the majority of my life stating I categorically never wanted kids. I had no desire to ever become a mother at all. To be honest, I quite disliked children.

When my husband and I met in 2016, he felt the same. But then three years down the line, that changed. People often ask what made us change our minds and want to try for a baby and honestly, I don't think either of us could give you an answer to that question. But even if we could, we don't owe anyone that answer - we just did.

After trying to conceive for a short time, on 28th March 2020, just five days after the UK went into lockdown, we found out we were four to five weeks pregnant. We were beyond thrilled, but knowing the journey we were about to take would be completely different to the norm was daunting, to say the least.

Partners were not allowed to attend any antenatal appointments, scans or even be present for the whole of labour. I dreaded the first scan. I think this is a normal feeling for most, with the fear of the unknown as you wait for confirmation of a heartbeat, but COVID meant this had to be faced alone whilst partners sat outside in the car park. What should have been a happy, joy-filled moment was severely dampened. When the time came for our gender scan, I couldn't bear to let my partner miss it, standing in the car park waiting for me to casually tell him whether it was pink or blue like I was picking what flavour crisps I wanted with a meal deal. We opted to get a private scan, where he was allowed to see his baby for the first time and we could receive the news together - albeit £65 for the privilege.

There were some upsides to being pregnant during lockdown. It made the early days easier in terms of 'hiding' our news as it's significantly easier to get away with drinking lemonade from a gin glass without being questioned via Zoom.

I do, however, work for the NHS. This meant for the safety of myself and my baby, I had to make my pregnancy known sooner rather than later for the potential risks to be assessed. As my pregnancy was not considered high-risk until 28 weeks, I carried on working face-to-face with patients throughout the first peak of the pandemic. This, in itself, was strange and anxiety-inducing when so little was known about the effects of COVID on those who were pregnant. Our staffing was low, with many people being moved to wards to care for the rapidly growing number of severely unwell COVID patients. Those that weren't reassigned had caught COVID themselves or had been placed into isolation due to being high-risk. With the new essential accessories of a surgical mask and dry hands from the constant alcohol gel, I gave it my all until that 28-week deadline, when I left my colleagues for the safety of home for the remainder of my pregnancy.

Approaching the third trimester got a little more difficult. I attended hospital three times due to reduced fetal movements, traces of protein and a high heart rate. As a first-time mum, having to attend with these scares alone was exactly that - scary. It was decided that the safest option was to get me booked in for induction at 39+4 weeks. Inductions, much like the rest of my pregnancy, had to be attended alone, with my partner being able to join me once I was in active labour. I was beyond thankful when I was first assessed and my waters could be broken, meaning my partner was able to return almost immediately.

After 10 hours of what seemed like plain sailing labour, things took a turn. I wasn't progressing past seven centimetres and an emergency C-section was proposed. At 11:49 pm on November 24th, Harriet Elizabeth Turner was born. Just six hours later, due to COVID rules, my partner had to leave and I was to be alone with our daughter for the foreseeable future.

Parenting a newborn completely alone, with no visitors allowed even for an hour, was not the way I had anticipated things to be. C-section recovery is harder than I ever imagined, sleep deprivation well and truly kicked my ass, there was the constant lingering thought that I was going to catch COVID by being in the hospital and I was feeling mentally and physically run down. At this point, the thoughts running through my mind were never-ending. *How do I change a nappy? How am I supposed to know why she's crying? Am I holding her right? Have I fed her enough?* With Dad unable to visit, I felt alone, lost, confused and very, very tired. Navigating the first few days of parenthood is tough under any circumstances, even more so single-handedly. Thankfully, the team of staff on the ward made my stay somewhat easier and I will forever be appreciative of that.

Equipped with enough medication to open up my own pharmacy, after four long and uncomfortable days in hospital, we could finally head home. Little did I know just two days later I would be re-admitted with pleural effusion, which would eventually lead to the discovery of peripartum cardiomyopathy - an uncommon form of heart failure that can occur during the last month of pregnancy or up to five months after giving birth. My straightforward pregnancy turned into a whirlwind medical journey that wasn't about to end any time soon. Nor was the pandemic.

Bloods, ECGs, a CT scan, an MRI and an echocardiogram later, my referral to a specialist consultant was looming. *Would I have to attend alone? How do I process this all by myself?* Fortunately, my consultant was warm, friendly and understanding of the importance of not receiving this kind of news alone. Protected with a surgical mask, gown and distance, he kindly allowed my partner into the consulting room with me, something which I will never take for granted.

Maternity leave during lockdown was weird. Weirder than weird. It took six months of my little girl's life for restrictions to be somewhat lifted. Six months before my colleagues - whom I spent every single day with throughout the pregnancy itself - could meet her for the first time.

Whilst I felt grateful for the freedom that the newly lifted restrictions gave us, there was a lingering sadness for what felt like a wasted six months of my daughter's life. With my new diagnosis, the thought was forever in my mind - is this experience going to be the only one of pregnancy that I will ever know? The likelihood is: probably. Health-wise I simply don't know if I can risk another pregnancy. I wouldn't go as far as saying COVID ruined my pregnancy but it certainly has a lot to answer for.

Regardless of everything within the strangest year of my entire life, Harriet, my little girl and my whole world, is safe, healthy and thriving. She has not let the pandemic affect her growth, and neither have I, as we both embark on the journey of parenthood together. She is a bright, strong and very much loved baby of the COVID-19 pandemic.

Alice Ann Turner, 30, lives in South Yorkshire with her husband, Adam, two-year-old daughter, Harriet, and their dog, Percy. She works part-time for the NHS and in her spare time runs her small business, Bolts & Hearts, making quirky acrylic statement earrings, homeware and gifts.
@itsaliceann

HEATHER CORDINER

Pregnant, gosh, that happened quickly!
Eat all the right things, keep healthy, exercise gently.
Read all the books, like 'What to Expect When You're Expecting.'
7 months in... wait, what's this? Pandemic, then comes the messaging:
Don't hug, wash your hands, come to your appointments alone,
Midwives are now just on the phone.
This is not what I was expecting

Getting closer but there's an issue. Scan says baby is too big!
How did that happen? I don't know what I did?
Induction or C-section, I've got to decide on my own,
Masks on doctors, *no your husband can't come, stay at home.*
I don't want to do this by myself
Why are pregnant women being put on the shelf?
This is not what I was expecting

Birth day is here and Dad is allowed,
but only for surgery, a quick hug, then de-gowned.
Bye bye, Daddy,
just you and me now buddy.
Onto a ward, but curtains drawn,
Midwives in masks and left alone 'til morn,
This is not what I was expecting

Tiny baby, he looks like a doll,
Can barely hold him, I can't even roll.
He's crying, hungry, what do I do?
No milk coming from my boob,
Tiny syringes given to me, "for colostrum."
How do I do that? I want my mum!
This is not what I was expecting

Press my buzzer but no one comes,
Then I hear a voice shout, "There's no more midwives on"
They take my food order but I can't get out of bed,
I've eaten my bag of snacks but I want to be fed.
A head pops around, it's a fellow new mum,
"Do you want me to get yours?" "Oh yes please, thanks hun."
This is not what I was expecting

Nobody to talk to, lots of messages on my phone,
but I've never felt so alone,

I want to go home, but what awaits?
The news talks of dying and my heart breaks,
This little man needs me to be tough,
But the next few months are going to be rough.
This is not what I was expecting

Home at last, but no one can visit,
Zoom calls and Skype, but it's not the same, is it?
No classes, no mum's groups, no places to play.
How many times shall we walk around the streets today?
Having a newborn is definitely a struggle,
But it's kind of nice: you, me and Dad in our bubble,
This is not what I was expecting

Nearly three years on and how you've grown,
Thank you for the love you've shown.
I worried that without friends you wouldn't speak,
but quickly you found your voice and cheek.
In a world that was chaos for a while,
You were my light, my calm, my smile.
This is not what I was expecting...
But, is it ever, when you go from *you* to *Mum?*

ANONYMOUS

Deep breath.

I found out I was pregnant for the first time in March 2020, about three weeks before COVID came to England. Even now, writing this sentence makes me sob. There's a lot of grief for what could have been and what was taken away by lockdown restrictions.

I used to check the RCOG website regularly - what could happen to my unborn child if I caught COVID? There weren't answers. In the early days, there were a few incidents from abroad of difficulties in labour and unwell newborns.

I moved my work home; I rested more; I lay out in the sun reading about hypnobirthing; I watched the queues of people snake past our flat waiting to enter the supermarket; I pretended I could see the good things about lockdown impacting my pregnancy. But I was scared. I went to the first scan alone - the sonographer grumpily agreeing to write the sex of my baby on a piece of paper so my partner and I could find out together, later, when I'd walked home from hospital, removed my mask, washed my whole body and changed my clothes. I went to all of the appointments alone. I saw different healthcare practitioners each time. We wanted to tell our families our news in person, but the three-month marker came and went with Boris announcing more restrictions...

We told them on Zoom. This was when you could meet one person outside to exercise. This was when there were cheese and wine parties at Downing Street. I was still studying at a painting school - hardly anyone knew I was pregnant. They only saw me from the neck up via a laptop for months.

I had a relatively 'easy' birth. Routine. Good on paper. But for me, it felt like anything but that. I am just so thankful that the hospital allowed my partner in. It had been a growing concern as the weeks went by, up until my daughter was born on her due date in late October 2020, that I might have to go in alone.

Retrospectively, my contractions began and I hadn't realised. My waters broke, we laughed about it and called the hospital. We went in, as we were told to, even though I knew we'd be sent home as I wasn't really having noticeable contractions. We were directed to triage and stopped by someone.

"Why are you here? Get out," they said to my partner. I was left on my own. I knelt by a chair to steady the growing contractions. Once I'd been checked and was sent home, we set up our lounge. It was late, we employed the candles, music, ball and TENs machine. I called the hospital and they heard me and thought I wasn't far along because I sounded calm. 'Wait another few hours.' After that, I began moaning, leaning on the radiator, feeling like I'd pull it off the wall. I felt like I needed to push. We drove to the hospital and this time were whisked into a birth centre room. I was 8cm dilated. The relief! I wasn't allowed any pain relief other than gas and air because I was too far along. I started pushing. She was born around 10am: 2.67kg.

I know for certain that not being able to talk to other mothers in baby groups about the intense experience of giving birth set me back. I needed to try to process it - not on my own.

We were sent home the same evening. I felt like we were taking up space for others. Staff were overstretched. The birth rooms were in high demand. We were told someone would visit us the next day - an empty promise. I've carried the fact we left so early as a terrible decision that we made as I needed more support, but when I hear how other women were treated in hospitals during the pandemic, how they were left and isolated in sterile environments, I think I got off lightly.

No one came to visit us. On the fourth day, I called the midwives crying. Someone arrived mid-afternoon, rushed and telling us they still had four families to see that day before finishing at 4pm, along with a gruff order that if my daughter didn't start gaining weight I'd be taken back into hospital and she'd be given formula. No support to help me get to grips with breastfeeding. Sleep deprivation took over. Breastfeeding was a struggle. In between trying to feed, change nappies and sleep, I called helplines. My borough is excellent for breastfeeding care but I couldn't drop in and no one could come to see me. It was bad. I spent so long trying to explain what I was and was not doing over the phone to a friendly, faceless voice who kept telling me it was going OK until a key piece of information was shared - my baby never comes off me, feeds are taking up to an hour. I mentioned depression, anxiety and intrusive thoughts. My healthcare visitor, who I only ever saw as a whole person without a mask once, referred me at five weeks postpartum.

The Perinatal Mental Health Team were my life-saver. I spoke to (not in person - just on the phone) a consistent and supportive Clinical Nurse Specialist who then planned my care with two other therapists on a weekly basis. She knew exactly how to help me. My family were also supportive but they couldn't be with me as normal because of lockdown restrictions. It's a haze now but they did come to visit and check on me - fitting around the ever-changing restrictions. My mom wore a mask the first time she held my daughter. The note from my therapist reads: 'She was understandably finding the isolation imposed by COVID-19 restrictions hard and was greatly missing the support from extended family and friends.' We now know that Downing Street were continuing their string of illegal parties around this time when I desperately needed to see friends, family and other new moms but I was stuck inside my flat because of government rules and only allowed out for cold, dull walks.

22nd December was a low point. We were clawing our way to Christmas - desperate to visit family and get some much-needed help. It was our hope at the end of a long, foggy, newborn, PND tunnel. Boris changed the lockdown rules for London and I received a message from a friend - she had COVID - she had looked after our daughter for a few hours whilst me and my partner went out for the first time. A costly 'Spoons meal, it turned out. We had to isolate. We couldn't go to see family. It was almost too much for me to carry. I spent part of Christmas Day in a test centre. The rest of it, my partner carried me through. On Boxing Day we drove to my parents - there was another new rule – 'support bubbles.' My partner packed the car, put my daughter in and locked up as I helplessly did nothing. I cried in the car. I was negative but still hyper-worried about passing on COVID. We went to my parents' house. I couldn't go in. I broke down and cried in the garage, too scared about potentially giving them COVID. We compromised. I went alone in the lounge. My two sisters stood in the garden, looking at me through the window. I felt like I was going mad. Then, film-like timing - I received the text from the test. Negative.

From then until 10th January, I was cocooned with my family. My partner had to return to work. A family member who has two small children met me to chat and give support - it was a freezing, dark evening and because of COVID we had to loop around the streets trudging in the icy snow just so I could hear some warm words. My nan finally met her great-granddaughter at two months old.

The new year. 2021. I started feeling myself more and more. I joined Melodies for Mums - online - and it made a huge, positive impact on me. Seeing 30 plus screens with other moms with PND made me realise I was not on my own. I walked in the cold with one friend at a time - feeling so tired but it made me feel better. In the spring, things began to open up. Baby groups were with masks and no welcoming circles to sit in, just separate, socially-distanced mats. I did my weekly fitness class online from my lounge. My daughter watched, bemused, from her bouncer. I made a note of who I could see - one at a time, of course - for laps of my local park. There were many al fresco nappy changes.

After the summer in 2021, I was discharged from the Perinatal Mental Health Team. I was ready and it felt right. My final session with the incredible Clinical Nurse Specialist was on the 19th October via a screen. The care they gave me was outstanding and it shouldn't be a postcode lottery - every mother should have a robust Perinatal Mental Health Service where they live. I returned to my studio practice one day a week from June 2021. My journal reads: 'I last wrote in October (eight months ago) but it feels like a lifetime ago and I feel like a completely different person but also exactly myself again.'

In January 2022 I took on a new studio space. I lost my original studio in the first lockdown. My art practice shifted into exploring motherhood and my place within that. Art exhibitions I'm selected for give me space to start making sense of what happened when I became a mom in a pandemic. My daughter began nursery - a postponed start date after COVID difficulties. We could go in for a tour but were no longer allowed in for settling-in days. Not a part of the 'new normal' that I liked. I once cried uncontrollably upon leaving the flats of two different friends who had recently had babies. Being around a newborn brought up some deep emotions. In February 2022, we stayed with friends who had just had their second child. This time I felt OK around a newborn. My friend told me how going back to the baby groups now they are normal makes her realise how much we missed out on when doing it around lockdowns. I love being with my daughter now. The COVID months were rough. There's still a lot for me to understand and there's still a lot of anger. I'm grateful for academic research, creative outlets, public surveys to push for systemic change and mothers being honest... There are many things to learn from the past.

KAYLEIGH

Giving birth in a pandemic was the stuff of apocalyptic nightmares. Lonely buildings, sympathetic smiles covered by masks, messages conveyed by eyes alone, solitary walks into the unknown, empty rooms, nervous new mums' voices on the other side of a curtain, emotionally torn midwives and heartbroken dads ushered away from their loves. We got through it, yes, but at what cost?

Becoming a first-time mum in May 2020 deeply changed who I am. I am less sure, less confident, just less... me.

I walked into the hospital alone to be induced, fear rippling through every fibre. A stoic girl, resigned to what was beyond my control, I lay in a room alone while my contractions started. Too afraid to be alone, I ended up in the car park with my husband until my contractions became too painful and I had to return to that room, alone. Hours of pain passed before I rang my bell and begged - *I unashamedly begged* - for my husband to be allowed in.

My beautiful boy arrived and I was whisked off to theatre. We were reunited for 20 minutes before my husband was asked to leave. I silently sobbed as I was wheeled back to my room holding my tiny new baby. One of the masked porters gave me a look that said, 'I hate this, too.' The whole thing was too sad, too painful, yet we couldn't change it. I was powerless.

Here is the poem I wrote before I went into hospital:

I didn't get to dress my bump nice
I didn't get lunches with friends
I can't have my mum at my labour
And there's no sign of when this will end

I won't get baby sensory
I won't get long days in the park
Picnics with the other mums
Reality appears so stark

I won't get to have tea and cake
With the girls or mother-in-law
Filling up lovely cafes
With prams taking up the floor

I won't have bonding time with my mum
Like every new mother needs
I won't get time with friends
To moan about the night feeds

My husband may be sent home

When it comes to the big day
What should be the happiest time
Feels very bleak this way

I worry I'll not love my baby
I worry I'll grow to resent
The feelings this has created
With the way I feel at present

It's kind of unspoken in our British way
With the motto 'Keep calm and carry on'
But it's so hard to remember that
When you don't feel very strong

Kayleigh lives with her husband and son in West Yorkshire. She works as a Security Awareness and Culture Leader in Information Security, loves to write and whiles away the hours playing with her little boy. She's incredibly proud to be included in this project and would love to dedicate her piece to her son, her inspiration.

LAURA FETTES

To my firstborn,
I'm sorry.

I'm sorry you had such a rough start, a horrible birth, feeding issues and parents who didn't know what they were doing. For months after, I had nightmares about your birth, how we could have lost you and what I, as your mother, should have done to protect you. You had hospital appointments the week that lockdown hit and you were robbed of the face-to-face follow-up help that you desperately needed. The help we needed to help you. I'm sorry.

I'm sorry that I didn't recognise that you had reflux. I didn't know the symptoms and the doctors weren't seeing people. It got so bad that you were losing weight before we got you help and I'll always feel guilty for that. You would cry with the anticipation of pain when I would attempt to feed you. The thing which should have comforted you would cause you distress and I didn't know why. I'm sorry.

I'm sorry that I cried so much every day. I couldn't help with your painful tummy and you wouldn't sleep for any length of time. We weren't allowed to see friends, our village existed over Zoom calls and bore no resemblance to what had been promised. I didn't know how to help you and couldn't recognise the slide into postpartum depression. I began to resent your constant cries and neediness. Instead of idolising you, I wanted to avoid you and that will haunt me forever. I'm sorry.

I'm sorry you were robbed of baby groups and social interaction. People will tell you that they are unnecessary and that other generations didn't have them, but I wanted them for you. I wanted you to play with other babies and not be scared of new people. I wanted you to giggle at baby sensory and to relax during baby massage. Instead, I attempted these alone, following YouTube videos, and you continued to be afraid of strangers in masks. I'm sorry.

I'm sorry that you started nursery before you had met a lot of your family. The amazing nursery girls knew how to comfort you before your granny did. I know you won't remember this but you learnt to recognise your family from photos and Zoom calls and they were robbed of your newborn cuteness. I'm sorry.

I'm sorry that I didn't trust my instincts and that I let all the guilt and societal norms dictate how I tried to raise you. The sleep deprivation and PTSD drove my inner monologue and I needed you to conform, to have a schedule, to sleep. I lost hours every week in a dark room, convinced I could teach you to sleep and instead, we both cried. I'm sorry I didn't just embrace the lockdown, cuddle you more and trust that I was all you needed. I'm sorry.

I'm sorry that your dad and I fought so much. I was lonely and felt imprisoned with you in the house. He was working from home, physically so close, but in reality, unavailable. He couldn't understand that your cries painfully pierced my heart and my dreams. That I simultaneously wanted to yell at you to be quiet but also never wanted anyone to berate you in that way. I struggled to bond as you didn't seem to want me the way you wanted him and I fear this time period may have influenced our relationship forever. I'm sorry.

I'm sorry that you came into a world so different to the one your younger brother now has. Residual mask-wearing and partners waiting outside the wards reminded us that maternity restrictions were enforced far longer than restrictions in wider society. Your brother's first months involved family, play dates and baby groups, none of which were afforded to you. Despite it all, you idolise your brother and have embraced our new normal without question. You show us the way with your resilience, your innocence and your happiness, and for that, I'm grateful.

Laura Fettes: proud Irishwoman who conceded to living in Glasgow with her husband and two small boys. She became a mother just before lockdown and now juggles parenthood and working as a scientist. Outside of work she enjoys listening to music, weekly catharsis on the hockey pitch and sharing the good and bad of life with her wonderful friends.

LAURA MARCIANTE

For Erin

The long, dark tunnel is shortening at last
Lockdown will soon be a thing of the past
From month two of pregnancy to month six of your life
We have been burdened with restrictions and unbearable strife

2020 - the year the world became a very different space
But, in October, you arrived and became our happy place
It hasn't all been rosy, those newborn days were tough
Sleepless nights, crying, feeling I wasn't good enough

Maternity leave spent on the sofa or another lonely walk
I long for adult company and some grown-up talk
The bond we have is incredible, an upside of being at home
Wishing for better days when we don't see family through a phone

This strange pandemic lockdown life is all you've come to know
It saddens me that only Daddy and I have seen you grow
They say that things will become a bit more normal soon
Not every day will be spent longing to get out of our living room

You will finally get to meet all the people in our lives who mean so much
It's been a long time coming but soon they'll be close enough to touch
It makes me so excited to get to share you at long last
But part of me is sad that the time spent just you and I will be forever in the past

We made the best of our time at home with lots of cuddles and playing
I know you so well that, even without a voice, I know exactly what you're saying
Your smiles and warm snuggles have helped me through the hardest of days
You're the best thing that's ever happened to me, it's true what everyone says

So now the time is near for me to repay you for these wonderful weeks
I'll ensure that every day your smile fills up your gorgeous wee cheeks
We have lost time to make up for and lots of things to do
I can't wait to take you on playdates and day trips to the zoo

Family and friends and outings, so many places to go
Others will finally get to share the special moments as you grow
I'm going to make these next six months as special as can be

We'll do everything I've told you about but no longer just you and me

I'll miss having all the cuddles and just doing as we please
But I know how much your family can't wait to give you a squeeze
So many precious days to come and memories to be made
I'll always be right with you, my darling, no need to be afraid

New people, places, smells and sights are exciting, but strange, too
We will take it slow at first, I don't want to overwhelm you
I can't wait to show you the world, there's so much beauty to share
I want to teach you everything and show you everywhere

My darling girl, the time is near for you to experience all the joy out there
I'll never forget the time we had alone when the world was in despair
I'll always be right behind you, you can lead the way
I promise to ensure you feel safe, loved and happy every day

Laura Marciante, 36, originally from Scotland, now resides in Hampshire with her husband, their nearly-three-year-old daughter, Erin, and two pet cats. She works four days a week as a Recruitment Manager and thoroughly enjoys her Wednesdays off with Erin, having lots of fun and adventures. In the rare time she has to herself, Laura enjoys meals out with friends, theatre trips to London and music festivals - although these are less frequent than they used to be! A glass of wine and an episode of a good TV show are a little more realistic nowadays.

DEANNE LOGAN

I guided my mum and dad through a lateral flow test in their kitchen so they could hold their five-month-old grandson for the first time. That 30-minute wait felt cruel.

I went into the Tommy's clinic for our six-week supportive scan, alone. Already crying. Already expecting the missed miscarriage like in our previous two pregnancies. My husband in the waiting room.

I baked and baked, until I ran out of ingredients, to quieten the anxious noise in my brain about the 12-week scan the following day. My husband couldn't attend.

Alistair stripped off as soon as he got home from the supermarket whilst I, in gloves and a mask, began washing down all of the shopping with antibacterial wipes.

All I did was walk the dog. Furloughed and pregnant, my days were long and full of nausea.

One of my sisters didn't even see me pregnant. The joy I thought I'd share felt like some hidden secret. Even as I returned to work after being furloughed, for the eight weeks before my maternity leave started, I had to tell people why I was off again soon as they had only seen my head and shoulders on a Teams call.

There was the kind offer of a virtual baby shower. *But what if my baby dies like the previous two?* I didn't want to celebrate too soon.

My husband was at home. We had lunches in the sunshine and the evenings were long. It was like a school summer holiday and, yet, like nothing we'd ever experienced before. We painted the nursery and dried baby clothes in the soft breeze.

My pregnancy was 'high risk,' which meant so many appointments all alone or over the phone. Making huge decisions about my birthing preferences and advocating for myself amidst waves of anxiety.

I studied for a postgraduate qualification whilst pregnant and furloughed. It was inspiring and enabled me to connect with people again. It gave me hope.

I felt pushed into an induction – alone, waiting for labour to progress so my husband could join me.

A shit-show of a birth, two days on a high dependency unit which were blurry, painful and emotional and then onto the postnatal ward with visiting limited to four hours per day.

I felt so alone, abandoned, terrified and exhausted. I was astonished that I had undergone an emergency C-section, had pre-eclampsia, lost two litres of blood, had additional surgery straight after the C-section as they cut my urethra, my blood pressure was still insane, I could barely move and I was still left alone to care for my baby.

I cried and cried during that week in hospital. I was exhausted and in pain. I was so sick of eating baked potatoes. I needed a poo but couldn't go. The afterpains were intense. I needed help. I needed my husband.

I remember sending a lot of texts – "he's perfect," "so grateful," "we're on the mend."

Oh, Deanne, you didn't need to pretend. It was awful. It was hard to enjoy the early days of motherhood when they were clouded with everything that had gone wrong.

Breastfeeding was the only thing I was good at. I only realised this when Isaac was 12 months old. Despite the birth complications and not meeting my son until six hours after he'd been born, we were able to breastfeed. We used nipple shields and topped him up with formula to help his jaundice levels.

What if my baby dies of COVID?
What if my baby stops breathing?
What if he dies and nobody has met him?
What if he dies because I fail him somehow?

Intrusive thoughts filled my days, for months.

Isaac had tongue tie which was missed during a virtual consultation with a breastfeeding specialist. I searched Google to find someone who was doing face-to-face consultations during the pandemic and, once there, she quickly detected tongue tie. We did the procedure there and then – blood, tears (mostly mine) and milk to soothe. It was gently snowing when we left and I wondered if now, at 10 weeks, our feeding journey would improve a little.

Every afternoon, Isaac would nap on my shoulder – nowhere else would do – and once I surrendered into this wonder, I allowed my breathing to match his and watched lots of Netflix. We introduced him to everyone on Zoom. ON

ZOOM. A virtual baby. Almost not real to others, but so very real and wonderful to me.

Despite the pandemic forcing our isolation, I felt like I was failing by not seeing any other humans. So, I joined several online baby classes. I hoped to meet some other mums but the reality was I would often be feeding Isaac or he'd be asleep on my shoulder. Yearning for connection and doing baby sign language to myself.

Postnatal depression consumed me. Postnatal anxiety consumed me. A complaint letter to the hospital triggered both the birth debrief and a referral to the perinatal team. I had such wonderful and consistent support there. I was put on some medication and had weekly calls with the mental health nurse. It was step by step.

The birth debrief was one of the most powerful things I did in those early months. It helped me put words to my experience. It helped me ask the questions I was in no way able to think of or ask at the time of the birth.

We spent nine weeks of my maternity leave in Guernsey with my in-laws in 2021. There was barely any COVID there. Watching from afar and enjoying such freedom was incredible. I felt lucky, yet lonely. We were escaping COVID but I missed my people.

Isaac was my first baby. I didn't know any other way. Lockdown forced us to look inwards, to see and feel ourselves. The awakening of deep anxieties. The beginning of pacing my life. Permission to slow down and rest.

Deanne Logan, 38, from the Midlands, lives with her husband, Alistair, two-year-old Isaac, and cocker spaniel, Ruby. She has her own business, Mulberry & Mint, which provides coaching, mentoring and learning and development consultancy, which she runs part-time, so she has two days a week with Isaac. Her coaching focuses on supporting women through their maternity journey and into motherhood. She is passionate about being in nature and seeks out animals on all of her countryside walks.
@mulberry_and_mint_coaching

HELEN McCLEN

To my first-born,

It wasn't until you were born that I realised how much my own mother sacrificed for me. Little did I know how much we would all sacrifice in the coming days and months.
First child, first grandchild, first niece.
First separation, first lockdown, first pandemic – hopefully, the last.
I carry the guilt of hiding you away from the world,
But also the relief that I knew you were protected.
I carry the guilt that you had no social opportunities,
But the reassurance that you were safe at home.
I carry your red book – empty, incomplete.
No weight chart to look back on. No visits from health visitors. Just the memory of a few phone calls. It must be colic. No, it isn't. It might be eczema. It might not.
Frustrated, helpless, alone.
I carry the memories of walking through the pouring rain to get you to sleep.
The routine broken when we entered another lockdown.
Tired, broken, lonely.
Our support network waiting to reach out.
Furloughed, redundant, separated.
I carry the photographs of you meeting your grandparents through the living room window.
And the guilt that they never experienced those newborn cuddles.
I carry the heartache, the memories, the grief.
And I carry the trauma.
The stress, the depression, the anxiety.
But I'm dealing with it. Never forgotten, but I'm healing.
I'm here and I'm present.
I carry it all for you.
And when you're older and you compare your baby book to your sister's, I'll put on a brave face and I'll tell you about the year you were born.
But inside, I'll feel all the emotion and I'll carry it all so that you don't have to.
Because that's my job now and it's what my mother would have done for me.
My journey into motherhood was not as expected but it will not be overshadowed by the pandemic. Because you, my darling girl, were the best thing to come out of 2020.

Helen McClen, 31, from Newcastle upon Tyne, lives with her husband and two children and works part-time supporting families in the local community.

HANNAH BOYD

One of the things I had looked forward to in pregnancy was being out and about and receiving that knowing look and little smile from other people when they saw my bump that said, 'ah, how lovely.' Wearing a 'baby on board' badge. Feeling special. I thought it was going to be a time when I would feel looked after, that my every whim and desire would be met with an, 'of course!' Because when else can you make extreme demands if not when you are pregnant? Yet, my experience of pregnancy and what was to follow couldn't have been further from the picture I just painted. My reality was the polar opposite.

My first scan at King's College in London was exciting, though I was extremely nervous. I hadn't really wrapped my head around the fact that this was happening and I don't think I'd processed the idea that my husband wasn't going to be allowed in with me. As we approached the doors, we saw that security guards were standing there. It felt a little strong-handed and we were both crushed. My husband had been looking forward to it and to see his face made me feel heartbroken. I had to go in alone. I was instructed to go to the desk to speak with the receptionists, but with a tall plastic screen and masks I couldn't hear what they were asking me. I felt embarrassed at asking them to repeat the simple questions several times. Not feeling quite so special now, it took the shine off the whole experience. I sat down in the waiting area and looked around at all these women – alone - at different stages, feeling glad that birth was not as imminent for me as it was for some.

When I was called for my blood test, I walked past a room where I could overhear a woman crying and two sonographers talking about calling in the lady's husband from outside. I immediately began to feel anxious myself, not because I was particularly concerned that my fate would be the same, but because I had an overwhelming wave of feeling so alone in what would probably be the biggest change that was ever going to happen to me, and I had to face that by myself. I felt forgotten.

At my 20-week scan, which I attended alone, we were to find out the sex. I took out my phone to take pictures of the scan to show my husband but was told I was not allowed to take pictures or videos of my own baby due to GDPR reasons. It was starting to feel like the world was against me and at every corner I was being thwarted, unnecessarily so. Sparks of anger were beginning to grow, yet I felt too vulnerable, lying on my back with a transvaginal scanner inside me, to even muster up an ounce of the irritation I was beginning to feel. I just lay there and took her response as a given.

My pregnancy was classed as low-risk. I was healthy, taking online yoga classes and eating well. All my scheduled appointments that were laid out at my initial midwife meeting, which at the time felt important, were now cancelled and I was scheduled for few and far between phone calls, each time with a different midwife. They didn't know me and I didn't know them, there was no relationship with these people and I had to sit on the phone whilst I listened to them catch up on my notes. There was not one healthcare professional that knew me. Even at week 25, where you usually have your bump measured, your urine taken and other blood tests, I was not seen. My concerns and questions were falling on deaf ears, particularly as I was "low-risk."

At week 36, I received an extra routine scan. I suppose you could see this as a blessing or a curse, depending on how you look at it. I was told that I had a big baby and the term 'gestational diabetes' was thrown around. The oral glucose test confirmed I had GD and as I was creeping into week 37 the time in which I had to turn things around was limited. My rage was beginning to bubble. This was a concern that I had asked to be checked at week 25 and was told not to worry about. I still find it amazing that this one test detrimentally offset the path of my birth in a whole new direction. All hopes of having a home birth or a water birth were stripped away, I was immediately placed in the 'high-risk' category and the talks of induction began. The rug had been pulled from under my feet and I was confused, distraught and anxious. I had read enough about inductions to feel confident enough that this was not for me. My repeated attempts at quoting research, facts and figures as to why induction would not be the best option for me were met with comments about shoulder dystocia, stillbirth and complications, because not only did I have a suspected big baby but I also now had GD and the risks were higher. I was being scaremongered into an induction.

Whilst each one of these experiences may not seem wildly upsetting or traumatising, they were each slowly altering my narrative on pregnancy. A story in which I felt I was repeatedly ignored, not shown care or compassion and robbed of all the 'normal' experiences I should have had. Going into my final weeks of pregnancy and birth, I was no longer prepared mentally. Instead, I felt like I was preparing myself for a fight, but a fight in which I was exhausted and had no voice.

We arrived at the hospital for the induction and my husband was asked to sign a form that said there would be no re-entry if he was to leave. He was ejected at 8pm that night, leaving me in a ward full of women talking on their phones to their loved ones. A young lady in the bed next to me was crying about being alone. I felt for her, because I was her. I was scared; trapped between the known and the unknown. Knowing there was an impending birth yet no idea what was going to happen to me, how it would all feel or how long I would be alone. Frustrated at knowing the 'rule of six' meant my husband could leave to go to the pub with his friends if he wished. Some ludicrous rule that told me pregnant and birthing people did not matter. I. Did. Not. Matter.

The birth was bad. I was cracked wide open. But what followed in the days, weeks and months after felt like barbaric torture. The oxytocin 'high' just wasn't there. Breastfeeding was a non-starter as my broken body failed me yet again and this was coupled with severe tongue tie. Here we go again. Another failure. Another loss that I felt deeply through and through. I was already mourning the loss of the birthing experience I had wanted, feeling I had been tricked into a shit show of a birth. No one to talk to, nobody to see.

The midwives that we had to travel to see wouldn't allow my husband into the room.

"The room is too small to hold that many people, but would you mind a student midwife being in the room?"

Sobbing and shaking with anger, I tried everything to keep my husband by my side but was met with no empathy. Could they not see my pain? See me? I wanted to be heard but, instead, it was just another blow to my confidence and my mental state. I took the first sledgehammer at the birth and the blows kept coming. I was so lost and flailing in this new world. Overnight, I had become de-skilled, failing at all these new activities and I was not coping. Why couldn't they see?

Every phone call to a midwife or health visitor left me in tears as they told me they couldn't come. I felt like screaming (in fact, I think I did.) I was begging for help, for someone to see my baby and support me. I desperately needed reassurance that never came and the feeling of isolation hit like a wave. It felt so insurmountable that I couldn't see my way through it. I wanted to run away, even if just for one night, but where could I go? There was nowhere. Nowhere at all. Being let down, pushed aside and discarded, my frustrations and anger began to manifest as rage. A deep-seated rage that still sits with me, even now.

With my parents living so far away, it was weeks before they could come to visit. I was holding out for Christmas until the announcement was made on the 19th of December 2020 about the new 'tier 4' lockdown rules. The pressure cooker building up inside of me couldn't take any more and this news caused it to blow. It was another thing that was taken away from me at the point I needed it the most and it sent me spiralling down into a deep, black hole. I didn't know there was a place darker than where I already was, but I was wrong. A place I've never been to before, nor do I wish to return.

I was a prisoner in my own home, I hated my house and every room I entered. Each room held a nightmare. The kitchen - because I would often be pacing the floors from 11pm until 2am. The bedroom - because I had to anxiously cradle a crying baby for hours. The toilet - because it was painful to go. The bath - because I would hear Reuben crying again whilst I was in the tub. The living room - because it felt too large, too open and exposed and I wanted to shrink into the smallest thing I could be. I no longer felt safe anywhere in my own home. I was on edge, anxious and irrational. I had no sense of what was normal or what wasn't and the one person I should have been able to confide in and take comfort from felt like an alien to me now. My husband tried his best, but who was I? I didn't know this new person that I had become overnight. Anxiety sat in me like a stranger that just wouldn't leave and it was unknown and unwelcome. Utterly consumed, I had no real sense of when all of this would end and I felt every tick of the second hand that went by.

So, I ran.

Home, to my parents, in Yorkshire, I took our baby and I broke the rules. The rules that nearly broke me, my marriage and my relationship with my baby.

I can't distinguish between what was postnatal depression, newborn hell or lockdown madness. I just know that it wasn't just sadness that I was feeling. I had been robbed, I was bereft and thoroughly defeated by every experience. I truly began to feel unimportant and that I didn't matter. Each comment, experience and feeling began to, brick by brick, build a wall, which I used to protect myself.

I don't know what it's like to have a close circle of NCT friends to text in those dark hours of the night. I don't know what it's like to joke about those newborn hazy days or see the funny side of birth stories. I don't know what it's like to breastfeed your baby or not wince at a breastfeeding woman. I don't know what it's like to look back at baby photos with fondness and warmth. I only know that I cannot answer questions about my experiences simply. For me, there is no simple.

I cannot say I wish that none of these experiences had happened to me (though, in part, I do) because then I wouldn't be the 'new me.' Though some of my story has tainted memories, I'd like to think I am a softer, more compassionate and empathic version of myself, who is learning to make peace with what was and what is. I believe I am stronger, braver and changed irrevocably.

And that can never be a bad thing.

But, tell me, would you do all that again?

Hannah Boyd, 38, is a down-to-earth, leopard print-loving Yorkshire lass from Wakefield, West Yorkshire. However, you will now find her living in London with her husband and their beautiful almost three-year-old son, Reuben. She is a part-time primary school teacher by day but her real passion lies within health and wellness. She has completed a Naturopathic Nutrition degree and is embarking on her next adventure later this year to train as a fully qualified Kinesiologist.
@4the_love_of_leopard

LAURA YOUNG

I know the first time I felt like a mum. The night after your 20-week scan, I woke up to find I had been crying in my sleep. The scan hadn't gone as planned, we were sent home with minimal information and were told to wait for the test results. Every instinct in my body wanted to protect you, to be your mum, but we had to wait and see what the future would hold. Those two weeks were the longest of my life as we waited for news. In the background, the pandemic was emerging and everything was unknown. We drove to Brighton that weekend to see the sea, to get away from it all, and to wait.

The results came and it was the best-case scenario. We still had a medical journey ahead, but we were happy.

And then lockdown hit.

Suddenly, the world was turned upside down. We were confined to our home, unable to see the family and friends we'd avoided for the last two weeks as we were unsure what to say. All my antenatal appointments were promptly cancelled.

The months before your birth were mixed. Your wonderful nurse, dressed in PPE, did garden visits at a distance, to help prepare us for your first year. We went for walks. Your dad did the supermarket shop because we didn't know what was safe. I had antenatal appointments, on the phone or at endlessly changing locations, booked last minute and always with someone new. I had to explain your medical condition over and over again. Three days past your due date, contractions started. We arrived at the hospital very early that Saturday morning – grateful for the ease of weekend hospital parking. Your dad was asked to leave after he'd dropped me off. I entered triage alone. A few minutes later, things took a turn and the midwife warned me that she was about to push the emergency button. From that point, everything moved quickly.

I remember shouting your dad's phone number as I was wheeled away. He hadn't even made it to the car park before he was called back and allowed to join me. I was scared. Those following hours before you arrived, I think I was in shock – I barely spoke – as the scenario changed. They prepared us for a C-section but then stood us down.

You arrived that night. You were beautiful, big and loud. We were together - a new family - for merely an hour before you were whisked off to special care and your dad was asked to leave. Sent to drive home to an empty flat - a new dad - in the middle of the night.

I was put on a ward with lots of mums and babies before the nurse realised that I was without mine and so moved me to another ward with other special care mums. You hear of those who experienced the comradery of COVID postnatal wards – women on their own supporting each other - but our ward was different. We were all scared and starting a new, unknown journey, completely alone.

The intercom to special care was the first time I called myself your mum. I was your mum! I'd set off to find you in special care – again, alone. I began our routine for the next 11 days as you learned to feed. We were the lucky ones – both allowed to see you but not at the same time, so we swapped – learning all the firsts (how to feed, change and comfort you) alone. You came home at 11 days old. You fit into our lockdown bubble perfectly.

Your first year was an adventure. You came on lots of rainy walks with me (it was the only way you'd nap.) You met relatives – often outside, unable to even come inside after having driven for hours to see you. There were lots of medical appointments for both you and me. We tried baby classes when restrictions eased.

At three months old, we took you for your first operation. Another journey we couldn't do as a family. I took you in, alone, fighting back tears as I handed you over to your wonderful surgeon. Then, I left the hospital so I could wait outside – in a deserted London – for six long hours with your dad.

That first night was one of the hardest of my life. You were in pain and I was overwhelmed and alone. At 4am, another mum, after hearing me cry, asked if she could watch you for ten minutes while I took a break. I felt like I was failing you, unable to make your pain go away.

The next morning, I swapped with your dad. I walked through central London back to a hotel, dazed and emotional. I cried. I cried a lot.

Your first year ended with another operation. We had to cancel the big birthday party we'd planned for you as we had to restrict contact before the hospital. Instead, we celebrated with family in the garden. Not what we planned, but perfect just the same. The photo of our family of three and your first birthday cake remains one of my favourites.

You had your second operation, again with just one parent present. No second person to help remember what doctors said or to grab a cup of coffee.

But, you are a fighter. You healed and returned to my happy, cheeky, bouncy little boy.

Your first year was not what I expected. I often felt alone, overwhelmed and scared. But it also brought wonderful moments of joy: your love of your online music class, your dad, ever-present as he was able to work from home, and new pandemic mum friends – bonded by a shared experience.

It wasn't the first year I planned. But it was the one where I became a mum. And I am so glad that I'm your mum.

Laura Young, 34, lives with her husband and three-year-old son and is preparing for a new addition to the family shortly. She works as a civil servant but outside of work, when not spending time with the family, she loves to run.

LIZZIE BRACE

To my beautiful son, Beau, and my supportive husband, Joe. To the pandemic mums, babies and families. We had to dig to depths we never knew were possible. We are survivors.

I want to acknowledge that the journey of conception, pregnancy, and birthing babies can be incredibly tough. Some people go through horrendous, heartbreaking and traumatic situations that are unimaginably hard. This is by no means any form of comparison or a sob story. However, this is my personal story of how the pandemic impacted my first pregnancy, birth and post-partum journey. Writing and sharing this has been part of my healing journey.

During the later part of 2019, my husband Joe and I started to think about relocating from London and starting a family. I conceived Beau in March 2020. During the same month, we sold our flat and progressed with a house we liked in Malvern, Worcestershire. Finding out I was pregnant in April was a mix of emotions; excitement, fear and overwhelm. Having had an early miscarriage a few months before added a layer of worry. There were many life changes happening all at once as well as the escalating pandemic.

Little did we know how huge the unfolding pandemic would become. It added a layer of additional challenges to our situation; worrying that any decision made could put me at risk of getting COVID and hence potentially harm me or my baby. I was already a health-anxious person who had struggled with emetophobia (fear of vomiting) since I was a child. These anxieties were exacerbated by COVID-19. It was also challenging working from home, living, eating, doing workouts and watching TV all in the same room in our flat (and doing this whilst growing a baby!) I have much admiration for families who had to live through the lockdowns in limited space.

Due to a few worries at around eight weeks, I went for a scan. Going on my own was really tough as my anxiety was high and I was so worried about being in a hospital. Everything I touched led to me anti-bac-ing my hands. Joe was in the car park and could not work out if my tears on exit were a good or bad thing. Luckily, they were positive as I had been told there was a little heartbeat.

On reflection, I had not appreciated how the many stressors and huge life events in this period of time put me in a more vulnerable state to cope with the events that followed.

Our move at the end of July 2020 provided some positives; like being in a house instead of a small flat and being able to mix outside more as restrictions eased. However, there remained a continued feeling of worry as a vulnerable person and we continued to socially distance. This was far from an ideal scenario after restarting our lives and moving across the country! Antenatal classes and pregnancy yoga sessions on Zoom were the closest I got to meeting new people.

When I heard about the second lockdown in October 2020, many thoughts raced through my mind. *How would I cope without family being able to visit? How would the grandparents get to meet their grandchild?* The only good news was that 'bubbles' could now be formed for parents with a child aged under one. This was to be my mum and dad, who lived in Devon. This news was a relative "win" during a time of great uncertainty.

Our baby measuring big meant more monitoring and appointments, which I had to attend solo. There was a discussion of induction from the consultants. A low point came during my final meeting with a very blunt consultant, where I felt backed into having an induction. I needed Joe there for support, but of course, the closest he got was the car park. Him being excluded like this was a repeated and upsetting experience.

After no signs of spontaneous labour, we started the induction process on the 6th of December. Four days later, after multiple pessaries and other invasive procedures, doctors detected a lowered heart rate so I was rushed to delivery and my waters were broken. I went through a very long labour, which eventually ended with a terrible three-hour wait to enter theatre, with pushing contractions and no decent pain relief as it was too late. Finally, due to complications and his positioning, my big boy Beau was delivered by emergency caesarean at 9.33 am on Thursday 10th December weighing 9 pounds 5 ounces! It was a scary experience and I was extremely drained, having been in hospital for four days with very little sleep.

It didn't really hit me straight away that Joe was sent home just 1.5 hours after my surgery. I was on a busy hospital ward with the anaesthesia wearing off, in a complete bubble, on a comedown, almost an out-of-body experience. Staff were so overworked and understaffed.

We were discharged the following day. I woke that night feeling hot and ill. *COVID?* I delved into my bedside drawer and reached for my ovulation stick, which confirmed my high temperature of nearly 39 degrees. Something wasn't right. I knew we had to call the ward.

They confirmed we must come back in. We managed to grapple a few belongings for Beau and I into a bag and get a screaming, hungry baby into the car. Joe drove us back to the hospital where we were placed onto the "COVID ward." I was prodded, poked and tested, then placed on an IV with antibiotics and fluids. I remember drifting in and out of sleep. I was in pain. It was hard to move. I had to wear a mask. I had to be separated from my husband. In the middle of the sweat, the aches, the pains and the mental and physical exhaustion, I saw a text from a family friend saying, "Congratulations... I hope you are thriving as a three." Thriving? I could not have been further from thriving. We had been delivering news to family and friends that our healthy, gorgeous little man had arrived, yet I felt overwhelmed and poorly. It was such an emotionally conflicting time.

The COVID test was negative and it was confirmed I had "generalised sepsis." Joe was restricted to two hours of visiting per day. I cannot explain the desperation or depth of overwhelm at being in hospital during these six days after birth and how this experience, albeit a relatively short time, had such an impact on my motherhood journey. It was an accumulation of traumatic events; having an induction against my instincts, a long labour with complications followed by delayed emergency surgery, re-admission to hospital due to sepsis, being heavily medicalised, in an understaffed hospital with a newborn who could not feed properly, no partner at a time I needed him the most, plus the standard hormonal changes and vulnerability of becoming a parent. I had a newborn baby but could not give him the attention I would have loved to as a first-time mum. That led to guilt.

It was the maternity visiting restrictions that I found the most traumatic out of everything. Pre-pandemic, the visiting hours were 12 per day and sometimes included overnight stays. I'll never forget the surge of happiness when I saw Joe enter the ward, but also the sadness, despair and anxiety when he left. I begged a maternity assistant to be discharged. I was so desperate to go home.

The next day my results indicated it was safe for me to return home and continue antibiotics there. Once home, I was hit with more reminders of the impact of the pandemic. Meeting the grandparents metres apart or from the doorstep in the cold, and anxiety over whether Beau and I had got COVID. It was far from what I ever envisaged.

Beau was still struggling to feed and it was incredibly painful, but there were no NHS tongue tie services readily available and no home visits from any professionals. After some weeks, tongue tie was confirmed after booking a private specialist. A week later, the pain eased and I finally felt there was some form of success.

Once back home, we had some beautiful moments. Watching our gorgeous son thrive and meet milestones was incredible. At times, we forgot about the pandemic and its impact. We were back in a lockdown from January. There were some positives, like not being overwhelmed by visitors and that my husband was working from home, but there was boredom and isolation. I had a limited network. I wanted to meet people, share the journey, experience motherhood collectively, share stories and help to heal. We had family that wanted to help and visit, but they could only see us outside. Having my mum be there for much of our early days was a saving grace. I wanted my sister, who lived over two hours away, to visit. She wanted to help but couldn't. On our reuniting in March 2021, once travelling further afield was allowed, we met in a random town midway. We ran to each other and leapt and squealed with happiness. There will always be that bit of sadness that we missed out on those early baby days together.

Once released from hospital, I experienced an elation period. However, as the weeks passed, I noticed avoidance of certain things associated with the hospital or birth. Feelings of resentment related to the birth and afterwards, were swirling around inside me. Looking back, it is clear that the experiences we had gone through added an extra layer of complexity and negativity, like a heavy, grey cloud, to those typically challenging periods with a small baby and that some of these were trauma responses. I felt conflicted about what to share and who to, because I felt I should be grateful to have my healthy baby. A midwife said to me, "Draw a line under your birth experience. It doesn't always go the way we want." These comments fed into my self-doubt over whether my feelings of sadness and resentment were valid. That can be damaging to a person's emotional well-being, especially when those feelings and emotions are raw and you are at your most vulnerable.

I felt guilt, too. The pandemic had killed lots of people. I had a husband, a new home and now our healthy baby. All these factors made it difficult to offload how I was truly feeling. I felt emotionally stuck, and responsible for the way I was feeling, as if it was my job to fix it. It is only over time that I've learnt that the impact of traumatic experiences does not just disappear, the brain processes them differently from non-traumatic experiences.

There were many triggers over my postpartum period. Any conversation around the topic of birth or postpartum would strike a feeling in my chest. I felt conflicted in wanting to help friends and be supportive, yet those discussions impacted my mental health negatively. The fact that women now had the option of their partner's presence at hospital appointments and scans, and did not have to carry the anxiety of being unvaccinated and catching the virus, or experience the loneliness of early motherhood in lockdown, I found difficult. It was not easy to balance trying to help with looking after myself.

A person I will be forever grateful to, who made a difference to my mental health, was Jo, the co-founder of Becoming Families Worcestershire. Over the 18 months following Beau's birth, I reached out to her in times of need and distress. Jo helped me to understand that all the things I felt were valid and signposted me to other support services such as EMDR sessions. At times I thought things had healed, but then another birth would happen or I would hit other challenges and the raw emotions came back. I decided I needed more support and I saw a perinatal counsellor, Elise, who was also a big part of my healing journey. I realised it was not just about the birth, it was everything that had happened over a few years. This started my journey of self-compassion, helping me to recognise that whilst I had not lost someone, there were many losses along our journey. Because of the pandemic, as well as our networks being spread out and having started over again, some of our foundations were not grounded, which increased our vulnerability.

Over two years on, I appreciate the many positives in our lives. Whilst the experience of the pandemic will always live with me, the support has helped me process, understand, allow emotions and accept things as best as I can. I feel proud of myself. I allow myself to acknowledge that it was fine to feel a loss.

Beau is two years old. He is an amazing, fun-loving, fast-moving, hugely affectionate, blonde-haired, blue-eyed little boy and I love him more than anything.

Lizzie Brace, 34, lives with her two-year-old son, Beau, and her husband, Joe, in Malvern, Worcestershire. In addition to being Beau's mummy, Lizzie works part-time as a youth worker. Lizzie originates from Essex. She previously worked as a social worker in various children's services roles in the south east before her move to Worcestershire in 2020. Lizzie loves beautiful surroundings and hence loves walking on the Malvern Hills. She also enjoys being with her family, yummy food, adventures and keeping fit.

RACHEL M

It feels suffocating. I find it so hard to be responsible for someone else when I feel like I can't even look after myself at the moment. Not having anywhere else to go for a change of scenery or different faces. Particularly when Tom's at work and it's just me and Micah for hours and hours. Everything that HAS to be done, it's exhausting and I just feel like I'm failing. Even if I manage to get one task done OK, I mess up the others and feel like the whole day has been a failure. I'm so fed up with feeling down and like a failure, but I can't see how I can get out of it. I want to find a way to be my old self again but I feel like I can't. And I feel like I'm being unfair to T and M, having to be around me when I'm like this.

I wrote this as a note in my phone on May 10th 2020. I remember feeling like I needed to get out what I was feeling, even though I found it hard to understand or explain my thoughts at that time. Reading it back brings me straight back to where I was when I wrote it. Three years on, I feel guilty reading those words.

My first child was born in October 2019, so was five months old when we entered the first lockdown. I can recall the mixture of feelings I had at the time - the fear and anxiety of not being able to be with the people I loved and needed to be with, but also the naivety of thinking it wouldn't last long; maybe a few weeks, but no longer than that. I'd had a straightforward pregnancy but a traumatic birth and breastfeeding journey. Although I knew I was still working through that, I thought I was doing okay until around January 2020. I noticed my mental health had taken a blow after an impressive panic attack, seemingly out of the blue. I contacted my GP and health visitor to try and get support early on. I made sure I was getting out of the house and seeing people, ensuring I wasn't isolating myself, which seemed to be helping until lockdown came along and well and truly pulled the rug from under my feet. In the blink of an eye, all my support was stripped away. All the measures I had been putting into place to try and keep myself afloat had been whipped away from me and I felt I had nothing left. Instead of being able to see people and meet up with friends, I was pacing the streets, just me and my boy in the pram, in all weathers, just to get out. I vividly remember walking at top speed in the pouring rain just to try and stop myself from having another panic attack. I tried to keep connected by joining virtual groups and baby classes, but it wasn't the same. I needed to be pulled out of my house to somewhere else, not just sat on the floor in front of my phone trying to do a virtual music class with my baby, feeling like I was failing him.

My GP suggested I start antidepressants. I was reluctant, as it felt like it added to my feelings of failure. I hated the idea that I couldn't function day to day without medication. I hated that my husband was having to take days off work to care for our son as I couldn't even look after myself at some points, let alone a baby. Everything in me wanted to manage without them, but I couldn't, so I finally gave in and started taking them. Although I was hesitant to start the antidepressants, I felt I was being listened to.

    I received no response from my health visitor after my plea for help and to this day, no one ever got back to me about supporting me and my dwindling mental health, despite reaching out so many times. I dread to think how many other mothers' needs were missed. When I talk about the lack of support during lockdown, I often get the response of, 'Well, times were hard, services were stretched.' I get that, but it still isn't OK. Those services are vital and they weren't there for me when I needed them.

    It wasn't all negative. I was fortunate enough to have the support of an invaluable infant-feeding worker. I had been attending her breastfeeding groups since my baby was born, and these continued virtually over lockdown. She regularly checked in with me, offering a listening ear, helpful advice, and making referrals for me when I couldn't bring myself to do it. Thanks to this, I received support from a local charity called Acacia and then had some talking therapy with Birmingham Healthy Minds. This, combined with the medication, just about got me through the hardest months of my life.

    In August 2021, I was pregnant with my second child. I was in a good place mentally, I was off antidepressants and thought I had managed to put the trauma of lockdown behind me. However, as my pregnancy progressed, I realised that so many of those feelings were still there. The fear was still impacting me. There were still restrictions in hospital for scans and appointments. It all felt so real again. I went back onto the medication and had another referral to Acacia for support. I felt like I was failing again, but desperately trying to make sure I didn't get back to the place I ended up in before. I would say I managed to succeed in preventing as much of a spiral as the previous time, but my second maternity leave was still impacted greatly by the effects of lockdown. I felt so cheated the first time around that I felt I had to throw myself headfirst into all the activities I could the second time. It meant I never really stopped to simply enjoy the time with my second baby. The juggling of two children was made even more intense by giving myself so much more to do than I think I would have done if I hadn't experienced a maternity leave where I wasn't able to do anything. I have so much guilt that my second child has had none of the intense one on one time that I had with my first. During lockdown, I had nothing to focus on other than my baby. Whilst that wasn't entirely helpful or healthy, I still miss elements of it.

    I still get a pang of jealousy when I see first-time mums experiencing a maternity leave without the impact of lockdown affecting their decisions, and I hate that. I hate the guilt of finding my experience of early motherhood so negative, despite having such a wonderful boy who I love so immensely. I hate remembering the feelings of isolation in the times when I should have been able to introduce my baby to my friends and family and meet up with others for a chat over a cup of tea. I hate the guilt of my little boy seeing me crying and completely broken, and the fear of how that may impact him. I still hate it when he sees me crying.

Lockdown took away so much from so many. We're still trying to recover from what we lost and come to terms with what we needed but didn't get. I needed connection. I needed to be heard and to be held. I needed family. I needed some element of normality and the life I knew before.

Rachel, 32, from Birmingham, lives with her husband, two children and their two cats. She is a Paediatric Nurse and now works in the community. When she can find the time (and energy) she enjoys going outside for walks and bike rides, or squeezing in exercise at home.

LOUISE ACKERMAN-MURPHY

Vision of 20:20

Hands, Face, Space!
Tick tock, TikTok!
Ground control to Major Tom
Clap your hands or bang a pot.

Delayed 007, spy on your neighbour instead
Bake a sourdough, don't let your starter end up dead
If someone's flouting, call the police
No excuses - society must now cease!

Baby safely kicking and my little girl cries
Grandma keeps calling as time flies
Days seem never-ending, another walk to visit the ducks
In a prison of biology, running out of fucks!

Where is my village? All staying home.
Zoom Zoom, but I just want some space.
My Belly keeps growing
like the curve in my face.

There is chalk on the pavements
Rainbows on the wall
The swings remain empty
and so does the school.

Who is the man with the straw-like hair?
He enters our sanctuary on and off throughout the day
Flanked by his experts with intention to scare.
Anxiety is rising, so in the garden, we play.

Waiting in my car for the ladies in blue.
The sky remains empty; we cannot escape
unaccompanied, wee dipped, but not touching you.
My belly keeps growing and I sit and wait.

This is not the story I had on my page.
It said *slowly breathe out and then in while holding a hand.*
So, I cry in the bath, from the fear and the rage.
I CAN'T BREATHE - get on your knee: make a stand.

The world is so silent, streets like a ghost town
Yet there are so many new words:
furlough, transmissible, covidiot, lockdown.
The shelves are so empty and deliveries are few.

My belly's stopped growing and I am not doing well.
Carrying my bags alone, I go in.
Their faces remain covered like a dystopian hell.
Calming blue ladies, their eyes try to grin.

People are dying so, just suck it up, take one for the team
your needs aren't important so quietly do your part
no yoga balls or birthing partners allowed, feels so mean.
Negative, he's allowed in: time to push, this might smart!

I contract, push and tear full of fear
Men and their rules, not a damn of what we endured
Staff run ragged, put at risk, but they get a Thursday cheer!
Men happy with backhanders, inability to procure.

MP's drunk on prosecco while I was alone, left to scream.
Snogging their aids but I did as I was told!
Drunk on gas, this could all be a nightmarish dream
The year was 2020, but now hindsight is bold.

Louise, 39, originally from London, set up home in Bristol eight years ago with her husband, Stuart. She is mum to three little girls: Emelia, 5, Penelope, 3, and baby Meredith who was born at Easter 2023. She works part-time with a charitable organisation to support disabled people with their mobility. Louise reignited her passion for writing during her first maternity leave with the help of The Mothership Writers. Louise uses her writing as an outlet for motherhood and to share her journey of grief since losing her beloved father just before the pandemic. Sushi enthusiast and tea addict Louise has fully embraced the local culture and describes herself as a Neo-Bristolian. You can enjoy her funny, yet honest, account of life as she knows it via her Instagram @alifeaslouknowsit

NICOLA HAMILTON

Trigger warning: Miscarriage

13th March 2020

Friday the 13th... a date that many people associate with bad luck, and boy, can I relate to that! On Friday 13th May 2017, I was lying in a hospital bed, coming around from anaesthetic, to be told I had liver cancer and needed life-saving surgery, or worse... a liver transplant!

Talk about bad luck!

Today, however, was a good day. I found out that I was pregnant again. I was full of excitement, but fear at the same time, after having had a miscarriage in November 2019. I was determined to think positively. It was a beautiful day in Glasgow, the sun was shining and I couldn't wait to tell my partner he was going to be a dad.

16th March 2020

COVID was the subject of our daily handover at work. Everyone was making a big deal of it. We were asked if we would be able to help out with the acute services in the hospital if required. Panicking, I felt I had to confide in my manager that I was pregnant, even though I didn't really want to. After the last time, I wanted to wait until I was 12 weeks. It was too painful to think about telling people again if we had a second miscarriage.

Was COVID really such a big deal?

23rd March 2020

The UK was placed into a national lockdown. I watched the news bulletin and was horrified to find out that being pregnant placed me at a higher risk of complications should I develop COVID. Cue - a panicked text message to my manager to ask what I should do. I was told to stay at home for the meantime until she had spoken to senior hospital management.

6th April 2020

We were allowed out of the house for one hour per day to exercise. Thankfully, the Scottish weather was being kind and blessing us with gorgeous sunshine. I arrived home after our daily walk to a massive bleed. I was absolutely heartbroken and convinced that we were miscarrying again. I was told I had to wait for a few days for a scan appointment at the early pregnancy unit.

I was told that Stevie couldn't come in with me. I would have to go back to the same place that I went to back in November, when we were told we had lost the baby, but this time I would be alone.

Absolutely terrified.

8th April 2020

I arrived at the hospital at 8.30 am and had never seen anything like it in my life! There was hazard tape everywhere and security guards at the front door asking people why they were there. There was no chance of Stevie being able to sneak in with me - security put a stop to that. I kissed him goodbye and made my way down a lonely corridor to the EPU and, ironically, sat in exactly the same seat as last time. I couldn't stop crying, memories came flooding back and I had no one to comfort me. Stevie had been at every hospital appointment I had ever been to. Even when it was bad news, he was there to hold my hand and tell me it would be OK. Today, I was completely alone.

60 minutes later, I ran outside to Stevie, sobbing with relief. Everything was OK! I saw our little rainbow on the screen, wriggling around with a perfect heartbeat. I had two precious pictures to show him, which were supposed to make up for him not being allowed in.

16th May 2020

I managed to book a private scan so Stevie could come with me as he wasn't allowed to come to the upcoming NHS 12-week scan. I was terrified that it was going to be bad news but we were both over the moon to see our wee rainbow waving at us on the screen. The sonographer was lovely and reassured us that everything was looking as it should be.

18th May 2020

It was time to go for that all-important 12-week scan. Even though we had seen our wee rainbow two days ago at the private scan, I was still a bag of nerves. What if something had changed in the past 48 hours? Stevie wasn't allowed to come with me. He wasn't even allowed in the building! I had to sit in the waiting room by myself, seeing pregnant women with their huge bumps come and go, worrying that would never be me. I didn't have anyone to hold my hand or give me a reassuring smile. I understood the reasons why, but it didn't make it feel any better.

Finally, my name was called. I still don't know how I managed to walk into that scan room. My legs were like jelly. I burst into tears when the sonographer told me everything was perfect and I was actually measuring at 14 weeks. It was so unfair that Stevie missed out on that special moment.

Finally, we were able to tell our friends and family our special news. Everyone had been asking me why I was shielding at home and I had to blame the cancer. We were still in lockdown and not able to see anyone, so cue lots of FaceTime calls (not the way I had ever planned to tell people I was pregnant.)

30th June 2020

I was really struggling with lockdown. Working from home when you're an NHS nurse is not fun. There were lots of worried parents phoning me, looking for advice, and I genuinely didn't know what to tell them. The government advice was changing on a daily basis and I was confused by it. No wonder parents were stressed out!

At the hospital today, I was told that antenatal classes had been stopped. I was given a link to a website that had some information on pregnancy and birth.

August 2020

Due to my previous liver cancer, I was recommended to have extra growth scans to monitor the baby's development. I was super excited as Nicola Sturgeon announced that partners could now attend all antenatal appointments, so Stevie would finally get to come in with me. Lockdown restrictions were eased in Scotland with bars, restaurants and shops all open. Finally, things were looking like they might be returning to normal!

Unfortunately, my excitement was short-lived, after being told that he could not attend the next scan. Apparently, partners were allowed to attend the 12 and 20-week scans but not for any additional monitoring scans thereafter! What was this madness?

I had no one to talk to and no way of channelling this anger. I sent an email to my local member of parliament, asking them to look into this. I also contacted a journalist from The Scottish Sun who ran an article in the local newspaper highlighting the issue, as each health board in Scotland seemed to be making up their own rules in terms of who could attend antenatal scans. Deep down, I knew that this wouldn't change anything, but I felt better for doing something.

September 2020

At my next growth scan, the madness continued. Stevie was STILL not allowed into the scan with me, but he could come in to see the consultant afterwards. I saw women with their partners waiting to go into their 12 and 20-week scans. The 'rules' didn't make sense. After my scan, I had to phone Stevie to come in when it was my turn to go in. Another utterly pointless rule that I couldn't understand.

After seeing the consultant, we were given a date for my C-section. I tried to not think about what restrictions would be in place by then, and instead, we went away for a few days to try to relax before the baby arrived.

October 2020

I was devastated to hear on the radio that restrictions were being brought back due to an increase in COVID cases. Hospitals would be imposing restrictions on visitors, with only "essential visitors" allowed. I sat in the car and sobbed.

30th October 2020

After a sleepless night, our wee rainbow baby, Sophie, was born at 11.27am by planned C-section and was absolutely perfect. Stevie was allowed to come in with me whilst I was being admitted and stayed with me right through until we were taken to the recovery suite. The theatre staff were phenomenal and couldn't have done any more for us. They made us feel relaxed and reassured me at every moment. The moment that they lifted the screen down to show us Sophie was magical and a moment that I will never ever forget.

Then, our magical little bubble was broken.

It all happened so fast. One minute, we were both cooing over Sophie, and the next, I was wheeled out of the room to be taken up to the ward, leaving Stevie standing behind me, looking like his world had just ended. He had to phone the ward to book a slot to come and see his newborn baby. I cried all the way up to the ward. A poor student midwife greeted me on arrival and didn't know what to say to me. There was nothing that she could say that would make the situation any better. I was numb from the waist down and had no one to help me lift Sophie in and out of her cot to feed or change her. I had to constantly buzz for help. The midwives, to their credit, were amazing, but by God, they were rushed off their feet.

Finally, by the evening, Stevie was allowed back in for his 'slot.' He was able to feed Sophie for the first time and change her into a wee outfit, but all too soon, it was time for him to go. Despite being in a room with five other women, I had never felt so alone in my life. It was just me and Sophie, and unbeknown to me at that time, our life was to continue in this way for the foreseeable future.

March 2023

Sitting here writing this brings up so many emotions. I'm angry that my entire pregnancy was tainted by COVID. Pregnancy after loss is difficult enough, but having to do it in the midst of a global pandemic is the stuff nightmares are made of. What makes me even angrier, is that whilst I was following the rules and doing as I was told by the Government, the politicians who were making those rules were doing the exact opposite. Some were having parties at Number 10 whilst others were travelling around the country despite testing positive for COVID. How was that fair?

I had to take Sophie, alone, for her immunisations. Stevie had to hide in another room when the health visitor came out to do her visits and I couldn't even see my GP face to face when I developed an infection in my C-Section wound or when Sophie developed reflux. There were no baby groups to attend to socialise and meet other new mums. I joined every Facebook group going, seeking reassurance that I was doing everything right as I had no bloody clue!

I cannot even begin to explain the rage I feel when I see new mums out and about, pushing their prams and meeting their friends in coffee shops whilst everyone coos over their newborn. I walked the deserted streets every day,

alone, pushing my pram. I sometimes still cry myself to sleep at night thinking about it. My entire pregnancy, and almost half of my maternity leave, were spent under some form of lockdown and I just feel so angry.
 SO FUCKING ANGRY!

Nicola Hamilton is a 41-year-old mum of one to Sophie, who is 2.5 years old. Nicola lives in Renfrewshire with her fiancé and works part-time as a Children's Nurse.

SARAH STOCKTON

Expectations

It wasn't as planned.
It wasn't a baby shower and stroking tiny clothes between excited fingers.
It wasn't a homebirth – strength, power, choice.
It wasn't cooing visitors and emphatic embraces.
It wasn't the same through screens.
It wasn't genuine smiles and making the best of it all.
It wasn't baby groups and mum friends and adventures.
It wasn't even coffee shops and solitude.

It was unnoticed blossom on the trees.
It was reaching ever closer, evermore ominous.
It was bulletins and announcements.
It was lockdown.
It was freedoms restricted, choices revoked, the yearned for, never-before-worshipped touch of another, denied.
It was leaving to go to the hospital late, later, later still.
It was a rush, a second-degree tear and three lives changed in unknown ways.
It was texting photos, through tears, of the most beautiful, precious baby to the screens of people that wouldn't know him – for months.
It was uncertainty, abandonment, stoicism.
It was heart-wrenching, gut-coiling, deep-down sadness as the well-meaning neighbours waved to the three of us; all sharing applause, praise, desperate eye contact and ebbing and flowing hope on doorsteps.
It was knowing it was only us that could love him – for now – forever?
It was visions of futures forever changed.
It was park-meets, holding baby up, like Simba, for aching hearts to see but not touch, not breathe in, nor shower with affection.

It was, ultimately, temporary.

But it was the not knowing that drove those moments.

- various visions of dystopia
- juxtaposed with everything we should have had. Unspoken.

I wrote to you

To diarise those days
hopeful you'd look back one day and feel the true emotion
– the vivid trauma –
maybe long, long after the blocked-out memories have faded
from living memory.

To convey my love, my hopes, like prayer – manifesting
a future in which you read my words –
a post-pandemic time when you – at least – survived.

To document my absolute, untold, un-witnessed love for you,
just in case.

To remind myself there's a future place,
a time removed from now,
a feeling different to this.

To cleanse my aching soul of some of the inexplicable,
unchangeable truths.

To focus not on bodies piling up in morgues,
suicide rates, helplessness, abandonment,
but to focus on love – mother to son – pure and true.

To ensure my voice will be with you – long after I've gone.

To paint, for you, a time when you represented hope, love, ambition
and a deep desire for you to carry that identity with you,
always.

Sarah Stockton, 33, from Birmingham, lives with her husband, three-year-old son, Theo, and three-month-old daughter, Willow. She works part-time as a Secondary School English teacher and has always written fiction to unwind and decompress. She has previously published the work of disadvantaged young people she works with as a way of building confidence and validating their experiences. In the very few moments of peace she has, she likes to garden and try to keep her houseplants alive.

CHARLOTTE FOX

March 16th 2020

    Just like that, I have to stop seeing friends and family. A 30-minute brief by Boris and I can no longer leave the house. All I hear is, "pregnant" and "vulnerable."

    I don't even have my pram, it's on order. I must break the rules tomorrow and collect it, I need to keep some control. I need my pram. I need my car seat. What about antenatal classes? I have no idea what I'm doing and I thought we'd make some friends; people to share experiences with; people to go for lunch with.

    No one is going to see me pregnant again. What about all those plans, breaking up for Easter, going shopping, starting maternity leave? They're all up in the air.

A week later

    Boris is here again. Now Jack can't go to work. We're now together 24/7. There's nothing on the TV but repeats and the only thing we can do is have an hour-long walk to keep us sane.

April

    I should be collecting friends; I haven't seen them for months... If only I'd known that months would become years due to travel restrictions and they'd never see me pregnant and never hold my baby.

    I should be having my baby shower but it's cancelled. My friends deliver treats and leave them in the porch. I don't want treats, I just want a hug, I just want them to stroke my belly and talk to my baby.

    "We'll have a 'baby is here' party," they say.

    I go to my twice-weekly scans alone. I pray on the way there that nothing's wrong and that I don't have to hear bad news without Jack's hand to hold. Afterwards, I come home, strip at the door, my clothes go in the wash and I go straight in the shower.

    I've cleaned the house from top to bottom, every cupboard and every drawer. We've painted all the rooms. The days are dragging. We clock watch. We've established new routines: 11am tea and biscuits. 3pm: tea, cake and Tenable.

    We've bought so little, yet now there's nowhere to buy from. Why me? What did I do wrong in my previous life? No one's seen me pregnant, and no one's asked when I'm due. I just wanted a normal pregnancy.

May

Baby is due this month. Maybe, just maybe, things will be different. I didn't plan to be this unprepared. We had shopping trips and date nights planed, our last before we become a family of three.

I've experience reduced movements for the second time. I travel alone, sit alone for hours and am told I need to be induced. I cry all the way home.

I enter at 6pm and Jack leaves at 8pm as he can't stay with me. I'm in a cubicle, curtains closed, all alone. I can hear other people coming onto the ward. I can hear their conversations and I relay these by text to a friend. We giggle about the fact that this is my only entertainment. I don't leave that cubicle, except to wee. It's six hours until I see another human, when my observations are done. Away she goes, and in another six hours I'll have some interaction again. I get no sleep. After 24 hours of induction, nothing has happened. I'm told if nothing happens within 30 hours, I will have to move upstairs and wait two days. I cannot go another two days in these conditions, it's torture.

30 hours and my waters are broken. Jack can finally be with me.

11.5 hours later and we have a baby boy. I want to go home and I make this very clear. 9pm: we leave.

My parents have their first grandchild and they can't meet him.

The days go by in a blur as we tag-team. There's no village to help us, no one to give us a break, to make us lunch, to cook us tea or to let us have a couple of hours to try and recharge. It's just me, Jack and the baby.

The health visitor comes. Jack has to go upstairs. He's missing out on so much.

We get cards and presents through the post. For the visits, we stand at the conservatory doors so we can be seen, with the kitchen door open so we can hear each other. I just want people to hold my baby and I want to make memories and take photos of him with his grandparents, aunties and cousins. We're living in a goldfish bowl with people looking at us through the glass. This isn't what I dreamed of. This isn't what I planned.

June

Jack has to go back to work. We've had four weeks as the three of us and now it's just Flynn and I. I've still not been to the supermarket. It's been 12 weeks since I last went, I think, I can't remember... Normality has gone. I started lockdown as me, Charlotte, and now I'm Mummy. Everything changed but I never got to enjoy those last few weeks as me, and I'll never be that me again.

Some days go quickly and others drag. I can't cope, I need some support. We decide to break the rules. We decide I need my mum and Flynn needs his granny. Masked up and wearing gloves, my mum gets to hold her grandson for the first time. He's six weeks old.

March 2023

My baby is nearly three years old. I'm still grieving the normal pregnancy, birth, postpartum and maternity leave that I didn't get. I am angry that everything I dreamed of didn't happen. I am so sad that this is my only experience of having a baby and I don't think I'll ever fully heal from that. If I'd known what we know now, I'd have broken the rules and I'd have saved my mental health sooner.

Charlotte Fox, 36, from Derbyshire, lives with her three year old son, Flynn. She works part-time as a primary school teacher.

JANINE RANDALL

3rd September 2020

    Dearest daughter,

    You are now four months old and today you are going to meet your Grammy and one of your uncles in Ireland for the first time. We have had countless video calls on WhatsApp but now they are going to finally cuddle you and see just how blue your eyes are in person. There have been barriers along the way, our flights were cancelled but we have booked with another airline and we are now on our way to Heathrow. Your daddy and brother are staying at home so it's just me and you. I have practised collapsing your pushchair one-handed when holding you in my other arm and I have rearranged the changing bag to try and make it as easy as possible. This is not how I had originally thought things would be when I found out I was pregnant in August 2019, and to say that you were born at a strange time is an understatement.

* * *

    When I found out I was having a girl at my 20-week scan, I was so happy to know that I would have one of each: a boy and a girl. I had suffered from postnatal PTSD after having your brother so I was worried about how your birth would go and if I would have the same intrusive thoughts as before. This was one of the reasons that I desperately wanted to have your daddy there at your birth.

    I finished work on 28th February 2020, using some annual leave before starting maternity leave, ready for your due date on 19th April 2020. I remember seeing signs up at work about anyone arriving from Wuhan in China needing to isolate because of a new virus. But China is so far away, I didn't feel like it was going to have any effect on us. How wrong I was.

    One of my pregnancy cravings with you was jam doughnuts. It seems strange that the last time I had a jam doughnut was on 10th March 2020. The next day, the WHO declared COVID-19 a global pandemic. As a pregnant woman, I was on the list of vulnerable people and advised to isolate. Our local maternity hospital set up a Facebook page that I was checking every day. The guidance was changed in the middle of March to say that only one birth partner was permitted and that we would be regularly updated. With a month to go until your due date, I thought this would only be in a place for a short time.

    There was panic-buying of toilet rolls, hand sanitiser and paracetamol, among other things. I was hoping that things would change before your arrival so that I would have toilet rolls for postpartum bleeding and painkillers to help after childbirth. Daddy and I took a hypnobirthing course and it said to make a list of worries before the birth. Lack of supplies, not being able to leave the house, not being able to see anyone, the possibility that I would have to give birth alone, not knowing how long I would have to stay in hospital for after having you and worrying about who was going to look after your big brother when I went into labour were all on the list. To take my mind off it, I made a different list – my labour playlist.

The Prime Minister addressed the nation on 23rd March 2020 to announce that there would be a nationwide lockdown, using the slogan "Stay Home, Protect the NHS, Save Lives." On 25th March, I had a midwife appointment which I had to attend on my own. I was told that if Daddy was showing any COVID symptoms he wouldn't be allowed in the hospital, so we agreed that none of us would leave the house, not even to go shopping. I will always be so grateful to our friends who went to the shop for us. It helped alleviate one of my worries at a time when it was impossible to even get a grocery shop delivered. I tried the 'midnight method' many times, trying to get a delivery slot with all the major supermarkets, but never had any success.

Your due date of 19th April 2020 came and went. The next day, feeling tired, uncomfortable and anxious, I decided to not answer any calls or messages and I turned off the internet on my phone. I know that everyone was interested to hear if there were any signs of you gracing us with your presence, but all the worry and uncertainty was becoming too much for me.

I woke up at 4am on 23rd April with contractions which got stronger throughout the day. One of your godmothers came to look after your brother so that Daddy and I could go to the hospital. On my way in, I started to have a nosebleed and the contractions were so strong I couldn't move. Luckily, a lady who worked there was coming out and got a wheelchair for me. Getting into the room, being told that I was in established labour and Daddy being allowed to stay with me provided some comfort as I knew that I wouldn't be on my own. I went into my hypnobirthing bubble and focused on my breathing. It was a Thursday evening and I could hear the sound of the 'claps for carers' as I had a contraction.

At 1.32am on 24th April 2020, you came into the world and completed our family.

By the time we had our six-week appointment with the GP, everything was physically fine for both of us, but I was struggling mentally. Our support network had gotten smaller and smaller. I was discharged from hospital with a list of websites and phone numbers but the last thing I wanted to do was talk to a stranger. I didn't feel that there was anything they could do to make it possible to have my 'village.' I cried when the doctor gave you a cuddle. I wanted so much for you to have been cuddled by family and friends, but instead, I could count on one hand the people who had held you. As time went on, I worried about if I was ever going to be able to introduce you to other people or see my family in person again. The health visitor called for your six-week check-up, but it felt like a tick-box exercise and they didn't ask how I was. I haven't heard from them since.

It seems silly saying it now, when we're travelling to Ireland, but when you were a newborn there was so much uncertainty. Everyone was getting used to the 'new normal' to keep the R number down. This meant wearing masks, keeping a two-metre distance, only being allowed out for one form of exercise each day and otherwise having to stay at home. Play areas in parks were closed, so on our first walk with you we went to the end of our road and back again. If we walked past anyone, we moved to keep our distance, walking into the roads, unusually quiet with no traffic. I tried to focus on things I appreciated, like having a garden so at least we could sit outside rather than being stuck in the house all day. With fewer cars on the roads, I woke up to birdsong, which is usually hard to hear.

At six weeks old, your uncle and auntie drove three hours each way so that they could see you from a distance at a nearby park and then stand outside our living room window for a close-up view. I have photos of this which I will show you when you're older. Your family would have loved to have met you properly back then, but it wasn't allowed. We couldn't register your birth until you were 59 days old. All these things that would usually happen early on were delayed. As soon as I got your birth certificate I applied for a passport for you, so that when travelling was allowed again, I could introduce you to my mum and brothers.

From 4th July 2020, the government announced that parents in England were able to get childcare from friends and family, but as our closest family live a three-hour drive away and our friends had formed their own support bubbles, it meant we were on our own. On 11th July 2020, your uncle and auntie came to visit again and this time they were allowed inside the house. I felt so emotional that they got to cuddle you and your brother and that they could give me a hug. It's hard to explain how much I needed it. On 17th July 2020, you got to meet Grandma and Grandad in person for the first time. It made me so happy that family were finally able to meet you properly instead of through WhatsApp video calls.

* * *

We have arrived at Grammy's house. Daddy drove us to Heathrow and said goodbye outside because he wasn't allowed inside the airport. I had my mask on the whole time, which meant my glasses kept getting steamed up, but it was worth it. It was your first time on a plane and you were great. I breastfed you for take-off and you were sleeping when we landed. There weren't many passengers on the plane so they were able to spread us out to maintain social distancing. When we landed in Dublin, your pushchair wasn't there when we got off the plane and I was told it was because of COVID. I had to carry you from the plane to the baggage reclaim. We got a taxi to Grammy's house and as we pulled up, I could see her and your uncle looking out of the living room window. It was a scene I will never forget. I changed you, had a shower and changed my clothes for the big moment. Your other uncle filmed the first time that Grammy and Mummy's other brother got to meet you in person. They got to hold you, kiss you and hug me. We are only here for 48 hours, and we will all be isolating for two weeks afterwards, to be safe.

After everything, this moment will always be special to me. When you're older, I will show you the photos and videos as I know you won't remember this, but I will. I don't know when we will be able to visit again, hopefully with Daddy and your big brother, but this has given us all the emotional boost that we so desperately needed.

Love you so much, my little lockdown lady.

Mummy xxx

Janine Randall, 38, lives in Hampshire with her husband and two children. Since graduating, she has worked in various education roles in Spain, Ireland and the UK. She volunteers with her local Maternity Voices Partnership to help improve maternity services. Outside of work and being Mum, she enjoys exploring new cuisines, travelling and reading.

LAURA WOODLAND

To my boy,

As we approach your third birthday it's time to reflect
On when we were left to fend for ourselves
Our needs not met

A global pandemic knocked us off our feet
We had to 'stay at home'
No one could meet

We moved house at the start and here we stayed
Hibernating and scared
Whilst the government played

Patiently waiting, naive to how hard it would be
Worried but excited
To be home as a three

We had scans bi-weekly to watch you grow
A little on the small side
But perfectly so

All of these appointments I attended alone
Fearing the outcome
But I tried not to moan

May rolled around and it was VE Day
You'd been a bit quiet
Not moving in your usual way

People partied in the streets
Whilst I was in hospital
Anxiously awaiting your heartbeat

There it was, you were okay
We went home relieved
Still willing the virus away

On the 5th of June, I attended an appointment
"We're going to induce you"
I couldn't hide my disappointment

I couldn't wait to meet you but not in this way
Three days of labouring alone
Before Daddy could stay

And then, the day was here, the 8th of June
You entered the world
We were over the moon

Daddy stayed with us for just two short hours
No one else could visit
No cards, no flowers

On paper, I was a "lucky one"
A straightforward birth
A healthy son

But these are the days that will haunt me for life
Frightened and alone
Because COVID was rife

At a time when I needed people most
I was deprived of that
It was not what I'd hoped

Days on end with the sleepiest bundle
I couldn't see a way out
No light at the end of the tunnel

Your weight was declining
I was so painfully worried
I couldn't stop crying

Trying to feed you but I just couldn't do it
It wasn't working for us
I couldn't improve it

"Why can't I do this? This is what I'm meant to do"
But sometimes you just can't
When there's no help for you

Four days passed and we could finally go
Daddy picked us up
And he drove us home slow

I was scared, your daddy too
We stayed home and hid
We wanted to protect you

Finally, at home, you started to grow
So thankful for it
But I still felt so low

Some time passed before we let people visit
"Stand outside please"
We didn't want to push it

Unsure if I'd given you my heart condition
We didn't want to risk anything
It was the right decision

The months that followed are some of the hardest I've endured
I felt like I was failing
I thought you deserved more

Important appointments over the phone
"Please just see us"
It was the fear of the unknown

I took you to some classes after the first lockdown
Desperate to feel normal
But I felt like a clown

Then it was back to staying at home
The virus wasn't leaving
We could no longer roam

We had a routine which we fell into daily
Get up, go for a walk
Then watch the telly

I'd take you for a walk on the Strawberry Line
Holding my breath as we passed others
Trying to act fine

We were so lucky that Daddy worked from home
We'd play next door
Whilst he spoke on the phone

I loved spending so much time with you
I just imagined it different
It was a lot to go through

I felt so distant from family and friends
"I'll try harder...
When all of this ends"

I felt so isolated but I pushed myself deeper
Embarrassed to reach out
Feeling weaker and weaker

They say it takes a village but there was no one to be seen
It will never not cut deep
The year that should have been

How difficult it was shocked me to the core
And still to this day
It feels so raw

How could grief, love and joy so easily co-exist?
It wasn't meant to be like this
There was so much we missed

Soon, it was Easter, and we were allowed to do more
We started to go out
We started to explore

And then came the day my maternity leave was over
I hated leaving you
But it brought us even closer

You stayed with a childminder and you settled well
You enjoyed it there
I could tell

Now, I don't want it to be all doom and gloom
For the year 2020
Also saw you bloom

My boy - you were my saving grace
You kept me going
You are my safe place

And please, my darling, know you did nothing wrong
Our beacon of light
You guided us along

Thanks for making me 'Mum'
Despite the dark days
I hope all you've known is warmth, love and fun

It's been an honour to spend so much time with you
Time I wouldn't have got
Had normal leave followed through

It's now 2023 and you're a big brother
A little sister you dote on
You make me the proudest mother

COVID is still here but it doesn't affect our daily life
We've been on holidays and day trips
I love seeing the world through your eyes

And whilst I'll bear the scars of it for life
I won't let it define us
As parents and son, husband and wife

As hard as it was, I'd do it again
I'd do anything for you
You're my best friend

My hardest days were met with my best
And now looking back
I wouldn't ask for less

For it brought me a love I never knew
It brought me my baby
Marley... I simply adore you.

Laura Woodland is 31 and from Yatton, Bristol. She is a wife to Marc, Mummy to her lockdown babe Marley, and Quinn, his baby sister. She loves being outside and going on spontaneous adventures with her little family, especially visiting National Trust sites and the beach!
*@laurawoodland_*

ANNA JAMES

Dear Lily...

My firstborn, of course, my world changed completely the moment you arrived, but the world had been changing daily in the weeks before you were born. My baby shower was the last time lots of us were all together in one room before everyone's lives were turned upside down. Anxiety and fear became commonplace as everyone struggled to adapt to the 'new normal.' It was hard to tell what was due to becoming parents and what was due to living in COVID times. COVID-19 was a war we were all fighting and while the world stood still for some, we struggled to navigate parenthood for the first time without the pre-pandemic support structure.

16th March 2020

A week before I am due to go on maternity leave, I text one of my team after watching the news: "Today was probably my last day in the office, then... I'll be WFH... see you when I've had the baby!" Self-isolation has been forced upon pregnant mothers as we are vulnerable. All my maternity leave plans are instantly dashed. No last-minute pampering sessions, no shopping trips to get more baby things, no 'ladies who lunch' with other mums or the blissful, hazy, lazy days I've been looking forward to before you arrive. Instead, we are only allowed to make essential trips. The thought of having to go into hospital for pre-birth check-ups terrifies me. What if I get COVID? What would it do to me? Or you? The world I knew has ceased to exist.

No international travel. All shops are closed, except those selling essentials. Schools have shut and parents are juggling homeschooling and jobs. Playgrounds are empty. Restaurants are shut, offering takeaways instead of dining in. Everyone has been told to work from home if they can and to avoid public transport. Essential workers, like Daddy, have to carry on working but try and protect themselves the best they can.

7th April 2020

One week to go...

Every day we watch the news, horrified at the reports of people dying in their thousands in our country. Around the world, the COVID death toll keeps on rising. I am terrified at the prospect of bringing a new baby into this and am scared I might catch COVID every time I go to hospital for appointments. I don't go out much and am becoming increasingly anxious about the potential of giving birth to you without your daddy allowed in as my birthing partner, especially as the guidance keeps changing. The idea of giving birth alone scares me, but it is a very real possibility. I sign every petition I see to allow labouring mothers to have birth partners with them. Depressing updates on the news make me worry. What if your daddy got COVID? How would he react to it? What if he got it and then had to isolate and miss the birth of his first child? My mind spins with potential 'what ifs.' My girlfriends set up multiple backup plans in case Daddy can't be there so that I won't be on my own. I feel much better when he is allowed to work from home for two weeks before your due date, in an effort to keep us all safe.

14th April 2020

"Baby's still breech," the midwife says. So, a C-section it is.

I wait alone on the ward while another mother is wheeled down, also alone, for her operation. I'm nervous about the recovery from such an operation. I can't lift anything other than you. How will we manage when only one of us is allowed anywhere?

Daddy is only allowed to be with me once I'm prepped in theatre, so we talk on the phone while I wait. I can see him in the corridor across the courtyard, pacing nervously. I wish he was here with me to hold my hand. The staff are brilliant and help to calm me down. When Daddy is finally allowed in, he is wearing an operating gown and mask, looking nervous. I've never been so relieved to have him by my side, holding my hand, excited to meet you.

When you are born he turns to me; "It's a girl, we have a daughter!"

I can't see you properly as I have the mandatory mask on and my glasses are steaming up. The three of us have a short time in recovery, cuddling and marvelling over how wonderful and amazing you are. Daddy is only allowed to stay for an hour because of the restrictions, so he goes home and then it's just you and me again. The hours tick by slowly. I am exhausted, drugged up and alone with a tiny human depending on me. My muscles don't work properly and I have to ask the nurse to pass you to me just so I can cuddle you. I rely on others heavily; I feel as though I can't do anything I should be able to.

I count down to visiting time. No one can come except Daddy and he is only allowed to stay for an hour. It isn't long enough. I want my mum and dad here to calm me, but they aren't allowed in to help. No one but me, Daddy and the hospital staff are allowed to hold you, which seems crazy. Four loving grandparents have waited as long as we have, excited for your arrival. I start to worry that everyone wearing masks will traumatise you or slow down your facial recognition.

I need someone else with me. I feel too alone. I'm desperate to get you home with Daddy where we will be safe. I can't stop watching you. Your tiny hands and legs jerk, feeling the air around you, discovering a world that is alien, almost as much to me as it is to you.

15th April 2020

I can barely walk when we are allowed to go home. I know I'm being told important things about what to do next but I am on so many drugs and my exhausted, anxious brain can't take it in and Daddy isn't here with me to hear it. I desperately want someone to share the responsibility with. I don't want

Daddy to miss out on any more bonding time with you. For this reason, we probably go home before we are really ready.

16th April 2020

We call the midwives a lot when you're a newborn. We are worried about everything – is this normal? Are you supposed to do that? There is no one other than Daddy to help me with you, everyone else has to stay two metres away and we are tying ourselves in knots that you aren't feeding enough.

We stand outside our house with everyone in our street, clapping for the NHS staff working hard in this pandemic. Grandparents and friends come to the doorstep with presents. We wipe everything down and leave cards isolated for 24 hours before feeling like it is safe to touch them. I can't let anything slip, just in case we catch it. I'd never forgive myself.

26th May 2020

Daddy is back at work and we muddle through the days on our own. To reduce the risk of contamination, we take clothes off at the door and wash them, and ourselves, immediately. Masks are an everyday staple to protect everyone and my anxiety rises when someone passes near you without one. There are no clinics open so whenever anyone asks how heavy you are, I have no idea. We can't open a bank account for you as you haven't been registered. They are only registering deaths, not births.

There have been several heartbreaking and painful moments when seeing your grandparents because it feels unnatural that they can't come in and we can't hug them.

I had a meltdown today after a particularly tough day. It is so hard doing this alone. Your daddy says, "We've done all of this on our own. There's been no one able to help us. We've had to do it all. Everything."

This must be why I'm finding it so hard.

15th June 2020

At eight weeks old, you and I are in hospital again because you have a UTI. We end up in hospital for nearly a week, in our own room, isolated from the ward and any chances of catching COVID. I know everyone is busy but you are so small and vulnerable. I don't like leaving you in the room on your own and there's no one else who can take over from me. Daddy isn't allowed to visit.

COVID is cruel. The news says we're past the peak. Schools are opening again. Why can't he come onto the ward to see you? He has to wait at the door to hand over clean clothes for us. It'll be Father's Day on Sunday - his first as a daddy. I'm so sad that Grandpa still hasn't held you yet. You're his first grandchild and it all seems so unfair.

I didn't know then, but we would only have two Father's Days with Grandpa before he died. I'll forever be grateful that we were allowed out for Father's Day.

19th June 2020

We're all still terrified of COVID, though restrictions are easing. My parents are so scared of it that I feel like they are withdrawing from us. My head swirls with what if's. What if you get this killer virus? What if someone else has it and it gets on our clothes and in the house, and you breathe it in? My mind is working in overdrive and spirals out of control. I am snappy, constantly anxious and my mental health is declining.

It's only looking back now that I think I should have been diagnosed with postnatal depression and I'm so sorry I didn't speak up earlier to get help. I tell you that one day things will be back to normal and hopefully you won't remember this.

This lockdown is hazy and sleep-deprived. I don't know what day it is, I'm stuck in the every-day-merges-into-one newborn phase. My feelings are constantly conflicted. I love so many special moments with you, yet feel so isolated and unable to properly share you. I do a lot of sitting around, breastfeeding you, snuggling you close and loving the cuddles. I desperately long for the day when grandparents can kiss and cuddle you.

1st July 2020

You are ten weeks old and we can finally register your birth. We let grandparents hold you. They are over the moon. It's the start of the return to some kind of normal and it's bittersweet that they are only just holding you, but I cherish those memories now, especially now Grandpa isn't here. Maternity leave is not what I had planned. Baby classes are online; screens are a blessing as well as a barrier to meeting other new parents. The village it takes to raise a child is all around, yet so far away. Going for coffee and cake with a friend is a walk around the park with a takeaway.

COVID is heartless and the restrictions are cruel. My heart breaks for all of those people who had to say goodbye to their loved ones over FaceTime instead of in-person and the funerals that took place with only a few attendees.

Loss, sadness, fear and anxiety became a part of every day. It makes me so sad that this was your first experience of this world, and how much I changed, too. Thankfully, you were oblivious and didn't know any different. I'm grateful you came along when you did. You are the raft that kept us afloat on the hardest days I've experienced in the past three years. I love you more than you will ever know, love Mommy xxx

Anna James, 40, from Sedgley in Dudley, lives with her partner and their three-year-old daughter, Lily. She works part-time as a Senior Bid Manager. She loves music, nature and a relaxing spa day whenever she gets the chance. A cup of coffee or afternoon tea is her go-to activity for a catch-up with friends.

SARAH LANE

No one saw us grow together,
from poppy seed to watermelon.
Nor placed a hand to feel you squirm,
as you pushed against the walls of your home.

No one celebrated with us or came to a baby shower,
no balloons, games or cupcake tower.
Never got to shop for a baby buggy,
online only, if we were lucky.

No one was there when I was prodded and pricked,
blood test after blood test to check you were fit.
Nobody knew your arrival date had changed,
due to a complication, an induction was arranged.

No one saw Dad dropping off Mum and bump
A feeling in my throat like a giant lump.
Saying an awkward goodbye was just so wrong,
"I'll see you later," neither knowing how long

No one felt my fear and fright,
As I walked off alone and out of sight.
Nobody there to settle us in,
Just a blue curtain and our own company.

No one was there for your dad at home,
alone, waiting nervously by his phone.
Trying to keep busy to fight off the worry,
thinking of me, and you in my tummy.

No one was there as the cramps set in,
your journey into this world was beginning.
No hand to hold as I clung to the wall,
and paced the length of the hospital hall.

No one saw the messages to your dad,
whilst in labour and getting so mad.
Messages that should never have to be sent,
we should have been together; that's what was meant.

No one came when I screamed out in pain,
Begging for the one I needed, my Mr Lane.

And then Dad was there and you had arrived,
We had done it, I was strong, I had survived.

No one was with us when they sent Dad away,
After just two hours, all we wanted was for him to stay.
Alone to figure out how to be a new mum,
not even sure how to fit a nappy to your bum.

No one was there to take the photograph,
something so little, it sounds a bit daft.
But it mattered to us and we wanted it so,
a photo of the three of us leaving for home.

No one was there when we had to go back in,
back to the hospital with hours of waiting.
Needing Dad, support and a comforting cuddle,
instead - just us two and my emotions in a muddle.

No one was there when I tried to reach out,
as the anxiety began and my head filled with doubt.
Your dad did what he could and he was my rock,
he was great, but I needed help to get back to the top.

No one was there, just a face on the screen,
as I tried to tell my story and felt seen.
'Think of an image,' the therapist said,
a broken heart popped into my head.

No one was there to run baby groups,
Every day the same, going around in a loop.
No new mum friends to meet for coffee and cake,
Just me, you and banana bread to bake.

No one was there for breastfeeding guidance
everything in the world was still so silent.
We couldn't check your growth at weigh-in clinics,
So we stood on scales and tried to wing it.

No one knows the broken dreams and grief that I felt,
but one look at you and my heart would melt.
My shining rainbow through the stormy cloud,
you made us whole and we are so proud.

Through all of this, just you, Dad and me,

alone together but the most perfect three.
Time has healed and you have grown,
The world has changed and we aren't alone.

Now everyone has listened and heard our story,
of how strong us lockdown mamas can be.
A time in history we will never forget,
and the time when mothers and babies first met.

Now everyone can see how I would do it again if I had to
out of it came the most wondrous you.
Because now we have you and you are so worth it,
our life with you is so blissful and perfect.

Now everyone sees how beautiful you are,
and how as a family we have come so far
They've seen your big blue eyes and button nose,
your silky blonde hair and your ten tiny toes.

Now everyone's heard your voice and it's the sweetest sound,
they've watched you take your first steps on the ground.
They've heard you speak, laugh and sing,
being with you is the most magical thing.

Now everyone has felt your kindness and your joy,
they've seen the way you play with your favourite toy.
The way you can be so caring at the age of just two,
and your curiosity about the world and all that is new.

Now everyone sees the mum and dad we've grown into,
and they've seen you grow from one to two.
We'll always protect you and forever keep you safe,
Our favourite sight is a smile on your face.

Now everyone can see the love I feel,
with being a mum comes a love so real.
My darling daughter, my bestest friend,
my love for you will never end.

Sarah Lane, 31, lives in Hampshire with her husband, almost-three-year-old daughter – Isla, and their dog, Django. Living life as a mum, working part-time and trying to build up her own business in dog training and behaviour, she is a huge lover and advocate of rescue dogs. When not working, she enjoys having some "me" time at bounce classes and dog walks and loves nothing more than spending the weekend with her family, making memories. @adogs_taledogtraining

VICTORIA GRIFFITHS

March 2023, Rhode Island, USA.

To some extent, I was already used to having and raising children in isolation from others. That is the life of an expatriate. Having had two children already in the USA, online chats with grandparents and the absence of a family member around to cook me a meal or to take older siblings for a few hours to give me a break during pregnancy, were already familiar struggles and disappointments.

What I wasn't prepared for during the pandemic, was how that sense of isolation would deepen further, and how it would result in me doing things that I never thought I could. Three years later, I am often still overcome with grief for what can never be regained, but also aware of the unanticipated period of empowerment and self-discovery it created. The more I listen to others' stories of giving birth at that time, the more I realise that it is entirely appropriate for these vastly different feelings to co-exist when you have brought new life into such a dark period of history.

In March 2020, when our corner of the world in the USA joined the increasing number of other places shutting down due to the rapid community spread of COVID-19, just one week before friends and family in the UK also went into lockdown, I was six months pregnant with my third child. Although it was a healthy pregnancy, it had provoked asthma and allergies, and I felt more tired in this pregnancy than in my previous two. In the absence of family support I had just decided to carve out more time for rest in other ways; increasing my three-year-old's preschool hours and having someone help out with housework.

Then, suddenly, those things and so much more were gone. It was not gradual, there was no period of adjustment. One week life was normal, and the next it was not. Worst of all, there was still so little known about the virus. How easily did it spread and could it be transferred on clothing, groceries, packages or even letters? Early indications suggested it was most dangerous for the elderly and those with underlying conditions, but were expecting mothers more at risk? Babies in the womb? Newborns? There were no certain answers.

I threw myself into helping my six-year-old finish her school year remotely. It was a welcome distraction, if exhausting in the final trimester of pregnancy with a three-year-old at home as well. I was just entering the point of the pregnancy when prenatal visits increased in readiness for the delivery. I sent a picture of myself to my family in the disposable mask I had been handed to wear at my appointment. *A valuable commodity*, I joked, fully intending to keep it afterwards for multiple uses as they were so hard to come by. As soon as I got home I stripped my clothes and showered so as not to potentially introduce anything contaminated into the house. In the back of my mind, the niggling thought was rising. What would this changing landscape mean for the birth?

My husband and I started to call the hospital on an almost weekly basis. How many COVID-19 patients did they have now? Had there been any cases on the maternity ward? What measures were in place to reduce the possibility of it spreading in the hospital? It was the one place that nobody wanted to be to right now, but when you're having a baby you don't have a choice. It felt like every question unlocked more questions, our minds desperately searching for anything we might not have considered. The fear that we might bring COVID-19 home with us from the hospital, as well as a newborn, was not the only thing that worried me. All of the comfort measures I had planned for this birth were disappearing, too. The virus meant that patients could not use the birthing tub at the hospital, or the nitrous oxide, commonly known as gas and air, still a relatively new comfort measure in the US. All I could do was watch as my carefully thought-through birth plan was decimated.

Rumours were starting to circulate of hospitals not allowing partners or other support people in. It was happening in New York, which was little more than a three-hour train ride from us. According to the rapidly changing rules and restrictions at our hospital, it looked like my husband might be able to be there for the birth (at least that's what they were allowing that week) but if he left to be with our two older children he would not be able to return. I would be left in the hospital, alone, with my newborn within 24 hours of giving birth, regardless of how it had gone and how well we were recovering.

He would have to leave the hospital, for who else would stay with our two older children during a global pandemic? My mother had been around to help during the births of my first two children, but, now stuck in the UK, she would not be there for this little one. She would not be there for the end of the pregnancy to see my bump, to hold down the fort as we headed to the hospital, to ready the girls to meet their new sibling, to hold her newborn grandchild or welcome it home for the first time. Those thoughts had to be buried. Decisions needed to be made.

I considered doing something I never in my wildest dreams thought I would ever do. Could I... could I really... what if... what if I had this baby at home?

Already in the final trimester of pregnancy, I didn't have long to decide. Maybe that was a good thing because looking back on the weeks that my husband and I wrestled with it - consulting doctors, midwives, doulas, people who we knew who'd had homebirths (a number that we could count on one hand) - it felt like a lifetime. There were endless late-night chats after our older two were in bed, as we weighed up possible scenarios and then tried to put them aside so we could get a night's sleep before the intensive days of juggling school and work under one roof began again.

A small percentage of people in the UK choose home births every year. In the USA it is even less common, as birth tends to be more medicalised and the vast majority of insurance companies will not cover the cost of midwife support at home where there is perceived to be more inherent risk. As a risk-avoidant person myself, I had always been in awe of anyone who felt like they could birth without the reassurance of having doctors, neonatal intensive care units and operating theatres close by. Of course, before hospitals, women had birthed at home for centuries with little to no medical support, but then, I thought, there must be a reason why people had switched to giving birth in the hospital. Surely it was safer, wasn't it? At least, I think that's what we've been led to believe.

I was acutely aware that it is one thing to choose a home birth because it is the birth scenario you have always wanted and another to choose it because the thought of birthing in the hospital is now more frightening than the thought of birthing at home. The lesser of two evils. Having experienced childbirth twice before, I kept playing over and over in my mind what it might be like to do that again, but this time in my own house.

There was one home birth practice in our small state consisting of three midwives and two trainees, and they had space for me if I didn't leave it too long to decide. Demand for home birth was, unsurprisingly, increasing. Finally, we satisfied ourselves enough that everything indicated that the risk to myself and the baby of birthing at home was low. We paid out of our own pockets to secure our midwife support, something I will always be grateful we could afford to do.

Two weeks before my due date, the death of George Floyd sent shockwaves through the US. Rioting meant that we were now receiving text message alerts to our phones with a curfew time to observe in addition to COVID-19 restrictions - yet another reason I was glad not to be travelling to a hospital. It was impossible to process the turmoil the country and the world was in; the world that I was about to bring my new child into. My social media feed, already saturated with how to create daily schedules for children learning from home and updates on COVID-19, was also filling up with advice about how to talk to your children about these heavy and important issues, the books I needed to buy and the voices I needed to listen to. I felt overwhelmed with the responsibilities I held as a mother, ones I had never anticipated that were coming thicker and faster than I could handle.

The day that my six-year-old finished her school year remotely and a week before my due date, I woke an hour after going to bed, with labour progressing fast. Nine hours later, my son was born to the sounds of his sisters singing along at the tops of their lungs to a musical in the living room downstairs. Within two hours I was able to be in my own bed with my baby snuggled up skin to skin, with his older siblings meeting him for the first time, something they would not have been able to do in the hospital. It felt completely wild to have chosen and accomplished something that felt so primitive in modern society, a choice that many people could not fathom, but under the circumstances, it also felt like more than I could have hoped for.

Though I may forget their faces, masked as they were, I will never forget the kindness and professionalism of the women who helped me birth at home during a pandemic. They could have closed their doors, but instead, they were there steadfastly holding space, even in the midst of chaos, for women like me to birth as free from fear as possible. They are quite simply, my heroes.

Those first few days of my son's life were exceedingly precious; cocooned at home with my husband doing the cooking, the occasional visit from a masked midwife and family greeting the new baby over the internet. In some ways, it felt simpler bringing a baby into the world with no other expectations on us to go anywhere or see anyone. But soon, the melancholy hit me. There was not a soul to admire and fuss over my new baby, few gifts, no deliveries of prepared meals from well-wishers, no one running the vacuum around for us or giving the older two some undivided attention. Now, I had three children under six, including a newborn, and my husband and I were on our own.

The worst of it was the knowledge that this virus wasn't going anywhere. Two weeks after the birth, I broke down and cried to the midwife, clutching my new baby, tears rolling down my cheeks and soaking his swaddling blanket. This wasn't how it was supposed to be. He was so small and I was so fearful for him. I had delivered him safely, but I was exhausted and alone and had no idea what would be required of me next. There was still no end in sight.

What followed was the longest, strangest and yet, somehow also sweetest summer of my life. Just as the rest of the world was starting to breathe a little, with the warmer months meaning that it was possible to meet up outside as virus cases dropped, we took the difficult decision to stay isolated. It was too risky with a newborn and my asthma, and we had no close family or friends around to create a 'bubble' with.

I embarked on 'summer activities camp at home' for my older children. I cradled my infant on my lap while I helped his sisters glue and stick things. I held him on my shoulder while I supervised experiments in the garden and I nursed while reading story books. It was such an intensive time with my children that required all of me, but also joyful. I expect the memory will eventually fade, even for my eldest child, but the smiling faces, the little hands, the warmth of my baby against my body, my constant companion, will not fade easily from mine.

That summer, and for many months afterwards, we took each day as it came. It was the only way to survive the continued uncertainty. So many things would have been overwhelming if we'd known how long they would last, especially how long it would take for our family to be able to meet our son for the first time. Even after the vaccine was rolled out for everyone over the age of 18 in both countries, the travel restrictions between the UK and USA remained in place. Grandparents would not meet my son in-person until he was almost 18 months old, and for some relatives, he would be two before they met him. Not one of our wider family knew him as a baby at all, except what they observed through a screen.

Though I wanted to hold back time for all those who were missing his babyhood, and while I wanted to treasure those early days that go so fast, paradoxically, I also spent so much of my son's first two years willing the time to go faster, for him to get bigger and more robust. *Just a few more months*, I kept thinking, *just get a few more months on you and you'll be able to fight this thing better when you get it... or if I get it you'll be able to manage better without me.* When my older children went back to school, I wrote a letter to all three, just in case I should end up in hospital.

In the spring of 2022, the virus finally caught up with us. By that time, I was vaccinated and found myself most affected by watching my son, now almost two years old, succumb to it. After doing everything within my power to spare him from exposure to this mutating virus, I felt that all too familiar grip of fear, helplessness and despair. While the virus wasn't considered much of a threat to those in his age range, seeing him look so unwell and so tired that he could not stay awake for more than an hour made me anxious for what might be happening inside his body that I could not see. I had kept him from it for so long, longer than most, but it still didn't feel like long enough.

I expect I will continue to feel a wide range of conflicting emotions for some time to come. Every birthday my son passes, it will be impossible not to remember the circumstances surrounding his birth, the stress and the struggle. Yet, I hope I will also remember the lessons it taught me; to pause and treasure the good and the beautiful, especially the beauty of new life, in spite of, or maybe even in defiance of, the anxiety and unknowns. And that humans are resourceful and able to cope with more than we think. Perhaps that is especially true of those of us with children, though in today's society, it is often considered a burden to be weighed down with responsibility for those who are dependent on their caregivers. In the midst of so many hard choices, gut-wrenching news headlines and sad stories, my children were bright lights that sustained me. They sustained me exactly because they needed me and just holding my son in my arms in that turbulent time was a gift of peace.

My children, I've come to realise, are my superpower, and even though it was not meant to be this way, I would not change this time for anything.

Victoria Griffiths (née Robb), 39, was born and grew up in the UK. In 2010, she moved to Boston, Massachusetts with her husband and over a decade later is now a mother of three living in Cranston, Rhode Island. Her passions include supporting children and families through work and volunteering, history, art, theatre and being part of the local church. She holds degrees from Cambridge and Birmingham Universities. Her happy place is an autumn day in New England.

JESSICA WATSON

You've imagined the most incredible moment of your life.
You're going to feel like it's been ruined by something
Far beyond your control.
You'll be home, as a brand new family of three.
You'll feel every single ounce of sadness that everyone is expressing to you.

It'll be hard.
The hardest thing that you go through, but you'll fall into motherhood,
In a way better than you ever imagined.

Your new baby is magic,
But Mama, so are you.

We sat alone, Freddie and I, just hours after he had been born. His dad stood looking through the window as my tears dropped down onto my newborn son's head. We had been treated like lepers for ten hours and told, as I entered the theatre for my caesarean, that the staff were on overtime having had to wait for my PCR test result, due to a policy change at 9am that morning. They said that if I was positive my husband, Perri, wouldn't be allowed to be present, despite us isolating and being cooped up in the same room all day.

We had danced to our wedding song, I had sobbed through starvation and we had laughed at how ridiculous the whole process felt. The time we had looked forward to had been stripped away from us. We were eight days into the lockdown and we were cared for from a doorway. Finally, 4.30pm rolled around and we were told it was time to go to theatre.

Walking in the room felt cold and crowded. When a nurse joked that they were on overtime, I felt like a burden. I laughed, hoping that I wasn't being too much trouble. Perri came in the room and my section began. They say it feels like someone washing up in your stomach but to me, it felt like ransacking a bag to get the job done. 5.28pm and Freddie screamed the room down as he entered this world, almost as if he knew how crazy it was outside his safe space.

We got to the ward at around 7pm and Perri was immediately shouted at by a midwife to leave. We looked at each other, he held Freddie for less than a minute and left. My whole body felt empty as I began to sob.

"Sorry, it's just policy," she muttered, clearly feeling bound by rules. I was told to buzz if I needed anything and we were alone again, Freddie and me. He side-eyed me (as he still does now) and I was besotted, yet heartbroken. I stayed awake all night, studying every feature that I had created over the last nine months. I took photos and videos, sending them to Perri as he had his last undisturbed night of sleep. I did laps of the room we were in and drank litres upon litres of water, determined to get home as soon as we could. Less than 24 hours later, we were discharged and made it home.

My parents live 70 yards away from us, on the street I grew up on. I needed to see them. They had isolated in case they were needed. We snuck in, placed Freddie in his car seat in the middle of the room and we stood in opposite corners and looked at him. We stayed for five minutes and then left. Grandparents - terrified to be too close to their first grandson. I had dreamed of this moment, picturing telling my dad that his first grandson shared his name as a middle name and watching my mum sing nursery rhymes to him as she cradled him in her arms.

The next day, Perri's family came to the back of the house to meet Freddie, also their first grandson. Unable to hold him and shower him with love, I sobbed again after they left. It felt unnatural to experience his first meetings like this. Cousins, aunts and uncles sent us messages of support and we had daily FaceTime calls with my sister, mum and dad. Cards and presents were dropped at the door, never seeing a soul. We were in our bubble of three, listening to Harry Styles, soaking up Freddie's every move. We took our hour-long walks, fearing anyone approaching his pram. Looks of sympathy were thrown at us, at a distance, from across the street.

Garden visits became a regular occurrence. We sat inside with the patio doors open and family members sat well over two metres away, craving the best glimpse of Freddie they could get. Wishing they could hold him. Me, wishing they could scoop him up and show him just how loved he was. I cried every single day. My eyes were swollen. I would end FaceTime calls early to avoid showing how I was struggling. *It's the baby blues*, I told myself over and over again. *It's just exhaustion. It can't be postnatal depression, I'm the happiest I've ever been.*

It was postnatal depression and I knew it. I could feel the anxiety building the longer we went without human contact. 10 weeks alone and I could feel myself becoming more and more anxious about him going near anyone else. Too protective, too scared and too broken. I needed family to hold him. So they did. In the garden, as the sun shone down on my mum holding my son, I felt terrified. Perri held my hand to steady the shakes. My dad held Freddie and their friendship was formed. I cried, again. Something so natural petrified me. How was I going to get over this feeling?

It was coming up to Freddie's nana's birthday. What better present could she receive, and what better present could she give me, than to help me begin to overcome this irrational fear? Perri asked her if she wanted to hold him and tears built in her eyes. My stomach was in knots and I felt like I couldn't breathe, physically shaking in fear. Perri held my hand whilst his mum cried as she rocked him.

How could I begin to admit that I was overjoyed but also felt a fog over everything? I continued to push back the thoughts swirling through my mind, despite my heart breaking over and over. The briefings on TV at 5pm knocked my stomach to sickness. I cried as dates were pushed further and further back.

I didn't want to share our beautiful boy with the world in a time full of loss and sadness. I struggled to share my anger as I read of rules being broken and pubs reopening.

After five months, I finally admitted that I wasn't okay. The weight began to lift as the words poured from my mouth. It felt like all I had done every day was love my sweet boy and cry. I started counselling. My counsellor told me my feelings were valid. I will always be thankful for her. I breathed a sigh of relief. I hadn't felt allowed to complain about our circumstances, for fear of looking ungrateful after being able to have my son.

Postnatal depression began to fade but the anxiety simmered (and still does) in the back of my mind. We were lucky enough to fall pregnant with our second son, George, in 2021. I attended appointments alone and Perri waited in the car park with other expectant dads, waiting to be summoned in for scans and consultations. George arrived seven weeks early and was admitted to NICU, upon which, my anxiety vanished. I felt like I had been fixed. The obvious worry that comes with a baby in NICU was present in the forefront of my mind but I was determined. I was ready to fight for anything he needed and for our family to be reunited. I felt stronger than I had in months.

Postnatal depression, anxiety and PTSD never entered my head as I forethought what it would be like bringing our boys into this world. I also never expected that I would still have the daily battles three years on: the panic as Freddie runs his favourite route he knows inside out, the shakes I feel in my hands as I approach the counter at work, the rushed visits to urgent care in the middle of the night when one of the boys is unwell and the fog hazing over my daily thoughts as I doubt myself. I'm trying, the same as we all are, to overcome it. To learn to live with this cruel norm. To live a motherhood where the start still seems so unfair. To live with the, "Oh, that must have been rough," when you tell someone your child's date of birth. To be envious of baby groups, baby showers and freedom.

We're part of a club. A shitty club that we never dreamed we would be part of. A club where we missed baby classes, met family members through windows and learned to hold our own when things got rough. We've bonded over Instagram posts and sympathised with each other. It's been a rough ride into motherhood, one that I would never have imagined for myself, but if I had the option to, I wouldn't change a thing.

Because my children are magic, and even if sometimes I don't believe it, so the fuck am I.

Jessica Watson, 34, from Darlington lives with her husband and their two sons, Freddie, 3 and George, 2. She works as a pharmacy dispenser and in her spare time she enjoys going on adventures with her family and the odd hour to get her nails and brows done for a bit of me time. In her quiet moments, she enjoys writing poetry and relaxing in front of bingeable series.

SAMANTHA

Trigger warning: Miscarriage

To my son, born in July 2020.
You are a little brother. You are a rainbow baby in more ways than one. You followed a miscarriage, but you're also the rainbow that followed the storm. Here's the story of the storm...

We were gleeful when two lines finally appeared in September 2019. One day, in October, I started to bleed. I remember feeling a 'pop' in my stomach later that evening. A few days later, it was confirmed that I'd had an early miscarriage.

I am one of the lucky ones - I conceived pretty much immediately after. That second line appeared again late in November 2019. There it was, our much-longed-for rainbow baby.

In January 2020, I attended the hospital for my 12-week scan. An accident on the motorway meant my partner couldn't get back from work in time and missed it. I lay on the bed while being scanned and managed to write a single, but crucial, message on my smartwatch to my partner: "All OK." A due date of 2nd August was confirmed. A midwife was trying to capture as many pregnant ladies waiting as possible to offer flu jabs. As she discussed what it would and wouldn't cover, she explained,

"We don't know how effective it is against the flu that's broken out in Wuhan in China that you may have heard of."

"Ah, yes," I replied, "I'm not worried about that."

9th March 2020

We had a week at Center Parcs. Only one of the shops had any toilet roll - it was like winning the lottery. This was suddenly much more serious than anyone had considered. We left Center Parcs knowing that the next time we'd visit would be very different as we'd be a family of four... but who knew how else it might be different? I had mixed feelings: sadness, worry, anxiety, hope and fear. The morning after, our daughter attended her weekend theatre school group. I took a photo of her and a friend sitting together, pretending to be sailors on a boat. Little did I know, this would be the last time they were together.

17th March 2020

My partner and I attended the 20-week scan. There were now strict rules about using hand gel before entering a hospital, except – there wasn't any. The stand was empty and the bottle wasn't there. It had been stolen, along with most public bottles of hand gel, and toilet rolls. The scan went well and I was relieved and grateful that my partner had been able to attend and see his baby on screen after missing the 12-week scan.

Our daughter's nursery was sending daily messages about what might happen. "We're going to stay open – we've only been advised to close and we don't want to." I was pregnant, I couldn't risk her bringing this killer virus home. It might kill her unborn baby sibling.

23rd March 2020

My partner started his new job. When he arrived home I said,

"There's a news conference tonight at 8pm. It's Boris... This is big."

We settled our daughter down to bed and when 8pm came we sat on separate sofas in silence.

"From midnight tonight, you must stay at home for three weeks."

We listened to the whole thing in silence. Afterwards, we just looked at each other, in shock. I rubbed my pregnant bump. I was scared. I was so, so scared. Our daughter had been with my partner's parents that day and was due to go the next day. They texted,

"Does this mean she won't be coming?"

We replied, "Yes."

The reality hit. We didn't know when she'd see her grandparents again. My partner then turned to work – he'd just completed his first day and was now being told he couldn't leave the house! What would this mean? Did he still have a job? With my impending maternity leave, I worried about if he would be able to provide for us.

"We have no idea what's going on," came the reply. "Stay at home tomorrow, we're telling everyone that, we'll be in touch."

The next morning I went up to my home office and logged on as normal. It was eerily different. Less phone calls. Less emails. My colleagues were as dumbfounded as we were. Nobody knew what it meant. "Oh well, it's only three weeks," we said. My partner was home with our daughter so they did crafts, played in the garden and made cakes – much to my delight!

"I'll go the shops this week," I said. "I could do with a change of scenery."

"No you bloody won't," came the reply from my partner. "You're pregnant, it's too risky. You must stop here."

I rubbed my pregnant belly and knew he was right. He went himself, returning home with tales of huge queues outside the supermarkets, aisles of empty shelves, clothing cordoned off as unessential and one-way systems.

A week passed and my partner and I were both put on furlough leave, along with all of my immediate colleagues.

"But I don't want to stop working," I said. "I need to work, it's my daily purpose, you know I need to work."

I had to agree to take a drop to 80% of my salary as the other option would be redundancy, because the work wasn't there. All business plans had been halted until the end of May to get us through this hurdle. I went with the flow and tried to think of the positives – I had additional time with my daughter before our second baby arrived.

We broke the rules after a few weeks and travelled a couple of miles to visit my dad, who lives alone with no other family. I needed to know he was OK. I took a photo of him, standing at his upstairs flat window, talking to us. *One to laugh at in the future...* That was the only way he saw my ever-growing pregnancy bump - from his upstairs flat window.

As I started furlough, my partner volunteered to go into work, leaving me looking after our daughter. I quickly moved into a routine which pretty much revolved around the CBeebies schedule with a walk outdoors each morning. In May, we were allowed back into parks. I have never, ever seen a two-year-old so happy to see a park. She ran and ran. She looked at everything and smelled every flower. It was like she had discovered freedom again.

A few days later, whispers between my colleagues were that something wasn't right. Our furlough was going to be extended.

"I'm so, so scared I'll be made redundant," I texted a friend.

"Don't be silly," she replied, "They're not going to make you redundant when you're pregnant."

My colleagues and I were invited to a call for an update. Something in my stomach told me this wasn't good.

"All business plans have been suspended for the remainder of this year, at least. As a result, there will be many roles put at risk of redundancy and I need you all to know that you may be affected."

Bam. There it was. I had my daughter sat on my knee, next to my pregnant bump, while I was told I might lose my job. *This can't be happening. Surely not.* My fate was out of my hands.

8th June 2020

A routine midwife appointment (thankfully, in person) discovered both mine and the baby's heartbeats were too fast. She wanted me to be checked out at the hospital. We had no option but to break the rules, so that my in-laws could look after our daughter. They'd not been able to touch her since 23rd March. The hospital asked me how I'd been and I explained I was about to find out if I'd keep my job. I asked if that was affecting my baby.

"Possibly," came the reply.

11th June 2020

I was told I was officially at risk of redundancy. I was due to start maternity leave in a few weeks! I was 32 weeks pregnant. How could this be happening? I sat on our bed after the call in silence. Numb. Alone.

13th June 2020

I had a call from my mum.

"I think I've had a stroke," she said, "I don't know what to do."

It turned out that she had a blockage in her neck which had caused a mild stroke. I needed to stay strong and positive, not only for our daughter, who I wanted to keep upbeat and happy, but also for our unborn baby. If I felt stressed, the baby would feel stressed and the hospital had advised me to stay calm. I had to breathe deeply and stay calm. I brushed aside any emotions I was feeling and painted a smile on my face. *It'll be fine. If I don't think about it then it can't affect me.*

9th July 2020

I was officially redundant. My employment would end three days after my baby's due date.

"I want to applaud you for the resilience you've shown throughout this process," I was told. "You've stayed so strong in what must be very difficult circumstances."

Because I'm so numb inside I can barely speak and simply don't have the energy to fight, I thought.

"Thanks," I replied.

The outplacement support offered was due to kick in at the end of July and early August.

"My baby is due, I can't take part in it," I told them.

"That's the agreement, I'm afraid," came the reply.

Deep breaths.

17th July 2020

I had to pack all of my work items into a jiffy bag for a courier to collect. That was it. Gone. Nine years of service packaged up in a jiffy bag. I didn't have any tears left. How could someone so heavily pregnant be made redundant? I reminded myself to stay strong. Ten days later, my waters broke unexpectedly. My in-laws collected our daughter and my partner drove me to hospital. I had to go in alone while he waited outside.

They were happy for me to go home until the contractions started but I declined, explaining I expected them to progress quickly based on my eldest's birth. They said I could be admitted onto the ward but my partner couldn't stay. I sobbed but knew that was the right thing to do. My partner texted me once he was home and I joked about the lovely window view I had. All of a sudden - BAM - a huge contraction hit out of nowhere. I knew this was it. Another couple passed about five minutes apart and I asked to be examined again.

"Six centimetres," she said, "You'd better tell your partner to come back."

I'd only been there for just over an hour!

Around two hours later, I felt the baby suddenly shoot down the birth canal. I looked at my partner and knew that this last push would be the last page in what had been the worst story ever written. At 5.27pm, our baby boy was born. Our rainbow after the storm had arrived. As I gave the final push to get him out, I felt the stress and tension of the last few months fall away. I cradled him in my arms for the first time and nothing else mattered anymore.

I was fortunate that my partner was able to stay in that room with us until midnight, when I was then transferred to the ward. As we dressed our son for the first time I reached into his bag and brought out a rainbow sleepsuit I'd packed. Our rainbow.

I didn't have a job any more, but my family was complete.

Samantha, 39, from Sheffield lives with her partner and two children; a five-year-old daughter and three-year-old son. She works full-time as a Learning and Development Manager, somehow juggling this with motherhood! Since becoming a mum, she is passionate about supporting and empowering parents in the workplace. You'll usually find her drinking endless cups of (cold) tea while waiting around at various kids' activities. Samantha is a Girlguiding volunteer where she always reminds herself that she has made a promise 'to do my best, to be true to myself!'

SARAH KNAPP

My first baby was born in 2017, and unfortunately, I had a very tough and traumatic birth with her. We tried for our second baby two years later and found out we were pregnant in October 2019. We were overjoyed, and as the pregnancy progressed, and after many hospital appointments and difficult conversations, it was agreed I would have a planned C-section. It wasn't what I originally wanted, as the recovery from the last section was tough, however, it was going to be the safest option for me and the baby. I was so desperate to have a better experience this time around and I was optimistic that it would be.

I announced the pregnancy to the world of Facebook with a family photo revealing my bump, along with the caption, '2020 looks pretty good to me!' If only I knew what was to come!

We found out we were having a baby boy in February 2020 and we were over the moon. There had been a few whispers of a virus called 'COVID,' but I didn't know much about it, nor did I feel the need to learn as I thought it was just another scaremongering thing the media were talking about. I was taking my then-three-year-old, Robyn, to a playgroup and one of the mums there said she didn't want to come back again after that session as she was too worried about COVID. I remember thinking how ridiculous and over-the-top that was, and couldn't believe someone was that concerned that they would stop doing something so normal! Again, if only I knew what was to come!

March 2020 came and COVID suddenly became this real, scary threat to our lives and of course, our normality. I was 25 weeks pregnant and it was advised that anyone 'high risk' should isolate. Being pregnant and asthmatic, I fell into this category. I felt scared, alone, hopeless, shocked and gutted. I had these overwhelming feelings so suddenly and each of them was all-consuming. I'm not sure if that was due to me being pregnant and perhaps more emotional than usual or if this would have been the effect regardless.

As time went by and the pregnancy weeks passed, these feelings stayed. I was so scared to go to any hospital or midwife appointments, in fear that I would catch the virus. I wore a mask and gloves and was so uncomfortably hot in them as there was an amazing, but intense, heatwave. I would wash my hands at every opportunity, even though I had been wearing gloves! I even put hand sanitizer on the gloves in case they had the virus on them! There was a time when the hospital didn't feel like a safe place, but instead, a place of danger, risk and higher threat.

The antenatal department was nearly always empty when I went in to have third trimester scans and it had this horrible, eerie feel to it; making me feel even more alone in my journey. My husband, Aaron, wasn't allowed to come to the appointments and it just felt so wrong and unfair. The worst hospital visits that I had to encounter alone were for reduced foetal movement. This is obviously a worrying thing to experience, even with your partner by your side, but to drive myself to the hospital, walk up to the antenatal department and then wait to be called, all alone, was extremely difficult. Thankfully, all five times that I had to go in for reduced movement, everything was okay. I couldn't bring myself to imagine how awful it would have been, to be there without my husband if something had been wrong. After one of the episodes of reduced movement, I came home after midnight, left my clothes at the front door and then showered, even though I was exhausted, I was just so worried about the virus being on me.

Whenever I had an appointment at the hospital, I would feel mixed emotions. The first being fear. Fear of going where there would be people. Fear there would be someone that got too close to me. Fear that I would touch something with the virus on it and I would get it and pass it on to my unborn baby or the rest of my family. The other strong emotion was relief. Relief at leaving the house. Relief at being in a different space. Relief to be outside, or in the car. Relief to know that life still existed outside of my own home. Relieved to be free!

After one particular hospital trip, I chose to drive the longer way home as it felt so great to be out. At the time, this would have been seen as wrong, but I needed it for my mental health. We are fortunate to live near the sea and it's always been my happy place and a space for calm and tranquillity. I needed that more than ever. I pulled over and got out of the car, which felt so daring and naughty. I walked up to the pebbles and down to the sand. I wrote 'HOPE' in the sand and felt incredibly emotional as I stood staring at the word. I felt hopeless yet so wanted to feel hopeful. I have always been an optimistic person so tried my best to keep thinking of life after this was all over.

My mum hadn't been able to touch my bump or feel my baby move inside my tummy; something so small, so normal, yet it was taken away from us both. When the government introduced social 'bubbles,' my mum was the first person we chose to see and be close to again. The day we hugged, for the first time in months, was truly magical and something I will never forget. She touched my bump and I felt overwhelmingly grateful that she could, at last, be more involved with my pregnancy journey. At this point, though, I had only 14 days to go.

We couldn't decorate a room for our baby. The room needed plastering and a few days before it was due to be done, lockdown happened. My husband made a makeshift wardrobe out of copper pipe just so I had somewhere to hang all of the baby's clothes (mostly second-hand, as shops were closed!) I couldn't do the whole 'nesting' thing and felt so sad that I couldn't get his room ready for his arrival. I felt less prepared for him coming, both physically and emotionally.

June 26th 2020 came and our baby boy, Marley, was going to be born. My husband was allowed with me whilst we waited for my time slot, was allowed to come into theatre whilst I was having the caesarean and to be with us in the recovery room for a few hours after the birth. We had been told that he would be allowed on the ward with us for a short time, to help settle us in and set us up with all that we needed for the night. I couldn't feel my body from the waist down as the spinal block hadn't worn off. I was being wheeled into the ward when the nurse told Aaron that he had to go home and couldn't come in any further. I cried in the corridor, desperate for him to stay. Emotionally, I wasn't ready for him to go and physically, I definitely wasn't. I began panicking, thinking, *how on earth am I going to get through the night looking after Marley when I can't even move properly?* The midwives reassured me they were there to help but, of course, they were short staffed and couldn't keep coming in every ten minutes. If I did something as simple as dropping something, I couldn't lean over to pick it up. I would have to call the midwife just for that and they were so busy, I felt like an inconvenience. Of course, had my husband been there, a trivial thing like that would have been sorted in seconds. It was such a horrible, almost desperate, feeling; being so reliant on the staff when they couldn't help. Marley cried constantly and I couldn't physically keep reaching over to get him because of the pain and because I still couldn't feel my legs. It was awful to not be able to care for my newborn baby or have any help from my husband. Aaron was allowed to come in for thirty minutes a day and had to wear a mask and an apron when on the ward. It felt so unnatural for him to hold his precious new baby with PPE on.

  We came home after three days in hospital (it felt a lot longer without the visits from friends or family) and it was wonderful for Robyn to finally meet her new baby brother. I was sad that she didn't get to come into the hospital to see Marley. I also really missed her as I had got used to being with her all the time in lockdown.

  When we were home, we didn't have the usual influx of visitors. I know for some, that was a positive, but for me, I missed that. I wanted to show Marley off to the world. I wanted him to be cuddled by my friends and family. I wanted strangers to look at him and say how beautiful he was. We didn't get any of that. We eventually decided to let our close family have a cuddle with him but they all wore masks and he had disposable covers wrapped around him so he didn't come into contact with their clothes. All of his early photos with anyone other than myself, my husband or Robyn, are like this. Whenever I look at them now, I feel such sadness. I feel like something special was taken away from us and we can never get it back.

  I broke down in tears within a few weeks of being home. Aaron asked me what was wrong and I told him how sad I was that we'd hardly received any 'new baby' cards. I knew this was because people weren't shopping as normal and some shops were still shut. Perhaps some people were waiting for that day they would be allowed to visit. But all the rational reasons didn't help me. I just felt like people didn't care he had been born or even remembered he had arrived. Looking back now, I know that wasn't true but at the time it felt so big and upsetting... just another consequence of having a baby in the pandemic.

  I was not able to register Marley for months after he had been born. There were so many deaths being registered due to COVID that everything was delayed. Once again, there was the feeling that Marley didn't matter, his birth wasn't important enough to be registered and we were just so small in this huge pandemic. All the problems it was causing came rushing over me.

It felt like no one was there to help and support me as a new mum. I couldn't go and get him weighed at the family centres; they simply weren't open. I loved doing this with Robyn; it was always so exciting to see how much she had grown each week and it felt rotten that I didn't get to experience this with Marley. There were no baby groups to go to. No chats with other mums. No sharing baby experiences with someone in the same boat as you. It felt lonely and sad.

Nine months after having Marley, I had an accident at home and broke my back. It was March 2021 and we were still very much in the pandemic. I was admitted to hospital and was there for three long weeks. I wasn't allowed to have anyone with me when I went into hospital and I wasn't allowed any visitors so I didn't see my then-three-year-old or nine-month-old for the duration of my stay. This was by far one of the hardest things I've ever had to endure but it was definitely made worse as all the feelings from when I had my 2020 baby came rushing back, whilst I was there lying in the hospital bed, alone. I think these feelings and memories will stay with me forever.

Fast forward to March 2023 - my best friend has just had her second baby and I was able to visit them in the hospital, a normal pleasure that was taken away in the pandemic. She showed me photos of her eldest child visiting his new brother and I couldn't help feeling jealous. I would have loved for Robyn to come and meet her baby brother in hospital when he was born. Still, nearly three years on, emotions run deep and strong. I think it's because we can never get those moments back and therefore a piece of our children's lives, and our own, were taken away.

The pandemic certainly taught me to be more grateful for the little everyday things. It taught me that I am a person who needs people, I am a person who is at their happiest when I am in the company of good friends and family and even just chatting to friendly strangers. It taught me that I am incredibly strong and I can face more than I would have ever have imagined. I have definitely been left with some scars. I am hugely triggered if one of my children are ill with something contagious and we have to stay in. Isolating was a huge mental battle for me and those feelings come racing back as if it were yesterday. I think I will always feel a sadness when I look back at how Marley came into the world at such a scary and lonely time. Those feelings will never go away and the memories can never be changed. I will, however, teach Robyn and Marley as they grow up, about how we got through it. How we were strong and brave. How we, as a family, came together and spent time together like never before. We played more and we loved harder. That is something I will always be grateful for. Love definitely won.

Sarah Knapp, 35, from Worthing lives with her husband, Aaron, and their two children, Robyn, 6 and Marley, 3. She works from home, part-time, running her beauty business. The rest of her time is filled with her being a mum to her energetic, strong-spirited pair! She loves to dance and socialise with her friends with a cocktail, or three!

CHARLOTTE TOKOLICS

I had a lockdown pregnancy, a lockdown birth and an on-and-off lockdown first year as a mum. I could write pages and pages about my experiences, as I'm sure we all could. I have been fortunate enough to have received lots of help from services, counselling, family, friends and my amazing fiancé. I feel that I have accepted a lot of it, and for my own sake, I just need to move on. But there are a few things that still make me sad and incredibly angry.

The best way I can convey my feelings around that time is to write in short bursts and imagine I am in the situation. They are not stories, they are not exactly poems, they may be messy but they are my experiences. A collection of writings...

Where it began

I found strength through it all that I didn't know I possessed. I found calm and silence. I found a routine, a system and a way through it all.

I found a way.

I've learned that many others did, too.

But, now it's all over and I am left with the rubble and ruins of my mind to clean up, alone.

There are no services for me anymore. There is no support. I am at the bottom of the waiting list with everyone else.

I managed and I got through. I am proud of myself. I am proud of the mum that I was.

But, now it all falls apart. The strength is wavering and the reality of the absolute clusterfuck that we went through is seeping through the cracks.

I am overwhelmed. I am tired. I am exhausted. I am envious of the new mums that have the experience I dreamed of.

I was aware of my fragility when I found out I was pregnant and I tried to do everything right. I was prepared, I sought help and therapy, I was looking after myself, eating the right things, taking the vitamins, I quit smoking with ease, reduced my caffeine, took it easy, I was learning to drive and was the happiest I'd ever been.

I had never felt better than I did two weeks before lockdown.

I had been discharged from therapy and I was feeling amazing. I was starting to show and we had started telling people that we were expecting. I was elated.

Then news started to trickle in, the odd rumour here, a bit of a news story there.

And then

BAM

It all changed.
It all went to shit.

And things were never the same.

Alone

I went to appointments alone, I found out the gender of our daughter alone, I stayed in hospital alone, I was induced alone, I spent all but five hours of my daughter's first couple of days alone, I cried alone, I struggled alone, all during the most traumatising, stressful and scary times of my life. I have never needed support more. I needed my partner, my mum, my sister and my friends around me.

I needed to have the same midwife, not a different one every time.

I needed doctors to make decisions based on what was best for me and my daughter, not tell me I should be induced immediately but then send me home because there weren't enough beds. Mistakes made by NHS staff who were exhausted and overrun.

I fully acknowledge and appreciate that times were tough, but it felt like I might as well have been in prison. It was cold and empty and compassion and care were hard to find.

What were supposed to be the best weeks of my life ended up being the worst.

That's hard to swallow.

How is it fair?

How is it fair
that while I was alone
In hospital being induced
In 30-degree heat
No fans allowed
No partner, no visits
no friends...

Just the midwives
Were by my side
In shifts of eight hours

That the country was eating
In restaurants and bars
'Eat out to help out'
What a farce

I was alone
Curtains drawn
To keep cool
Struggling to keep a brave face

No visitors allowed
The ward was so quiet
We were all going through
our own hell

The hospitals overrun
No beds upstairs
'We'll have to delay your induction'
Hot and bothered
Scared and alone
Doctors too busy to come

My fiancé could not visit
To offer support
He was waiting at home alone
A whole week wasted
Waiting for me
A week we couldn't enjoy
As a three

But he COULD
eat out to help out
In restaurants and bars
How ridiculous
What a farce

November 2020

I'm ready
I'm ready
Let's go out and explore
Let's sign up for all of the classes
I'm ready
You're ready
Let's go out and see
What the world is really like

Let's go swimming
Let's go to a class
Where you wear silly hats
and I laugh
Let's meet other mums
And make lifelong friends
Let's go
I'm ready
And excited

I can't wait to show you the world
I can't wait to meet your new friends
I can't wait to get out and about
I can't wait to be the mum I want to be

I'm so excited
Let's go to a dance class
Let's go for a cake
Let's go out for dinner
Let's go to the shops
Let's go and see family
Let's go out and play
Let's go to a play group

I'm ready
You're ready
Let's go!

BREAKING NEWS: COVID-19: PM announces four-week England lockdown

Oh

Never mind.

The small things

Your newborn joy was stolen from me
In those very first few weeks
One of them was spent locked away
In a cold dark hospital room
I tried to be strong
And I tried to be brave
To keep it together for you

It's the small things that catch me
Like a slap in the face
And
I remember our experience
Was different

These things don't really mean a thing
new parents with a newborn in tow
Out late at night
Going for a shop
It is nothing really
Not special at all

But we didn't do that with you

A late night meal in a restaurant
A sleeping baby next to Mum
She gently rocks the pram
While she eats with the other hand
Not special or exciting at all

But it hurts me to see this
we couldn't do it
It's silly, I know it's true
But these things
Catch me off guard
Like a stab in my heart
Because we could not do this with you

It hurts more than it should

***

I'd like to end on a positive note. Despite the incredibly difficult circumstances we faced - the isolation and the loneliness - I got to have my daughter all to myself for a long time. I got to enjoy her and watch her change every day. She got me through. She makes me better every day and has changed my life. Mothers find a way through the darkness and we are guided by our little shining stars.

10th February 2021

Dear E,

I have wanted to write to you for the longest time. I kept putting it off for so long and I never knew why.
I know now that I was scared.
Scared of disappointing the future you.
Scared that you would see that I was not the mother I intended to be for you.
Scared that I would let you down before I'd even had a chance to try, before you'd even had a chance to thrive.
Scared that I couldn't be the mother you deserved.
But
I am finding the strength to be strong for you.
I am finding the courage to be brave for you.
I am finding the patience to be calm for you.
I am finding the laughter to be fun for you.
I am finding the knowledge to be smart for you.
One thing I do not need to find is love for you

Charlotte Tokolics, 31, from Watford, Hertfordshire, lives with her fiancé, Ben, and their three-year-old daughter, Everly. Charlotte works part-time for a family mediation company and loves to write poetry about life and motherhood. She also enjoys making things and anything crafty. Inspired by the help she received during the first couple of years of her daughter's life, Charlotte is studying Counselling part-time and hopes to go on to support struggling new mothers in the future.

HANNAH JG RAMSDALE

My home,
Our Street,
My town,
England
February 2023

Dear Me, Myself, I and Mummy-me,

Remembering that time, those days, isn't easy. It's really hard. It was the slowest and fastest of minutes, hours, days and months. It was his first year. Our third and final little human arrived on Sunday 19th January 2020. He wanted to meet us – with a five-hour labour and at 10lb, he was ready. At nine weeks old, he was in lockdown with his mummy, daddy and two big sisters. And I was screwed. How the fuck was I going to do this? I focused on squirreling away toys to bring out on another day. I remember Boris Johnson telling us all from behind a desk, 'Stay home, Protect the NHS, Save Lives,' - the realisation of what lockdown meant and how scary it was felt enormous.

I've since told our eldest, on more than one occasion, that if she plays Tricky Words on YouTube when she is late teens, Mummy may have to go and sit 'all by her own' (in the words of our centre child) in a dark room and cry endless, snotty tears. To think. To pause. To remember what we did and wonder how on earth we did it.

Three under five years old. At home. All day. A husband at work full-time. A newborn. I was a mama owl, awake day and night. Groundhog Mama days. I remember blazing sunlight. I remember sometimes settling little brother for his sleeps in the pram outside. I remember the minutes I struggled to settle him for a sleep inside, in his moses basket. I remember being eternally grateful to the friend who had lent us their Sleepyhead. I remember boiling hot days. I remember thinking we would all be loving this spring had the world not shut down. Had the world not needed the reset. And now? We have simply forgotten why we needed to reset in the first place.

I remember attempts at Google classroom lessons, the computer being folded down and only the teachers voice being heard into the corners of our dining room, as the sea of faces just freaked my daughter out. I remember eventually opting out of home schooling. It was never going to happen. At home, her little sister giddy to have her big sister to play with all day, every day. I remember holding on to a pattern in our endless home days. The pattern of feeds and naps gave way for me to occupy and be with his sisters.

I remember the e.n.d.l.e.s.s requests for snacks. I remember spinning. I remember many minutes of play doh with the My Little Pony figures. I remember the Dinosaur King theme tune booming from the screen. I remember Miraculous, it's theme tune and characters. I remember Tiki and

Plagg cuddly arriving as a 'just because' gift for them, from us. I remember thinking of friends, redeployed and in layers of PPE. For two hours off and two hours on. I remember the sense of nurse responsibility. I remember knowing I was exactly where I should be and at the same time thinking I should be somewhere else. Helping, caring, reassuring, supporting and nursing those who needed it the most.

I remember feeding, burping, changing, playing, sleeping on repeat. I remember nappy bags stacked high on the mat outside the back door. I remember their birthdays and finding anything at home that would do, making celebrations from very little. I remember selfie photos of the four of us - me and my first, second and third on the playmat, holding my phone above us all. I remember the shitty chaos of paints outside in the garden. I remember painted rainbow pictures covering the garage floor to end up on the lounge window for the neighbours to see. For the one hour a day we had out of our homes, I remember sisters playing with their dolls and their games, lasting for what felt like all day. I remember FaceTime chats with Far Away Granny and Grandpa Parkes. I remember FaceTime colouring with Granny that gave me a moment to stand still. I remember setting up a shop in the garden with a play till and pretend food, bags and aprons for his sisters. I remember pumping up the paddling pool and finding leaves in it the next morning. I remember the occasional surprise gift from a friend - letterbox cakes or flowers that completely changed my world on the day they arrived. I remember feeling overwhelmed by my friend's kindness, their thoughts having found me. I remember the wonderful, shitty chaos of home. I remember feeling so unbelievably lonely with the house full to the brim. I remember HouseParty with our families and celebrating occasions on screens, raising glasses of fizz and saying cheers while we were all in different areas of the country.

I remember little humans with me as I needed a wee, a poo and eventually my post-partum bleeds. I remember being asked to make Rapunzel the doll a face mask. How? How the fuck do I do that? I remember taking deep breaths. I remember the minute by minute, hour by hour, day by day mantra in my head. I remember feeling upside down. I remember never attending one single Zoom quiz night with friends. I remember knowing I couldn't and didn't want to. I remember screaming (lots) - me and the children. I remember the 'Guess the chocolate bar' quiz on WhatsApp. I remember still recovering from birth trauma. I remember the pain, the treatment and the agony as my body tried to recover. I remember chocolate. I remember carbs, to keep calm and carry on. I remember not knowing or realising I needed more vitamins and nutrients. Not realising I needed to take a lot more care of my body during those post-partum days and months. I remember not knowing about post-natal depletion. I wished I had. I wished I'd taken much better care of me. I remember knowing, through a mummy spider sense, there was a little human waiting for me in the darkness of the night, she was standing patiently at my bed, waiting to get in with her mummy-me and her little brother.

I remember a pineapple arriving one Saturday in the shopping (not ordered by me, just came by chance. By happy chance) and it being put to bed by my little women and looked after all day. I remember being grateful for shopping arriving at home and not having to queue up for hours and waiting to go in, wearing a face mask and using even more sanitiser. I remember Frozen 2. I remember Anna and 'do the next right thing.' I remember Charlie Mackesy. I remember 'The boy, the mole, the fox and the horse.' I remember 'same storm, different boat.' I remember finding their games in every corner of the house. An envelope with a flannel, a clip and miniature figure. To them, it certainly made sense. I remember breakfast, lunch and teatime on repeat.

I remember clearing up and putting away constantly. I remember Sylvanian Families and my childhood wooden house and their games. I remember getting a little bit of an evening back, as the world continued to be locked away. I remember crying (lots) - me and the children. I remember sending 'Morning/Afternoon friend' WhatsApp's to keep in touch with friends, as if I was holding on to a float.

I remember hearing devastating news. I remember talking out loud to my friend at the sink, putting the washing on the line, while I was doing anything and everything, making me feel as if I was with her, supporting her, even though she was miles and countries away. And I couldn't talk and I couldn't support her in her pain and tragedy. I remember long, slow, tears for myself and so many others. I remember sore hands. I remember being told about Anna Mathur and feeling so relieved. I remember cracked fingers and split nails. I remember not knowing how my weaknesses were my strengths and how strong I was. I remember trying to cover the cuts with plasters, for them to get soaked again in less than an hour. I remember therapy through OxPIP and logging on Zoom to meet Jane with my son in my lap on the bed, while Daddy tried to work with his sisters charging around downstairs. I remember the visceral pain of breastfeeding trauma and grief. I remember curling up on the bathroom floor and crying.

I remember being extraordinarily grateful, relieved and overwhelmed that the children weren't being taken away - they weren't ever going to be evacuees. They were with me and staying safe, with me.

I remember thinking, *I need them to be taken away. I need them not to be with me. I wish they weren't with me. For a minute. An hour. Or two. Or five.* This is a wish that didn't come true.

I remember 5 Minute Mum and Daisy Upton giving me ideas, inspiration and patience to just keep swimming. Swimming in the thick, dark treacle. Swimming against the current is how it felt. Being swept away, often.

I remember trying to attempt a Joe Wicks PE class and it just being me left in the room.

I remember their smiles, their laughter. I remember we became cocooned and stayed safe.

I remember their games stretching far and wide into every corner of our home – inside and out.

I remember feeling as if I was a spinning wheel. As if I was a revolving door. Constantly open to having everything taken from me.

I remember. I remember. I remember.

With so much love to,
Me xx

Hannah Ramsdale, 39, from Abingdon, lives with her husband and three little humans – 7 years, 6 years and 3 years old. Having recently left nursing, she is finding her next role. During any window of opportunity since September 2021 she has been studying matrescence with Mama Rising. She held her first Mum-Me minute circle in September 2023. When she can take slow minutes you will find her writing letters to friends with a cuppa.

JULIE COLMAN

If we are going to blame anyone, I think it should be Nicola. It was a brilliant, blue Edinburgh day and we were walking through the park as both of our phones pinged simultaneously. Another Guardian alert, what would it be this time? How many more people had died? Was there a new strain? A new lockdown? A vaccine? How many more rules had Boris broken? Oh, wait, it was none of that. It was Nicola finally announcing the easing of lockdown restrictions in Scotland. My heart skipped a beat. The smell of tulips and cut grass, the warmth of the day and the joy of that announcement washed over my entire body. My wee boy would get to meet his extended family. He'd be born and able to live outside a bubble. We excitedly began to walk home, desperate to read up on the news, text family and start planning visits. Our pace quickened the more excited we got but then a few steps later, my waters broke, a month early. And so, it began.

COVID aside, I had a smug pregnancy. I was never sick, my skin was immaculate, I glowed the entire time and my ankles stayed skinny. I loved being pregnant, I felt so healthy and peachy and round. That all vanished, however, the moment my waters broke at 36 weeks and two days. Initially, I tried to pretend I had wet myself. I managed to get away with that for 24 hours until it was alarmingly obvious it was not pee continuously streaming out of me. Phone calls, appointments, face masks, scans and monitoring all alone, found that baby boy was perfectly content, but yes, my waters had broken and this wasn't ideal. My drug-free, healthy, zen pregnancy was about to end with a lot of drugs and a lot of intervention.

Goodbye water birth, goodbye birth plan. I hadn't even finished the baby books. I still didn't know how to breastfeed or burp a baby. I always presumed there would be more time. The chance of infection was too high, so I was monitored and 'allowed' to try and get to 37 weeks whilst trying to convince my baby that he really wanted to come and meet his parents. He didn't, not yet anyway. Like his mother, he was pretty smug with his current predicament and perfectly comfy and cosy. He had no desire to come and say hello just yet. We waited and panicked and painted the box room and scoured the internet for all the things we still had to buy – a car seat being the most important. No shops were open so we just had to guess which one would work the best for us. Blind hope.

37 weeks, I made it. Anxious as hell, babe still in belly, I marched off to the maternity unit. Alone obviously, no partners allowed. We'd start with a pessary and take things from there. It was in, secured and fizzing away at my cervix. I started watching something on Netflix to occupy my brain, Bake Off for florists, if I remember correctly. I was trying to take my mind off what the pessary was doing, but more the fact that I was alone. *It's fine, it will all be fine, everything is fine.* I was quietly content in my own room, with a window that I could open and air I could breathe in if I squashed my face against a wall and

angled my body in a bizarre shape. It was all going so well, until it wasn't. I sneezed and the pessary came shooting out of me, my cervix displeased at the drugs trying to open it up fizzing away. It wasn't meant to be.

And so began the next phase of intervention: multiple sweeps followed by an oxytocin drip. After 12 hours of bouncing on a yoga ball and a failed cervix, I was physically and emotionally exhausted. And so, in the wee small hours of the morning, a group of doctors appeared in my room telling me the only option was a C-section. I signed on the dotted line, my hand shaking, my signature not resembling the one I use in day-to-day life, trying to remain calm but internally falling apart. Was this it? I convinced myself it was and started to say my goodbyes. Bright lights, on the operating table, looking up at a sea of patient and kind eyes. Waiting. Watching all the movement in the room. Staring at my husband, trying to gauge his reaction to it all, wondering when I would go. Would I just fall asleep? Would I feel it? Would I be sad? As the thoughts of death and dying enveloped my brain I felt something in my core, a pull. I looked down and instantly felt a pop from my belly, something that had been so full and buoyant, now empty.

He was here. My baby. Aggressively but tentatively shoved towards my face, a tiny wee cry, a kiss, a cuddle, a sniff and off he went to be checked over and weighed while I was sewn up and moved onto a trolley. Wheeled away to a side room as a new family of three. We sat in awe, kisses and cuddles and love and the smell, the smell was magic. Naked bodies and boobs and fluids and blood and a baby. We had an hour together, our new family of three, until baby and I were wheeled away again. My husband was rudely told to go away at the door and didn't even get to say goodbye. I didn't have any of my belongings, it was just me and my baby. My bag eventually arrived but was placed at the bottom of my bed. Thanks to my drug cocktail I was paralysed from the waist down so could barely move to reach it. We were left abandoned, the two of us in a drug-fuelled exhausted daze. Staff came to check on us but didn't help. They hurried around other patients and checked the babies but ignored their traumatised and exhausted mothers. I will be forever grateful my time there was short.

My husband was in the car, in the car park. Sitting waiting.

Once out of the danger zone, we were transferred to the sun-filled ward. All the other new mums looked at me equally dazed and confused. A new community. A group of women forever affected in ways that we weren't even aware of yet. All alone at the most vulnerable moments of our lives, heavily reliant on the grace and kindness of each other. Quietly asking if we were all OK, giving knowing nods and smiles. Brief chit-chat and conversation through flowing curtains. Whispers of *It's OK, you're doing good*. Alarms and buzzers for midwives when things went wrong. Baby's crying, them crying, me crying. Waiting to be discharged, waiting to be with my people, waiting to start life as a new family.

We could finally go home. I could walk, I could carry him unaided and I had done a pee by myself. Granted, it didn't feel like I was the one doing the pee, or that it was coming out of me, but it pleased the midwives. Stomach cut open at 3.15 am on Thursday, home and on the sofa for 2 pm the next day. A stark reminder of the powers of modern medicine and the infinite power and strength of a woman's body. The trauma of the last week vanished when I saw my husband hold our son. My world, my loves. Home.

A month later, it would all change. Partners were allowed to be present and visitors could go in with negative COVID tests. If my son had been born on his due date, so much trauma would have been avoided, but my boy, headstrong, decided he wanted a different start and an extra month of life with his mum and dad.

We are here, we survived and we thrived, despite it all.

Three years of my hilarious, joyous, beautiful boy.

Three years of me as Mum.

Bliss.

Julie Colman, 37, from Edinburgh lives with her husband and darling son, Harris. She works part-time delivering projects in art organisations and charities. Any time she isn't playing Paw Patrol or baking banana bread, you can find her at her kitchen table completing sewing projects and feeling zen.

CLARE LANGER

Dearest Percival,

I don't know when you will read this but it's here for when you are ready, interested or perhaps as part of a school project. It's a snapshot of time, memories, and history, and an opportunity for me to be brave. You see, I was finally pregnant with you during a time of huge uncertainty and fear in the world. You were born during that time and our first six months together were under strict rule and isolation. The months, well, years since, have continued to be impacted as the world returned somewhat to how it was before. Being pregnant with you and becoming your mum was, and is, the greatest happiness and privilege of my life. I just wish it hadn't been during a global pandemic when we were robbed of so much we had dreamed about.

I thought it could be useful for me to open up and share my experiences from during this time. To realise that, although we felt alone, we weren't, and are part of a unique group of mums and now-toddlers who are connected by what we went through. Only we can understand each other. This writing will mean that our story is never forgotten and is there if people now want to listen, something that didn't happen at the time. We didn't have the opportunity to talk about what we went through, which has made life hard, and my mental health suffer, at times. Hopefully, others having an insight into what we went through will give us mums some validation and reassurance that learnings will be had and history not repeated.

So, here goes...

On 18th February 2020, your dad and I, after weeks of medication and preparation, went to have two embryos transferred into my uterus. This was our seventh round of IVF with embryos 8 and 9, frozen in spring 2019. We were full of hope and fear before the rollercoaster of the next two weeks, waiting to find out whether or not we were pregnant. Our results came back - we were pregnant for the fourth time. I got to see you and your heartbeat at our first scan on 13th March. Just two days prior, on 11th March, the World Health Organization had declared COVID-19 a pandemic. Three days later, our prime minister told pregnant women to stay at home and isolate for the next 12 weeks. A week later, the first national lockdown was announced, meaning we weren't allowed to leave our homes, except for strictly limited reasons.

These early weeks were extremely worrying for us, having lost three pregnancies prior and your dad working on the frontline of our NHS, knowing very little about this virus that was making people ill all over the world. We worried about getting the virus and losing you, each other or our loved ones. There was huge stress for your dad in A&E. He looked so drained when he came back from work each day.

My fear about the virus passed. A combination of my nursing knowledge and focusing on you growing inside me helped. I was so consumed by the fear of another miscarriage that it took my mind off things. I was beyond grateful to be pregnant again and hadn't waited almost my whole life for this experience to not enjoy it. However, I knew I needed lots of support. The realisation that I'd likely be spending all of my pregnancy in social isolation made me feel suffocated and sad. Your dad was already working extra shifts on the frontline whilst other people were able to work from home and be safe with their families.

I wanted to share and fully experience my pregnancy, making memories with your dad, our family and friends but realised this wasn't going to happen. I was angry, sad and frustrated at the situation but it was impossible to talk to, or share these feelings with, anyone.

I was already concerned about my mental health before the pandemic and was looking forward to getting on with my life again after many years of IVF. I never saw pregnancy as a barrier to anything but the Coronavirus was. Unfortunately, the pressures on our NHS meant that many non-critical services were cancelled or suspended. Our recurrent miscarriage clinic called to say that they would not be seeing me at all during my pregnancy. I was devastated and felt abandoned, scared and full of panic. I phoned around as many local maternity services as I could and every single midwife I spoke to said they couldn't help me.

"But I'm eight weeks pregnant after seven cycles of IVF and three miscarriages!" I cried. I was inconsolable and shocked at the lack of empathy or understanding. It was as if they were robots, not humans. I couldn't understand what was happening. Your dad was still going to work every day and caring for patients - why wouldn't someone care for us? I just needed to know you were there and safe.

I felt devastated for the thousands of women who wouldn't get a scan before 12 weeks despite their loss histories. Partners weren't allowed into scans, depending on the local trust. The disparities between care across the country were unfair and continued after the pandemic, robbing parents-to-be of once-in-a-lifetime experiences, support and memories.

A few days later, I experienced pain and bleeding. Frozen in fear that this was a repeat of the past, I called the Early Pregnancy Unit but it was closed on weekends. In desperation, I left messages in other places and after some searching found a 24-hour pregnancy advice line. The midwife was so kind and supportive. After following her advice and resting all weekend, we phoned for a scan first thing on Monday. Your dad had to wait in the car this time as restrictions were stricter. Straight away the sonographer saw you and pointed out the sac and umbilical cord. I rushed to tell your dad as soon as I could. He was beside himself, alone with worry, his eyes full of tears.

Finally being pregnant after all these years and stuck in isolation due to the pandemic was really gutting and a rollercoaster of emotions. As our pregnancy continued, we reached milestones but they weren't at all how I'd dreamed they would be. My booking appointment was much later than it should have been and via phone. I attended my midwife appointments alone. I felt that they were just a tick list and no one really seemed interested. I cried when they made the rule that we all had to wear masks. It was another barrier.

Lockdown was a very emotional time alongside our pregnancy worries. The many anxieties to balance were exhausting. I worried about all those working on the frontline and felt guilty I wasn't able to go back to nursing and help, too. Because I wasn't allowed to work I wasn't entitled to maternity pay. I missed freedom and London, in particular. Taking the train, feeling the buzz and seeing the sights. I started running when we were allowed to go outside and I searched for online pregnancy yoga - it was upsetting not being able to go to real classes. It brings me to tears thinking about everything us pregnant mums were robbed of.

The second month of isolation included my 12-week scan. Life was on hold and I wanted to scream because our life had already been on hold long before lockdown, with going through years of IVF. I was grateful but I was sad. I was happy but I wanted to be working and living my life with my bump. I was particularly grateful to have a successful round of IVF before lockdown, as IVF clinics were eventually forced to close due to the pandemic and those desperate for a chance to have a family were being told no. It was devastating and that could so easily have been us. I was burdened with the worry of if our parents got the virus and died before we told them we were pregnant, but we didn't want to share the news until further along in our pregnancy because we were so anxious. It was a lonely time.

Being in lockdown meant we couldn't announce our pregnancy in person so we had to get creative. We got our parents on the phone and shared the news via a photo message. Emotions were high and it was wonderful to finally experience the joy of others. We had to have virtual conversations with so many friends and family and celebratory toasts on Zoom. Some members of our family, like your auntie and my brother, never saw me pregnant in person, which is so sad.

It was at this point that my mood was often quite low. I had been in isolation for 12 weeks. I knew I was vulnerable before becoming pregnant but it was impossible to know whether this was due to pregnancy, coming off IVF medication, the impact of lockdown or the trauma of past years catching up with me.

Midwife appointments continued to be disappointing. I saw a different one every time, meaning there was no opportunity to build a relationship or trust with any of them. There was no continuity and I hated going alone, but hey, getting in the car and going to an appointment was something to do in those months of isolation and became the highlight of my week, like a trip to the supermarket when I was allowed!

As lockdown continued, you grew perfectly, and I started growing in my happiness and confidence that you would come home with us. As I became more reassured I enjoyed it more and it made me realise just how much of a burden infertility and IVF was. It was exhausting and I had been very sad for years. I reflected on how I wanted to begin to heal and work through this so I had more resilience to be your mum.

One of my happiest memories of lockdown, and ever, was when we found out you were a boy. At that point, we were allowed to have six people in our garden, so we decided to do a gender reveal. Your Grandma, Gramps, Nana & Pops came and your dad also had a long-awaited day off. We had a local photographer come to do a 'doorstep' photoshoot. This day was the turning point in my confidence growing, our connection with you, our baby boy, and making the most of the rest of our pregnancy, despite being in lockdown. Of course, it was coupled with the growing sadness of being robbed of sharing the joy, experiencing many things, generally being made a fuss of and showing off my bump!

For the remainder of our pregnancy, we made the most of any lifting of restrictions. Then, at 38 weeks, you arrived! Your dad had to leave just an hour after you were born and I couldn't even have a shower after a 36-hour labour. I was alone, with no help or support, until he returned seven hours later. Eight days later, we went into a third lockdown for the first six months of your life. This happened alongside a devastating terminal diagnosis of your Pops (Daddy's father) just a week before you arrived and he died when you were six months old. It all happened in a long, lonely lockdown.

Your dad and I know that if we hadn't gone through all these ups and downs then we wouldn't have you here with us now, and for that, we are forever grateful. We got lucky in the best of ways and both you, and time, are great healers. It has been, and continues to be, hard as we have a lot still to process to be mentally healthy, but all of those lessons and skills we can share with you will help you to navigate the highs and lows of life. We are doing the best we can and you teach us so much every day.

Love you always, I am so proud of you and us all. Much love,
Mummy xxx

Clare Langer, 41, from Surrey, lives with her husband, dog and two-year-old son, Percy. She works locally in a sustainable clothing and gift boutique, having previously been a clinical nurse specialist in the NHS. Her loves include cooking, baking, British flowers, independent businesses and supporting others going through infertility & IVF.
@lemon_ade_baby
@clareybelle

TERRI COLEMAN

"Where are the photos?'"
My daughter will say,
When I show her the albums
Of when she was born, that May

"Where was my family?"
My youngest will ask.
My darling, they were at home
Only leaving the house with a mask

"Where was my nanny,
And my grandad too?"
They were keeping their distance,
To protect me and you

Just some of the questions you'll ask
On those trips down memory lane,
A number of comparisons
But the love was just the same

Those late pregnancy months,
And your first year in the world.
So different to your sisters
When you were both baby girls

But whilst there's no proof
Of park trips and play groups,
No photos of visitors at hospital;
Beaming whilst holding you

There's so much more
To what you'll see,
Things that will always mean
so much to me

It's the messages from your family
So desperate to meet you,
The tears and need to hold you
And the sheer joy when they were able to

It's the cuddles, feeds and bonding
With nowhere to be,

Pram strolls over local fields,
Making memories as a family

It's the little moments just for us
When the world was fast asleep
When the roads outside were empty
But inside our house was complete

Those early days I'll always cherish,
When it was just us four.
Keeping those moments for ourselves,
Those early days were ours.

* * *

17th January 2021

      Mabel - my sweet little lockdown baby. You entered this world smack bang in the middle of a pandemic. I was seven months pregnant with you when the first lockdown started and I was petrified. It was all so new and scary, I was frightened of bringing you into a world so unknown. I wanted to keep you in my tummy where I knew you were safe, but then I wanted you safe and sound in my arms, too. Those last few weeks of pregnancy were worrying but we made it to your birth day and you arrived safely. Everything was perfect, but extremely difficult, with you missing out on crucial bonding time with your daddy and not meeting your family until you were three months old. It hurts my heart to think that such important memories were missed. I'm so sorry that you haven't got photos of cuddles with people when you were a newborn. Those photos of everyone finally holding you are so special to me. I'm so grateful that there was a time when restrictions eased so you got to bond with your family, and you were amazing. To say that your exposure to familiar faces was restricted, you took to people so well and are actually full of confidence. Your little life has been a rollercoaster with seeing people and then not seeing them, I'm sorry if that's overwhelming for you at times. You take it all in your stride, though. Life during a pandemic is all you've ever known and that makes me grateful but devastated at the same time. I'm grateful that you don't know any different, that this is standard to you and a masked face is the norm, but that is also so heartbreaking. You shouldn't have to accept this as normal, you shouldn't be used to seeing only eyes instead of a smile. I had so many hopes and visions for your first year. It's crazy to think that I should be ending my maternity leave and going back to work this month. Eight months together and so much left unfinished. I'm sorry that you haven't even stepped foot in a sensory room. No baby classes, park dates or bonding in a little cafe. I'm truly devastated as I know that you would have thrived from all of these things. We've got so much to catch up on when we're able to and I can't wait to show you the world.

Terri Coleman, 31, from Wolverhampton lives with her husband and daughters in their house of love and chaos. Lover of books, music, list making (rarely completing them) finding new places to explore and capturing moments in pictures. Enjoys the smaller details and simple things in life.

LARA ALI

What we lost	What we gained
Seeing family and friends, and sharing you moving around in my belly.	Your daddy and I had so much time to get ready for you. We spent hours walking and relaxing, talking about what meeting you would be like.
A baby shower and a leaving party from work.	Only your daddy and I felt you moving around in my belly. That's a special memory, just for us.
Having your daddy with me at appointments and after you were born in hospital.	I could give you my entire focus. You were my world before I went into the world again.
Taking you to baby classes, coffee shops, the office and to family and friends' houses.	We had an excuse to stay home and make our own little memories. We cuddled on the sofa and went for walks in the park. We didn't rush around. We just had each other.

Where to begin about the year you were born, little one?

I don't know when you'll read this, but by the time you do, I'm guessing you'll know me pretty well, so you'll know (and if you don't, then your daddy will have told you) that I LOVE to make a list. That's why, when I thought about explaining what the heck happened in the year you were born, I had to make a list of losses and gains. Because 2020 was a year of conflicts, yings and yangs, sunshine and darkness. A year where nothing happened but everything happened. Even now, I don't quite know what to make of it.

It started under a cloud. There was a looming "something" on the horizon. It seemed like an inconvenience at the time. Something that was going to make buying food and going out a bit more tricky. But we all ignored it. The really bad stuff was happening far away. It wouldn't reach us. So, we carried on. I took you on your first trip abroad, to California, for work. At the time, life felt relatively normal.

Little did we know that just after Mother's Day everything was going to change. We were told to "stay at home, protect the NHS and save lives." That all sounds scary and maybe my memories are weirdly warped because now, when I think of you being all wriggly in my belly, I don't think about scary, dark times. My overriding memories of being pregnant with you are of incredible warmth and sunshine.

I also remember teary days where I felt scared and sad that Granny and Auntie Nina couldn't feel you moving around in my belly. Where I worried that they wouldn't be able to meet you and that I might have to bring you into this world on my own, without Daddy. But those moments seem few and far between, in hindsight.

The day in June 2020, when you finally arrived, is probably a story you don't want to hear, so I'll spare you the details. It was hot. It was scary. It was painful. It was lonely, but I had you. A perfect little creation: fresh, innocent and naïve to everything going on. You kept me going until Daddy came to pick us up and we could finally start our lives as a family.

Those early days were so special. We missed out on a lot, like visits from friends and family, baby classes and trips out. But we gained so much more. We gained time together: just you, me and Daddy. We figured out how to get into our own little groove without too much interruption.

We gained extra rest from the hours we spent inside, snuggled up and sleeping on the sofa with the patio doors open to keep cool.

We gained precious memories of watching you change so quickly because we studied you closely. You were our perfect distraction from all the craziness. We learned that if you clicked your tongue you wanted milk and that you'd do a funny breath at the end of some of your sneezes.

We gained a lot of all-important steps and fresh air in the hours we spent walking around with you in the buggy. You, refusing to drop off to sleep, because everything going on outside was too exciting and needed to be explored.

I said earlier that I don't quite know what to make of the year you were born. There's a lot to be sad, frustrated and angry about but after writing all of this down, I guess I do know what to make of it. Yes, it was a horrible time, one that caused a lot of sadness and one that a lot of people don't want to remember.

But I do.

Because I choose to remember all that we gained in 2020, and that was you.

Lara Ali, 34, from Daventry lives with her husband and energetic three-year-old son, Oscar. She runs her own Marketing Agency and thrives on being busy. She does CrossFit in an attempt to keep up with the "always running" Oscar, but also enjoys reading quietly or doing creative projects with the tele on in the background.

CHARLOTTE SCANLON

January 2020

You arrive, a bundle of joy with no hair and a screaming cry. The birth is a blur but you're here and we've become Mummy and Daddy just like that. We toast your arrival with sandwiches and champagne. We watch rugby on my phone from the hospital bed whilst we wait to be discharged. You look tiny in your car seat. The midwife checks us over and we are off. I cry in the car on the way home; amazed that you are coming home with us, worried if you'll like our house. Your little hands clasp my finger and for the first time I say, "It's OK, Mummy's here."

February 2020

We show you off to everyone. There are cuddles with grandparents and proud aunties, afraid of dropping you or holding you wrong. You, in your blanket burrito, nestle in the arms of friends and family, smiling as they look down at your sweet, sleeping face. News reports start talking of a virus on the other side of the world. We don't take much notice in our little newborn bubble.

March 2020

We've booked dinner with your proud grandparents, our first trip out with you. The car radio talks of restaurants and pubs closing tonight. We arrive at a ghost town restaurant with the phone ringing and people cancelling. For the first time, we question what 'restrictions' mean and if we are 'doing the right thing.' We say goodbye after the food and wine.
"See you in a few weeks when this all blows over..."
Lockdown arrives and there's a novelty about spending all this time together. We are in a little baby bubble and it is magical watching you change day by day. There's no pressure to get out of the house and see people, we just do our own thing at our own pace. Daily bulletins puncture the bubble, you can't avoid the 'COVID' word now, but we try to stay positive despite the rising tide of bad news. It's hard not to let the anxiety bubble up; a potent mix of hormones, loneliness and fear.

April 2020

You have your jabs and we don't sit in the waiting room, we have to wait in the car instead. They call my phone and only I can come, so Daddy waits outside in the spring sunshine. We nervously glance at other new parents, masked up and carrying their little eight-week-old bundles towards their first experience of pain. Your cry echoes through the corridor. The nurse and I look at each other above the surgical masks we're wearing and remark on how odd all of this is. She calls you a beautiful baby and my heart bursts with pride, before it breaks when the needle pierces your skin.

For my first trip outside the house without you, I imagined a drink with friends, a coffee without the pushchair, missing you but relishing the moment as me, not Mum. But no; I'm queuing outside the supermarket, wearing a mask. I'm desperate to feel normal but also desperate to be at home, with you, where it's safe. I load my trolley up, diligently following the one-way system, hoping I can get home before my milk starts leaking out.

In the middle of the night, after feeding you and carefully placing you down without waking you, I scour the news and details of the pandemic jump out; what the new restrictions are and what has changed. Numbers and words swim in front of my tired, teary eyes. I look for ways to return to normality, whatever that looks like with a little person by my side. I yearn to see my family, friends and the other mums from our baby group, even strangers in a coffee shop. But then, it hits me, and it makes me sad... I really, just like you, want my mum.

I push your buggy over and over again across the patio, soothing you to sleep in the fresh spring air. Daffodils and tulips poke through the soil, new spring life contrasting against the bubble of fear that's permanently lodged in my chest. I can't pound the pavements to get you to nap because we're not allowed out of our house. I can't meet other mums to share stories and whisper, "This is quite hard, isn't it?" because we're not allowed out of our house. I can't manoeuvre the buggy through cafe doors, with people cooing over your cuteness, because we're not allowed out of our house.

The chime of another Teams call drifts downstairs as Daddy navigates working from the spare room. I'm frustrated and angry and, not for the first time, I shed a tear at what we're missing and how uncertain life feels.

May 2020

You're facing out in your carrier now with your little sun hat on. The weather is ready for picnics and playing in the park but all we can do is our daily walk when Daddy finishes work. We spend our days together; I feel I know every inch of your little face because I spend all day looking at it. All the books said, "Don't be bound by the routine," but they didn't predict a global pandemic, did they? The routine is the only thing keeping us sane. We Zoom-call your baby friends and do an online baby massage class. Two babies fall asleep, we mute and unmute so the crescendo of cries isn't too loud. The screen is filled with tired mum faces, trying to chit-chat about how weird this whole situation is. If only we were sat at each other's houses, eating biscuits and drinking tea, swapping stories about feeding and sleeping with the babies lying on a blanket together. Squishy faces and chubby little thighs, all looking at each other with wonder. It's not the same through the screen. It's just not the same.

June 2020

The ringtone of video calls connecting is normal now. We look forward to hearing the chimes, promising love pouring out of the screen, the closest we'll come to a hug at the moment. Tummy time with Granny and Grandpa has become watching them move on the laptop screen. It's grainy and there's a delay but it's a connection. It's familiar and it's what we need at this uncertain time.

A heatwave comes and we order a paddling pool. I'd dreamed of sharing this moment with family and friends, BBQ smells wafting through the air whilst you gleefully splash in the shallows of your own little pool. But no, it's just the three of us, Mummy and Daddy delighting in your shrieks and giggles. Toasting us, the three musketeers, three months into this lockdown unknown.

July 2020

It's time to give you food. I read another book. Weaning is a minefield. I thought we'd see friends and try first tastes together, sharing stories of broccoli purée splattered up the walls and drinking cups of tea whilst our gummy babies chew on rusks in their high chairs. Instead, it's me, you and a blender. Green purée one day, orange the next. Endless photos for everyone to see you taste veg for the first time. We listen to the radio whilst you smear the mess all over yourself. It's ironic that 'Eat Out to Help Out' is launched just when you've started having food. Maybe we will have lunch out together soon.

August 2020

Grandparents visit this week. We're still wiping our groceries with antibacterial wipes and wearing masks out and about, but we sit in the garden with other people, two metres apart. It is so good to see people who love you and want to squish you and to see your little toothy grin as you remember them and recognise their voices. Is this the new normal?

September 2020

As a teacher, I can't separate September from the new school year beginning. I'm not going back to work yet, but the feeling of starting afresh is palpable. I wonder if I'll take you into school to meet all my colleagues, have everyone cluster around and ask to hold you. My colleagues are excited to get back into the classroom, go back to normal teaching and no longer see their pupils in tiny boxes on a screen.

October 2020

You're a joyful nine months old and have been out in this strange new world for as long as you were safely cocooned inside of me. How different life is now, both because you're here and because of COVID. I feel sad about all we've missed. There were no baby classes in those first few months but here we are, at a Halloween party, all the babies in fancy dress and the parents accessorising with masks and lateral flow tests.

November 2020

I go back to work for some KIT days and I miss you with all my being. My body aches being so far away from you. Having spent so long in a little bubble together, even though I want to go to work, it physically hurts to leave you. I pack my bag, masks, water bottle, hand sanitiser and proof of a negative COVID test. You are safe at home with your grandparents and Daddy, whereas I feel like I am stepping into the dangerous unknown. The pictures popping up on my phone keep me going until the moment I get home and those chubby arms reach out for me. All of these 'normal' mum feelings are heightened after the anxiety of the past year and the unknown we still face every time the six o'clock news begins. It hasn't gone away and I can't work out what has changed me more: becoming a mum or a global pandemic.

December 2020

I love Christmas. The magic is magnified by seeing it all through your eyes. They widen in wonder at the fairy lights on the tree. You touch the tinsel and gurgle at this strange thing in your hands. You have your settling-in sessions at nursery and I sit and cry in the car whilst you have a happy time in the baby room. We're not allowed to come in and sit in the corridor, we have to wait in the car, masked. The staff marvel at your crawling and your gorgeous smile; my smile of pride almost cracks my face in half. This is what we'd missed: sharing the joy of our child with others.

January 2021

On New Year's Day, there is a sprinkling of snow. We go into the garden in pyjamas and wellies and you keep pointing at the sky. Watching these moments is magical and it's hard to think that my maternity leave finishes in a few days. I feel like it's been stolen away from us. We had so much time together, but so little time with others. It was glorious in parts; time with no pressure to do or be anything other than your mum, time with Daddy that we wouldn't have had otherwise and time where we really slowed down. But also, time was taken from us, time with relatives, experiences we would have loved to share with you but couldn't, all the things we wanted to do but couldn't and all the rites of passage the baby books had told us would happen in our first year.

I go back to work and another lockdown is announced. I spiral into anxiety, the unknown of all of this is devastating and feels relentless. You've started nursery and are loving it. Nursery stays open for key workers (a new title that we didn't have last year) so we keep dropping you off at the door whilst we work from home.

Your birthday comes around and it's a tiny party. You try jelly for the first time and cannot understand it! Daddy and I clink glasses and say, "It can't get any harder than this, surely? First child in a global pandemic means we've nailed it, right?"

I can't stop looking at photos from a year ago when you were a bundle of newness and I didn't know the word 'coronavirus.' We didn't know what lay ahead. How ill-prepared we were back then! But oh, how much has changed, how much we've been through together and how full you make our hearts.

Charlotte Scanlon, 35, lives in Hertfordshire with her husband and two children. A teacher by trade, she has spent much of her life in busy classrooms. Since having her son in January 2020, she's decided to pivot into supporting children in education in a number of different ways, including setting up 'Tiny Acorns Book Club' where she regularly reviews children's books and delves into educational research.
@tinyacornsbookclub

KYRIE CLARKE

I'm at an eye appointment with my two-year-old. The optometrist is taking some background information.

"Emergency C-section - and was that because of you or because of her?"

How could I begin to answer that?

I'd never really been worried about my mental health before. I'd had my fair share of experiences of grief, stress, heartbreak, anxiety and panic attacks, but overall I tend to feel pretty happy most of the time. But when I was alone, bedridden after being essentially chopped in half, and then in sole charge of the survival of a beautiful little person who would not stop crying and who I could not reach - that was when I started to worry.

Lockdown first started to fuck with my anxiety levels when I couldn't get in touch with any midwives before my 28-week appointment. All the phone numbers rang out, parading me through a chain of *call this person... oh no, you want that department*, until it eventually devoured its own tail and I ended up back at the start. In the end, a receptionist somewhere gave me all the mobile numbers she had and I sent them all the same text:

I'm becoming really stressed and anxious because of the lack of information or communication from the midwifery team. I know it's a crazy time but I have had no information or replies from anyone I've contacted about how antenatal appointments will work now. I have my 28-week appointment in two weeks and have no idea if it will go ahead. This is a really anxious time, it's not helping and it is not good for me or my baby. I am writing through tears as I am scared by the lack of help being offered. I know this is an extraordinary time but I have heard nothing from anyone since the outbreak started. Please can you call me on this number ASAP?

Finally, one rang me. I could barely speak. I was sobbing so hard. She was kind and apologised and sorted it out for me, but I was disturbed at how far it had pushed me. Was it hormones? Lockdown? Fear? Helplessness? I didn't know, but it scared me and held a mirror up to how vulnerable pregnant women were at that time.

My due date came and went. Baby didn't take the eviction hint from all the daily long walks and instead, stayed in the warm. I couldn't blame her, she'd probably heard there was a pandemic out there and decided to stay put. One morning, I woke up to a small wet patch. Waters? Or a renegade wee? We called maternity and they told me to come down to be seen. The midwife looked at my sanitary towel and said it was my waters. I asked if she needed to examine me and she said no, which seemed strange, but what do I know?

"If nothing happens in 24 hours, come back and we'll have to induce you."

Reader: Nothing happened.

The next day, at 8am, I went to the hospital to be induced. I waited. By the evening, the only midwife around, who was doing the best she could to manage two wards, came to give me the induction.

"Because your waters have broken, we're going to skip the first stage of induction and go to the second one."

Still, nobody examined me. If they had, they'd have seen the waters were alive and well up there. The gel went in and I waited on the ward. Contractions started and there was a shift change. Another lovely midwife came on and whispered encouragement.

"You'll be moved down to delivery at 10pm, then your husband can be with you. You are a tigress, you can do this."

10pm came and went. By midnight, I told my husband to get some sleep.

I was taken down to delivery at 2am, where I met the most inappropriately named midwife ever - Comfort. She snorted at my birth plan, shoved consent forms for an epidural that my plan said I didn't want at me then said my husband couldn't come until I was five centimetres dilated. She examined me and snorted again – "not even one centimetre," and left the room. I threw up.

At 6am the doctors came around. Their first question was - where is your birth partner? I told them what Comfort had, non-comfortingly, said. They shook their heads. "Call him and tell him to come now. You shouldn't be doing this alone."

With my husband came a shift change, thankfully, and cold Comfort was replaced by an amazing cheerleader of a midwife. But Comfort had got into my head. I went for an epidural as the third stage of induction ramped up. Hours passed. Nothing happened. She examined me, looked back at my notes and whistled.

"Your waters are intact," she tapped the notes disapprovingly. "I know the midwife you saw in triage and she should have done better. A doctor should have come to examine you. She knows that."

I didn't need to be induced in the first place. Oh well. Too late now. She broke my waters. The epidural gradually stopped working and pain radiated through my uterus. After 30 hours and several examinations, I was still only 2cm. It was so disheartening. I cried as the doctors spoke about having a C-section. *Failure to progress sounds like I've done something wrong. I've failed her.*

The C-section in the big, bright, modern theatre was the most surreal, upbeat and positive part of the whole scenario. Everybody in the room was so full of energy, chatty and happy we almost forgot we were in a pandemic. High on whatever they put in you to make you not feel that you are being cut in half, we went off to the recovery suite where I was in and out of sleep and feeling drunkenly happy.

"You have until the timer on that drip runs down, and then you have to leave," the midwife said apologetically to my husband. I was so out of it that the time flew by, and before we knew it he had to go and my daughter and I were wheeled up to the ward.

My mood plummeted the next day when the drugs wore off. *Get up, do this much wee, walk even though your body is screaming no, don't twist to pick up your baby, call one of us to do it for you but nobody comes so you have to do it anyway.* I don't think I brushed my teeth during the two nights I was there.

We struggled with breastfeeding and my daughter cried a lot. I couldn't put her down. I heard one of the other mums mutter something and I broke down. *I can't do this. I can't give her what she wants. I have no idea what I'm doing and I can barely move to pick her up.* Yet another brilliant midwife helped me put myself back together when I was the most broken I've ever been and was worried I had lost it.

"You aren't mad, you aren't doing it wrong. We're having to be midwives and doctors and partners and mothers because none of you have that at the moment and it's not natural. You are doing great."

I have never been so happy to cross the threshold into my own home. The relief was extremely physical, like nothing I've ever felt before. Me and my baby were back in a safe, calm, comfortable, loving environment, reunited with my husband, which is what we should have been able to have all along.

My husband shouldn't have missed the first day or so of his daughter's life. None of the women in that hospital should have gone through the first days and hours of bringing somebody into the world, alone. But that's what happened. And it almost broke me.

"Was the emergency section because of you or because of her?" my daughter's optometrist asks again. I don't know how to answer her. There's not one word for it. There's no space on her form for the failings caused by a pandemic and a health system operating on fumes.

"Because of me," I say.
The conversation moves on.
Because of me.
But the trauma stays.

Born, raised and still living and working in East London, Kyrie, 37, lives with her husband, almost three-year-old daughter and two annoying cats. She's a qualified Teacher of the Deaf, currently missing full-blooded coffee, dubious sushi and unpasteurised cheeses whilst pregnant with baby number two.

REBECCA FOGARTY

The year that we missed

I'm happy for you. She meant it, I'm sure
Despite the half-hearted voice down the phone.
Happiness is hard to come by when you're
Weighed down by worry and weddings postponed.
But what did I have to complain about?
Loss, grief, separation infect the news.
Roll up your sleeves, carry on, paintbrush out
We spent our lockdown preparing for you.
It is only with time we will unclench our fists,
Let the weight fall upon us of the year that we missed.

Parades of men give televised updates
Back in boardrooms make the rules of my life
Women not welcome to have those debates,
Excluded for that trip taken to Fife.
Invisible while we shielded at home,
Made to give birth without a hand from others.
While our hormones raged, did testosterone
Put face masks on us labouring mothers?
The ordeal of birth so easily dismissed,
Our champions were missing in the year that we missed.

My tummy round like a huge Christmas pud,
Two hundred miles from me to my mother,
Not much in the world could be as it should,
Last-minute decisions split one another.
Fridge fully stocked but in the wrong city,
Turkey for six shared in Swansea by friends.
For one day can we forget Chris Whitty,
Johnson and Hancock, the slides and the trends?
Be sure to tell Santa as he's checking his list -
Christmas is cancelled in the year that we missed.

Grandpa-to-be takes the call late at night -
Daughter in labour but he stays at home.
Sat in pyjamas, he waits for the light,
More than new parents were left all alone.
Rule change forms a bubble stretching for miles
Finally, they meet their baby's baby.
Relief! And rest... and inflating those smiles

Flattened by Zoom for those stuck overseas.
Never mind that your skin just cries out to be kissed.
Cuddles are outlawed in the year that we missed.

I do get it, Mam. You mean it, I'm sure.
You've heard all my - no, our - stories before.
We kept you at home while they broke the law
Drove up to Birmingham, foot to the floor
Too few in photos and selfies galore
Reunion on green, faraway shores
I pushed down these feelings, deep to my core
Lucky to have you, who would ask for more?
Yes, it was total, but meant to be shared, our bliss
And I'll always be missing the year that we missed.

Rebecca Fogarty is a local politician in South Wales, alongside being a mother, mediator, wife, friend, activist, public speaker and project manager... She constantly wrestles to remind herself that all these parts are precious, even if they are sometimes contradictory! She met her husband while travelling the world but they have now settled in Swansea, where they had their son, Steffan, and can't imagine living anywhere else.

VERITY CHANCELLOR

After trying for a baby for almost a year and having fertility tests, we were over the moon when we found out we were expecting a baby, due in May 2020. We joined NCT classes and planned a baby shower, and family and friends were beyond excited. Little did we know what was coming.

We, like the rest of the world, didn't realise how bad things would get. The first sign of this was when our NCT teacher told us we'd have to wash our hands before entering the class and that we could no longer hold the baby dolls. We all discussed how crazy it was and even laughed, not realising that would be our last one face to face. The rest of our classes went online, even the 'reunion' where we all planned to meet up once our babies were here. We all felt deflated.

I was still working in an office in March 2020, about to go on maternity leave in April, when the news came out about the potential danger of COVID-19 if you were pregnant. My mum worked in the NHS at the time and rang me to say I had to get out of there and go home immediately. I told her she was overreacting and I couldn't just up and leave. The next day, not only I, but every single one of us in the office had to pack up our computers and work from home for the foreseeable. It was an overwhelming feeling, no real 'send-off' and, instead, all leaving together at once. I think this is when I realised the severity of the situation and it dawned on me this wasn't going to be the lead-up to the birth or maternity leave I had envisioned.

I had a routine midwife appointment, which I used to look forward to, but I suddenly had to wear a mask, call when I was outside and could only see her in the car park. I was in tears as she walked towards my car in full PPE. We just looked at each other, both in disbelief at this turn of events. She welled up and kept saying she was so sorry it had to be like this. She didn't have answers for me. Everything was uncertain.

My husband was a key worker, so while it felt everyone was stuck at home together, I was alone. When he came home he would take off his uniform at the door, put it in the wash and shower before coming near me. He was constantly worried about bringing the virus home and the uncertainty of what this would mean for the birth, as whispers began about partners not being able to attend. As someone who not only wanted my husband there but also my mum, my anxiety was through the roof. I kept saying to myself, *I cannot do this alone.*

We decided it would be safest for my husband to isolate at home with me prior to the birth because we couldn't risk getting COVID. His boss was understanding but said it would have to be unpaid. My son was five days overdue and I did everything to try and induce labour in the hope that my husband could be there. We decided to watch a programme about babies and delivery and as we pressed play, my waters broke. My contractions started pretty quickly so we rang the hospital and made our way in. They told me I would have to go in alone. That walk was the most daunting of my entire life. They confirmed my waters had broken and told me to go home, have a bath and wait, because my husband wouldn't be able to join me until I was in active labour. Luckily, this happened around an hour later, so when we returned he was able to come in with me.

Nothing seemed strange at this moment other than the midwives being in masks and gowns. I was just so grateful to not be alone. We managed to get my mum on FaceTime to see the birth from the windowsill in our room. At 4:37am, our lives changed forever: my baby was born. He was perfect. Nothing else in the world mattered at that moment and we were in newborn bliss.

Unfortunately, I had to have stitches, lost a lot of blood, couldn't get out of bed and had a catheter put in. Soon after delivery, they were quick to test me for COVID. I had hyperemesis (severe sickness) for most of my pregnancy and I was still being sick during labour, so a stick up both nostrils and a sweep around my throat did not help. I felt like a science experiment. What else would my body go through? I was put on anti-sickness and fluid drips as I couldn't keep water down. They can typically make you drowsy, but I felt completely out of it, slurring my words and eventually falling asleep. My husband did the first feed, the first nappy and changed him. When I came around, I felt like I had missed out, but had no time to dwell as I was told my blood test showed a sky-high liver result and I'd have to stay in the ward for more tests. It was at this moment they told my husband he would have to leave as COVID rules meant no visitors were allowed. I was absolutely hysterical. As they wheeled me off to the ward, with my husband waving goodbye, one of the nurses told me to breathe and stay calm. How could I? I didn't know what I was doing with a baby, I felt like I'd been hit by a bus, was on all kinds of drugs and had been told I'd be doing the rest of the hospital stay completely on my own.

I planned to bottle feed him from early on, so I had formula with me and asked one of the midwives to help me. She said they were busy and only helping the breastfeeding mothers. I gave him a whole bottle over an hour or so, only to have the same midwife return and tell me I'd over fed him. She wrote in my notes, 'mother overfed baby.' I'd never felt so lonely and overwhelmed in my life. I felt like I'd already failed at motherhood. That night, he cried in the cot next to me and I just stroked his face because I was in too much pain to get up. I tried to swing my legs around and lift him but I couldn't. A midwife came and took him so I could sleep for a few hours. When I woke up, he was back next to me, changed, fed and swaddled. I was on the phone to my husband constantly, crying that I wanted to come home, simultaneously already feeling mum guilt for being upset for his first day in the world.

I had to have an ultrasound on my liver and they wheeled me off in a wheelchair while they took care of him. I was crying again, not wanting to leave him, but with no visitors allowed I had no choice.

Later that day, my catheter was taken out but I hadn't managed a big enough wee to be allowed home. I asked for a jug of water to drink, determined to be able to go home. Luckily, my results came back clear and when the doctor came around, I begged her to discharge me, telling her I felt absolutely fine, even though I felt the complete opposite. She agreed and my baby boy was carried out in his car seat to my husband waiting outside. I have never felt such relief in my life, but at the same time terrified about motherhood, hoping we knew what to do at home by ourselves, with no one being able to visit.

After waddling up to the front door, we were home at last, instantly in the newborn bubble. No time to reflect, straight in at the deep end but feeling love beyond words. We had "visits" from everyone, looking at him through the shut patio doors or kitchen window. It was heart-breaking to see my parents meet their first grandchild that way and equally I felt I really needed my mum myself.

His first and only appointment was to be checked over and weighed. I had to take him in alone. I asked if someone could check my stitches because it felt so painful, I didn't know what was normal and was too scared to look. They told me they were only checking the babies and not the mothers. I came out of the appointment sobbing and my waiting husband was baffled.

I had only one phone call from a health visitor who asked, 'How's baby girl doing?' It turned out that the hospital had registered him as a girl. I felt sick to my stomach thinking about how many babies had gone under the radar. She asked one question about me.

"Are you OK, mentally?

To which I replied, "Um... I think so?"

"Great! We'll see him when he's two."

I couldn't believe we were left to our own devices after just one weigh-in. No checks at home and no one to check my recovery. I was given a health visitor name and number to use if I had any questions, but after sending three text messages and receiving no replies, I gave up.

After about three weeks, we were allowed a 'bubble' which meant my mum could come over. That first hold was so emotional, she already felt like she had missed so much and he'd changed already. My husband went back to work and it was a constant daily cycle of outdoor walks in the pram (crossing the street if we encountered anyone else) watching Boris on the TV (hoping for good news) and video calls with family and friends. I remember desperately wanting to show him off. I looked forward to the Thursday night claps for the NHS just so I could hold my baby at the door for the neighbours to see, yet didn't want to take him to the supermarkets because he wasn't protected with a mask like I was.

In time, restrictions lifted. I managed to take him to some baby classes and it felt like finally making up for lost time, although by the time things were becoming more normal, I had to go back to work. I felt that the maternity leave I'd built up in my head before even becoming pregnant, had been ripped from underneath me. I appreciate the amazing quality bonding time we had just us, figuring everything out in our own way and time. I just wished I could have done more with him.

He joined nursery and I went back to work. The nursery explained how the 'lockdown babies' were much more interested in the adults than the other babies, because many of them had never played with other children. At work, people would constantly ask me what it was like having a lockdown baby and at that time I didn't have the words to respond. I missed my boy. This huge chapter in my life felt like a blur.

To my darling boy, Roman, you were our light during such a dark time. Everything in the world was uncertain, but knowing you were mine was all I ever needed. I'm so blessed and I can't wait to tell you all of these stories from your year of birth, in years to come. Love, Mum x

Verity Chancellor, 30, from Taunton lives with her husband Stuart, three-year-old son, Roman and one-year-old, Penelope. She works part-time as a Marketing Manager and runs a TikTok account created in lockdown, dedicated to motherhood. (@veritychancellor)

EMMA BARRIE

14 December 2019

I find out I'm pregnant the day after I pass my driving test and on the one-year anniversary of my mother passing away from breast cancer. She has sent a beautiful gift.

16 March 2020

I buy my first car; little did I know I would only do 255 miles in my first year of driving and it would sit for most of 2020 on the driveway.

23 March 2020

We're having a Chinese at our best friends' house. Boris Johnson tells us we're going into lockdown. You can't reschedule a pregnancy; everything is now uncertain. We hug our friends goodbye, we don't know when we will next see them.

End of March 2020

5% house deposits get pulled off the market. All hopes of moving out of our tiny rented accommodation before baby arrives diminish. My work colleague drops a computer monitor on my driveway - payroll are 'key workers.' We start rolling out furlough pay and making all of our processes digital. We are working from home. My husband is furloughed – he's playing his game system in the same room I'm working in. The house suddenly feels smaller.

April 2020

I start my payroll management course. All tutorials and essays and exams are moved to an online platform. Instead of discussions with classmates, we have a WhatsApp group.

I must go to our second scan alone. I feel isolated in all areas of my life.

13-14 July 2020

Had a beautiful weekend at my baby shower when originally I thought I wouldn't be getting one at all. Never more than SIX people in the garden at one time and lots of sanitising.

No one can feel my bump or feel him kick but hopefully, things will be better in time for them all to have newborn cuddles.

7 August 2020

Celebrating the start of my maternity leave with a lunch date with my dad. A quiet, spacious garden restaurant, sanitiser pumped by foot.

15 August 2020

I hand in my CIPP essay earlier than the deadline, which is on my due date.

16 August 2020
Mini maternity photoshoot at home. No professional maternity or newborn photoshoot, so this is done by my husband. No antenatal classes either and no opportunities to meet other mums-to-be and make friends for life.

22 August 2020
The day I fall in love at first sight.
I have the most wonderful birthing experience.
Contractions start at 4am and are rather irregular until 4pm, when my waters break and things start to ramp up a bit! We both have a COVID swab. I get straight into the pool and have gas and air. I move onto land for the delivery. A student midwife helps me, guiding my pushing and breathing. An 8lb baby with only minor grazes.

25 August 2020
Alfie meets his grandparents for the first time - they are wearing face masks.

19 October 2020
Alfie has his first vaccinations and then we finally register his existence in this world (which is supposed to be within 42 days of birth) delayed by the backlog caused by COVID.

31 October 2020
Mortgage offer accepted on a new build property - 5% deposits have returned!

14 December 2020
One year since I found out I was pregnant. Our journey was not as expected.

25 December 2020
Alfie's first Christmas - we're supposed to choose which grandparents to spend it with.

26 February 2021
Alfie's first time on a swing.

23 March 2021
A whole year in lockdown. I can't believe it. I remember seeing on the news about COVID in China and didn't even consider it would come to the

UK. Boris' announcement made it real. I recall rubbing my bump, wondering what sort of world I would be bringing my son into. I spent my whole pregnancy terrified of catching it, not for the sake of my own health but because of the tiny little life I was carrying. I was so blessed to bring him into the world, safe and healthy, even if I had to keep him all to myself.

31 March 2021
We move into our new home.

July 2021
Alfie's hearing is tested and he is reviewed for autism. Nothing to report, apart from the impact of COVID on children's socialisation causing many delays.

22 August 2021
We celebrate Alfie's first birthday with ALL of our family and friends.

9 September 2021
I return to work and leave Alfie for the first time with his grandparents... He gets COVID.

Emma Barrie, soon to be the big 3.0, lives in Northampton with her husband, David and her nearly three-year-old son, Alfred. She is CIPP qualified after completing her studies whilst on maternity leave, working as a payroll executive for an accountancy firm. She has enjoyed getting back out into the world post-COVID, especially bottomless brunches.

SHONA ANDERSON

My first Mother's Day was not what I expected.

I'd imagined spending it surrounded by family, celebrating becoming a mum. My mum holding our newborn whilst I slept or sat with some tea and cake. Instead, we made the decision to protect our newborn, and his grandparents, from coronavirus and spend the weekend just the three of us, and the dog. Alone, but safe.

I remember crying a lot the day we made the decision, the first thoughts and questions appearing in my highly anxious mind. *But when will I next see my mum? What if I can't see her again for a while? Look at what's happening in Italy, are we next? What if we get coronavirus and can't look after our baby? What will we do without any help? Especially if we are ill? Or worse, what happens if my baby gets it and gets sick or dies?* All I wanted was to protect my baby and keep him safe. This decision alone, to visit my parents or not, felt impossible. Maybe because I knew not going was accepting that coronavirus was real. But the guidance made it clear, this was highly contagious and we shouldn't be mixing.

My baby group cancelled our lunch, where we were going to see each other for the first time since we were pregnant, to meet each other's babies. Others were making the same awful, yet sensible, decisions. My husband agreed that we shouldn't take the risk and we should stay at home. *As upsetting as it might be, we can see everyone in a little while once things have calmed down.* He isn't an anxious person like me, so if he was worried, that meant we should stay at home.

By Mother's Day, having had a traumatic birth five weeks earlier, I'd barely left the house and had spent this time dreaming of all the things I would do once I was more mobile and had more energy. Barely able to walk, the furthest I'd ventured was around the block, only just able to start the physio I desperately needed so that I'd be able to sit down again without being in intense pain. I wanted to leave the house and start doing normal things so desperately, but I couldn't take the risk.

By the 22nd of March 2020, I'd already researched COVID-19 to an obsessive level, vigilant about hand washing, my hands red and raw. Everyone thought it was my anxiety again.

"Oh, it's all being exaggerated in the news."

"What are you doing for Mother's Day?"

"Make sure you get out, it's good for your baby's immune system".

Surely, protecting my baby from an unknown virus was best for his immune system? So, if anything, when the lockdown was announced the next day, my initial reaction was relief. Relief that I didn't have to make any more decisions and was being told what to do instead. Stay home, save lives. I also felt vindicated. I hadn't been exaggerating, it wasn't my anxiety, I was right. It meant we'd made the right decision to stay at home for Mother's Day.

But, that was before I knew the long road to come.

I didn't know that after that Mother's Day, my mum wouldn't hold my baby for months.

That she and my dad would be told to shield and not leave their house for months, for they were at high risk of dying if they got COVID.

That even when we could see them again, we would isolate for two weeks, terrified we were still doing the wrong thing.

That there would be more gut-wrenching decisions, like deciding who we should allow to get close to our baby and which grandparents we would see when 'bubbles' were introduced in December of that year.

That people would be panic-buying in shops and infant Calpol would sell out, causing more worry and anxiety.

That we would wipe down the shopping so we didn't let the virus into our home.

That every day we would wake up to a new death tally, made to feel like we were responsible if we broke the rules.

That all parks would be closed and it would be illegal to drive up to the common.

That I wouldn't even be able to get a takeaway coffee.

That my physio would be cancelled so my coccydynia wouldn't heal and my episiotomy would get infected again and no one would look at it or give me an appointment because physio and postnatal checks weren't essential.

That it would be six months before I could sit up straight, not in pain.

That this would mean spending months sitting alone, on a sofa, with a baby.

That I wouldn't see a health visitor or have my baby weighed, all doctor's appointments would be over the phone and we wouldn't be allowed to bring in the red book because COVID lives on paper.

That I wouldn't go to a dentist in years, even for a single check-up, my MATB1 form useless and not extended.

That I would reach out for mental health help and end up having to push for months, eventually receiving terrifying and conflicting advice: *Do not take your baby outside as he could catch COVID and die.*

That I would still be waiting for a call back from the health visitor who said she'd check in, after I stated that I was struggling mentally.

That the fear of one of us getting COVID would grow each day, intensified by the newspapers: 'Baby six weeks old dies of COVID.'

That I would get no help whatsoever - no one to hold the baby, no cups of tea, no one to speak to in person other than my amazing husband, who was so helpful, but had to work (from our tiny two-bed flat).

That I'd feel guilty as I knew others had it so much worse: frontline workers, the elderly and people with weakened immune systems, so why was I complaining?

That people would keep saying, 'Isn't this the perfect time to have a baby?' Because we should have been enjoying the time together and bonding, but I didn't agree, and I'd feel guilty, ashamed and ungrateful.

That all the baby groups I'd spent years imagining, would all be online, and when in person, we'd all wear masks and not be allowed to sing, because singing spreads COVID, and then they'd all get cancelled again after a month. Enough to get a taster of normality before it being ripped away.

That I'd only be able to meet one other mum and walk at a social distance from them around the park, or sit in small groups, none of us knowing if babies were included in the numbers, so awkwardly having to decide who was in our group of three and one of us having to leave if another mum came into the park. More awful, anxiety-inducing decisions.

That we couldn't let our babies touch each other so we'd pull their hands away, stopping their natural social curiosity. Keep them close, keep them safe.

That we would be the only people to understand each other and our situation.

That our weekly Zoom catch-ups and messages would be one of the only things keeping me going.

That these women would become my closest friends, and would remain so years later.

That other friends would stick it out and be patient with me and they will never understand how much they mean to me or how much I appreciate them.

That my relationship with my husband would be tested and we would strengthen our bond, able to say that we truly know each other inside out.

That voice notes would fill the void for human contact for a while.

That I'd never go back to my office and none of my old co-workers would ever meet my baby.

That some friends wouldn't understand the decisions I was making or why they hadn't held my baby yet.

That I'd feel the old me slipping away more and more each day.

That we wouldn't agree with the decisions and choices other friends or family made, but would be jealous of the social contact we so longed for.

That as the anxiety and depression grew, I would stop getting invited to even the virtual quizzes.

That I'd get so depressed I'd email a charity saying, 'I have been having thoughts about how everyone would be better off without me.'

That when I finally got therapy through the NHS in September 2020, I'd be told that to keep my mental health well I should socialise, attend groups and see people - all things I knew.

That when I questioned what, in that case, would I do in another lockdown, I'd be told there wouldn't be another one and that it was over, only for there to be more lockdowns.

That this would send me back into a depression which I wouldn't get additional help from the NHS for, because mothers are only a risk to themselves if their baby is under a year old.

That our babies would all get used to having COVID tests stuck up their noses and their temperatures taken.

That after isolating for so long our baby would pick up so many consecutive illnesses, making up for a year inside, and that we still wouldn't be able to get a doctor's appointment for these.

That my baby wouldn't meet the rest of his friends and family, including his great-grandparents, until he was over a year old.

That I would worry about my baby's development.

That I would worry my mood swings were damaging him for life.

That we would spend his second and third years re-learning how to do things with a child that we hadn't done in the first year, like getting trains and buses.

That I would have to measure and buy my baby's first shoes myself online, no trip to Clarks.

That not only would we spend my first Mother's Day alone but also Father's Day, our birthdays, our first Christmas and my son's first birthday.

That this would all last for years, still a threat at my baby's second birthday.

That even when it 'ended,' it never really did, it just faded into the background.

That my anxiety would continue to spiral, and with it would come a rage and jealousy I'd never known before.

That I'd never again be the person I was before 2020, unsure of how much of me changed because of becoming a mother and how much because of COVID.

Maybe I didn't get it right that first Mother's Day. Maybe I should have taken the opportunity to see my family all together one last time, living a bit longer in blissful ignorance before I was placed on home arrest for the crime of becoming a mother. Yes, maybe on that first Mother's Day I should have ignored the news and taken the risk.

There was, however, one member of our little bubble who was unaware throughout, who turned the disastrous year into a beautiful one. My baby boy; the other half of our dyad. On my first Mother's Day I saw his beautiful smile for the first time. His perfect, innocent face looked up at me and broke into a smile that reminded me there is always a little hope and happiness to be found. That smile was really what Mother's Day is all about. Keeping him safe will have always been worth it, and the bond we created in the darkest of months and hardest of years is something indestructible.

    My Jura, I love you.

Shona Anderson, 31, lives in South West London with her husband, three-year-old son, Jura and dog, Harris. She recently moved from her career in buying to train as a Breastfeeding Peer Supporter and Counsellor, something she is very passionate about. In her spare time, she enjoys walking her dog in the common or practising her calligraphy, with a chai in hand.

SARAH STOKES

Stay at home, wash your hands
Don't go out unless needs be
We welcomed our second baby to this world
But nobody was able to see

Our household was a new kind of different
In a world that none of us knew
The days moulded into weeks
Our anxiety and worry grew

They say the second time is easier
But that was not true at all
I wanted my mum to tell me I would be OK
But not from the end of a call

Just a weekly shop delivery
Brought fear like never before
Anti-bac wipes over everything
Left everything outside at the door

A walk a day was our luxury
Planting flowers at home was our best game
Pictures filled up my phone daily
Sending them via messages just wasn't the same

Now we look back at that time
The world seems to have moved on
But my children are still struggling
From the time all socialising was gone

So, I hold their hands a little tighter
I tell them we will be just fine
As we reintroduce them to this changed world
One little step at a time

Sarah Stokes, from Lincolnshire, lives with her husband, three children and four dogs. She is a very busy stay at home mum who loves writing, walking and a nice cup of tea. She is at her happiest when she's making memories with her little family.

MADELEINE ABEL

I was 28 weeks pregnant when we were first all told to "stay at home." It's hard to believe it's been over three years since then. Initially, we weren't too worried as I was lucky to have had a straightforward pregnancy and the initial messages were that pregnant ladies were not any more at risk. The magnitude of everything first started to dawn on us when we did an online food order and only three items were delivered. As my partner visited more and more empty shops in an attempt to fill our cupboards, we began to worry.

Courses that we'd booked started moving online including pregnancy yoga, NCT and hypnobirthing. We had the option to get our money back or join the courses virtually. We didn't want to miss out but at the same time the whole reason for booking NCT was to meet friends and we wondered if it would be the same in a virtual environment. Hypnobirthing was all about relaxation and creating a calm environment, would that be possible online? It was disappointing to find ourselves having to choose whether to cancel or to go ahead knowing it wouldn't be quite the same.

Hospital appointments also started to change. Midwife contact was suddenly over the phone instead of face-to-face. Whilst I was grateful to be considered 'low-risk,' it meant that my appointments largely consisted of being asked if I was OK, and that was it. I never spoke with the same person twice. I reached my third trimester and felt like no one really cared.

Then came the 35-week scan, the first one I needed to attend alone. Stories were being regularly published about women having to attend scans alone, some being given devastating news. How would I cope if it happened to me?

It was as the due date approached and the subject of induction was raised that the negativity really kicked in. COVID restrictions meant an induction would involve being alone on the antenatal ward. That, together with the various negatives associated with induction, meant I wanted to avoid it at all costs. There was incredible pressure at this stage to book in. I agreed to go in for a discussion but my intention was still very much to decline. I met with the obstetrician and was backed into a corner and pressured into agreeing. I called my partner and a close friend for advice and, after two tearful calls, I begrudgingly agreed. Not long after the procedure, a concern with the baby's heartbeat was raised. I was left for hours watching the monitor. I stared at the machine, wishing for the right results that would allow me to go home.

My heart sank when I was told I would need to stay in. My partner went home to get my things and was allowed back again to drop them off. We went for a short walk. He did his best to keep my spirits up but I was devastated, knowing what was to come. We hardly said a word. He took me back to the ward and we said our tearful goodbyes. I held on to him, not wanting to let go, and then suddenly, he was gone. My worst fear had become a reality.

I was shown to a shared bay. We had planned to set up a homely feeling with fairy lights, LED candles, music, essential oils and family photos. That had been one of my partner's roles. Naively thinking this bay was only a temporary measure until I got my own room and my partner was allowed in, I left it all in the bag. There was so much focus on being in 'active labour' that it felt like I was just left to it. Staff would occasionally come in to check on me and look at the monitoring, trying to work out whether the numbers were good or not. The beeping of the machine is a noise that will probably never leave me.

Even at this stage, I was clinging to the hope that I could still achieve the most 'natural' birth possible. It was as if I was waiting to start the whole process again once my partner arrived and do things properly, but things were slowly starting to progress and I had no control over any of it. I couldn't stop it to wait for him and I couldn't speed it up so he was allowed in any earlier. Despite my preparation, I didn't seem able to use any of the techniques to try to stay calm and keep the anxiety at bay. When the contractions finally started to ramp up I found myself obsessively monitoring the contractions app on my phone to see if I was any closer to 'active labour.'

I could handle the pain at first, but it was the worry that I couldn't deal with. Why did we keep having problems with the heartbeat? Why wasn't it stabilising? Why were things not progressing? What was wrong with my baby? The idea of the baby being in distress was almost too much to take. As the contractions stepped up even more, I began to cope less and less. Exhaustion started to kick in and the pain became unbearable. I was crying out and wailing for help but no one came. Never before had I felt so incredibly lonely and scared.

Someone came in to do a COVID test. I was gagging and trying not to throw up whilst in the most excruciating pain. I thought to myself, *if they can come in and test me mid-contraction as easily as that, why can't they test my partner and let him in?*

That morning, I was told that if things didn't progress they would need to break my waters. They said they would be back at 5.15pm so all my focus was on that deadline. Obsessively clock-watching, I waited, and no one came. A few people popped in but the message was always 'the doctor is coming, it's just incredibly busy.' It was 9pm when the doctor came. Unfortunately, there was meconium in the waters but no one seemed too concerned. For me, on the other hand, it felt like yet another thing to worry about. I was told that they would be back in another four hours to check on me and that, perhaps then, my partner would be allowed in.

A while later, things took a turn for the worse. The curtains flung open, the lights turned on and what felt like 20 people rushed in. The midwife had pulled the emergency alarm and the tone of the room immediately changed. My mind went into full-blown panic mode. The alarm had been raised as the baby's heartbeat had dropped for a prolonged period. At this point, I was so traumatised and couldn't take anymore.

I was finally moved to my own room. It was clear that neither the baby nor I were coping well. Physically and mentally exhausted, it felt like I was on another planet. I wanted to give up. They gave me something to slow the contractions to protect the baby and suggested an epidural to allow me to get some rest. My partner finally arrived and whilst it was a relief to see him, I was so out of it I could hardly converse with him. It felt like I'd been in hospital forever, yet at only three centimetres dilated it seemed like the entire birth process was still ahead. I couldn't imagine how I was going to survive, so when a C-section was suggested, despite it being my absolute last choice, my main feeling was relief.

The C-section was incredibly frightening, but went as well as we could have hoped. I closed my eyes, listened to hypnobirthing through my headphones and held on to my partner's hand for dear life. I didn't want to hear what the doctors were saying or listen if anything went wrong.

After my son was born, instead of being passed to me immediately, he was taken over to the other side of the room to be given assistance. He needed some help clearing his airways in order to breathe. I couldn't hear anything, I couldn't see anything and I didn't even know the sex of my baby yet.

At last, I held him in my arms. Everything was calm and peaceful and it felt like the ordeal was finally over. That feeling was short-lived, however, as we were then told he needed antibiotics and he was taken to the baby ward. My partner went with him which left me alone again. After what felt like forever, they finally returned. This was the first and only time the three of us had any significant time together in the hospital – precious, but way too short. After about an hour, my partner had to leave. Suddenly, I was responsible for this tiny being, yet I couldn't even look after myself.

With both of us on antibiotics and me having had a C-section, we had to stay in. Every day, they would check his infection markers. His poor little feet became like pincushions from all of the tests. His levels remained dangerously high and did not seem to be coming down. They took him away to have the tests which was absolutely heartbreaking. I desperately wanted to go with him but wasn't allowed. The doctors were not happy with his progress so they recommended a lumbar puncture. The news hit me like a dagger to the heart. I simply couldn't cope with my tiny baby going off on his own to have this procedure and not being there for him through the pain. Even though I was used to him being taken away at this point, this particular occasion was unbearable. I cried and cried.

The first few days felt like a complete blur. I completely underestimated how difficult things would be post C-section. I could hardly move, let alone pick the baby up. That first nappy made me feel like a failure. There was no working it out together, laughing at doing it wrong or supporting one another in trying to get it right. It was painful, upsetting and involved a lot of tears for both me and baby. The lack of sleep and sheer exhaustion was like nothing I'd experienced. A midwife came round in the early hours one morning and could see I was struggling. She offered to take him for a while so I could sleep. I was so grateful for the rest but also felt like a failure. How different things would have been if my partner had been there to share the load.

One night, I found myself sobbing uncontrollably, so incredibly alone and worried. The ward was split into six bays, each with its own curtain, closed due to COVID. It was strange to be surrounded by people but not able to see anyone. As I cried, I heard a voice from the bay opposite asking if I was OK. I couldn't find the words to reply but I appreciated this kind stranger reaching out. The following day we started talking through the curtains. It was bizarre to be making friends in such a way but we had gotten used to restrictions. After a couple of days, we dared to open our curtains and it was a relief to see a friendly face. As time went on, women around me were discharged. It was so hard not knowing when it would be my turn.

Although I had meticulously packed my hospital bag, I hadn't prepared for an extended stay. My partner was allowed to bring some bits in for me and was permitted to the entrance of the ward, but not allowed to enter. Sadly, I wasn't allowed to take baby to the door, so I was torn between wanting to see my partner and leaving my new baby completely alone in our cubicle. On one occasion, my partner's visit coincided with meeting the doctor. She was able to explain to him in much better terms what was going on. From that point on, we did FaceTime calls every time the doctor came so he could listen in and hear everything first-hand. The pressure of having to remember and relay such important information was too much for me.

After six long days, we finally turned a corner and were told we could go home. It took a few moments for me to believe it. I immediately burst into floods of tears, so incredibly overwhelmed with emotion. After a week of constant bad news, this was the best news ever. Words can't describe how I felt at that moment.

I was so relieved to be home that I didn't realise there would be a whole aftermath to follow. Maternity leave was nothing like what I'd hoped for. My partner's leave was practically over by the time we got home. Instead of two weeks, we got three days. They say it takes a village to raise a child but, because of COVID, my village was nowhere to be found. There was no queue of visitors. No family on standby to give me a desperately needed break. No friends popping by with meals. No home visits by the health visitor. No baby classes to meet up with other new mothers. The first meetings were all outdoors at a distance of two metres apart. Walks with family, friends and the NCT group managed to keep me sane.

Certain things were incredibly triggering, like other people having babies once restrictions had started to lift. I was genuinely happy for them but also felt an uncomfortable envy, a pang of 'why couldn't that have been me?' On one occasion, I was watching a birth scene on television that should have been one of those feel-good moments, but I just completely fell apart. I found myself avoiding anything that reminded me of birth. I dreaded driving past the hospital and would avoid looking at it. The changing COVID rules had me feeling such anger. It was difficult to comprehend that shortly after giving birth under those circumstances we were then being encouraged to 'eat out to help out.'

After about six months, things started to take their toll. There had been wonderful moments during my maternity leave but it had also been the toughest time of my life. Christmas had just been cancelled and the country was in lockdown again. Winter meant that park walks and meeting up outdoors had more or less stopped, but there was no indoor socialising or leaving the baby with anyone to get a break. COVID made becoming a parent for the first time so much more difficult. I found myself in a supermarket car park one day, crying my eyes out, and decided that I needed some help. I was very lucky to be fast-tracked for therapy.

It wasn't until my second pregnancy in Autumn 2021 that I realised the effect the trauma had had. Constantly being asked about my first birth experience was particularly triggering. I was allocated a case-loading midwife and also received support from a therapist and the consultant midwife. Together we found strategies for dealing with the worry and fear. I was incredibly lucky to have such a strong support team. Most importantly, my partner did not leave my side for one moment. My second birth experience was a truly healing experience. Despite this, I'll never get over the circumstances under which I gave birth the first time. Being a lockdown mama was never part of my plan, but it is now a permanent part of my story.

Madeleine Abel, from South East London, lives with her partner, Will, and their two young children, Monty, 3, and Emilia Rose, 1. She works as both a Personal Assistant and more recently a baby swim teacher. She is kept very busy juggling hectic family life and is currently undertaking home renovation project number three. She is at her happiest when on holiday with loved ones or making memories with family and friends.

LUCY FAIRBROTHER

To my pandemic baby,

Life isn't how I imagined it would be when I thought about bringing you into the world. It doesn't look or feel how I thought it would, and some days I question if it was the right time, but then I look into your beautiful eyes and I know that it was. The world feels topsy-turvy right now but in the midst of the chaos, there is YOU.

Your world has been very small so far but know this: there is a big world waiting for you, full of adventure and love. Until then, I promise to fill your world full of love, security and fun. I promise to give you my full attention, make up games for you to make you belly laugh and cuddle you whenever you need it, even if that's every nap. I understand that your world is pretty much just me, but that's okay, because you are my whole world, too. You are the hope given to me in the darkest of times and have been the biggest star that has brightened up my days since the moment I knew you existed.

I hope you know that behind the masks are smiles, beyond the social distancing are loved ones waiting for cuddles, beyond the travel restrictions are family dying to meet you and behind the closed doors there is fun waiting to be had.

I know I need to stop putting pressure on myself to be the mum out of the books and the blogs because those babies weren't born in a global pandemic – those books and blogs haven't been written yet! I am going be the mum I always wanted to be, despite what we are facing in the outside world. I will continue to shower you with attention and love because you are my everything and I promise to keep you safe and happy.

I promise I brought you into a world that is more than just a pandemic; so much more! I brought you into a world full of people that can't wait to properly get to know you when they can, where we don't have restrictions and we can do life our own way. It's a world full of unwritten memories just waiting to be made and places to explore.

I hope the world is a kinder place for you when all of this is over and that people continue to make an effort with each other. I hope they still call, Zoom, Skype, or better yet, just turn up on the doorstep to see us and we can let them in the house! I hope we still go on walks with loved ones and make bucket lists for the future, enjoying actually ticking things off the list, too!

I hope we read this together in years to come and I tell you all about living in a pandemic, because it's just a story to you. I hope we have found a new way forward that is full of joy of happiness.

May you always know how loved you are and how much you changed my life. You gave me purpose and allowed me to cope in the most trying of times, because you were, and are, so much more than my pandemic baby. My very own Ruby Buttons, I'm so glad you are mine and I am yours. Thank you for choosing me to be your mummy x

Lucy Fairbrother, 32, from Cheshire lives with her husband, Marcus, and three-year-old daughter, Ruby. She works part-time as a UX Principal and loves to spend time with family and friends, especially if it involves hot chocolate and cake. She is currently expecting her second baby and is finally experiencing what life is like when pregnant outside of lockdown!

MAYA LAMPARD

Monday 8th June 2020.
Letter no.36 to my baby.

Wales. 35 weeks pregnant.

This weekend was tough to get through - a mixture of hormones, ongoing lockdown and external events.

On Thursday, your daddy's Aunt Emma came to stay without much warning. She has terminal cancer and has been isolating in various places, but as we've all isolated and not been allowed to move around (including Great Aunt Annie who has to sit two metres away when she comes to visit us in the garden) we all agreed Emma would stay with your granny and follow the same protocols to keep us, and more importantly herself, safe.

She arrived at lunchtime and had decided that she wasn't going to do any of that. She came right into the kitchen and sat down. I think we were all a bit startled. Nobody got up. We were following the rules: don't hug your family member who you could be seeing for the last time. She brought you a present - a hand-crocheted blue and green blanket. It was beautiful, but my thanks were disingenuous due to not knowing how to behave and worrying about breaking the rules (as if Boris or his friends were watching).

Your daddy and I stayed in our room because we weren't sure what to do. Emma got upset and said she didn't feel welcome. Over the next few hours, everyone tried their best to make amends, albeit within COVID restriction rules. On Friday evening, she shouted at your great-grandmother and decided to leave the next day. The whole debacle upset everyone. Your great-grandfather cried all of Saturday. He has slowly been coming out of his depressed spell, which he has suffered from since the lockdown started. It was hard to watch.

At dinner, we talked about it. It seemed that we were all on the same page about what we thought should have happened under the current government guidelines and that made me feel momentarily better. Not without question for your future. What will it be like for you, born into a world where we cannot express our natural human connections? Family dynamics destroyed due to rule-following? Will you know only me and Daddy? What relationships will you grow with your wider family? Will you ever know what it is like to hug, hold hands, have contact with friends and sit together in contentment, rather than in fear of catching a disease? Will you be able to spontaneously visit family, like we used to? If the last few days are anything to go by, then probably not.

It rained for the remainder of the weekend. We used our 'exercise allowance' to walk around Garn Goch, an iron age fort in Bethlehem, which helped to clear my head.

We got home to scratching in the roof. It seemed mice had moved in: my worst nightmare. Your daddy banged them away with a rake and put some poison down. This was quite stressful and on top of this, my 34/35 week pregnancy symptoms were Braxton hicks, which felt like an uncomfortable tightening of the bump where I could not sit or stand easily.

In 11 days, we will go back home, after being away for almost three months. We had left in a hurry, knowing an indefinite lockdown was imminent and that spending it on a huge farm in Wales with your great grandparents and Auntie was better than being stuck in a small flat in London.

As the time gets closer to your arrival, I am thinking about going back to my own space and being able to prepare. I will make your bedroom nice and wash all your clothes. I will set up a home for you.

I wonder if Great Granny, Great Grandfather and Auntie's voices will be familiar to you, as well as the sound of the chainsaw and the feel of walking the uneven ground in the mud around the farm. Will you recognise my family, who we have not seen in the entirety of the lockdown? Will you know that I don't normally wake up and work from my bedroom, that I go to an office, that I go to parties, dinners, restaurants and theatres? That there are usually more people in my life than those you hear from inside my body?

Sometimes I'm overwhelmed by the lockdown. Sometimes I can't stop crying because we aren't free. I can't see a way out of this. If they lift the restrictions, how will we go back to how life was? All those germs and I'll have little you to keep safe. Will I overcome it? Will I be able to take you to normal places, like baby groups, or will my whole essence of motherhood be wrapping you in bubble wrap?

I think about how everyone is beginning to talk about returning to 'normal.' It will still take a while and I'm not convinced it is safe yet, by any means. But, it feels like time to move forward, or at least think about moving forward.

I feel grateful to have enjoyed my pregnancy here, on the farm, without the stress of the 100mph London life, but at the same time, there are so many things I miss. Getting a coffee, going to the supermarket for snacks, going to meet friends and family for lunches and dinners, going round to my parents' house, driving around in my little beat-up car whilst listening to music. I miss being inspired by the people I encounter in a day, hearing snippets of their lives, their weekends and what's on their minds. Now, I just read it all from a screen. Will the next time I am doing those things, be with you? If so, it'll be a delight.

Lastly, a little news update for documentation. We've passed 40,000 deaths - the second-highest death toll in the world, after the USA.

But, don't worry, whatever it'll be, you'll be with me and Daddy. We will keep you safe.

Love,
Mama

Maya Lampard lives in Surrey with her husband and three year old son, Freddie. She works full-time in London, as well as being a mother and in her spare time (if she gets any) she enjoys writing diary entries and letters to people she loves. She loves to spend time walking in the forests and mountains, gaining inspiration for writing and gathering thoughts.

KIA BROWN

A baby during lockdown – you really couldn't make this stuff up. A pandemic, a real life pandemic. It was like something out of a *Black Mirror* episode. It was April 2020 and the coronavirus had been declared a pandemic by the World Health Organization. At the time, I didn't really understand what that meant. What I did know was that I was a BAME pregnant woman, classed as vulnerable. Every day, as I watched Boris Johnson give us the 5pm updates, I saw my chances of having two birth partners and any visitors decline. My partner told me that all that mattered was me and the baby, but this wasn't the experience I wanted. I cried every time I watched the news, seeing our freedom being taken away from us. What had I done to deserve this as a first-time mum? My partner tried to distract me as much as he could with board games, our daily hour walk and cuddles. His love gave me safety in a world that felt unsafe.

I remember getting a taxi to the Day Assessment Unit. Every shop had their shutters down, there were barely any people around and the roads were empty. It felt eerie, like a ghost town. I'd called the DAU as a precaution, really. I couldn't feel the baby kicking as much. As I looked around the ward, I saw consultants and midwives wearing PPE. It was a strange sight, everyone looked flustered, faces covered, gloves and aprons on. I could overhear midwives complaining about having to take blood while wearing gloves. NHS workers were scared but were trying to hide it. Even with all of that PPE, I could still see their nerves. This was not how I imagined giving birth to my first child.

According to the news, I was due to give birth during the peak of the virus. Before the virus, my main concern was how my mental health was going to be impacted by birth and motherhood. Well, you know what they say: misery loves company. All I could think about was how I was about to give birth to a baby in a world where no one could visit us. I wanted my mum and sister by my side. I wanted this baby to meet their aunties, uncles, grandparents and friends.

One minute it was Easter Saturday and I was looking forward to my last week of independence before the real hard work began. Then, the next minute, that freedom was taken away. A check-up appointment in the DAU ended up with me being held captive by the masked midwives. I was trying to figure out the ones who were friendly, looking for smiles in their eyes. One came over with a sympathetic look in their eyes and said, 'I don't think you're going home today, love.' Later, the stoic consultant confirmed what they had been whispering. No one wants to tell a highly emotional pregnant woman that they're not allowed to go back home.

Four hours later, heavily pregnant and with a rumbling stomach, I cried on my partner as he dropped off my hospital bag. I didn't know it, but this would be the last time I would see him before I gave birth. The last time I would touch him, smell him or be close to him as just the two of us. I had to say goodbye to him outside of the hospital as he wasn't allowed in, not even to carry my bag. Begrudgingly, I entered my new home (if that is what you can call it) with my mandatory mask that made me feel even more uncomfortable. The mask was a reminder of what was happening. I felt like my feelings had been silenced. My patience with everything was dwindling. This wasn't fair, why was this happening to me? As I accepted my fate, I tried to remain calm. The NCT guidance that we had received on Zoom had recommended I make the environment as homely and comfortable as possible. I made sure my partner brought my favourite red blanket and my Harry Potter dressing gown.

I wasn't due to have my C-section for another five days, but I knew I wouldn't be going home before the birth. The next few days were a combination of sleep deprivation, Zoom calls to my partner, pretending to read, getting used to the bland hospital food, being monitored constantly and having masked midwives continuously sticking needles in me. I was also high-risk as I had pregnancy-induced hypertension and gestational diabetes. By this point, I'd had enough of being pregnant. I was sick of waddling, having to pee all the time and not being able to sleep properly. I just wanted my body back (no one tells you you don't really get it back, though.)

After growing concerns, my C-section was pulled forward. Overwhelmed with excitement and fear, I was ready to meet the little one who had been snug inside of me for eight and a half months. The masked surgeon presented her to me, and my partner shakily announced that we had a daughter. We both cried tears of joy. I had never felt so much love in my life. She was perfect, undeniably pure and innocent. Her eyes were wide and awakening. I forgot that there was a life-threatening virus in the world. All that mattered was that my daughter was here. Not only did I give birth to a beautiful baby girl, but also to a new version of myself. I was entering an unknown world; I knew the road was long ahead of us, but I had a feeling that we were going to be okay. I could feel it. We would beat this virus.

Kia Brown, 32, from Bristol, lives with her fiancé, Tom, and two daughters, Lottie, aged 3 and Harriet, aged 1. Kia works part-time as an Assistant Disability Adviser, and she is a Trustee for Bluebell Charity which supports parents' mental health during and beyond pregnancy. Kia also volunteers on the Mum's Advisory Board for the Motherhood Group Charity, which focuses on supporting and advocating for black mothers. Kia has an MSc in English Language from The University of Edinburgh, writes in her spare time and her happy place is with a coffee in one hand and a book in another.
@ladybookly

LAURA McALLISTER

Conceived before COVID was ever a thing,
So excited for all this pregnancy would bring.
Excited to experience appointments and scans
All with your daddy holding my hand.
When the first lockdown came, we just didn't know
How much we would lose and how COVID would grow.

Trapped in a room, working from home
Scared for you, for everyone, and all alone.
Daddy – a key worker – risking his life,
No one to understand, not even the midwife.
Appointments and scans all on my own,
Eager, yet scared, to see how you'd grown.

Daddy missed out on hearing your heartbeat,
Parenting classes now obsolete.
Left to wonder and ponder and learn by ourselves,
While you started kicking and my tummy swelled.
No gimmicky announcements or gender reveal,
Nobody saw us, the pregnancy didn't seem real.

Alone on the ward while I was induced,
Daddy on video call but it was no use.
I needed support or a hand to hold,
You're not in labour enough, is all I was told.
So, I struggled alone for several hours more,
Until Daddy was allowed to walk through the door.

The birth was hard, but you were worth the wait,
Born happy, healthy and a hefty weight.
Love at first sight as you lay on my chest,
But Daddy had to leave at the government's behest.
I cuddled you close and held on tight,
As we battled alone through our first night.

After a scary few days in neonatal,
We made it back home with you in your cradle.
Happy to become a family of three,
Relieved to have Daddy taking care of you and me.

Looking forward to family coming to visit,
Sadly, though, lockdown made that illicit.

So, there we were, in lockdown number two,
First-time parents, alone, without a clue.
We did it on our own, as COVID dictated,
But watching you grow kept us elated.
Maternity leave was not what I pictured,
No baby classes, new mum friends or newborn pictures.

There was no village to rally round,
Life became quite profound.
But I wouldn't change a thing, for if I did,
I wouldn't know my strength, or have you as my kid.
I'm proud of you and Daddy and all we have achieved,
We've overcome the odds, but I still feel aggrieved.

Laura McAllister, 35, is from Bacup, Lancashire. She currently lives in Middlesbrough with her husband and daughter who will soon be three. She works as a Project Manager for a computer software company. In her spare time, when not chasing after a rambunctious toddler, she enjoys baking and rugby. Laura has written poetry since childhood as she was encouraged by her uncle to use it as a release for her emotions.

HANNAH TILLBROOK

Reflection - 23rd March 2021

Today marks the first anniversary of the day the world turned upside down for Britain. The first lockdown was called and we knew our experience of becoming parents wouldn't be what we'd hoped.

My husband, Mike, and I started trying for a baby shortly after we got married in May 2016. We didn't know if we'd be able to have children without medical intervention as I had Polycystic Ovarian Syndrome (PCOS). After three years, we were blessed to find out Amelia was on her way. I was anxious throughout pregnancy, as the statistics for miscarriage when you have PCOS is three times more likely than for women without. We made sure we celebrated each week and each new fruit she was as big as, and we enjoyed seeing her at our scans. It wasn't an easy pregnancy because Amelia wasn't growing well. However, she beat the odds and at 36+1, three days after the first lockdown was called, Amelia was born at 4lb 5oz.

We were in hospital, alone, for three days.

* * *

This time one year ago, we arrived at the hospital and Mike was turned away at the ward door. The receptionist met me in the corridor to warn me that there were men already in the waiting room with their partners because they had arrived before the restrictions were brought in that morning. If only our appointment was 30 minutes earlier, he would have been allowed in. I was angry and broken. I sat alone, in tears, whilst other couples were allowed to be together because they had been lucky enough to have an earlier appointment. The midwives had to take my blood pressure twice because I was so distressed.

I needed Mike at all those scans because there was so much information to digest from the Foetal Medicine Consultants, due to Amelia's growth. This was our last scan and it would be decided how our daughter would be born. It was awful going in without him because I was scared, but also because this was his baby too, why didn't he have the right to hear about his child? Thankfully, the consultant was happy after the scan for me to call Mike so we could discuss the plan on speaker - that was so important to me and I couldn't thank her enough. I feel for the women who had to go to multiple scans alone, especially where there were concerns, because it was awful having to do it just once.

As we were booked in for a C-section, Mike was allowed to be with me from the start. I didn't worry about whether I'd be able to cope with labour, I was just worried about the possibility of our tiny baby being poorly and me having major surgery. The C-section was quite traumatic as I found the surgery painful. Amelia was born tiny, but perfect, that afternoon and Mike was able to stay until 4pm. Sadly, because of the restrictions, once Mike had left the hospital, he wasn't allowed back again, which meant he missed out on the first three days of her life, and I had to do it alone. I understand that three days is nothing in the wider scheme of things, but I was stuck in hospital, recovering from a C-section, with a tiny, premature baby, on my own without a clue what to do. I struggled to breastfeed and was feeling out of my depth. I don't know what I would have done without the lovely hospital staff and being able to video chat with people. I chose to give Amelia formula alongside my breastfeeding attempts simply because I needed to know she was getting the food she needed and that there was a better chance of us leaving the hospital on day three. I needed to go home and be with my husband.

When we got to day three, Mike and I were on a video call when the paediatric consultant came around. We were finally cleared to come home and I think Mike was already in the car before we finished talking! Finally, we were a family again. Toby, our Jack Russell pug, was less thrilled but still a lovely big brother.

So many mums didn't get the support they needed. I was desperate to breastfeed but it was a difficult journey. I was in pain and felt like I was failing. The only help available was online zoom sessions with the local maternity support service. Although brilliant, there is only so much that can be done through a screen.

We had always said we wanted a week with no visitors to let us settle in, but that became two, three, four weeks... Suddenly, Mike had to go back to work and I was alone with this tiny munchkin and a depressed-looking dog. No parents, family or friends were allowed any further than the window. Uncomfortable and abnormal, as if we were a zoo attraction.

The first person (not including medical staff) to hold her was my mum, when she was eight weeks old. Eight weeks. I was much more emotional than I thought I would be and whilst she held her in full PPE, I leaned over, rested my head on Mum's apron and sobbed.

Amelia has a photo album of first cuddles, where I will have to explain why she looks so much older in each one and why no one came to see her. This has been Amelia's life and I am so angry and sad about that. I recognise that she won't remember, but we will. We will remember the endless days and nights with a screaming baby, dealing with it alone when usually we could have called someone for a five-minute break.

> Those who had prayed for her safe arrival were not able to see her.
> Tiny newborn cuddles were only for us.
> We did it all with no village.
> We were robbed of celebrating the arrival of our baby with our family and friends.
> Maternity leave was incredibly lonely.
> Amelia only knew most people through a screen.
> She wasn't able to develop relationships with her family or other babies.

She didn't get to meet some of our family members until she was eight weeks old.

She didn't meet another baby until much later.

We couldn't do as many activities as a family that we had planned.

I'm tired of hearing people say that you should be grateful to have a healthy baby. A few people have said this to me, and it's always been with the best of intentions, but it isn't helpful. Please don't tell a mum who has just had a baby (in lockdown or not) to be grateful that she has a healthy baby. She is. But you can feel more than one feeling at once. Feelings aren't a competition of who has had it worse. I know many have had a more difficult time throughout this pandemic than we have. We have a roof over our heads, money in the bank, food on the table and, thankfully, have not lost anyone to COVID. We don't have to worry about lots of things, and for that, I am incredibly lucky and thankful... but when you tell a new mum she should be grateful that her baby is healthy, you make her feelings irrelevant, which they are not. It is like saying *it doesn't matter what trauma you went through, get over it, because you have a healthy baby.* A healthy baby is wonderful, but they need a healthy mum.

Through this pandemic, I've seen friends go through incredibly traumatic things, alone. It's appalling that you could go to the pub with your mates but couldn't have a loved one with you for support on one of the worst days of your life. This should never have been allowed.

I will openly say that the first four months of my maternity leave sucked, not because I didn't have a beautiful and healthy baby, but because after Mike left to go to work, I was completely alone with a baby who screamed for hours. I had no one to physically come and help. What I would have given for someone to pop around and cuddle her, even for 15 minutes, so I could have a break. That is what most women get: family and friends who will pop round and cuddle the baby, so you naturally get a break at times, but that wasn't allowed. There were no baby groups to meet other mums.

I am so thankful to those who supported both Mike and I through video calls, window visits and conversations, especially in the first four months, because you helped preserve my sanity. I don't think I would be where I am currently, without you.

Am I thankful that Amelia is healthy? Absolutely.

Am I thankful that we haven't lost anyone close to us through all of this? Absolutely.

Am I grieving the maternity leave Amelia and I should have had? Absolutely.

I am still emotional about these things that began a year ago today. However, I am challenging myself to remember there have been many wonderful moments, too. Our support bubble with Keli, our childcare bubble with Naomi and Jeremy, video chats with my mum and stepdad, all of which held me together - I can't thank you enough.

I'm so sad that our experience of becoming parents to the little girl we tried and prayed for for three years, wasn't as it should have been, but we are still blessed with a daughter who we are very thankful for. This is not the first year of Amelia's life we had hoped for, but I'm praying the second will be amazing.

Final Reflection - March 2023

As I sit here writing this, my daughter has just celebrated her third birthday, and I'm looking back on our journey as a family and the impact the lockdown had on us.

Being a sociable person who benefits from having people around, the lockdown impacted my mental health and although I was never diagnosed with post-natal depression, I sincerely believe that was only because I chose not to return the survey. I knew whatever the GP service could offer, it wasn't what I needed.

In January 2021, I spoke with Mike about finding a private therapist to work through the trauma of an infertility journey, a difficult pregnancy, giving birth and being alone in hospital and lockdown. He recognised how important this was for me and despite being on a tight budget due to me only receiving maternity and part-time pay, I found a wonderful therapist who I felt comfortable enough with to start working through things. Over ten months, I worked through a lot of things with the therapist, which made me feel better. However, when 'partygate' was first announced on the news, I felt like I was back to square one. I was so angry that whilst I'd fought my way through what should have been the happiest year of my life, the politicians putting me in that position had been doing whatever they wanted. I will never get the chance to relive my daughters first years. I am angry about that - although I know I can't change it – but they could have. They could have allowed my husband to visit me whilst I was trying to process the lockdown, with a premature baby, trying to take care of her after a C-section in hospital, but they didn't. They made me go through it alone, but they absolutely needed their cheese and wine parties.

The most difficult challenge I face now is the jealousy when I see people announcing their pregnancies, knowing that they will be able to have their partner, family and friends visit them, have people there to just give them five minutes when their baby won't stop crying, support from baby groups and just being able to have that village around them that I didn't get. I am so thankful that my friends don't have to go through restrictions, but I just wish that had been the same for me, too. It sounds tiny in the wider scheme of things, but knowing that my child didn't meet some of her family members until she was two years old is so incredibly sad.

I recognise that, although I have pictures where I look happy in the first couple of years, I know I didn't enjoy Amelia as much as I should have done. I'm sad that I was so caught up in the world around me that I wasn't able to just focus on our daughter. I will forever be sad that the experience I had waited so long for will always be tainted, and I hope that one day it won't affect me every time it's the 23rd March, but for now, I am focusing on trying to be the best mum I can be.

Hannah Tillbrook, 34, from Oxfordshire, lives with her husband, their three-year-old and their Jack Russell Pug. She works as a Social Worker and is an active member of her church. She enjoys spending time with her friends and family as well as reading and watching medical/crime dramas.

EMMA MORGAN

Mummies Tummies

Some girls at school used to say "*We knew each other in
our Mummies tummies*" and I held my best friend's hand
harder, because we had only known each other since the
buggy upturned on my face outside her nurse Mum's
house. My daughter will never have a
>   *Friend She Knew From A Mummy's Tummy*
because bump-her kept inside, bar one walk a day;
bumped along two metres from another body.

Each week, so-called too neat, bump and me
went to hospital. Sat in a room full of Mummies
all with babies in their tummies, each with a safe
radius and a mask to contain us. Too scared to say
Hello! We'd forgotten - what do you do with
a stranger? My daughter will never have a
Mummies Tummies friend, but maybe
>   *Knew Each Other Since Our Mummies Were Brave,*
>   *Once They'd Re-opened Soft Play*
will be their post-pandemic friend trend.

Elastic Tension

Waiting newborn, feeding feeding, soothing easing.
Tape on chairs, a plastic-covered nurse for wiping,
disinfecting in the wake of leaving.
Tops of faces, delays, all day, feeding feeding,
soothing you, empty me. Cafe's closed. Short staffed - delays.
Eyes avoiding, tears falling, baby rocking, soothing soothing.
Never held by loved ones, examined by gloved ones,
tight for drawing blood, alone for an ultrasound.
No mouths, no-one to form the happy shape.
Tears falling, waiting, feeding, soothing.
Lives lost. Waiting for a name to be called.
One moment, a single mask drawn down, forgotten.
Would you like some water? Hand on shoulder
ease elastic tension - can you wait a little longer?
Yes. We can wait a little longer.
Thank you stranger.

Emma Morgan is a single mum and poet from Oxford. She juggles working as a Graphic Designer with caring for her young daughter. Emma writes poetry on motherhood and nature, during the spare moments, and when she cannot sleep. She loves signing with her daughter, who is profoundly deaf, and has hopes to make accessible poetry in British Sign Language. Find more of her work on Instagram @emmorpoetry

TORI BEAT

We took a while to decide, my husband and I, whether we would try for baby number two. I had suffered some undiagnosed postnatal depression following the birth of our daughter in 2017 and, whilst she brought a kind of love and joy to our lives that we didn't know was possible, parenthood had not come without its challenges (who knew?)

We had the serious now-or-probably-never conversation on the drive down to Cornwall for a long-anticipated family holiday, during that Forget The Pandemic And Get Yourselves Out Of The House period encouraged by the Government in August 2020. We had made it through the first lockdown and, fortunately, emerged relatively unscathed. Neither myself nor my husband were getting any younger and we felt like we needed to make a decision before it was too late.

When we went into lockdown in March 2020, our daughter was two and a half. I don't doubt that any developmental stage with a child in lockdown had its challenges, but two and a half felt like a particularly tricky time to be locked in the house. She was testing the behavioural boundaries like never before, needed way more entertainment and, crucially, had DROPPED HER NAP. It was quickly apparent that I'd be doing a full seven 'til seven shift without a break, every day until nursery opened again. And we had no idea when that would be.

That said, she was a super sleeper and we had just about nailed potty training. Not that that mattered as we weren't leaving the house, but it felt like a big tick off the to-do list. And she was healthy, thank goodness. So, we had lots to be thankful for and she was at an age where, a few tantrums aside, she was wonderfully entertaining company. That stage of development fascinates me, when they're finding their place in the world, questioning everything and chatting constantly. But, I was totally knackered.

In October 2020, I found out I was pregnant. We were thrilled – a late spring baby, something for everyone to look forward to, due to arrive a few months before our daughter turned four and started school in September. By this time, on the COVID front, we were already deep into a second wave, given that everyone had been eating out to help out in August and schools and universities had started to open back up. We were, of course, being cautious, but also wanted to try and get on with life as normally as possible within the limitations that were still in place. Our daughter, now three, was back at nursery – a notorious breeding ground for all the germs – but we wanted her to have as normal an integration back into social life as possible, in preparation for starting school next year. But, as I started attending my midwife appointments, it became clear that the maternity care offering was anything but back to normal.

First of all, I had to attend all appointments alone. This was not a surprise. I'd heard many stories of mothers giving birth without their partners and some receiving dreaded news alone, while the outside world was being encouraged to get back into the swing of normal life for the benefit of the economy. Theatres, bowling alleys and soft plays were starting to open up their doors, with people mixing as if nothing was happening outside, but people were still dying, and women were, yet again, being let down by the capitalist patriarchy.

We were still, ever so cautiously, visiting my 93-year-old extremely vulnerable grandmother, only once a week, to minimise the risk of passing anything on to her, despite the fact that she was otherwise alone. We had been spun the line that she would be safer if we kept our distance, even though she was desperately lonely and longing for the regular, uncompromised visits with her great-grandchildren to resume. But, we stuck to the rules and kept physical contact to a minimum. In hindsight, I wish we had ignored the guidance and lived what, we didn't know then, would be her final year to the full. Hugs and all.

The outside world looked largely similar to how it did before the pandemic, you just had to wear a mask sometimes and could only sit in a bar in groups of six, whatever difference that makes. But if you were having a baby – you know, actually keeping the human race going – you had to cope with the myriad physical and mental trials of scans, antenatal appointments, heck, even giving birth, on your own. With just a few well-meaning but, ultimately, stretched-to-the-limits-of-what-is-possible healthcare professionals for support. I began to spiral into an anxiety-ridden hole about what this pregnancy might look like.

Three weeks after I'd attended my midwife booking appointment, I started to get severe pelvic pain on my right side, amongst other symptoms indicative of an ectopic pregnancy. I put my feet up and tried to ride it out but the pain, and my anxiety, got progressively worse. On 12 November 2020, at ten weeks pregnant and one week after England had entered the second national lockdown, I was advised by the pregnancy assessment unit of my local hospital to go in for an emergency scan.

I knew that I would have to attend this appointment alone, as those were the rules. We had suffered a missed miscarriage during our first pregnancy back in 2016 which, devastatingly, was only discovered at the 12-week scan. The thought of going through that process again, without my husband, filled me with dread. I knew there was a possibility that this pregnancy wasn't viable and that I might need potentially life-saving surgery if it happened to be an ectopic pregnancy.

What I wasn't prepared for that morning, though, was my husband testing positive for COVID, which threw a spanner in the works. It hadn't affected the possibility of him coming along to the appointment – that was never going to be allowed anyway – but it did mean that I now felt duty-bound to tell the hospital that I was living with someone who had COVID. My test was negative but there was a possibility that I was carrying the virus, too, and I was about to go into hospital and be in the same vicinity as other people who were pregnant and healthcare workers who were risking their lives just being there. I couldn't not tell them.

I called the hospital and told them that I was supposed to be coming in for an emergency scan to rule out an ectopic pregnancy but that my husband had just tested positive for COVID. After much umming and ahhing, the receptionist said he would have to speak to the midwives, and put me on hold. Although he didn't put me on hold. I could hear the entire debate going on about whether or not I should be allowed in to have a potentially life-saving scan.

"She can't come in here, she might have COVID," said one member of staff, after the receptionist had explained my circumstances.

"But she's been referred for a query ectopic," said another. "She could die if it's missed."

"Well, we should probably ask her to wait until tomorrow, after she's done another test?" suggested someone else.

"I'll see her," said a heroically brave midwife, who I'd later meet, named Nikki. "Prepare a separate entrance for her and tell her to come in at 1.30."

I went into the hospital that afternoon through a separate entrance, without touching anything or coming into contact with the main waiting area. I was extremely anxious. Nikki greeted me warmly and told me not to worry, leading me gently into the specially-prepared sonography room. She talked me through the process and put me at ease, mindful that I'd had a harrowing experience of early scans before. As I lay trembling, she showed me the tiny bean growing inside me that would become our beautiful baby boy.

Nikki was so kind to me. She knew I might have COVID and treated me anyway. She spoke up for me when others were, understandably, at odds with what to do for the best. The scan had a happy outcome but neither she nor I knew what lay ahead when she put herself forward to see me that day and she never once made me feel like I was troubling them unnecessarily.

Happily, the rest of my pregnancy was relatively uncomplicated. I was anxious about how things were going to pan out, particularly during the early months as we bumbled from the second lockdown to the third, not knowing when – or if – things were ever going to get back to anything like normal. I always kept in mind those women who, just a few months before me, were forced to give birth without their partners, labouring whilst wearing masks and left behind by the over-stretched postnatal care system. I was in a much more fortunate position as we moved from the first to the second year of the pandemic and the outside world had already found lots of ways to cope with the new normal.

The pregnancy yoga class I had done whilst pregnant with my daughter had moved online and, despite the lack of face-to-face contact, became an invaluable support network for advice on maternity care rules and birthing plans. I missed things like swimming and other exercise classes but I managed to spend lots of time outside, walking and keeping generally active. I was trying to get my head in as safe a space as possible, knowing that this pregnancy and birth would probably be quite different to the previous.

In May 2021, I gave birth to a wonderful, healthy baby boy. The midwives were incredible. How they managed to do their jobs under such intense pressure and challenging circumstances will never cease to amaze me.

The next day, we brought our son home to meet our daughter. The look on her face when she caught the first glimpse of her new baby brother will stay with me forever. Whilst restrictions were starting to ease, there were still some in place regarding social gatherings, so our friends and family visited cautiously and gradually over the first few weeks, with us mostly spending time outside in the early summer sunshine. The postnatal care continued, with home visits and essential appointments at clinics still going ahead. Breast-feeding support workers were, fortunately, available, despite such heavy demand on the system. As our pregnancy yoga cohort had all had their babies by mid-July, we were able to meet face-to-face for post-natal yoga as soon as the restrictions were eased further.

Even though I began my Motherhood 2.0 journey during Lockdown 2.0, I feel like one of the lucky ones. Lucky - that we had an uncomplicated pregnancy with no major issues, despite our early scare. Lucky - that Nikki was willing to see me for the emergency scan, despite my husband having COVID. Lucky - that we were still able to see friends and family, albeit cautiously, for much-needed love and support. And lucky – and forever grateful - to the incredible people of the NHS who enabled me to give birth to our son in a truly magical way, with my husband holding my hand.

Tori Beat is a freelance writer and mother-of-two, based in Derbyshire. She has written opinion pieces for publications such as Sonshine Magazine, The Robora Magazine, and came runner-up in the 2022 Green Parent Magazine writing competition. Tori was selected to guest-edit Issue 10 of Freelancer Magazine in 2023, with articles on her experiences of work, identity and leaving her former career as a lawyer. Alongside copywriting for small businesses, Tori is currently working on her poetry collection and her novel-in-progress, Class of '99, was shortlisted for the Watson, Little x Indie Novella prize 2023. You can find her on Instagram @tori_beat.

SARAH BIRCH

A story for Charlotte.

February 2020. A nasty virus that we didn't know a lot about had come to the UK. In the lead-up, the news channels were showing video footage of people collapsing in the streets in China. Dad and I were petrified of catching it from work colleagues who had been travelling, especially as we were trying to keep tiny you safe. Supermarkets looked very different, with a toilet roll panic and flour and pasta running low on the shelves. We chose late-night trips to the supermarket to get provisions for the week. Sometimes the shelves were empty, only able to bring back whatever we could find - frankfurter pasta with cheese, anyone?

The first week of March came, along with a 12-week scan, the last appointment that your dad was able to attend for a while. He was amazed by you flipping around like a tiny dolphin on the screen and I was relieved that you were there and healthy! I told my manager that I was pregnant on the Tuesday and by the Friday we were told to work from home. I didn't have the chance to tell my colleagues I was pregnant.

Zoom quizzes, FaceTime with family and a lot of homemade banana bread later, it was time for the 20-week scan. Dad waited in the car park and I had to go in alone. Despite my nerves, you were growing well. I made a separate gender reveal for Dad on a little card and I ticked the pink box for a girl. He opened the envelope in the car when I got back and he was so happy he was having the little girl he'd wished for.

We missed out on all of the in-person shopping, since non-essential shops were closed, and so had to order everything online, including your pram. We had to watch many videos of people putting them up and down and trawled reviews online to see which we liked the most.

Every week, we would go out and clap for the NHS. In hindsight, it's odd that it was the only time we saw other people, other than the weekly shop. It felt sad that it was neighbours and strangers who saw my bump growing in person and not our friends or family.

A few weeks and a 4D scan later, 26th June 2020 was etched in my mind as the day we found out everything was going wrong. I was just going into my 29th week of pregnancy and had my first in-person appointment with a midwife. Up until then, I was considered low-risk. This time, my iron was low, blood pressure high and my bump was measuring small. I was put onto daily monitoring for the foreseeable future.

36 weeks came and I was working at home. I locked my computer and went for my morning monitoring. I hadn't felt you move as much as normal so they did some investigations and you were compressing your cord which was causing dips in your heart rate. You were small and had low fluid, and they said

this was likely a sign you were distressed, advising that I needed to be induced. I was thinking, 'Oh gosh, I haven't even logged off yet!'

They took me straight to the induction ward and I texted Dad to tell him he could go home as he was waiting in the car park. We made the best of a bad situation, the other ladies and I chatted with each other through the long days on the ward. Some already had children so were giving tips and we shared magazines.

Your dad was sleeping at my parent's house as they were only 20 minutes away from the hospital rather than the 50-minute journey from our home. I felt so angry that he could 'eat out to help out' at a pub or restaurant with his friends but he couldn't be there with me when I really needed him.

Labour ramped up after my waters broke spontaneously. The next hours went by in a blur and I held it together until it was my turn to go to the labour ward. I instantly took up the offer of an epidural and wanted to hug that anaesthetist as the pain went in an instant. I was already 10cm dilated and in the pushing stage by the time Dad was allowed in from the car park.

Your heart rate was dipping and not coming back quickly. All of a sudden, a swarm of doctors came in at once, Dad got his gown on and it was all systems go. Forceps and big pushes later, you were out. You let out a big, loud cry and I let out a big sigh of relief, and you were whisked off for checks and to be weighed. It felt as if I was on another planet at that point.

You were wrapped like a little burrito and given to Dad. I met you both later in the recovery room. Around an hour post-birth, once my vitals were OK, Dad was told he needed to leave. They wheeled you and I down to the postnatal ward. I couldn't believe how beautiful you were, staring up at me, studying my face. I fell asleep before I'd had any tea and toast!

We had three long days together, mostly on our own - Dad was allowed to visit for an hour a day. I found it hard being alone and spent a lot of that time in tears. One night, we had a whole ward to ourselves and I have never felt so lonely.

Because you were so small, only 5lb 2oz and early, you were under the care of the midwives and health visitors for a while. You had a feeding plan and we had scales dropped on our doorstep to weigh you ourselves. It was strange not being able to meet other mums and compare notes. I felt like I spent so much time Googling and asking the other mums inside my phone, who became my version of a village.

10 days in, I went to an overnight intensive breastfeeding class with you. I was only going there to learn how to pump. I think there was a misunderstanding and they wouldn't let me formula feed you, which meant you cried for four hours because you were hungry. At that point, I was completely and utterly broken. The healthcare assistant came to check on us and found us both sobbing. I was in the bed, with you in my arms, wondering why I'd brought this on myself. Again, I felt so alone.

The lovely mum in the cubicle next to me said, 'You're doing so well, you're a great mum,' from behind the curtain that divided us. I can't tell you how much these words meant to me.

At around eight weeks, we made a childcare bubble with Nanny and Grandad, and Grandad got me brave enough to start taking you out. I was so frightened that you'd cry and I'd look incapable, or of you getting unwell. He took us to the park and later on we braved a café. You were so interested in all the people and it wasn't half as bad as I'd imagined.

We didn't get to go to your first baby class until you were nearly nine months old. I got a bit tearful seeing you looking at all the other babies, wondering if you'd feel robbed of this time one day.

Flash forward and you're three years old. I can't believe any of this happened. Masks and social distancing are a thing of the past. In the future, I hope you're able to learn about the time you were born, when the rest of the world was standing still.

Sarah Birch, 32, from Essex, lives with her husband and her three-year-old daughter, Charlotte. She works part-time as an Operational Analyst in Banking. At home, she loves baking and decorating cakes and curling up with a good book.
@sarahl0us

ELLIE BRIGHT

Trigger warning: IVF journey

IVF. Delayed.
Inject your skin for the process to begin
One needle at a time
The fear of "am I doing this right?"

Masks on. Sanitise. Walk in. Sit. Don't take up space
Walk through empty corridors to lay on blue paper
Intrusive questions
Prodded and poked
Internal ultrasound leaves me choking for air
Please help me
Get me out of here

Process repeats
Prescriptions collected

Keep shooting
Keep bloating
Keep choking

Sat in a ward
Alone
Scared for your life
Alone
Scared for the outcome
Alone

Called into the theatre
Don't touch anything
Lay on the bed.
Strapped in by the legs and arms. Velcro pulling at your skin.
It's cold in here. It's busy but you're alone in here.
Anaesthetic takes you, you are glad for the release from fear.

Awake. Panic. Pain.
Wait for the call.
Eggs collected, eggs have fertilised.
One good embryo to pin our hopes on.
All comes down to this day... Let's go. No. Wait.
Wait in the car to be called in.

Small talk and holding hands, checking the phone. Two hours late.
Then "come now" to sit alone for another hour

Harsh bright lights
Cold air
Rude doctor - "Lay down, legs up, shut up"
Tears streaming down my face
Please, a hand to hold?
Some reassurance?
Escorted out, door closed.

Wait
Wait
Wait

Positive test
Excitement
Relief
All is meant to be

Travelling to tell loved ones
Meet outside
Stay two meters apart
Don't get close

Sickness
Never-ending sickness

Grow
Stretch
Hide from the virus
Stay at home
Not safe to be at work
Grow
Stretch

Blood.
Panic.
Help me.
Call. Drive. Wait.
Labour ward.

Breathe. Breathe. Breathe.
Waves of emotion.

Brain disengaged, I am floating away in time and space
Empty but full at the same time
Dizziness - Who is who?
Hands held. Relief.
Not alone. Relief.
Help requested and arrives. Relief.
Breathe. Breathe. Breathe.
Breathe. Breathe. Breathe.
Transition tears apart my soul
Screaming and shouting to make it stop
"Cut this baby out of me"
I'm in too much pain, I'm going to die, can't you see?
Push they say, breathe they say.
Quiet - "You're scaring other patients"
Silenced by fear and pain and death and trauma and strapped to a bed on my back.
Strapped down once again - flashback.
Pushing pushing breathing pushing
Baby here
We did it

Stitch

A trail on the floor
Red
D
R
I
P
S
A tale of life
Red blood
Drops signifying pain
Splashes of heartache and heartbreak
Dashes of fear
Jellied clumps "no bigger than 50p please," the new size of me

A trail on the floor.
Of me,
no more.
Baby born,
Belly abandoned,
Wishes realised.
Back to reality.

Reality now being bright red
D
R
I
P
S
A line drawn in blood between then and now
Shower,
Wee,
Discharge,
Go.
Be.
Boom. no time for reality to hit.
Sink
Sink
S
I
N
K
Sink in the drips that used to belong to you. When you were one. And now you're two.
Two and tiny pieces of you
left on the floor in each drip.
Birth forgotten, on with your job now. Not medically well, not even fixed.
But here you are, now you must go.
Drip
Drip
D
R
I
P
Down the corridor home we go.
Home.
Home.
Home.
I want you to visit
But don't... stay far.
Don't touch her.
Holding my breath while they do anyway.
Silence your fear. Bury it deep inside with the pre-pregnant you.
Beautiful newborn bubble. Beautifully raw. Beautifully blue. Beautifully me and you.
The world is opening up
I'm late to the party

Afraid of the party
Keep me away from the party
The world has forgotten
But you're still so small
Cases rise and fall
But nobody following rules
You make space but now the space is theirs to take
Cases rise and fall
Still terrified of it all
Keep her safe
Keep her safe
Hold her tight
Readjust
Little steps
Making progress down the path
Little steps of one mile, two miles,
But then, fifty miles. Fourth trimester is over.

Ellie Bright (she/her), 29, from the West Midlands, lives with her wife and daughter. She is a stay-at-home parent who enjoys singing nursery rhymes, messy play and reading stories. In adult company, Ellie likes to do arty things and yoga. She is a sucker for anything with a rainbow on and the TV show Friends.

LUCY HORNE

Trigger warning: IVF, fertility struggles.

Our journey to have a baby was not an easy one. My husband and I got married in 2015 when we were in our mid-twenties and naively thought sex = baby. I had already stopped taking the contraceptive pill about a year before, so my periods had returned and were regular. Around 12 months later, after a lot of unprotected sex, nothing had happened and so we visited our GP. To start with, I didn't feel supported and was told time was on our side (that ever-present woman's ticking clock) and to, pretty much, keep calm and carry on. This was not good for our mental health! I started ovulation tracking and sex became a loveless task with me keeping my legs in the air for 30 minutes after. Each period was met with such sadness and our relationship struggled. So, we went back to our GP.

Cue an 18-month process of rigorous testing, being poked and prodded (internally and externally) an operation and my husband doing many sperm tests. We were told that no one knew why we were not getting pregnant. Everything physically was as it should be so maybe we needed to try and stress less! This was impossible - by now, most of our friends had babies and weekends were full of baby showers, first birthdays and christenings. At each event, I felt a shining spotlight on us, highlighting our childlessness. I was severely depressed and the only thing that would help was a baby in my arms.

We were referred to have IVF. IVF is the hardest, most gut-wrenching and exhausting process. I was having three injections a day and an internal scan and blood tests every other day. This gave no guarantee of pregnancy, but a chance, so they were things I was willing to endure.

We did round after round of IVF. I just kept pushing myself; each time I thought I hit my limit I would keep going. After a miscarriage and two chemical pregnancies, our worlds were turned upside down. COVID-19 hit. The government decided to shut all IVF clinics and all cycles were cancelled. This was devastating for us. We had no idea when things would start back up again and my biological clock was ticking even louder.

Everyone was impacted by COVID. We all had worries and concerns. Would our loved ones get sick? Would we be OK financially? Would we survive? Would we lose that chance of having a baby?

I believe the lockdown actually ended up being our saviour. I had been going through round after round like a woman possessed and COVID stopped that. It meant we had time to reflect, for my body to recover, to grieve and accept that perhaps we wouldn't become parents and perhaps that would be OK. We had each other, something that COVID made you realise you couldn't take for granted.

We still had two embryos in the freezer and I couldn't turn my back on them, so once the clinics were allowed to open again, we decided to use those last two but with a more relaxed, accepting approach. We accepted that whatever the outcome was, it would be OK, as we had each other and our loved ones.

In October 2020, I found out our ninth round of IVF had worked. COVID was still present and after such a long journey to pregnancy I wasn't going to risk anything, so I spent the entirety of it shielding. I sent my friends and family photos of my growing bump. I had to record my 12-week scan because my husband wasn't allowed in. My pregnancy was nothing like I had imagined, I was overwhelmingly scared and nervous and I couldn't accept that the dream was real. I had the usual fears that come with pregnancy but with the very real underlying threat of COVID. This was pre-vaccinations, at a time where we didn't know how COVID affected pregnant women and their unborn babies.

In June 2021, I gave birth to the most amazing, wonderful, miracle little boy. COVID changed the experience for us – I was expected to wear a mask for the start of labour. It was decided I needed a C-section, however, before I could go to theatre, I needed to take a COVID test, despite the fact that I had just been panting away over the midwife. The restrictions also meant my husband was only allowed to stay for a few hours after the birth.

I limited who could meet our newborn. Whoever did, took a COVID test first and wore a mask. My postpartum care was a quick phone call to check I didn't have postnatal depression and that I was physically healing OK. We didn't get to go to any baby groups. There was no support for me as a first-time mum, whose journey to having a baby was so fraught that I struggled accepting I now had one in my arms, and lived in fear of something bad happening.

We are now in March 2023 and our little bundle of joy has grown into the most fearless, strong-willed 21-month-old. He really is the embryo that *could*.

As much as COVID took away how I experienced my pregnancy and birth, I feel it gave us a moment to pause. It gave us a moment to breathe. It gave us a moment to reflect. And it was this break that meant our next round worked.

So, I hate COVID, I hate the fear it brought, I hate that it broke our stability, I hate that it took lives, I hate that the repercussions are still felt now, but I love that it allowed us to pause. Maybe this was the one thing we needed to finally have our dream come true.

Lucy Horne, 32, from Ramsgate lives with her husband, her dog and their two-year-old son. She works part-time as a Studio Manager at a post-production studio. She lives a short walk away from the beach which is her calm place - most days she will pop down there even just for half an hour! Luckily, her son shares her love for the coast, so the two of them can usually be found there – rain or shine. Lucy and her husband are just starting the IVF journey again in the hope of giving their son a sibling.
@ivfan_dme

HELEN WHALE

Reflections from the lost

Strange times pass
Many parts are forgotten
Then a trigger and it hits me
Tears fall like reels of cotton.

It wasn't supposed to be that way
That time back in 2020
It should've been full of newborn joy
But it was fear and hand washing a'plenty.

I was scared of everything
I was worried for everyone
I tried so hard to be okay
But I was emergency schooling, not being a mum.

I was nursing my newborn, too
And recovering from birth
And re-learning long multiplication
And digging up the earth.

I took too much on
But felt I needed it to survive
To shoulder all their worries
And try my best to help them thrive

It was a time of so much unrest
The fear of death so close
The rules we had to stick to
In case we caught a COVID dose.

The pit of sadness as we missed out
Not seeing my family's smiles
Loved ones not seeing my babies grow
Doorstep chats, a distance that felt like miles.

Groundhog days for months
The desperation to go and explore
The longing for a hug with Mum
Fear that enveloped me at every door.

I feel grateful we're all okay
I feel guilty for saying and writing this
For putting pen to paper
For there were also times... that I now miss.

The slow, long days and country walks
The extra cuddles and no rushing
The chance to be a teacher
The play setups and online disco moshing.

Being with my husband and best friend
The best lockdown partner there could be
Our relationship got stronger
We are a solid unit with our wee three.

The walks with small groups of friends
The simple focus just on us
Settling as a family of five
Realising... this was in fact, a plus?!

But... was it really a plus?
I don't really know
A rainbow of emotions to work with
We all need to take it slow.

To let our hearts and heads heal
To be kind and lead with love
For everyone's story is different
So, while we can, let's hug.

Helen Whale, 40, lives in Gloucestershire with her husband and three children; Lily, Jack and Lottie. She works part-time as a Marketing and Business Co-ordinator for a small HR Consultancy. Between working and juggling the school/pre-school runs, Helen can be found tending to her veggies and flower patches at her allotment. She loves being outside and going for long country walks and adventures with her family, observing the world through their little eyes.
@whale_plot_four

REBECCA BRYANT

Trigger warning: NICU stay, parenting a child with a disability

When did you fall in love with your child? When they were playing football in your tummy? When you saw their little body bouncing around on the scan? When they nuzzled into your chest for the first time? For me, it was sometime in May 2020, early evening I'd say. We were both alone, in a hospital room at Great Ormond Street Hospital (GOSH) and a researcher from genetics had "popped along" to take photos of my little S for their studies. I'd agreed to it a few weeks prior, after finding out we would be there as the respiratory ward at GOSH tried to solve why my little S couldn't breathe properly. At first, I was OK with her snapping away at all the so-called features that made my daughter stand out. But, as the minutes rolled on, I became more uncomfortable with the situation. My daughter, the mystery. My daughter, born with a rare disease during a global pandemic. My daughter, the science experiment. I was reducing her to just that, when really, she was my beautiful little girl who I wanted to protect, keep safe and take home to cherish.

The problem was, I didn't really know how to act in this situation. I was a first-time mum. When people asked me if she acted differently from other babies, I had no idea. It was like asking me about progressive rock in the late 90s - I really didn't have a clue. You see, S came so quickly. My whole pregnancy felt like troubled waters with scans, tests and lots of anxiety. S was measuring small from around 20 weeks and didn't grow from about 28 weeks. At 30 weeks, we were told for the sake of her health she needed to come out at 32 weeks and the safest way was via a C-section. I hadn't even bought a buggy, let alone considered my birth plan. I was still working and wanted some time. But time we didn't have. If I'm honest with myself, I was a wreck in the run-up to her birth, see-sawing between "what ifs" and "it will be OK." I was obsessed with finding answers on Google, Facebook, anywhere that would offer reassurance that my little one would be OK. But then, she wasn't. She was alive, but not "OK" in the sense of what society perceives as being "OK."

My beautiful girl with a head of golden curls was born on 9th March 2020, or what the papers notably called "Black Monday," weighing only 1.2kg. She was so tiny and fragile and whisked away as soon as she was removed from the incision across the lower half of my body. I was taken to a separate room to recover while Daddy went to get her settled in NICU. This didn't come as a shock to us. We knew she'd have to spend some time in NICU as the doctors had pre-warned us. I guess we just got on with it. My parents were there and they were able to see this little creature in her incubator, with so many tubes attached to her, looking like something from a sci-fi movie. It was the first and last time they saw her for almost five months. Her hair was a beautiful white-gold, so unusual and unique.

The days after remain a bit of a blur. I'd almost forgotten I'd been cut open and was walking around soon after. My milk came in easily and I started filling up syringes with colostrum. I learned how to pump and was soon filling up bottles to feed the little one. I spent a few hours with her in NICU and back on the ward, while in the background we started hearing about the disease which was spreading around the world. We'd hoped that my parents could stay for a few days but we sent them home the following day. As for my husband's parents, they were further away and didn't get a look-in. We were in a quandary. Should we leave the hospital or try and stay? We were fearful that we could catch the disease and not be let into NICU, where rules were strict in normal times. We soon found out those rules would become a diktat for our daily lives during COVID. Eventually, we returned home, empty-handed apart from a hospital-grade breast pump, which I would use to fill up bottle after bottle with milk, hoping that she'd come home soon. It wouldn't be that long, surely?

Days turned to weeks and weeks turned to months. Too scared to take public transport or take a taxi, we ended up walking the almost-six-mile round trip to and from hospital. This started a week after my C-section. Luckily, I had recovered pretty quickly from this major operation. Was this the best course of action? I have no idea, but it was the only way we could get to see her and deliver my milk to her every day.

If you've ever had a child in NICU, you'll know how difficult it can be. Now, imagine that time spent with your vulnerable baby is reduced to just three hours a day. Three hours for you, three hours for your partner. Not at the same time. Now, imagine that a month after spending your days trudging in to read, pump, read, attempt to breastfeed, hold, change, feed and pump again, you get a phone call from the doctors in NICU telling you to come in. You miss the call, of course, because you switched your phone to airplane mode to listen to some Radio 4 drama while walking to the hospital. You wanted to save your battery so you could take photos of your baby in NICU. The flurry of messages appear and the NICU nurse says that the doctor wants to see you and your husband together. This doesn't sound good. You ask if it's serious, while standing in NICU surrounded by seriously ill babies. They don't know. You call your husband who asks you if he's really needed. And yes, yes, you think so. Then "Dr Doom," as we started calling her for reasons that will soon become apparent, delivers the news that your child has a chromosomal deletion.

"What does that mean?" I asked. Dr Doom didn't really know. It could mean a lot of things. We both sat there trying to be optimistic. Dr Doom said she couldn't find anyone else with a similar one but it probably meant something. Great. Then came the part where we had to deliver the news to the rest of the family, by phone, obviously, because we were in the midst of deep, dark COVID by now. We weren't really sure what to think apart from "Fuck this." Our first child was stuck in hospital and we found out she wasn't going to be "OK," in the general sense of the word. Unable to see our family or friends or do anything normal to be able to help us process all this information, it felt like a bloody nightmare or a seriously sick joke.

More inconsequential, yet bleak, news came from Dr Doom over the next few weeks alongside some apnoeic episodes where S temporarily stopped breathing. I pretty much read up everything I could find on the internet about this chromosomal deletion, talked to a genetic counsellor at GOSH and still felt in the dark as to what it meant for my little one. There were weekly chats with a family psychotherapist from the hospital. I remember talking with her and not being sure how this would help us. It wouldn't change anything. And the one thing which is my "therapy" - exercise - I wasn't able to do. I couldn't even exercise the grief out of my system because it hadn't been eight weeks and the mother's check-up, which was about as useful as chatting with an unqualified acquaintance, hadn't taken place yet. My family paid for me to talk to a very expensive Harley Street shrink because they thought I was depressed. Thankfully, their conclusion was: "she's not clinically depressed, she's faced with an incredibly difficult situation during incredibly difficult times." The fact I was even getting up and getting on seemed like a "win," looking back on it now.

I saw babies come and go in NICU, graduate to SCBU, then home, while we were still stuck in this funk of NICU hell. Spending my maternity leave waiting for my slot to see my daughter, Marie Kondo-ing my sock, knicker and clothes drawers to pass the time, was not exactly the plan. I wanted her home, I wanted to breastfeed, I wanted to hold her and not be scared she'd break. And I'd have given anything for her to be "healthy." Yes, she was alive but needed medical care to keep her that way. All these feelings and fears ruminated, taking up time and energy, leaving me feeling exhausted. We were told, after almost eight weeks, that she would be moving to GOSH. For how long? A few days?

It turned out to be the whole month of May, the glorious month she was actually due.

Eight weeks after giving birth, I dusted off my bike, filled up my pannier and cycled the six miles to GOSH to be with her. Cycling would give me the freedom to come and go without relying on anyone else, so we could all be safe. All I can say is thank goodness for Netflix because this would be my company for that very long month of May. I'd never 'binge-watched' anything before now and saw it as a waste of my life. Netflix, however, was a saviour of mine. You see, only one parent was allowed to be with the child at a time. And yes, you'd think we could swap but that one parent then had to stay for two weeks at a time. Since I was on maternity leave, pumping milk for her and ready to be her mother, it made sense that it was me. No matter how hard, lonely and trying it was, I had to be there, I had to stay in that hospital room with a hospital shower, toilet and not much else apart from my little S.

My dad told me to write or edit some of his work but I wasn't in the right frame of mind. I felt pretty numb and traumatised by everything going on. What with specialists "popping in" to tell me more about my child's diagnosis, none of it good, I'd end up with a sour taste in my mouth, angry that I had to bear the weight of all this bad news on my own. How dare they come in unannounced, trying to humanise what they were about to say. I needed my husband, I needed someone to share all this information with. Despite knowing they'd come at some point, I felt like my space had been invaded when they'd simply turn up.

Then there were those closest to me who were still trying to understand what was happening with their granddaughter. I'd call them to talk and end up slamming the phone down because they'd tell you the doctors were exaggerating or medical science these days can cure a number of things. It felt like they didn't get it or didn't want to. I was angry at them but forgot that they, too, were having to find their way around this extraordinary situation. When does denial turn into acceptance, I wondered, and still do today when people come out with, "she'll get there in her own time." Where, exactly? Where is my little disabled daughter trying to get to?

The people I met at NCT for all of the two sessions we attended had all had their babies by now and were sharing newborn anecdotes on the WhatsApp group. Little S was nil-by-mouth, tube-fed and still is today. She was not, and never will be, like what you imagined your child to be. I felt like an observer from afar, desperate to be part of a group which I very much wasn't. While they were worried about breastfeeding and sleeping, I was worried about whether my daughter would be able to breathe without oxygen prongs stuck up her nose. Not to downplay their worries, I would have been the same in a parallel universe where I had taken home a healthy first child, but at the time it felt like my worries were on a completely different scale. And no, I didn't have anyone around me to help at all, because no one had an answer. No one around me could understand what we were going through because it all felt so unreal. An unreal situation in unreal times. Pinch myself, I'd wake up and it would all be sunshine and rainbows. I would be outside reading in the garden with the baby beside me in the cot, sleeping. Instead, I was in what amounted to be a souped-up version of a prison cell in the West End.

Don't get me wrong, I tried to make the most of an impossible situation, including taking my little S outside for the first time on the roof garden of GOSH. It was a beautiful sunny day and she was wearing a little sun hat. Eyes shut because of an eye condition but my baby girl could bathe her little face in the sunshine for the first time. I sang songs to her, read her stories and brought a mobile to hang from her cot. We would zoom around the ward together using her buggy, attached to oxygen, like a little doll in a girl's pram. She had her first bath in GOSH, a momentous occasion for a new parent. We'd do anything to take away from the sterile environment where we were staying together. Kind nurses would pop in throughout the day and night.

I managed to get some fresh air every few days as I decided to go home and see my husband for the night. My husband cleverly hacked Ocado to get ourselves on the list for online shopping which meant I'd have a stack of meals to take back with me to GOSH. I spoke with friends and family every day and felt grateful for their support. My husband would spend his Sunday walking down to see me. He couldn't visit S. We'd wander around the outskirts of Coram fields, like a ghost town, then walk back afterwards. We both missed each other terribly and it was equally hard for us. Me in hospital and him, in isolation, at home without his wife or baby who he was just getting to know.

Did we get home eventually? Well, yes, after a month of tests, we were able to come home with our little one on oxygen. The day we left hospital was a mixture of happiness and madness as we walked from GOSH, through North London pushing a tiny baby in a pram, bike and panniers plus rucksacks. We don't have a car and this seemed like the only solution. Finally, we could start our lives with little S and all be together. Due to her feed times, we had to route march it home, where we were greeted at the bottom of the flats by a little welcome (albeit socially distanced) party. It felt so good to be home at last. Little did we know we'd be back in hospital and PICU two weeks later, but in that moment I felt sheer joy.

I continue to feel joy when my little S is well and happy. She's following her own path. And we did have our time together, our daily walks, my terrible singing, all isolated, just me, S and her Dad. I finally returned to work after nine months, albeit from home, and the hospital stays started again as she was hit hook, line and sinker by every bug nursery could throw at her. I was pregnant with my second child by then, which made every stay more difficult. COVID and its consequential hangover meant S didn't, and doesn't, receive the right amount of care. Imagine trying to do a physio appointment via video. I didn't have a clue what they were asking me to do. Or the social worker asking if I thought talking to a counsellor may help. To which I replied, poker-faced, no, actually practical help would be good because I'm about to have my second child and am spending most of my time on a hospital ward.

There's no fairytale ending to this story. We've almost lost her a couple of times. We spend way too much time in hospital, writing emails and arguing for what she's entitled to but I think any parent of a disabled child would say the same. Would we change our experience? Probably. What this experience has taught me is some things are out of our control, to be happy and just go with it.

And, on the whole, we are happy and have a beautiful little family. What S lacks in terms of walking and talking, she makes up with her beautiful smile. Of course, every parent will say their child is beautiful and sweet but S is very endearing, and you want to cuddle and look after her. With two little girls, we have so much going on that I will not bore you with the tedious and time-consuming details. I'm not going to sugar-coat it, either. At times, it's not easy, and quite frankly it can be impossible to keep all the plates spinning, but there are moments when we're together and everyone's well, which are simply magic.

Rebecca Bryant, 40, from London lives with her husband and two daughters, Scheherazade, 3, and Isadora, 1. When she's not looking after two little people, she enjoys working in marketing, running when she gets the chance and ballet class on a Sunday morning. As a relative newbie to SEND parenting (Rebecca's first daughter was born with complex needs), she is passionate about disability rights and inclusion. You can follow all her latest escapades @becsinter

JADE CANNON

The Forgotten Mothers

Deep breaths through a mask
In a lonely waiting room,
behind a door
Awaits a grainy picture of a womb

When I close my eyes
I can smell the freshly bleached floors,
Erasing tales of sadness
But forever opening sores

Waiting for a heartbeat with baited breath,
No hand to hold,
Hands shaking,
Waiting to be told

The euphoric dose of joy,
Followed by an ounce of sadness,
Missing my mum,
Sick of this pandemic madness

Labour in masks,
Isolated decisions,
Clutching onto my birth plan
Once written with precision

Unplanned,
our first night alone,
A dark and crisply silent ward,
Paralysed by the unknown

But we were lucky,
You were born healthy and pink,
We took you home,
Our missing link

But what about the others?
The ones that laboured alone,
Or had to tell their husbands about a loss
Through that square on a phone

How do they recover?
How do they feel?
The Forgotten Mothers...
How do they ever heal?

Jade Cannon lives in Greater London with her wonderful family and has worked in events for the last 15 years. Jade loves creative writing and during the pandemic found an immense passion for writing about motherhood. She describes herself as a humanitarian, and has enjoyed creating committees to raise money for various charities as well as women's networks; to try and move the dial when it comes to leadership in the workplace. Her interests include politics, fashion and getting lost in a good book. Her happy place is when she's by the sea with family!

LUCY WEBB

Trigger Warning: Self-harm

It could have been worse.

Eleven weeks pregnant. Watching the death toll rise on the TV each evening becomes our new normal. Tomorrow, we will drive an hour out of town and pay £80 for a private dating scan. I am convinced my womb is empty and that the numerous pregnancy tests I have peed on are all lying to me. My mind tells me that I do not deserve this child and that karma will get me for some unknown evil I have undoubtably committed in a past life. I am terrified of attending my first scan alone in the hospital. But these are the rules and they cannot be broken.

"Everyone gets anxious during pregnancy," I am told dismissively.

I feel nauseous but not from the hormones. Panic has taken root, deep in my stomach, just behind where the baby is supposedly growing their little fingers and toes. How could there be anything in my belly when I feel so hollow? Like everyone in the country, I am scared and uncertain.

We hand over our debit card at the private clinic and we are allowed to see our daughter on the screen for the first time.

We are together.

My partner is smiling behind his mask. I squeeze his fingers for reassurance.

The small seed of panic I felt earlier has settled. Unfortunately, not settled in contentment or relief, but settled as it was planning on staying for a while.

But it could have been worse.

I am now thirteen weeks pregnant, and my stomach is starting to swell. I have started to mark my skin with scratches. Once with a blade.

I am so lonely.

Today is my first appointment with the mental health midwife. I burn with shame as I tell her that I am regretting my pregnancy. I do not want to bring a baby into a world with this much trauma and death. I cannot keep my baby safe. I have no control and I am petrified.

I am due my next health check in three weeks and must attend that alone. I tell the midwife my fears and my need for support. But these are the rules, and they cannot be broken.

But it could have been worse.

Nineteen weeks pregnant and I have spent six hours in A&E.
Alone.

Earlier I examined a lump of bloodied mucus clinging to the side of the toilet bowl. It looked like a strawberry someone had chewed up and spat back out. I am convinced it is part of my baby.

No one has acknowledged me since the receptionist instructed me to take a seat in one of the plastic cubicles in the waiting area. She told me firmly that my partner had to leave. A man struggles with his vomiting toddler. He has no one to help him. Other patients try to assist by handing him paper towels and cardboard sick bowls but are told by staff they need to keep their distance.

My phone has no signal inside the walls of the hospital. There is no way of getting in touch with my partner who is waiting worriedly in the car outside. I think about the plans we have the following evening. We are going to my favourite restaurant for my birthday and I will be surrounded by up to five members of my family. We will eat noodles and they will drink beer (orange juice for me) whilst sharing stories, jokes and hopes that this pandemic will soon be over.

Back in the waiting room, I am frightened and crying. In this moment, I would trade the meal with my family. I would give up the stupid rule of six. I would sacrifice all the pubs, bowling alleys and hairdressers that are allowed to open, just to be allowed someone next to me, holding my hand whilst I wait to find out if my baby is alive.

Shortly before 2am, a doctor beckons me into an empty room. He and his chaperone stare out over their masks with tired, dead eyes as they prepare their examination. He pushes one of his latex-covered fingers into me and tells me to come back tomorrow morning for a scan, where I would see my baby alive and in one piece.

Two days later, the UK enters its second lockdown.
But it could have been worse.

I am waddling along the sea front, taking my one permitted walk a day. Benches line the promenade but it is illegal to sit down and rest. My back aches and I soon stop leaving the house. The news repeatedly informs us that we must keep two meters distance; people are dangerous and they could breathe out deadly air infecting me and my unborn child. I am no longer allowed to work in the office as the risk is too high. I go days inside the same four walls. I do not want to speak to anyone.
But it could have been worse.

I am thirty-six weeks pregnant and my intrusive thoughts are paralysing. I am convinced that people want to hurt me and my baby. I leave the house sporadically, but everyone is a threat. It is hard to rationalise that thought when it is all I have seen, heard and read about for the last year.

I phone my midwife and ask her to go over what would happen if there was a terrorist attack in the hospital whilst I am giving birth.
But it could have been worse.

My support worker tells me to leave the house and go to see my parents. I am about to become a mother, but I need my own. This is not permitted under current lockdown rules. The government say we are allowed a support bubble if we have a child under one. My child is still in my womb, so I am not eligible.

I take her advice anyway and go to my mum and dads for a cup of tea. I sit with my legs shaking, waiting for the knock on the door from the police to arrest me. I almost vomit from the anxiety.

But it could have been worse.

It is my due date and I am in labour.

A midwife sticks a swab up my nose in between my contractions. I come into the hospital already nine centimetres dilated and I am pushing for just two hours before my daughter arrives, purple, screaming and covered in meconium.

I must stay 24 hours in the hospital due to the potential complications from my anxiety medication. My partner is allowed to stay with me the whole time. When I later retell this story, I am told I am lucky to have had a mental health birth plan that allowed such considerations. I am full of so much love as I hold my newborn baby girl with my scarred arms. I am so grateful that I am not alone, but I do not feel lucky.

I think about the women in the rooms next to me, their birth partners shoved out the door just a couple of hours after squeezing their babies out or having their stomachs cut open. I feel guilt and rage on behalf of them.

Luck stems from good fortune. I think about how traumatic the last few months have been. How my mind has struggled with the consequences of being pregnant during a global pandemic. How isolation and lone appointments have nearly broken me. To be allowed support during the most vulnerable time of my life should not have been reduced to 'luck.' This should have been a basic human right.

But it could have been worse.

Two weeks after the birth.

There are no baby groups, but I can go to the pub if I want. I want to hurt anyone who comes near my newborn. An inquisitive child peers into the pram and I want to shove them. I have heard of mothers' instinct, but I wonder if this is normal.

I use so much bleach to kill any germs that enter my home that my hands stink of the chemicals. Every time my baby cries, I am convinced I am burning her with my acid fingers. I talk through these thoughts in my therapy sessions and cry with relief when I am told they are to increase my medication. I want the thoughts to stop.

But it could have been worse.

Everyone went through the same thing, I am told. It is time to get over it.

The BBC report that the mental health crisis from COVID was minimal.

My pregnancy was healthy. Hundreds of thousands of people died. I could have given birth right at the beginning of the pandemic. I could have had no support at all. I could have had twins.

It could have been worse.

Two years later, I am still grieving for my stolen pregnancy experience.

I attend friends' baby showers and feel tears clawing at my throat as we play silly games and eat too much cake. I watch strangers coo over baby bumps and burn with rage.

I wonder what type of mother I would have been if the virus had not taken over the world. I wonder how different my child would be if, for the first six months of her life, she saw the full face of her family members, not eyes peeking over blue medical masks.

I am scared all of the time. I am still in therapy. I panic with any kind of change.

I try to talk about my fears. My worries. The impact the pandemic had on me and my mental health during my pregnancy.

I grit my teeth and try not to scream when people reply;

But it could have been worse.

Lucy Webb, 30, from Grimsby lives with her partner, Daryl, and their two-year old daughter, Lyra. Towards the end of her maternity leave, when COVID restrictions were finally starting to lift, Lucy decided to join a local writer's group. She writes a lot about her experiences of motherhood and mental health issues, but this is the first time she has been brave enough to share.

MARTINA BYRNES

It's usually now, when the hour is late and the sky is dark, that I get a melancholy feeling in my heart.
I think back to when everything was new, and it was just us two.
An evening, in August, at sunset. The dizziness in my head. The very next day - two positive lines on a test.
Telling my family and friends over video call was never what I'd imagined, at all.
Sharing this news over the phone. No one allowed to see us or watch me grow. No baby shower in person, only via Zoom. Every appointment on my own, alone in a waiting room.
No maternity clothes or pre-natal lunches. No one feeling my tummy for your first kicks or punches.
No buying baby clothes, prams or cots. No buying toys or trips to the shops.
YOU MUST STAY AT HOME. Waiting on a vaccine whilst the Tories partied on.
Cheese and wine, if you please.

Time to leave the city and move to the coast, leaving without a proper goodbye is what hurt the most.
I didn't know what to expect, perhaps an arm around my shoulder. Instead, I got driveways and garden furniture.
But you were on your way. "Just a little longer," I would say. So, I kept plodding on, one walk a day.
The labour was long, tiring and tough but you will never be that tiny again, so I soaked every moment up.
The nurses were under pressure, some were unkind. The doctor wasn't much better but at least now, you were by my side.

On day five, the midwife arrived. Oh, how I cried. I couldn't shake the feelings from my mind.
The weight I felt psychologically, not just physically and emotionally. The worry about my new responsibilities.
The intrusive thoughts and the bad dreams - but no one warns you about these things.
The equal weight of fear and adoration. This little person who ran off with my heart and I just let them take it...
Despite these difficult beginnings, those lonely tears and abandonment feelings
Being lost and completely alone, my mental health feeling so low, I would look in the mirror and search for the person I used to know.
"Gurl, time to pull yourself out of this rabbit hole."

I rose like a phoenix and took on my role as your mummy, but clawing my way to 'me' was a long time coming.

So, when someone says, 'You had a baby in COVID? That must have been tough.' It's only when you look back you realise how hard it really was.

Grateful for my resilience, grateful for my capability, because, after all, it was no longer all about me.

Martina Byrnes, 35, born in Ireland and raised in London, now lives on the Essex Coast with her fiancé, Scott and their daughter, Fiadh. Martina is a part-time administrator. When she is not writing poetry, she can be found at her local yoga studio or enjoying dinner and a glass of wine with friends.

EMILY HAWKES

When my eldest was a baby, I decided to keep a notebook of letters written to her on her birthday or notable occasions, to give to her when she is older. So, naturally, when my son was born in March 2020, I wanted to do the same thing. However, his first year was very different to how I had expected. I found myself at home with a newborn and a three-year-old, while my husband worked nights as a key worker. These are the first two letters to my son in his book.

June 2020

Hi Alex,

My darling, when I set out to write these keepsake notes I intended to write on your birthday. But why should I limit myself? You are three months old and the world turned upside down when you were born! We'd heard about COVID-19 from the start of the year, I guess, but on 11th March it was declared a global pandemic. I was sheltered from the news, being in hospital, but it became apparent that it was going to change a lot of things!

You were born on a Tuesday morning and we were in hospital until the Friday. By the following Monday, your due date, a national lockdown was declared and we self-isolated according to instructions from Boris Johnson, our Prime Minister.

I'd had a blood test booked at the doctors surgery that same day, as I'd lost so much blood when you were born. Upon my arrival, I was angrily asked if it was essential that I was there, as they were only seeing essential patients. Scared, I replied that I didn't know if it was essential and cried. They told me to sit down as they checked my notes and conceded that it was important, but that appointment broke me. I didn't have any further midwife appointments and saw the health visitor only once. She stood outside, six feet away from the house, while I collected the scales from the doorstep so you could be weighed. I didn't have the six-week postpartum health check. They phoned me at nine weeks. The doctor asked how my mental health was.

"Not good, we've been in lockdown since my baby was born."

The doctor was sympathetic and said it was understandable. Nothing further happened.

I asked the doctor if you could be weighed at your next immunisation appointment, as you'd not been weighed since you had your tongue tie cut and I was afraid you weren't thriving. I turned up to the appointment and the scales weren't there, the message hadn't been passed from the GP to the nurse. The nurse couldn't get them as she was in her PPE. I cried. She called for another staff member to bring them to the door of the room where she could collect them. I felt like I was being unhelpful and demanding.

Anyway, I digress. We were only to leave our homes for essential food shopping as infrequently as possible, for exercise once a day and for essential medical reasons. And that's how you've lived most of your life so far. Just the four of us, in our home with one walk a day.

Restrictions are now slowly being lifted. We can see people, as long as it is outside at a distance of two metres apart. Face coverings are becoming more commonplace and are essential for things like public transport. Shops are starting to open.

I feel all the emotions. I'm sad that friends and family are yet to meet you, and the few who were lucky enough to meet you before the lockdown have missed so much and they won't be holding you any time soon.

I'm isolated – Daddy goes to work and has done since you were five weeks old – he's a key worker. I've spent all my time with you and Elizabeth. I've laughed, I've cried, it's been hard, it's been wonderful. But, I miss people, I miss the plans I had to see people, do baby classes and just go out for a coffee. I miss quiet. Though it's quiet now as I listen to you breathing, asleep in the cot next to me at 11pm. Daddy is at work and Elizabeth is asleep in her room.

I'm scared that one or all of us will get sick – I'm doing all that I can to try to stop that from happening. Daddy thinks I'm overreacting but he doesn't know what it's like to be at home all the time with no other adults to talk to.

I feel so happy to have had this time with you both and to watch you bond with your sister – she loves to play peek-a-boo with you and you smile at her. It makes my heart happy.

The last two points might contradict each other a bit – but that's OK, you can feel more than one feeling at a time. Anyway, I seem to have gotten sidetracked.

All this to say, it's not been the start to life that I'd hoped for or expected for you. I'm sure it won't affect you in the long run, at least I hope it won't. Let's hope things improve once all the restrictions are lifted.

All my love
Mummy
xxx

March 2021

My darling boy, happy first birthday!

Little did I know when I last wrote to you in June that we would still be in lockdown when you turned one! There was a second wave of infections after Christmas and we've been in lockdown since early January. I hope by the time you are reading this that COVID-19 is very much a thing of the past.

As a result of this latest lockdown, we aren't supposed to meet up with anyone, except one-to-one outside, for exercise. Under-fives don't count. Schools went back on Monday as a first step to easing the restrictions. Not that either you or your sister are at school, but it's a step closer to normality.

We managed to make the most of your birthday. Not being allowed to do a 'cake smash' photoshoot (we weren't allowed a newborn photoshoot, either) we arranged our own at home. Perhaps these are 'first-world problems,' but I would have loved to have been able to do the things I'd planned. You loved crawling up and down the space I made at the back of the living room, it was like a race track for you. You started tentatively with the cake, a kind of *am I allowed to do this?* But quickly you were straight into the icing! You looked like you'd eaten a smurf (do look it up if you don't understand the reference.)

We were pleased to have Grandpa over in the afternoon. We last saw him on Christmas Day when the rules said you could have up to six people in your house for the day. As a paramedic, Grandpa has had his vaccinations and takes two tests a week, so it was nice to have him around. You weren't so sure, though!

On that note, you've recently started nursery and I can't say it's going well. I'm back to work a couple of days a week next week (working from home) and so far I've had to go and collect you by lunchtime most days. Of course, it's a very alien concept for you, you've spent your entire first year with me or Daddy, usually with Elizabeth at home. You've not had a babysitter (Grandad had you for an hour in October while I had a hospital appointment, you were fine and spent most of it asleep.) You've not been to baby classes or soft play. So, being looked after by strangers, amongst the noise of several babies and lots of new toys, is new and scary. I'm sure you'll get there in time and everyone will get to know the happy, smiley baby we know at home.

All my love,
Mummy
xxx

Emily Hawkes, 37, from Devon lives with her husband, six-and-a-half-year-old daughter, Elizabeth, and three-year-old son, Alex. She works as a Project Manager and Data Analyst. When not working or mumming, you will find her reading, enjoying an exercise class or sewing; she is determined that one day she will be brave enough to cut into her kids' baby clothes to turn them into a memory quilt.

LEIGH McCOMISH

20th April 2020

We were so excited at the thought of starting a family. I suffer with endometriosis so knew it could be difficult. However, this was a monumental day. I had done a test in the morning and saw the faintest line. OH MY GOODNESS! I was ecstatic and could not believe it. I had to go and get another test. Frantically, I googled the best pregnancy test to detect early pregnancy.

It was my gran's birthday. On the way to her house, I nipped to Boots for the test. She was on the phone when I arrived, so I darted up the stairs and took the test. I couldn't believe my eyes - another certain positive. I danced around in the toilet, bundled the test into my handbag and kept the secret to myself. I couldn't tell anyone until I got home to my partner.

When I got home, I shot up the stairs. My partner was just home from work. I was so excited to tell him our amazing news! I got the test out my bag and handed it over. His smile beaming, "Are you really!? Oh my god this is the best news ever!" We hugged, stared at the test and chatted about our future as a family of three. How exciting our next chapter was going to be.

At my first scan, I sat in the waiting room on my own. I desperately wanted to have my partner by my side to experience the wonderful joy of seeing our little baby for the first time, however, he had to wait outside the hospital main doors. It was a dingy, wet day. My name was called. Lying on the bed, the sonographer advised me that the nuchal at the back of baby's neck was slightly thicker than normal.

"Oh, what does that mean? This is my first baby."

"Well, this could mean your baby has something, but it's fine. That's you for today." I got off the bed, completely gobsmacked, confused and in a state of panic that something was wrong. I had no one to turn to.

I made my way back to the front doors of the hospital, my partner standing there, excited to see me and hear everything. I burst into tears. With no context, he panicked and was worried. We got to the car and I explained everything that was said and what happened. I called my midwife as we were both unhappy at the treatment received, the wording used and how this was delivered with no compassion or support. I felt so vulnerable, lost and devastated at how this woman had been so cold and matter of fact, particularly when I was alone. My phone rang. It was the head sonographer. She apologised profusely, advised that she would be having a meeting with said employee on how she handled the situation and that staff training would be provided. I was offered another scan the following week, where it turned out everything was fine and the nuchal was perfect sizing.

We couldn't attend antenatal classes. Everything, everywhere was closed. COVID, what was this? How was it going to affect pregnant women? No one knew and no one could give any answers. The country was in complete lockdown. Whilst I attended antenatal appointments on my own, hearing my baby's heartbeat for the first time and recording it for my partner to hear to experience it too, Boris was having a party! We all missed out on so much as we stuck by the rules. I did enjoy my walk every day until I was around 20 weeks pregnant and I started experiencing symptoms of constant urine infections. My midwife assured me this was common in pregnancy, but I was advised to go up to the assessment ward, provide a sample and have observations and bloods taken.

"Hm, Leigh, you are growing a very unusual bug. We are going to speak with microbiology to understand the treatment required. Are you willing to stay for this evening?"

Instantly, internally I was panicking, primarily because of the lockdown. *How can my partner come to visit me? I'm going to be on my own, in a room with no one to speak to, already feeling vulnerable with an 'unusual bug.'* I had to be strong.

Blood culture after blood culture was taken from me and I was hooked up to IV antibiotics. Thankfully, by day three, I was able to have a visitor pass for two people to visit me. I was in a side room, hidden away from the world with only the beeping monitors and my trusty Kindle for entertainment. My partner eventually popped his head through the door. I was so happy to see him. After a cuddle, we looked over my observation chart, not fully understanding the scribbles, but being a serial Googler, my research started.

"Could this be sepsis you are treating?" my partner asked the doctor as she was inserting a new cannula into my wrist.

"No no, Leigh has a very complex and unusual bug growing so we are treating this with what you could refer to as clinical bleach to eradicate the bug."

I stayed in for a week, which was difficult during lockdown as only my partner and my mum could come and visit.

27th November 2020

Finally, after months of being in and out of hospital, I was going home. I was ecstatic to be going back to my own surroundings to a home cooked meal and a nice cup of tea! I was 36 weeks pregnant and leaving my final scan, when I fell down a flight of stairs in the hospital. The pain in my right foot was agony and I was rushed straight to A&E, alone.

Double break in my ankle. I was devastated. I was in a moonboot, weeks away from having my bundle of joy in my arms. How was I going to navigate this?

December 18th 2020

We were in lockdown number three in Scotland, and our beautiful baby girl was born. My partner was able to be by my side as my birthing partner – what a relief! One thing I didn't have to go through by myself. We walked along to the theatre. The rush of emotions was so intense and the most surreal feeling. Meeting our baby girl for the very first time was everything. Knowing everything was perfect was the reassurance we needed after all the issues throughout pregnancy.

COVID stripped away a lot of the usual positive, exciting experiences that are supposed to come with pregnancy such as antenatal classes, meet ups with other mothers-to-be and baby classes. Although I was in this amazing baby bubble with my new little family, it was also extremely isolating and some days were tough. I was certainly caught up in my own thoughts, overthinking, worrying and criticising everything, which really affected me. Speaking with NHS professionals over Teams calls rather than face to face was difficult, the calls were rushed and I felt that the support wasn't there. My first six months of motherhood were extremely challenging. Baby blues, crying but not knowing what for, and being unable to be fully active due to my injury took its toll on how I felt. I felt isolated and inadequate due to not being able to support my family much. I relied heavily on my partner to not only look after my baby girl, but me too, as I couldn't do much on my own. It was debilitating. With the lack of visitors being able to come and see us, I felt it was just us against the world. Even though I had everything I had always dreamed of, I felt useless.

Despite all of this, the pandemic didn't stop our experience from being the most magical, beautiful, amazing and life-changing one, with so many positives to come out of a negative global pandemic.

I have an amazing support network around me, including a great group of mums who are my best friends. Round the clock, 24/7, they were there, albeit virtually. At the end of the phone, by text, through the night when feeding, they were there. We all pulled each other through the tough, early stages of motherhood, but also the pandemic as a new parent.

JENNIFER McLAMB

We have started calling our baby boy by his name. It's beginning to feel real that he will be on the other side of my big pregnant belly in a few months' time.

Today, Boris Johnson announced that pregnant women are in the high-risk category for contracting coronavirus, along with people over 70 years of age and those with respiratory conditions. Over the weekend, there were cases of pregnant women in York and London catching COVID and then passing the virus onto their newborn babies. I have been googling the few small studies there have been. There was a sample in China where a number of pregnant women who contracted COVID had premature babies.

Our visit to Nanny was cancelled earlier this month because the car broke down and now, because of COVID, we definitely won't be able to see her any time soon. I called her early this morning. It was difficult not mentioning COVID and I didn't have much news for her since I'm not leaving the house. I did manage to talk enough about her future great grandson to keep it light and make her happy.

I was struggling as I approached six months of pregnancy, with work travel as well as climbing up and down the stairs to my team's office. I don't have to deal with that now I am working from home. The instructions are to keep a distance from people and isolate ourselves as much as possible. This includes family. Jake's mum won't see us at all because she is more likely to catch COVID at school. Two other teachers have already had it.

The lockdown restrictions have got tighter. We are only allowed out of the house for essential trips like grocery shopping and once a day for exercise. I wonder what the rest of my pregnancy will be like, staying at home for the next few months. Then I'll be on maternity leave, so it's likely I won't see my colleagues or be in the office for well over a year.

I have been worried about Nanny the most, and Dad because of his chest infections. I miss my parents and sister. I miss the closeness and a hug from someone that isn't my husband. I don't know what the situation will be like when I actually give birth or whether our baby boy will be able to meet our family.

I find out that two members of staff in work have died from COVID. I go into a panic for most of the day. I call Mum, Dad and Kate, telling them to take the restrictions more seriously and limit their visits to shops. I send each of them a long email with places that they can get online deliveries from. Most of the major supermarkets' delivery slots are booked up for weeks in advance now.

Nanny is quite ill. COVID has caused massive shortages in care staff meaning that her routine has gone completely. There have been a few days where she didn't have her dementia medication at all and she got a bad UTI, which made the confusion worse. She's been admitted into hospital. I had sent her a birthday card and an Easter card, neither of which she will get now. In each, I wrote about my growing belly and feeling the baby's kicks. The cards were signed from me and Bump. I've been finding excuses to send her post regularly, to keep us and the baby in her memory somehow.

At our first midwife appointment since lockdown was announced, Jake isn't allowed to come in with me, so he drives me there and sits in the car outside. I go in, dressed head to toe in protective clothing - mask, gloves and apron. When she listens to the baby's heartbeat I record it on my phone and send it to Jake. I finally manage to film the baby doing some good kicks. I have wanted to for ages so I could share it with our families. I get sad thinking that my mum can't put her hand on my belly and feel her strong little grandson in there. Mum says the video made her so happy that she re-watches it whenever she needs cheering up.

My dad has his 61st birthday. We set out cake and presents on the driveway for a socially-distanced celebration. I asked Mum to take a picture of Jake and I with the bump. It was nice to have a chance to get a nice bump photo, even if Mum did put on sterile gloves so she felt comfortable using our camera without passing germs between us.

I'm only doing three days a week for the last few weeks of work. I am finding it hard. Work was a great distraction from not being able to see family and friends. I try to persuade Mum, Dad and my sister to give up on the rules and give me a hug, but no one is willing to take the risk, especially while I am pregnant.

My final day of work is strange. I don't walk out of an office or say goodbye to anyone, instead, after my final meeting of the day I log off and put the laptop away. I go for a walk in the sunshine, eating an ice cream, and then come back to the house as if I'm getting in from work. Jake has put up a poster saying *Happy Baby Leave*.

Just before 38 weeks, it is my 30th birthday. We have a socially-distanced picnic in the park, with friends arriving at staggered time slots (a maximum of six people can meet together outside.) Later, we go to Mum and Dad's for a birthday tea. Mum has prepared us each a separate bag of sterilized packaged foods, like couscous salad, dips and falafel, and each of us sit at opposite corners of the room. It's not the 30th birthday that I had planned, but it makes me so happy.

I wake up after having a dream about hugging my sister. That was the entire dream, that Kate and I had a hug.

At 42 weeks pregnant, I burst into tears at the table. I say I just want a hug from my mum and dad. Jake amazes me by saying, "Okay, we can call to see if they're alright with it, but let's go."

Just hours after those hugs, I go into labour.

When we say goodbye at the lift up to the ward, Jake says something loving and I respond brightly,

"Don't worry, I'll be with our baby." I feel guilty about this. He has to leave the hospital, after the birth of his son, to go home alone.

The neonatal doctor comes to tell me they are taking the baby for a CT scan and then to intensive care. He is one day old. I am on my own and I can't take it in. I call Jake and repeat the words that I've been told but it still feels like a dream that I don't understand. I am squeezing my breasts for colostrum, syringing it into tiny 5ml tubes to bring to my boy downstairs in NICU. It's all I can do right now so it has become my focus.

At five days old, my baby is returned to me. I am delirious as he feeds all night from about 10pm to 5am. He cries and I cry. I have never heard of cluster feeding before.

Finally, we are discharged. Jake is coming to pick us up later today. I am bringing our boy home.

Jennifer McLamb worked in the voluntary sector before taking care of her son and daughter. She began writing after the birth of her first child in 2020. She primarily writes poetry about family and new motherhood. Her work has been published by Mum Poem Press, Positive Wellbeing Zine for Mums and the 6ress, and she has read her poetry at the Cheltenham Literature Festival. @jennifermclamb_writes

HAYLEY ENGLAND

Where do I start? I found out I was pregnant with my first baby in December 2019. Excited, in a new-ish relationship with someone I had known for a while, apprehensive and nervous. Although I was feeling lots of different emotions, I had no idea what was about to unfold.

Before the whole world shut down, I was able to see friends and family and tell them face to face, which was nice. Some were shocked, but mostly they were happy for us. I was lucky enough to have my partner with me for the first scan. What an amazing experience that was - seeing my baby on the screen for the first time and also finding out I was further along than I thought - bonus! It was very emotional, after three months of extreme tiredness, intense sickness and just generally feeling rubbish - this scan made that all worth it.

I had told work quite early on as I ended up taking some time off due to sickness, and it was around this time that people started talking about this 'COVID' situation. I had never really watched the news so didn't entertain it much, brushing it off with, 'They scared us about bird flu before, so it's probably something like that!' Jeez, how wrong was I? The following day, I was told by my work not to come in and to work from home. What the hell was going on?

It all happened really fast and was terrifying. I turned into an avid news watcher, googling it, scrolling through social media and trying to see what other people thought about it all. The number of people dying from COVID was going up by the day. Even though my pregnancy symptoms had eased, I felt anxious. Once we were told that we couldn't leave our homes and that the country was going into lockdown, I was contacted by my midwife who explained that I would need to attend my appointments and scans alone, wear a mask and use hand sanitiser.

Stepping out and attending my next appointment on my own was daunting. I parked up at the hospital and walked towards the entrance where there were lots of security guards standing around. You were pretty much interrogated as to why you were there. I had to provide proof of my appointments, slather my hands with sanitiser, have my temperature checked and then wait until I was given the green light to go ahead to my appointment. Once I reached the ultrasound department, I had to queue two metres away from the next person and then sit in a waiting room with about six chairs in it, all separate from each other. I think we were scared to look at each other. Through no fault of their own, the staff were preoccupied with what they were trying to deal with, so were not as warm and friendly as before. There were a couple of times I had to go in to get checked out because I had reduced foetal movement and each time I went through the same process, alone.

I don't look back on this time with fond memories, which is sad as it should be a happy time. My relationship was also rocky at this time, so along with the unknown of the pandemic, I spent a lot of my pregnancy crying. I hardly saw my friends, who had been really excited about me having a baby. I couldn't have a baby shower. I couldn't go out and purchase baby items because the shops were shut. It wasn't how I thought it would be.

When it came to giving birth I was a mess. I had been on a hypnobirthing course (via Teams) which was amazing, however it still didn't prepare me for how my birth actually went. I was almost a week overdue, it was a Sunday, my partner was out and I just didn't feel right. I called the hospital and they said to come in. A friend drove me there and I went in alone. I was hooked up to a monitor in triage and left for about an hour, wearing a mask. After a sweep and no movement, I was taken down to a ward and an induction was started. I sat on the bed, not knowing what was going to happen. I didn't see a nurse again for about two hours, in which time I had started to have contractions. I was scared, in pain and alone. I tried to remain calm and time them but I couldn't do it as it was so painful. I managed to hobble off the bed and found a midwife and I explained that I was feeling a great deal of pain and needed something. She brushed me off and said she would come back in a minute. I sat there for what felt like hours, until she returned and said, 'I don't think you would be contracting now, it's too soon, I can get you paracetamol.' *I really don't think paracetamol is going to cut this,* I thought. She told me another midwife would come and check on me in half an hour. I got it - they were short-staffed - but I had never felt so invalidated.

When the next midwife came along I was in tears. Concerned, she had a look at the monitor and realised that it wasn't giving correct readings. After some re-jigging she could now see how intense my contractions actually were and offered me gas and air. In my birth plan, I hadn't wanted to use it but at this point, I would have taken anything. I was then left on my own again until the change of shift, when my new midwife examined me and moved me to a birthing suite.

The doctor then did his rounds and noticed that my baby's heart rate had slowed down. He asked to examine me and found that my waters had gone already. I didn't have that big 'gush' that's spoken about so I hadn't realised. He then said the dreaded words to me, that I would need to have an emergency C-section and that I would be first on the list. In between contractions, I had to call my partner and tell him to get here as soon as possible! It was all a mad rush and I was in so much pain. Being left like that, alone in a big clinical room, is so overwhelming. My partner managed to make it just in time, literally as they were taking me down to theatre. I managed a quick 'hello' and had to go. Whilst in theatre, I remember shaking with fear as I was placed on the bed for my epidural, trying to keep still during contractions. Once I was laid down and covered up, my partner was able to come in. I saw him and cried, relieved that I finally had someone there with me.

My boy didn't have the easiest start, when they got him out the cord was wrapped around his neck twice, it had a knot in it and he had swallowed meconium. He didn't cry for what felt like ages. My heart sank. He then let out a gasp and my partner and I just looked at each other. I cried. He was then brought over to me, I looked at him and then he was taken to NICU. I didn't get to see him again until 12 hours later. My partner had to leave as soon as I was taken to a ward. Luckily, I was given my own room, but it was isolating. Not having my partner there was very lonely, and we were not able to process what had happened together. The first time I met my boy and cuddled him, I was wearing a mask, so it felt like I couldn't even kiss my baby. Whilst he was in NICU, myself and my partner were not allowed in there at the same time, which was incredibly hard. I found it very difficult, after having a C-section, trying to move and look after him. I really wanted to breastfeed but unfortunately it didn't work out. I just didn't get the support that I needed. It was tough and I still beat myself up to this day for not being able to breastfeed and not pushing for help.

After three days, we were discharged from hospital. I couldn't wait to experience my baby in the comfort of my own home.

I think with everything that went on, it lead to me feeling depressed. I'm grateful for my health visitor who noticed this and referred me to the postnatal mental health team. Although, at the time, I thought I didn't need help, I'm glad they pushed it, because I wasn't in a good place. I ended up having telephone counselling. I don't think it solved anything but it was good to talk, although weird doing it on the phone and not seeing the other person.

I still found motherhood extremely hard and not having that support that's usually there, like face-to-face appointments, family hubs, mother and baby groups and generally the help from friends and family, made it a strange old time. My relationship ended about eight months after my son was born and luckily the world was opening up a bit more at this time, so I was able to see friends and family.

I find it difficult to look back on this time. What should have been a very happy time in my life is tainted by bad memories. In a way, I feel like I was robbed of having a lovely experience and I wonder, if it hadn't been in the middle of a pandemic, would it have been different? Would I have enjoyed it more? Would I have suffered so much mentally after giving birth? I guess it's hard to know.

Two and a half years on, and although I am a single mother and it's hard work, I am now finally getting so much joy out of my son and seeing him grow up into, thankfully, quite a confident young boy.

Hayley England, 36, from Essex is a single mum to an almost three-year-old son, trying her best to navigate motherhood whilst setting up a virtual assistant business from home. She enjoys going for walks and spending time with friends and family. She hopes to one day own a converted van to travel the UK. @hayleyvengland

KEZIA LOCKHOUSE

Becoming a mother in early 2021 came with many things: pain, grief, boredom, depression, a tiny, soft, 'easy' baby, a wave of creative inspiration, and COVID. 22nd February 2021, the day I was in active labour, the Government published a four-step roadmap to getting out of lockdown in England; 8th March - schools reopened; 12th April - socialising outdoors; 17th May - some socially distanced socialising indoors.

In the two years since, words have tumbled out of me like a wellspring; poetry has helped me heal. I looked back through all of the poems I had written and found only two or three direct mentions of 'COVID' and a couple of indirect references to the pandemic. COVID played a huge role in what made becoming a mother so challenging for me, so why wasn't I talking about it?

It's as if I permitted myself to be traumatised by the paralysis of an epidural, the forceps, by sustaining a birth injury (prolapse), by having had a baby who was taken away from me instantly with breathing difficulties, cleaned and returned after a long enough period without effective communication that I asked my partner whether or not he was alive; but I glossed over COVID. Do I belittle the pain caused to me directly because of COVID (and an NHS in crisis) because my story isn't a story about losing a loved one to the disease? Because we all fully accepted that the restrictions were a given, a necessity and even when we disagreed with them - unalterable. Who could I blame? Shout at? Boris? The Tories? The NHS? No, I should just keep calm and carry on.

By the time I regained enough confidence to leave the house with my newborn - I could. I got to meet other mums, go to Buggyfit, Baby yoga, Sing & Sign, and feel a bit normal. I felt lucky because I'd seen my sister-in-law and two close friends become mothers in 2020 and miss out on these things. But, accepting your lot because others have had it worse, when what you did have was still less than what you needed, is just another way of discounting. What is the story that I'm not telling, and how could sharing that help me heal, and perhaps help someone else feel validated in their own feelings and experience? It's a story of aloneness, separation, isolation and lack of support, peppered with a fair amount of anxiety during my pregnancy. I'm sure lots of mothers outside of pandemics feel all these things too, but COVID intensified them all.

My not-husband (thanks to a COVID-cancelled wedding) had been able to come to the 12 and 20-week scans, but not my two booking appointments at two different hospitals, blood tests or midwife appointments. Years later, at my pessary appointments, I was completely taken aback to see unaccompanied men in that waiting area. It dawned on me that they must be waiting for their partners and I couldn't stop my tears. It was so unfair.

My partner was not there at any of my additional scans. First a growth scan, then a positioning scan, then a scan to check fluid and blood flow which resulted in a recommendation for an induction that I was never comfortable with for many reasons. Alone with the registrar - my partner on speaker phone

- I argued against the induction and she kept dismissing my concerns. Firstly, she said it wasn't true that it would put me at risk of further intervention in my delivery (which came to pass) and even when I told her I was worried about the effect of being alone on my mental health, she didn't engage with me on that level. Instead, she said they were just trying to avoid stillbirth, a comment which peaked so much anxiety that I believed my placenta might give up at any moment, immediately killing the baby inside of me. At home that night, in the early hours, I convinced myself I was experiencing reduced movements. We went to hospital for monitoring and my partner waited in the car park. The baby woke up from his sleep and everything was normal but it gave the consultant on-duty cause to push my induction forward to as soon as possible. I was admitted to the antenatal ward 14 hours later. No visiting. My virtual start-of-maternity-leave Zoom send-off was scheduled for that evening, I joined from my hospital bed.

It was obvious the ward was overfull and understaffed. The midwives had no time for small but important things, the things that make you feel seen and cared for. I had to ask four or five times for a birth ball before one arrived. No medical professional ever spent longer than a few minutes with me at a time - I felt like an item on a to-do list. The induction process started the morning after I arrived. After hours of pain without progress, I asked the doctor if I could stop being induced and go home and wait for the baby to come by itself. She made me feel irresponsible for asking (the baby needed monitoring, there was an urgency to give birth.) She then forced her way into my cervix and told me they'd be able to break my waters and I was happy because that meant I'd be able to go to the delivery unit and my partner could join me.

The delivery unit was full, so I was kept waiting alone for two days and two nights, for a bed and a midwife to become available. So much for my birth being an urgent priority.

And, in fact, all of this was okay - I mean, it was shit - but it wasn't traumatising, my spirits were high, I was excited and calm, I had no fear of birth or contractions and felt very connected to my support network - albeit through the internet, but then it was lockdown number three so I was well used to that.

After a traumatic birth experience, where I was in an extremely heightened state of fear, exhaustion, anxiety and confusion due to hyponatremia[1], the COVID trauma came at the doors to the postnatal ward, having to say goodbye to my partner who was being sent home. He was locked out of the ward and would only be allowed in for two hours per day for the rest of our three-day stay. A part of my soul was being torn away, my heart was breaking and the pain of that separation was so great and so destructive. At the time I most needed someone to care for me, I had no one except a tiny, hungry, amber-hatted[2] baby, who I had to care for. The physical separation between mother, baby and father left a huge wound which pulled through our relationship - as a couple and as a family - for months afterwards.

We were discharged, delighted to be reunited and finally able to take our baby home to enjoy that newborn bubble we'd heard so much about. I felt safe and allowed myself to switch off from survival mode and feel the weight of the trauma, and I felt hopeful (and hormonal). But the next day, the health visitor came and sent us back to hospital as our baby had lost too much weight. Knowing I was being sent back to the place I'd been traumatised, and that I'd have to be alone again - for who knew how long - was some of the worst news I have ever received. I was hysterical. After an hour-long wait in paediatric A&E, we were finally admitted to the feeding ward and I was almost inconsolable. The staff seemed to assume I was worried for my baby, even though I kept telling whoever would listen it was because I was being separated from my partner again. I knew my baby was safe but I didn't believe I was safe. I was more worried for myself and my mental health then, than I have ever been before or since. I was convinced I would get PND, be unable to bond with my baby and be at huge risk of suicide. In the sleep-deprived night I spent on the feeding ward I felt like a Victorian madwoman being force-fed in an asylum, except it was my baby who was the one being forced with a bottle. Everything was wrong and I was alone again. I didn't know how long for.

A third ripple of separation hit two weeks after the birth. My partner was midway through a PGCE and wasn't entitled to paternity leave, but managed to arrange two weeks off with the course supervisors. I spent the first week in hospital. For the second week, we escaped to my parents', with whom we childcare 'bubbled' – both of us feeling too traumatised to be able to look after ourselves and our baby at the same time. The day those two weeks ended was the day schools reopened: 8th March. I was so jealous of my NCT mums whose partners could work from home, whilst I was alone with the baby for 10-hour days. As we'd bubbled with my parents, it meant my mother-in-law couldn't come and help. My own mum is a stroke survivor, without the mobility to look after us in the cook, wash-up, tidy, hold-the-baby kind of way I needed, and my dad is her carer. My partner would come home from work and I would instantly need him to do whatever it was that I had wanted to do and had not been able to that day (whether through newborn care or temporary disability due to my prolapse). We had, at least, given up on him showering as soon as he returned home from his COVID-y classroom, like we had been doing when I was pregnant.

We were displaced. We had moved to a new city early in my pregnancy for my partner to retrain, and although we instantly felt at home there and decided it would be a permanent relocation, we were only just establishing a network of friends. It turns out that making new friends is hard through online antenatal courses, socially distanced get-togethers and lockdowns. Our NCT group managed one in-person meet-up whilst pregnant – walking two-by-two on a cold December day. I was lucky to find an online network of local mums via an established local pregnancy Zoom yoga class, whose teacher administrated WhatsApp groups for us. The support I found there can't be overstated in the context of a time when the only person who came into our house when my baby was weeks old, aside from my parents, was a washing machine repair man (twice; because it kept eating washable breast pads). He had such Dad vibes and I found his presence as comforting as I did anxiety-inducing: was he exposing us to COVID?

For six months, I felt submerged and ever less like myself. I excelled at motherhood. I cried a lot. Slowly, I bonded with my baby and started to feel active love and joy for him, alongside my earliest feelings of responsibility, fascination and comfort. I made friends. Sometimes I would wail and moan huge sobs of grief. On a handful of occasions, I wondered whether it would be easier if I didn't exist. I was in a lot of pain from my prolapse and was, for a time, scared to move. I found walking extremely hard (crushing for a person whose COVID-cancelled honeymoon was going to be walking from John O'Groats to Land's End). I had tried to seek NHS support for my prolapse but was put off when my first physio session was on Zoom. What I needed was a qualified professional to put their finger in my vagina and tell me what was wrong, not generalised information I had already found out for myself. So, I went private, where I was able to attend, masked and in-person. My formal NHS diagnosis came one year after the birth due to the length of the gynaecological waiting list. I didn't even bother to try to get mental health support from the NHS. My birth experience resulted in a total loss of trust in the NHS' ability to care for my perinatal needs. The 6-8 week check was combined for me and my baby and I had no physical check-up. The baby was checked by a nurse who asked me how I was (I was tearful at the time) and I told her I was suffering emotionally and physically with my prolapse, but was fine. She was vaguely sympathetic in that sort of oh-yes-that's-normal-motherhood kind of way. She asked about contraception and whether I was due for a smear (sorry my vagina is broken, traumatised and closed for business, though always feeling uncomfortably open.) I was frustrated, disengaged and feeling let down, with a self-assessment mental health questionnaire that I probably failed but didn't call anyone for. I did have six sessions of private counselling for birth trauma with a therapist through my work's Employee Assistance Programme, which helped me start to process what had happened to me.

I was so scared of PND in my early postpartum period that I only realised I had suffered from it around 20 months after giving birth. Through all of this, my partner and I were reeling from the effects of a cleaving at the core of our relationship. We lost our first opportunities to bond as a three and struggled to make up for them whilst my partner was doing full-time work and I was doing full-time childcare. We'd never experienced anything like that level of inequality in our relationship before. We didn't understand the damage that had been done to us for a long time. When you find yourself alone you put your guard up, and it makes intimacy harder. My partner felt excluded from the family. I had a desperate need for my partner but was often emotionally unavailable due to my trauma and PND. We suffered and felt helpless.

My mind turns to a woman from my pregnancy yoga class who took her own life a month after all COVID restrictions were lifted in England – and I wonder how COVID might have counted for her. She was in my thoughts when I wrote this cleave poem alongside my own what-ifs, and gratitude for the women both in-person and online who supported me through the most challenging period of my life.

```
    finding myself      traumatised
           feeling      betrayed and
 broken postpartum      abandoned
          I found       women giving
   hands to hold me     up

                 privately

          offered       too late
           freely
```

Having taken a moment to look more directly at COVID's role in my experience, I now see something in this poem that was always there, but I'd missed before: the cleave itself, the story I wasn't telling. A separation. The negative space, only defined by what it isn't. COVID is the gap and the only word that exists within it is 'privately.' The private is always political. Lockdown mums and their struggles were - as a point of policy - moved out of the public sphere and into homes and hospitals, alone, even when football stadiums were full. Only through collective effort to publicise our privates, may we be counted and heard. Only in collective hearing can we hope to find recognition and support that was so sorely withheld from us during lockdown.

---

[1] Drinking so much water during the labour alongside a 'no solids' policy with the induction, which meant I diluted the sodium in my blood, like marathon runners get sometimes. Which put me at risk of death.

[2] The hospital used red, orange and green hats on the postnatal ward as an obvious traffic-light system for their staff to know which babies needed which level of additional care and observation.

Kezia Lockhouse, 32, is based in Cambridge with her husband and two-year old son. She works freelance in management roles in the theatre industry and writes poetry in the breathing spaces.

4AM DOODLES

@4am_doodles is a mum of two tiny humans, and as the name might suggest puts sleep-deprived doodles on Instagram that relate to experiences of parenting in the early years. She had her second tiny human in March 2021, towards the end of the Covid-19 pandemic but when a number of restrictions still applied to new parents. She doodled about some of the challenges of being pregnant and raising a tiny human during that time, collating her experiences in a book called *Pregnancy, Parenting & Poo in a Pandemic,* which she sold to raise money for Pregnant Then Screwed.

LISA DUBROVINA

Trigger Warning: NICU stay

WHO EVEN IS MUM?

'You can't eat here, Mum. MUM.'

I turn around and see a neonatal nurse looking at me sternly as I hold my half-peeled banana. I've become 'Mum' overnight and I'm not used to it. I feel like my entire pre-existing personality and life have been obliterated and now I'm C's mum, existing only in relation to this new baby of mine. I have been promoted to a superior being who should be attuned to the baby's needs and ready to ignore her own. I'm not feeling it.

'I haven't eaten anything since I went into labour.'

'You can eat in the kitchen, it's down this corridor.'

I look in the direction she's pointing with a sinking feeling: it'll take me a while to hobble down the long hallway.

As I walk to the kitchen, I overhear a woman say on the phone: 'I can't come out now because I'll need to feed her in ten minutes.'

How does she know? She seems so confident that her baby will need a feed soon. I don't know what my baby needs, the nurses have to constantly explain things to me.

'Why don't you try some skin-to-skin, Mum?'

'Your baby is hungry, Mum'.

And what about Mum herself? She is no longer allowed to have needs. No showers for her on the ward as she is not a patient. One toilet to share with staff. Long corridors to walk with a body that has just been cut open. She can, and should, sleep when the baby sleeps on a fold-out plastic armchair to the sound of beeping machines. She should, however, also be ready to wake, jump up and feed the baby.

Who even is Mum?

HOPE IS LAST TO DIE

'The doctor said he needs to be put back on oxygen.'

'But they told us they'd discharge us today.'

'I know. But it's not looking likely.'

'I don't understand, they said we'd all go home. Why would they have said it if they didn't mean it?'

'I don't think they expected the oxygen saturation to go down again.'

I wipe the sweat off my forehead. My milk came in today and I keep getting extremely hot, then extremely cold. I am like a human microwave heating the milk for my newborn. Then, when he's done, I turn into a fridge to keep the milk fresh for the next feed. I am sweaty, my breasts are leaking and I am still bleeding heavily from the birth. I am staying in NICU in a makeshift room so that I can establish breastfeeding, but I am not a patient, so there isn't a proper bathroom for me to use. I haven't showered in two days.

'I don't know if I can face more of this,' I say quietly, trying not to cry into my mask for the millionth time today.

'We have to face this, we have no choice.'

'Maybe tomorrow the levels will go up and we will go home.'

I say these words even though I don't truly believe them but at this moment I need some hope to keep me going.

SEPARATION

The ambulance people arrive and they start getting everything ready for the transfer. We are hoping to get some answers today, after a week in the limbo of beeping machines signalling an unknown health issue.

'It's time for his feed. Can I feed him now?'

'It's best to avoid so that he's not car sick on the way there. Sorry, Mum.'

They put cannulas into both his hands in case something happens on the way. He screams. I cry quietly into my mask. There's nothing I can do to comfort him.

The NICU nurses say goodbye and see you later, everyone has assured us that we will just go to the paediatric hospital for the echo of C's heart and then we'll be right back here or, perhaps, even discharged. It's hard not to cling to this tiny glimmer of hope.

We can't be in the ambulance because of COVID rules so we get a taxi across London. It is a crisp winter day and the sun is shining. There are families out in the park near the hospital. This is the first time in a week that I go outside for more than five minutes. It is strange that the world hasn't stopped and that the weather is allowed to be this lovely.

We're at the new hospital. It's shinier than the shabby local hospital, with walls decorated with cartoon animals. It's a place you hope you never have to go to, but if it turns out that you do need help for your sick child, this is the place to be.

The technician starts the echo. C is calm. The lights are off. It's quiet apart from the rhythmic beeping of the machine. I doze off on the plastic chair. I have only managed two or three hours of sleep per 24-hour period in the past week. After what feels like an eternity, the doctors arrive.

'This is not the news you were expecting. We have to operate on Monday morning. You will be admitted to the ward, only one parent allowed and no visitors because of COVID.'

We sit in shock, unable to process what just happened. We both cry while we wait for a room to be arranged for myself and C.

The room is ready. I try to stay calm at the prospect of at least four days looking after a newborn on my own. My husband says goodbye to his one-week-old son.

WIRELESS BABY

I wake up and it's snowing outside. It's a Sunday and I imagine that in a parallel universe outside the hospital walls, people are having fun playing in the snow. My husband calls me to say he's arrived. He can be in the waiting room but he's not allowed onto the ward. He hasn't seen C in three days. That is a third of C's life so far.

'I'm here and I brought more food. Your mum made bliny for you.'

'Thank you. My poor mum – one month in locked-down London and still no baby to cuddle.'

'I know, but I'm sure she's glad to be able to help in some way... Wait, come to the window, I think I can see you.'

I move closer to the window and see my husband waving at me through another window across the snowy courtyard. For one fleeting moment, I think that I could bring C to the window so that his dad can see him. Then, with a sinking feeling, I remember that C is wired up to lots of monitors and can't be moved too far from his cot.

'Have you asked the nurses if they will let me see him before the operation tomorrow?'

'I have and I keep getting conflicting responses.'

'Can you please ask again?'

'Yes, of course I will. I wish I could at least show him to you through the window but he's connected to all the machines.'

My husband sighs heavily.

'I am really ready for a wireless baby now.'

COMFORT MUSLIN

'It's 4am. You need to stop feeding him now.'

I take C off the breast, grateful that, for once, the feed went well. I pray that he will sleep for as much of the four hours until his operation as possible, wondering how on earth I will soothe a hungry 10-day-old.

The nurse suggests that I keep a muslin with me overnight to give to C as he's taken into the operating theatre. She says my smell will comfort him. I do as I am told, even though I am sceptical that it will help. We only just met 10 days ago and I don't feel like I've done a very good job of looking after him so I doubt my smell will help much.

I manage to doze off hugging the muslin; I wake up a couple of hours later and, just like every time I've woken up since C got put into NICU, I'm convinced that I am hugging him. I realise that it is not the case and I'm relieved I haven't squashed him but also sad that he's not nestled in my side.

C is mercifully still asleep. The operation should be at 8 which is half an hour away, I should be able to handle his unsatisfiable hunger for that long.

The nurse tells me the doctors are delayed. C's awake and hungry, wailing, and there's nothing I can do.

It's now been nearly six hours since C ate and the cardiologist is finally here.

'Congratulations on the birth of your baby.'

It feels odd to be congratulated when I am about to sign a consent form which states that the operation my newborn is to undergo carries a very small risk of death.

INVISIBLE WALLS

The nurse pushes the pram down the hospital corridor with a screaming C inside. My eyes are blurred with tears which flow down into my face mask. The nurse looks at my teary face and says 'aww, bless you,' in a slightly rehearsed tone which suggests that, while this is my own personal hell, she sees much worse on a daily basis.

I am pointing my phone at C's face so that my husband can see him on FaceTime before the operation. He is in the waiting room only a handful of metres away, but we are separated by the invisible wall of COVID restrictions.

C screams harder than ever. I've been forced to deny him my milk for six hours to prepare him for surgery. I know I should be holding him right now instead of letting the nurse push him in the pram, but I can barely walk because of the pain of the C-section. We stop to wait for the lifts and I am able to catch my breath.

'Turn around,' my husband says on the phone.

I do as I am told and I see him at the end of the corridor. The automatic doors have opened and he is standing just beyond them. The path to reach us is clear and would only take him a few steps, but he doesn't move. We follow the COVID rules to the letter until the end.

We get into the lift and a moment later we're in the operating theatre. I hold C's tiny hand as he goes under general anaesthetic. This is not what I expected to be doing on day 10 of new motherhood.

EMERGENCE

I need to do something with the milk in my breasts while I wait for C's operation to finish. I have a handheld pump somewhere but I can't find it. Over the past few days, the nurses have occasionally suggested I pump but I don't know how to do it. Am I just supposed to know how to milk myself? As I frantically search for my bag, breasts ready to explode, the nurse comes in.

'He's awake. Would you like to see him?'

I want to run and I would if only the stitches let me. They told me breastfeeding might be difficult after the operation. I don't know how it can get any harder. Sometimes I think that I'm being tested to see how many meltdowns it will take for me to finally run away. But I carry on, as fast as I can to the recovery room.

C looks tiny in the big hospital cot. I ask the nurses to hand him to me immediately so I can feed him. He latches on and seems surprisingly unfazed by what just happened. I take a sigh of relief. He is put onto the high-dependency unit and I am moved to a room on the other side of the hospital. It is university-style accommodation – grim, with communal bathrooms and no heating. It is at least a five-minute walk from the ward and I don't know how I will do the night feeds.

After moving my stuff from the ward to the new room, I walk back to the high-dependency unit. It's loud in there, with more beeping and a toy blaring nursery rhymes. The doctors are back for an initial check to see how the operation went. The heart looks good but the pulse is very high. More beeping to indicate that something is still not quite right. I brace myself for more time living in hospital, feeding a baby connected to machines. The nurse convinces me to skip a feed so I can sleep for a couple of hours in my new room. My husband tucks me in and goes home. I fall into a deep sleep.

I wake up two hours later, frantically checking my phone to see if the nurses have called me. I am picturing all sorts of nightmare scenarios. His pulse must be through the roof. The oxygen saturation levels have dropped. He is crying inconsolably from the post-operation pain. We must stay in the hospital indefinitely.

I get out of bed and start walking down the endless labyrinth of corridors. It is after hours and the hospital is quiet but for the occasional lone doctor or nurse rushing somewhere. I enter the high-dependency unit. C is peacefully asleep. His pulse is fine. Everything is fine. I take a seat next to him to wait for the next feed. I dare to hope we will be discharged the next day.

SUPERHEROES

I'd never realised that I am surrounded by superheroes until those 11 days in NICU with my newborn. I saw so much courage - the quiet, and often invisible, kind. The courage to keep helping others when you desperately need help yourself, to keep giving when you have nothing left to give.

The mother with one twin in NICU and the other in the postnatal ward who ran between the two so she could breastfeed them both.

The couple who shared a makeshift room with us and who finally got to go home with their baby boy after 10 weeks in a hospital during a pandemic.

The mother of the little boy who'd been living in the high-dependency unit for months and who kept showing up every day, as she watched new kids being admitted and discharged while her boy carried on living in the hospital.

The nurse whom I overheard telling the other nurses that her brother had died of COVID that day and yet she still had to do her shift as normal. She quietly looked after all the babies through the night, changing and feeding them as I breastfed C on and off for five hours. After I'd been there for a couple of hours we started talking.

'You are strong for persevering with breastfeeding in this situation,' she told me. To me, she seemed like the strongest person I'd ever met. The morning after our conversation, we were transferred to a paediatric hospital, told that C needed heart surgery and that my husband would not be able to see him until we got discharged because of strict COVID rules. I cried a lot in those four days. In the moments where I felt like I could no longer keep going, I would repeat the nurse's words in my head: 'You are strong, you are strong, you are strong.'

The operation went well and we were discharged the next day. I made it through and I got C through it.

I suppose I have some courage, too.

EPILOGUE

We finally went home after eleven long days at the hospital. My mother got to hug her grandson. C got to see his parents' faces without masks. I got to sleep and feed in my comfortable bedroom next to both my husband and my son. It was blissful for a moment, and then we had to start healing from the trauma of what had happened, alongside the usual challenges of looking after a newborn.

The extreme sleep deprivation took a toll on my body. I was nearly admitted into hospital again the day after we came back because I'd got a uterus infection. At six weeks postpartum, I struggled to walk from the pain of the C-section.

I grieved not being able to enjoy the newborn bubble in the comfort of our home without having to fear for his health. I remember very little of C in those initial days – I think all my memories are actually artificial reconstructions from the photos and videos that my husband and I took.

If someone had told me that I'd have to face all of this, I would've thought it was impossible for me to get through it and that I wouldn't have the strength. Turns out, you always find some strength because you have to.

Lisa Dubrovina is a writer and dancer living in London with her husband and young son. She had her baby in lockdown and since then has been telling her stories of motherhood through words and dance which she shares on Instagram @lisadanceswrites.

ACKNOWLEDGMENTS

Thank you to Arts Council England for believing in this project and for understanding the significance that creativity has to people's lives.

Thank you to the participants in this book for trusting me with your stories. Your positivity, excitement and passion for the project has kept my focus, brought me confidence and given me a huge sense of purpose.

Thank you particularly to Kate, Issy and Gill who provided me with knowledge and support regarding media and PR – a world I knew little about.

It would not have been possible to bring this book together without the unwavering support of my family, particularly my mum, Debbie, sister, Mollie, and husband, Adam. Balancing this project, alongside working almost full-time and being mum to a pre-schooler, has been one of the most challenging things I've ever done. But, through the hard, they have always believed in me. It is only with their love that this book is here.

Lastly, thank you to my own lockdown baby, Lily. Your journey into the world is what prompted this book, which, in turn, has helped so many. You have always been the shining light through it all.